T0271240

THE MISSISSIPPI SECESSION CONVENTION

THE
MISSISSIPPI
SECESSION
CONVENTION

Delegates and Deliberations in Politics and War, 1861–1865

TIMOTHY B. SMITH

UNIVERSITY PRESS OF MISSISSIPPI • JACKSON

www.upress.state.ms.us

The University Press of Mississippi is a member of the Association of American
University Presses.

Copyright © 2014 by University Press of Mississippi
All rights reserved
Manufactured in the United States of America

First printing 2014
∞
Library of Congress Cataloging-in-Publication Data

Smith, Timothy B., 1974–
The Mississippi Secession Convention : delegates and deliberations in politics and
war, 1861–1865 / Timothy B. Smith.
pages cm
Includes bibliographical references and index.
ISBN 978-1-62846-097-1 (cloth : alkaline paper) — ISBN 978-1-62846-098-8
(e-book) 1. Secession—Mississippi. 2. Secession—Mississippi—Sources. 3. Missis-
sippi—Politics and government—To 1865. 4. Mississippi—Politics and government—
To 1865—Sources. 5. Political leadership—Mississippi—History—19th century. 6.
Political leadership—Mississippi—History—19th century—Sources. 7. Voting—Mississippi—History—19th century. 8. Voting—Mississippi—History—19th century—
Sources. I. Title.
F341.S66 2014
973.7'13—dc23   2014008804

British Library Cataloging-in-Publication Data available

TO
DAVID G. SANSING

CONTENTS

PREFACE

A NORTHERN NEWSPAPER REPORTER COVERING THE MISSISSIPPI SECES-
sion convention wrote a seemingly odd line given the situation early in 1861.
Looking on the crowd of delegates debating such aspects as secession, connection to the new Confederacy, and war, the *New York Tribune* reporter
wrote, "You feel that the future historian may well say of these times: 'There
were giants in those days.'" This statement gives rise to thoughts of heroes or
villains as far as secession is concerned, and there are many even today who
flock to each school of thought. But while this book attempts to understand
both those delegates and their deliberations, it does not seek to lay blame or
canonize. Instead, I choose to hone in on the reporter's reality that a future
historian would examine these men. That is exactly what I propose to do in
this study.[1]

"The great historical riddle of secession," historian Christopher Olsen
has called it, has actually been the subject of much writing through the
decades. Well-known historians such as William Freehling and David M.
Potter have covered the topic in great detail. Concerning Mississippi specifically, one of the state's foremost historians, Percy L. Rainwater, has written the seminal text on the subject, *Mississippi: Storm Center of Secession*.
To Rainwater, the secession movement was primarily an effort to protect
slavery. Writing in 1938, he argued that secession was "a political device for
preserving a social system which was believed to be in greater danger in the
Union than out of it." He described Mississippians as being "thin-skinned"
in defense of slavery, thus resulting in the major 1860 move toward secession. In the end, he concluded that "her valor in defense ran far ahead of her
discretion."[2]

That was certainly a novel thesis in 1938, parting ways as it did with
the famous Dunning school of historiography as well as the Lost Cause
mentality. Yet its accuracy is very apparent today because many other historians have followed Rainwater's blazed trail. These individuals have examined Mississippi's secession story from deeper and varied angles, such
as Ralph A. Wooster in his quantitative examination of the delegates. His

deeply researched *The Secession Conventions of the South* (1962) provides an overview of each state's process, focusing mainly on the delegates themselves in terms of economic, social, and political quantities. He concentrated on Mississippi alone in 1954 in the *Journal of Mississippi History*.[3]

William L. Barney's *The Road to Secession* (1972) and particularly *The Secessionist Impulse* (1974) argue that economic and racial factors were predominant in Mississippi's movement toward secession. The middle class of lawyers and young planters needed secession to keep up their self-esteem by remaining masters to blacks and superiors to poorer whites. To get poor whites on board, who had little stake in leaving the Union economically, they used race and warned against Lincoln-led black equality in areas such as marriage, education, and jobs. Moreover, nonslaveholders saw in secession a chance to advance into the slaveholding class, and small-scale slave owners saw a chance to become big planters. Thus most support for secession came from new cotton counties opened since the Indian-suppressing days of Andrew Jackson, when new citizens formed and maintained an almost unyielding bond with the Democratic Party. In those new areas, the chance for upward mobility was greatest. Conversely, older cotton counties along the Mississippi River, containing large numbers of rich planters and old Whigs, saw little to gain in secession and thus were much less enthusiastic.[4]

Most recently, Christopher Olsen's social history of the movement has added another layer of analysis that seems contradictory to Barney, but they may in fact not be mutually exclusive at all. While Barney focuses on party functions between Democrats and old Whigs on the national and state level, Olsen argues that Mississippi and probably other Deep South states seceded because of an antiparty political culture at the most basic county and precinct level. That antiparty culture revolved around masculinity, honor, violence, and community and caused a severe reaction to Lincoln's election that led to ultimate confrontation. Where Barney sees white supremacy and racism as the key to understanding the nonslaveholders, Olsen sees a personal and communal reaction leaning toward Jacksonian Democracy. It was, after all, under Jackson's leadership that many of those young citizens settled into and became rooted in their locations in the 1830s. In contrast, border states had a more developed party system and less dependence on personal responses, thus shaping their delayed reactions.[5]

Other historians have devoted similar study to the subject, beginning with Luther W. Barnhardt's 1922 master's thesis, "The Secession Conventions of the Cotton South." Mississippi historian John K. Bettersworth's important *Confederate Mississippi* pays some attention to the secession convention as the beginning of the state's Civil War odyssey. Bradley G. Bond examines secession in the context of the nineteenth century as a whole and argues that secession was a reaction to the fear of losing freedom, namely the freedom to own slaves. In addition, there is a plethora of similar studies dealing with the road to secession in other slave states. Clearly, the road to Mississippi's secession has been well analyzed.[6]

Despite so many studies, there is still a glaring gap in the academic treatment of secession in Mississippi. While Wooster and Barnhardt deal with the convention delegates and the deliberations themselves, most of the major sources on Mississippi secession look primarily at the politics, society, and events leading up to the actual convention. Rainwater, Olsen, and Barney all study the period prior to 1861, some reaching as far back as the 1820s. The capstone of each of their works is the convention itself, with the passage of the ordinance of secession three days into the convention as the final act. They seek to explain why secession came by looking at the various facets and angles of the years prior to it. William L. Barney, in examining secession in both Mississippi and Alabama, interestingly wrote, "In the main the conventions were not deliberative bodies in the sense of carefully assessing various alternatives and then hammering out compromises." He went on to explain his reasoning, focusing entirely on the act of secession itself: "The secessionists knew what they wanted and had the voting strength to push across their program regardless of what the cooperationists said."[7]

Nothing could be farther from the truth, at least in a larger context. While the act of secession was indeed the climax of Rainwater's, Barney's, and Olsen's studies, and fittingly so, there is much more to the Mississippi convention than merely the act of secession. The Mississippi convention *was* a deliberative body. It *did* carefully assess various alternatives. It *did* hammer out compromises. And the decisions made there were extremely important to Mississippi then and after the war, and in some cases even now. Basically, the rest of the convention that took place after the January 9 passage of the act of secession, including a second session in March, has never been treated with any detail at all in any of the earlier studies, but it led to a realignment of politics in Mississippi, setting the stage for Mississippi's wartime political governance and impacting that which came after the war as well.

While certainly the climax of the secession movement, the convention was nevertheless also the birth of another era of Mississippi politics. The secession question was finished with the passage of the ordinance on January 9, but new issues arose after that, and the delegates, as a microcosm of the people themselves, split into new factions if not full-fledged parties. Amazingly, those who had been polar opposites on secession suddenly became staunch allies and battled those who had formerly joined them in supporting departure from the Union. These new issues included taxation, economics, joining the Confederacy, joining with border states, and even reopening the Atlantic slave trade. The chief issue, however, and the one that would actually shake the Confederacy to its core, was the matter of state versus federal authority, or federalism versus centralism. The Mississippi secession convention thus was a capstone to one movement, but was also a foundation for another political construct that would last decades. This aspect of the convention and its role in future Mississippi politics have never been treated in detail.

The question, then, is where to begin the study of the convention. Pre-1861 Mississippi politics have been thoroughly studied and need no elaboration here. William L. Barney has correctly written that "its roots may be traced back about as far as one wishes, but the immediate justification and impetus for the movement were a direct outgrowth of the 1860 presidential campaign." Barney's insight is accurate and serves as an example for this study. While Mississippi's secession movement could be traced back to its statehood and even earlier, perhaps even to the United States' "secession" from England, Lincoln's election seems to be the fitting beginning of a study of the convention and its delegates. The previous well-done studies may serve as introductions for this book.[8]

While most historians of secession have put the vast majority of their focus on the buildup to the 1860 canvass and the convention's eventual actions up to January 9, my focus will thus be on the events primarily after January 9. The December 1860 canvass and even the organization of the convention and the vote for secession are thus treated in detail here as important parts of the convention, but they are nevertheless seen as prologue to the main story of the deliberations and their lasting effects. Thus this book is not so much about the "secession crisis," but about the consequences of Mississippi secession.

Unlike the preconvention secession historiography that has produced a minor cottage industry, I am ranging far into uncharted waters in taking this approach, mainly because there is a dearth of work on the various conventions themselves after the actual act of secession occurred. Indeed, only minuscule examination of the entire Mississippi convention has appeared. John K. Bettersworth spent only a few paragraphs on the convention after January 9, and a similarly small section on the March session. He did, however, see the convention as the beginning of Mississippi's wartime political life. I took Bettersworth's insight and carried it forward in *Mississippi in the Civil War: The Home Front* (2010), arguing that the convention served as the foundation for the political, economic, military, and at times social stances Mississippi took in the war. The convention, I argue, tried to deal with all issues it could conceive would emerge during the war, and sought to put remedies to those possible problems in place. While those remedies proved far too limited and short-sighted, the convention was nevertheless the foundation for Mississippi's activity in the war. Having conducted a much more thorough study of the convention in this present book, I stand by my initial abbreviated findings contained in *Mississippi in the Civil War*.[9]

Yet the treatment of Mississippi's convention ends there, and other states' conventions have received similarly little attention. There are a few small books, articles, and theses dealing with the other conventions as part of the entire process, but very little has been done on a single convention itself. Those few studies are very dated, with some appearing in the 1910s. The closest we have come to anything dealing specifically with a convention are reprints or edited works of speeches or journals of the conventions themselves, including William Freehling's editorial work on Georgia and Virginia leaders' speeches. Thus this book on the Mississippi secession convention is the first of its kind in terms of a modern, academic, full-scale analysis of a secession convention.[10]

Perhaps part of the reason so little attention has been focused on the convention itself is a lack of sources. Unlike the deliberations of the Continental Congresses or the Constitutional Convention, which contained many larger than life statesmen who carried on a vast correspondence and whose papers have been saved, there is relatively little of that type of source material for the Mississippi convention. There is an official journal, but it is a bare-bones rendition of what occurred. It is augmented by a pamphlet John L. Power published in 1861. The convention paid him $4 a day and gave him "exclusive privilege" to print its proceedings in book form for five years. His *Proceedings of the Mississippi State Convention, Held January 7th to 26th, A.D. 1861* is a small book, but it is invaluable, adding many interesting details to the dry rendering in the official journal. One newspaper reviewed Power's book in 1861 and declared "in future times [it] will be valuable indeed." And so it is, as it contains many speeches that are absent in the official journal. Fortunately, many more speeches are found in newspapers from across the state. The most voluminous material is in a larger collection of Power's notes on the proceedings held in manuscript form at the University

of North Carolina's Southern Historical Collection. Apparently Power began his work hoping to provide a full coverage, but reduced his published
version down to the most important and interesting aspects. Beyond these
sources, there is very little manuscript material in the form of letters written by the members themselves detailing the nature and ambiance of the
convention. I have utilized all I could locate, those from James L. Alcorn,
Charles D. Fontaine, William R. Barksdale, Hugh R. Miller, Thomas Woods,
John L. Power, John W. Wood, David C. Glenn, and Alexander M. Clayton.[11]

Other contemporary sources existed at one time, but these have been
lost. The example of Wiley P. Harris, who was the unchallenged spirit of
the convention, is particularly unfortunate. He later wrote that he kept a
journal "beginning with the assembling of the convention in 1861" through
the Montgomery convention in February. He preserved it throughout the
war, "fearing that it might fall into the hands of the authorities of the United
States," he said, but it "had been mutilated by accident or design, and the
fragment left was destroyed by mice in its place of concealment, in my
house."[12]

Still, there is enough evidence and sufficient sources to piece together
a cohesive narrative of the convention, tedious though it was, and readers
should shun the temptation to get bogged down in all the deliberations
and detail and keep a firm eye on the larger picture, mainly the work and
ordinances of the major committees. In the end, my emphasis is less on
whether these members of the Mississippi secession convention were literal
or figurative giants and more on providing an objective view of them and
their work. Delegate Thomas Woods wrote long after the convention that
"God alone knows the very right of it all, and only future generations can
speak the voice of impartial truth." I can only hope that I speak with that
impartial voice.[13]

*   *   *

Many people aided me as I wrote the history of the Mississippi secession
convention. My first goal was to create a database of information on the
members. I spent over a year compiling as much information on the various delegates as I could find. This task took me all across Mississippi and in
surrounding states into archives, courthouses, and libraries. Fortunately, the
Internet made my task much easier, but there are a small number of individuals for whom I still could not locate even their death dates. Numerous
people aided my search, including Jennifer Barnett, Theresa Ridout, Jesee

Lawson Smith, Monica Wilkinson, Francis Britt, June Ellis, Ken Dupuy, Harold Graham, Clara Jane Ahrens, Richard Bullard, Judy Sanders, and Ken Spellman. Biographical researcher extraordinaire Bruce Allardice helped fill in several gaps and sent along pertinent material he had discovered as well as a photo.

A number of other individuals also aided in the preparation of this manuscript. Clay Williams, director of the Old Capitol Museum in Jackson, Mississippi, supplied material and answered questions. The staff at the various archives such as those at Duke University, Louisiana State University, the Mississippi State Library in Jackson, the University of Mississippi, and the University of North Carolina were, as always, very helpful, as were the staffs at the various county courthouses. In particular, the staff at the Mississippi Department of Archives and History were extremely helpful, encouraging, and delightful public servants. Their professionalism is one of the reasons I continue to research and write on Mississippi subjects. John F. Marszalek, as always, was a cheerful and extremely helpful editor and friend. The manuscript is much better for his having read it.

I have dedicated this book to one of Mississippi's favorite sons, David G. Sansing. In addition to other mentors, he has had a tremendous influence on my career, first setting the example of what I wanted to be when I took his Old South course at Ole Miss. He has continued to teach me through the decades as well, and I appreciate his kindness and friendship.

My family, as always, has supported this new project wholeheartedly, and I thank God for their love and support. My dad, George Smith, once again aided my research at various places throughout Mississippi. He and my mom, Miriam, were great hosts as we spent numerous nights with them on research trips. As always, Kelly, Mary Kate, and Leah Grace are my special angels, and without them nothing I do would be worthwhile or enjoyable.

TIMOTHY B. SMITH
ADAMSVILLE, TENNESSEE

THE MISSISSIPPI SECESSION CONVENTION

DRAMATIS PERSONAE

The Major Actors in the Mississippi Secession Convention

THE SECESSIONISTS

JOHN J. PETTUS—The chief secessionist in the state, Pettus is governor, chief executive officer, and chief promoter of leaving the Union. He is forty-seven years old, and his rise to power in the state has been long and continuous from his birth in Tennessee during the War of 1812. He makes his home on a plantation in Kemper County, from which he was elected to the lower house of the legislature as a Democrat in 1846. He has also represented the area in the higher branch of the legislature, spending nearly the entire decade of the 1850s in that office. At times, he has risen to even higher duties, such as president of the senate and, in that office, serving as acting governor for five days in 1854 when the governor of the state resigned before the new one took his seat. Pettus reached the height of his success when he was elected governor of Mississippi in 1859 on a strictly secessionist ticket.

Pettus is very well off, having made a fortune in crops and slaves. His personal wealth is around $70,000, and he owns many slaves. But his personal life is not as prosperous as his economic and political efforts. His wife, Pamelia, died several years ago, leaving him with four children to raise as best he can amid his political duties.

Pettus is bombastic and not afraid to use overblown rhetoric to get his point across. He is also rough, common, fond of chewing tobacco, and an avid talker and storyteller. More ominously, he also finds it difficult to stay on task, is not a visionary, and is considered by many to be anything but the calm, reasoned leader the state needs in such a time of crisis. But it is in large part due to Pettus's determination that Mississippi is at the brink of secession.[1]

WILEY P. HARRIS—By far the most esteemed member of the secession convention, Harris is only forty years old, but has made the most of his years. Unlike most delegates, he is a native of Mississippi, and despite losing his father at a young age, he was reared with all the blessings of aristocracy that existed in the still somewhat frontier antebellum Mississippi countryside. He is of solid patrician stock, his ancestors hailing from Virginia and claiming titles of privilege, including general officers in the Revolutionary War and kinship in the Washington family. Harris has actually been raised by his uncle of the same name, who was a prominent citizen himself, being a state legislator and state adjutant general.

Harris's career has been one of success. He has studied at the University of Virginia and in Lexington, Kentucky, with some of the most prominent lawyers in the nation. He became a judge at age twenty-nine. He has served in various political seats, such as the 1851 state convention and a term in Congress in the mid-1850s, which he accepted when his party deadlocked on opposing candidates for 150 ballots. He agreed to serve as the consensus candidate but would not seek reelection. He is a die-hard Democrat.

Harris lives in the state capital, Jackson, where he practices law and is married to the former Frances Mayes, a judge's daughter herself. They have four children. He owns no slaves but has made a modest fortune in the law. Although not extremely wealthy, he is the uncontested leader of the bar in Mississippi. Religious and witty, he has an interesting eccentric streak in which he talks to himself constantly, except when in deep thought immediately before speaking.

Harris is so esteemed that he is immediately hailed as the elder statesman of the convention, despite his relative youth. He is tall, calm, and courteous, and wields a charming wit when necessary. His ability is every bit as convincing, and he quietly leads by example. One member of the convention goes so far to compare his words to "the voice of an oracle."[2]

WILLIAM S. BARRY—One of the most seasoned politicians in the state, Barry is thirty-nine years old. He comes from a distinguished line of Virginia aristocracy, although like his confidant Harris, he was born in Mississippi. His Southern birth has not limited his education, however; Barry graduated from Yale in 1841. He has had a distinguished law practice in Columbus, but recently retired to work his several plantations and many slaves. He is also a politician, having served in Congress in the mid-1850s and more recently in the state legislature. He has been Speaker of the Mississippi house. A solid Democrat, he is highly regarded in almost all circles.

Barry is a Presbyterian, though not a practicing one, and is married to the former Sally Fearn, and they have one child. He is very well off, mostly due to his agricultural pursuits, and is estimated to be worth $65,000. He is comfortable in the life of retirement, but has made an exception to return to public life during the critical election and secession crises.

Barry is polished, fluent, energetic, and solemn, and he will prove to be a force in leading the convention in a solemn direction. He is acknowledged to be one of the best orators in the state. If he has any weaknesses, they are his habit of talking too much and his somewhat frail physical constitution. He overcomes his physical ailments with a strong mind, however, and is able to use his sharp and critical thinking ability to bend the will of hesitant Mississippians toward his ultimate goal, that of secession.[3]

L. Q. C. LAMAR—A sitting U.S. congressman, Lamar is the soul of secession at the convention. He is only thirty-five, but has had an impressive career. He is of solid tidewater Virginia stock that transplanted to Georgia in the late eighteenth century. Lamar has a solid education from Emory in Atlanta and married even better—Virginia Longstreet, the daughter of one of the South's finest educators, A. B. Longstreet—later head of the University of Mississippi. The couple has three children. In addition to a law career and agricultural pursuits on his plantation, Lamar has served in numerous political offices, including the state legislatures of both Georgia and Mississippi. He is also on faculty at the University of Mississippi in Oxford, where he makes his home. He is a staunch Democrat, serving as a delegate to the 1860 party convention and as a congressman for multiple terms. Lamar is so convinced of secession that he has been writing a draft of an ordinance, which he brings with him to Jackson.

Lamar is a man of wealth, owning as he does a plantation and thirty-one slaves. He also makes money through his law and political careers, and is estimated at having a net worth of around $35,000. He is a devout Methodist.

Lamar is a hard worker, possesses a masterful intellect, and is able to deduce the prevailing mood of the people and events surrounding him. He is sometimes brooding when countered, and is not always in adherence with the majority, but he is strong, capable, and determined. It will be largely on his shoulders that the convention delegates will lean as they advance toward secession.[4]

DAVID C. GLENN—Destined to be one of the hardest-working members of the convention, Glenn is a force to be reckoned with, his sheer will often carrying debates and decisions. A native of North Carolina, he came to Mississippi as a teenager to live with an uncle. He has lived across the state, first in Holly Springs as a child and then later in Jackson. He has since moved to Harrison County, where he practices law in Mississippi City, on the Gulf Coast. He is thirty-seven years old, but has held important positions such as two terms as Mississippi's attorney general, the first coming when he was only twenty-five. He was a Democratic delegate to the stormy 1860 convention.

Married to Patience B. Wilkinson in 1846 and the father of two daughters, Glenn is a widower. He espouses no religious preference, but is an avid secessionist, and is probably the most able speaker in the convention. One observer noted he was "unquestionably the most Ciceronian speaker in the state, combining with his fiery intellect, a splendid person, graceful manner." He is very much an intellectual and is able to forcefully carry his opinions with eloquence. He is also witty and humorous, and knows how to play to a crowd whether speaking in a canvass or on the floor of a deliberative body.

To the forceful Glenn the convention will turn for guidance concerning a new Confederacy, and what place Mississippi will have in it. His wise counsel and active mind are perfectly situated for the task, and he will not disappoint.[5]

SAMUEL J. GHOLSON—One of the foremost national statesmen in Mississippi, Gholson is a federal judge in north Mississippi. He is a native Kentuckian, now fifty-two years old, and has practiced law in Alabama as well as Aberdeen, Mississippi. He has served in the state legislature as well as two terms in the U.S. Congress before he received his judgeship.

Gholson is also a substantial planter, owning ninety slaves. His personal worth is over $100,000. He is married to Margaret, and is a firm secessionist, an old-line Democrat, and a Baptist.

Gholson will bring his considerable résumé to the convention, thinking that his positions and past garner for him much acclaim. He is thus talkative, probably too much, and is also very sensitive and reacts to anyone who confronts him. Such an attitude almost got him into a duel in years past with Francis Marion Rogers, also of Monroe County. Now Rogers is the county's other delegate to the convention. Gholson will thus be at the center of some of the stormier debates in the convention.[6]

HENRY T. ELLETT—One of the most widely known statesmen in Mississippi, Ellett is a native of New Jersey. He received a first-rate education at Princeton and began his law career there before moving to Port Gibson, Mississippi, in 1837. Since his arrival in Mississippi, he has held numerous important offices, such as in the state legislature. He also won a seat in Congress to fill the vacated position of Jefferson Davis in 1846, but he refused renomination. He is a very capable lawyer, and owns a plantation on which his seventeen slaves work.

Ellett is forty-seven years old. He and his wife, Rebecca, have four children at home. He has amassed a personal fortune worth $60,000, but still has politics in his blood. He is a devout Democrat and a Presbyterian.

An avid secessionist, Ellett will be called on to provide the convention with leadership. Friends describe him as simple and practical; there is nothing ostentatious about him. But he is firm and strong, one contemporary calling him a "splendidly-balanced man." The convention will need men like Ellett who have experience and wisdom in knowing how to run a convention, especially in its first organizational days.[7]

JAMES Z. GEORGE—Although not nearly as prominent in societal circles in 1861 as he would later become, George is thirty-four years old and makes himself a force at the secession convention by often taking part in the debate and offering numerous amendments, primarily regarding the institution of slavery. Despite his problematic childhood in Georgia, where he lost his father at age one and thereafter lived under the severe direction of a usurping stepfather, George is by no means a weak delegate. He is well regarded in many circles as a Mexican War veteran in Jefferson Davis's regiment and as an up-and-coming lawyer. He currently serves in the position of court reporter for the state's supreme court, where he rubs elbows with the leaders of the state. He is a die-hard Democrat and supports slavery, expansion, and secession across the board.

George is married to the former Elizabeth Young, and they have six children, one born every other year. He claims to be Baptist, but depends on his wife's devotion rather than his own membership in the church. He is an affluent planter in Carroll County, where he owns land and sixty-five slaves. He is among the wealthiest delegates to the convention, having a personal fortune totaling over $63,000. Yet the secession winter is one of overbearing sadness for George. His seventh child and namesake, infant James Z. George Jr., died on December 20, 1860, the very day George was elected to the convention by his fellow residents of Carroll County.

Despite the grief, George puts his personal sorrow aside and makes his way to Jackson in early January for the convention, setting up shop in his court reporter office on the third floor of the capitol building, where the convention is being held. He is shy, reserved, and not interested in society at all, but realizes he needs to come alive in the debates and convention if he is to succeed in the act of secession that he so dearly wants.[8]

THE COOPERATIONISTS

JAMES L. ALCORN—At age forty-four, Alcorn is the undisputed leader of the anti-secessionists at the convention. Born in Illinois in 1816, he is of solid frontier stock, his father having commanded an infantry company under Andrew Jackson at the Battle of New Orleans. He grew up and attended college in Kentucky, where he also served for a time in the state legislature. Since then, he has taught school, practiced law, and served as a peace officer. But it is in planting and slaves, he owns seventy-seven, that Alcorn has made his fortune. He owns a vast plantation in Coahoma County, and that led to his high status in society and politics. As a die-hard Unionist Whig, he has in years past often been a representative in the state legislature, and was defeated for a seat in Congress by fellow convention delegate and leader of the secessionists L. Q. C. Lamar.

Alcorn is the husband of Amelia Glover (his second wife—the first having died in 1849). He is the father of a hoard of children who live at his plantation at Friar's Point. He has made a fortune in life, being worth $110,000. By 1861 his land assets are his highest concern, as demonstrated by his unyielding work on the state's levee board, which tries to shield plantations such as his from the raging floodwaters of the Mississippi River. This concern for his plantation, livelihood, and fortune prompts him to oppose secession. He realizes that war means destruction and destruction means poverty, especially along the Mississippi River, which no doubt will become a major contested thoroughfare in the action. He had been a member of the Mississippi state convention of 1851, where he helped defeat the secession movement. Ten years later, Alcorn arrives in Jackson in January 1861 again dead set on stopping, or at least delaying as long as possible, secession—as much for his own economic interest as for those of his state.[9]

WALKER BROOKE—One of the most respected members of the convention, Brooke is forty-seven years old and has had an illustrious career. He is of solid Virginia stock, where he was born, and is a graduate of the University of Virginia. He has studied law, after his graduation, with some of the most renowned lawyers in Virginia and has even taught school in Kentucky before moving to the newly opened lands of Mississippi. He has been involved in a number of careers, including teaching school, the law, and politics. He is not a major planter like many of his contemporaries, but he does own five slaves. He held a seat in the Mississippi legislature in the 1840s and 1850s, and more recently went to Washington, D.C., as a senator from Mississippi. Brooke has always been a die-hard Whig but transferred to the Union Party in the mid-1850s. Now, with the demise of his party, he is somewhat in a state of flux, but still describes himself as a Whig. Nevertheless he is solidly pro-Union.

Brooke lives in Vicksburg, where since his refusal to run for reelection to the U.S. Senate he has devoted his time to the law. He is married to the former Jane Eskridge, and they have eight children. He has a net worth of $75,000 and is a Presbyterian.

Brooke is calm, careful, practical, and described by a contemporary as "a man great in appearance, in bearing, in intellect, and in speech." He is cultured and very courteous in conversation, but he can turn forceful and dynamic in debate. Brooke is careful to consider the cost of secession, and is not convinced it is the best route for Mississippi. And he represents a thoroughly cooperationist county. He is thus determined to do everything in his power to halt or at least delay the act of leaving the Union.[10]

JACOB S. YERGER—Of Washington County on the Mississippi River, Yerger is one of the most die-hard anti-secessionists at the convention. He is fifty-one and has led an illustrious life. He is a native of Pennsylvania, but his parents moved him to Tennessee at an early age. He studied law in Tennessee before removing to Mississippi, and he is now known as one of the most able lawyers in the state. He built up his law practice in Vicksburg and began a political career there, serving numerous terms in the state legislature. More recently, Yerger has moved to Greenville, farther north, where he continues his law activity and his representation in the state legislature. He has also lately served as a circuit judge in his home district. In politics, Yerger is a devoted Whig, and has been a delegate to national conventions and a state elector. He represents a cooperationist county, where the people fear the war, destruction, and economic turmoil that their closeness to the Mississippi River will bring.

Yerger is married to the former Mary Bowen, a native of Tennessee, and they have a number of children. He is an Episcopalian. Yerger is sociable, polished, and entertaining, but in serious venues such as politics or law he is candid, detailed, and careful. He is well known for his integrity and is open and honest. Even though he disagrees with the majority of Mississippians, he is still very respected and listened to. Yerger is convinced secession is not the answer to Mississippi's problems and puts his considerable vigor to work to stop it.[11]

JOHN J. THORNTON—As one of the younger members of the convention at thirty-four, Thornton will become one of the most determined and exasperating delegates at Jackson. He is a native of Virginia, but has made a life in Brandon. He is a physician by trade, but has other interests such as politics. In comparison to his fellow delegates who have made careers in the state legislature and even in Congress, he is still a local statesman, serving only on the town board of aldermen. His major interest is in the military, where he is an officer in the local militia. A die-hard Whig, he is opposed to secession on any grounds.

Thornton and his wife, Rachel, have four children. He is not extremely well-off, having a net worth of only around $6,100, but he does own five slaves. He claims no religious affiliation.

Thornton is determined, stubborn, dedicated, and sometimes vulgar. He has been elected by the people of Rankin County to oppose secession, and that is exactly what he intends to do, to the very end.[12]

JOHN W. WOOD—Probably the most belligerent of the cooperationists, Wood is forty years old and represents the people of Attala County, where he is a lawyer in Kosciusko. He is from Virginia, where he was born around 1821. He is an Episcopalian in religion, and despite his clear Unionist leaning, claims to be a "Southern Rights Democrat."

Despite his work in the law, Wood has not made much headway toward a fortune, claiming a real estate worth of only $100 and a net personal worth of only $5,000. He owns no slaves, although he talks of coming from a family that does so. He and his wife, Margaret, have six children ranging from infancy to manhood.

Wood is a good speaker, is confrontational, and does not mind standing up for his beliefs, doing so with a great deal of logic. But he is also brooding and tends to sulk when opponents do not take his advice. This volatile mixture of emotions and personality will thus create the most impulsive reaction to secession, which Wood is determined to stop.[13]

- 1 -

ELECTIONS

November–December 1860

THE STATEHOUSE IN JACKSON, MISSISSIPPI, WAS ABUZZ WITH ACTIVITY on the final Monday in November 1860. The state legislature had gathered, which was always a festive event, but this time it was not for its normal bi-annual meetings. This gathering was in reaction to national developments. Abraham Lincoln had been elected to the presidency, causing a massive and potentially violent reaction from the Southern states, from which he had not received a single electoral vote. Assuming that if they had no say in a presidential election they would have no say in other major matters of the day, Southern political leaders began to seriously think about the old weapons of nullification and secession once again. To be sure, these weapons had been wielded numerous times in the past, but only as threats. Most of the time the North had backed down. But now in 1860 there was an almost universal feeling that this time things would be different and that war was likely looming. In fact, one observer in the university town of Oxford noted, "the whole state was a scene of military preparation."[1]

South Carolina was already threatening to leave the Union and was even then making plans. That was no surprise; after all, South Carolina had previously gone the farthest among the Southern states in threatening the use of nullification and even secession. The most notable event was the early 1830s confrontation over the nullification of tariff legislation, but the ever active mind of Henry Clay fortunately fostered a compromise. Unfortunately, there was no Clay in 1860, and even worse, it seemed that the fire-eaters of South Carolina were not alone this time. Other states were also rattling their sabers, and Mississippi was on the verge of taking the first step in that direction.[2]

The Mississippi legislators gathering on that November 26 day were doing so in response to a call from Mississippi's fire-eating governor, John J. Pettus, to secede from the Union. South Carolina could do all the bluffing it wanted, but until another state or states joined it, the action would be seen as mere drama and bluffing yet again. But the equation would change if another state or several joined South Carolina. Secessionist papers in Mississippi touted the state's power in thus "forc[ing] the other Southern States out." In that case, the potential for trouble suddenly mushroomed.[3]

Yet just how to proceed was much in debate, as it had never been done before. The closest any state other than South Carolina had ventured toward secession came in several regional conventions to debate reactions to unwanted events. The Hartford convention of northeastern states in 1814 was a distant memory, but the 1850 Nashville convention was more readily on everyone's minds. Then there was the aborted Atlanta convention of Southern states that was to have taken place in April 1860; the Mississippi legislature had elected delegates, but the event never materialized. Realizing the slim chance of forming numerous states together on any issue, Southern fire-eaters in late 1860 seemed to be leaning toward individual state action rather than sectional conventions that rarely produced any results. Certainly that was the way South Carolina was moving, and it was also the dominant feeling in Mississippi as the process began to move forward. No less than one of Mississippi's most notable statesmen of the time, Wiley Harris, stated flatly that Fall: "We have had two experiments of appointing delegates to Southern conventions. If this is to be the end of the present movement in Mississippi—a convention to beg once more, and delegates to hunt up a Southern convention, we had better pause now."[4]

Almost everyone realized that the issue had not erupted overnight and would not be settled that quickly. Indeed, the issue that came to fruition during that specially called legislative session had been brewing for months and in many ways for years. Since that eventually anticlimactic Nashville convention in 1850, dramatic events year after year had served to drive a wedge further and further between North and South. But no event during that tumultuous decade of the 1850s, even John Brown's aborted slave rebellion, served to ignite the passions of the South to the point of leaving or even threatening to leave the Union. Northern politicians with Southern sentiments labeled doughfaces kept the lower section fairly content through those trying years. A series of compromises and accessions to the institution of slavery likewise fueled their contentment even during the growing sectional crisis. Yet with the election of Abraham Lincoln in November

1860, Southerners decided that their influence with the central government would be over on March 4, 1861, when the Republican would be inaugurated. Lincoln openly advocated stopping the expansion of slavery, and his views convinced Southerners that his real intentions were even harsher. Mississippians were ready to stand up, even if it meant a major confrontation; on Election Day, the Herbert precinct in Neshoba County contained a banner that read, "Death rather than submission to a Black Republican government."[5]

Not surprisingly, Mississippians turned out in record numbers but did not offer a single vote for Lincoln in the election; he was not even on the ballot in most Southern states. Governor Pettus later bragged that Lincoln had received "not one electoral vote in all the fifteen slave States." Mississippi went heavily for the Southern Democratic candidate, John C. Breckinridge of Kentucky, who was the sitting vice president. A sizable amount of support, mostly old Whig Party members, also went to Constitutional Union Party candidate and fellow Southerner John Bell of Tennessee. The turnout was high; it was a tremendously important election. But when all was said and done, neither Mississippi nor any of the other Southern states could keep Lincoln from taking over the reins of the federal government.[6]

The vote in the state foreshadowed the opposing lines in the secession movement and even afterward. Some 69,020 people voted in Mississippi in the presidential election, and Breckinridge received nearly 58 percent of the vote. Bell and his status quo ideals received some 36 percent, while Stephen A. Douglas netted a mere 5 percent, and Lincoln received no votes at all. The only counties voting for Bell and thus against the fire-eating wing of the split Democratic Party were all grouped along the Mississippi River, in the Mississippi-Yazoo Delta, and around the capital. Only Adams, Bolivar, Coahoma, DeSoto, Hinds, Issaquena, Madison, Panola, Tunica, Warren, Washington, and Yazoo counties went for Bell, and these counties were the largest slaveholding areas in the state. Obviously the largest slave owners in Mississippi did not have the fire-eater mentality.[7]

Yet those counties were far in the minority, and secessionists such as John J. Pettus ruled the day. And secession sentiment was continually emerging more and more throughout the state. Even in the Bell counties such as Hinds, DeSoto, and Madison, secessionists held "conventions" in the days preceding the meeting of the legislature, intending to send a clear message about what they wanted done. For example, despite having voted for Bell earlier in November, Hinds County secessionists organized a meeting on November 14 at which luminaries such as Wiley Harris advocated separation. When these major figures spoke, they swayed public opinion; "Wiley P. Harris is expected by his friends (and their name is legion) to take a prominent part in the exciting contests which is [sic] now upon us," declared one Jackson paper. Luminaries in other counties also took the lead. In Madison County, another pro-Bell area, former governor William McWillie chaired the convention meeting on November 19, and prominent men such as T. C. Tupper, Albert P. Hill, and Richard Winter served on a committee to draft resolutions. Meeting to "consider the position in which the South is placed by the election of Abraham Lincoln," the committee drafted resolutions which "cordially approve[d] of the act of our Governor." The resolutions firmly called for secession in order to defend slavery. Other politicians addressed the crowd, such as Otho R. Singleton, a member of Congress and whom one newspaper described as "something of a whale amongst Secession minnows." Absalom M. West, a member of the state senate from a neighboring county, also spoke. Similarly in DeSoto County delegates passed resolutions against "the progress of abolitionism" and spoke villainously against "Black Republicanism."[8]

All the while, such secessionist sentiment in Breckinridge counties only grew. At a meeting in Lowndes County on November 19, the courthouse in Columbus was, one observer noted, "filled to the brim, every face expressing intense interest in the expectant proceedings." Politicians and local luminaries such as George R. Clayton and William S. Barry drafted resolutions, and statesmen such as Israel Welsh and Congressman William Barksdale addressed the crowd to great applause. While never mentioning slavery, the resolutions did use the oft-mentioned variations such as institution, property, and labor. They further stated the convention "ought to declare that Mississippi resumes the powers and functions delegated to her." The secessionists in Lowndes County even formed a dragoon company before the day ended. In Lafayette County, a meeting took place at the courthouse during which "the speeches plainly led in the direction of secession and armed resistance, if necessary," one local remembered. He added, "Every Union man in the town wheeled into line."[9]

Perhaps the most important meeting after Lincoln's election came in Jackson itself on November 22. Governor Pettus invited the state's congressional delegation to meet with him to evaluate his next move. Except for John J. McRae, one of the representatives, all of the state's members of Congress, including Senator Jefferson Davis, were there. The others came with heavy hearts, knowing what they must do. L. Q. C. Lamar in fact wrote a few days earlier that "the election of Lincoln has diffused a general feeling of dissatisfaction throughout the State. Some are anxious and dejected (myself among them)." At the meeting, Pettus asked if he should push for immediate secession in his address to the legislature, and Lamar and the two senators, Jefferson Davis and Albert Gallatin Brown, counseled moderation. They argued Mississippi should depend on the actions of other states. The other three congressmen in attendance, William Barksdale, Otho R. Singleton, and Reuben Davis, all advocated immediately leaving the Union. Because of the tie vote, the fire-eater Pettus cast the deciding vote to call for immediate separation, which Reuben Davis noted was "practically a declaration of war." The same vote occurred on a resolution to persuade South Carolina to do the same thing. Word of pro-secession statewide meetings that filtered into the capital with the various legislators as they arrived for the special session only added to Pettus's determination.[10]

The excitement was thus high when the legislators convened on November 26 in their respective chambers on each end of the second floor of the massive capitol building in downtown Jackson. Both houses came to order at noon that day, their respective officers going through the motions of organization to get down to the real business at hand. After a few minor details, such as the appointment of a new clerk in the House of Representatives, each house sent members to inform the governor that it was prepared for business and would hear from him at his convenience.[11]

Governor John J. Pettus was ready for the role of his life. He had summoned the legislature to Jackson for the specific purpose of calling a convention, and he was prepared to explain to the members what he wanted done. Having worked for some time on his address to the legislature, Pettus had his recommendations, justifications, and reasons well prepared and delivered them to each body that very day. When the respective clerks began to read the governor's message in each house that afternoon, the full reality hit that they were at a crossroads in the state's affairs.[12]

Indeed, when the clerks began reading Pettus's "quite lengthy" message in the two houses, the atmosphere changed from excitement to serious attention as the weight of the moment became clearer. Pettus got the attention of his hearers immediately by first telling the legislators, "It is with deep regret that I am constrained to forego the usual congratulations for peace, prosperity, and bright hopes for the future." Yet, he said, it was his "imperative duty" to convene the legislature to consider what he called the "greatest and most solemn question that ever engaged the attention of any Legislative body on this Continent." He perhaps spoke more than he knew when he declared, "on the solution of which hangs the destiny, for weal or woe, not only of this generation and this age, but of all generations which come after us, for an indefinite term of centuries, the end of which no prophet can foretell." Pettus was no prophet, but his words would prove correct.[13]

With the rhetoric out of the way, Pettus got down to his basic arguments. "The existence or the abolition of African slavery in the Southern States is now up for a final settlement," he warned the legislature. He spoke of how Northerners had deemed slavery "sinful and must be destroyed" and how they dictated, with the limitation of expansion, that the South must choose "whether it shall be a peaceable and gradual abolition, or speedy and violent." Pettus declared, "these are the hard terms offered to fifteen States of this Confederacy—as if they were conquered and not co-equal States." As for Lincoln's election, Pettus warned that letting the Northerners run the nation "would be as reasonable to expect the steamship to make a successful voyage across the Atlantic with crazy men for engineers, as to hope for a prosperous future for the South under Black Republican rule."[14]

Much like the original Declaration of Independence, Pettus then listed a litany of abuses he felt the Northerners had waged against the South, including "a low selfishness in seizing all the Territories, which are the common property of all the States"; nullifying the Fugitive Slave Act; waging a campaign of hate against the South; inciting slave rebellions; and even bribing congressmen to vote with them. Pettus unequivocally declared, "I see but one path of honor and safety of Mississippi," and that was to leave the Union. And he backed up the right to do so with evidence from numerous Northern state constitutional ratification conventions proving that the states willingly joined the Union and could by choice leave it; Rhode Island's ratification stated that "the powers of the Government may be re-assumed by the people, whensoever it shall become necessary to their happiness."[15]

At the end of the document, Pettus became almost enraged and used a biblical analogy. He asked the legislature to "go down into Egypt while Herod reigns in Judea." Interestingly, he then left open the possibility of reuniting in the United States at a later time; when those tearing the nation apart "are dead," he advised, "you may come up out of Egypt."[16]

Finally, a more practical Pettus told the legislature exactly what he wanted. First and foremost, he wanted legislation calling for a convention. He also desired permission to appoint commissioners to other slave states to bring concert of action and to let them know Mississippi "does not intend to submit to that administration." He also asked for authority to pay militia troops that were beginning to muster, to adopt a coat of arms for the state, to prohibit the importation of slaves owned by masters who had no intention of becoming citizens, and a stay law on suits and debts. Obviously Pettus was gearing up for independence and wanted the military, political, and economic preparation to begin immediately to undergird the state's new status. Then, with one final warning against leaving "our fair land blighted—cursed with Black Republican politics and free negro morals, to become a cess pool of vice, crime and infamy," Pettus turned the matter over to the legislature.[17]

The legislators were quick to act, one Jackson newspaper reporting "the members addressed themselves energetically to the important duties which they were assembled to perform." Over the course of the next five days, the legislature debated and passed most of what Pettus wanted, the exception being the stay law. Passage of legislation went very quickly through the committee processes, and the two houses mainly stayed on task because of a self-imposed joint resolution to deal only with items in the governor's message. Even then, however, they could not help but roam away occasionally and pass a few bills regarding corporations and relief of the destitute. But the major action came on Pettus's requests, such as legislation dealing with the prohibition of importing slaves, a state coat of arms, sending commissioners to other states, and a military bill that "really looks war like," one opposing newspaper reported. "It is notorious that the Treasury is already bankrupt," it complained, "but this debt is to be created and six percent interest paid on it."[18]

Obviously the major piece of legislation coming out of the weeklong session of the legislature was the bill providing for a convention. Managed by a special committee of "the ablest men in the House" and chaired by Charles Clark, the bill went through the legislative process quickly, guarded as it was by the house's Speaker, J. A. P. Campbell. In the senate, Henry T. Ellett ushered the bill through the process, as senate president James Drane oversaw the effort. Ellett's bill became unnecessary once the house passed its bill, so the senate began work on it. The bill eventually passed both houses of the legislature unanimously, seeing very little debate on the floor of each—only a few amendments dealing with representation. Once each house agreed with the other's amendments, the bill went to the governor and became law with his signature.[19]

The bill itself had seven sections, which laid out in general form how the convention and its delegates would proceed. The election of delegates to the convention would be held on December 20, less than a month away, and would follow normal state election laws. Since the timing was so close, the various sheriffs of the counties were required to advertise the election in newspapers and by placing public notices in at least four places throughout each county. The legislature decided to limit the number of delegates to the same number as were members of the state House of Representatives, 100, with apportionment along the same lines, based on county representation in the house. The law, after some amending to the original, stated that the delegates had to be citizens of Mississippi, had to be at least twenty-one years of age, and had to have resided in the state for twelve months and be citizens of their county for four months. The legislature likewise set the date of the convention for January 7 at the statehouse, and provided compensation for the delegates on the same level as the legislature. Any vacancies to be filled or disputes to be ruled upon concerning the seating of delegates were left up to the convention itself once formed. Most important, the legislature gave specific instruction concerning the duty of the convention: to "consider the then existing relations between the Government of the United States and the people of the State of Mississippi, and to adopt such measures for vindicating the sovereignty of the State, and the protection of its institutions as shall appear to them to be demanded." Thus the bill was specific enough to continue to the next step, but vague enough to garner total support. One Vicksburg newspaper cynically wrote, "Of course, in that shape, it was acceptable to all." After leaving much of the decision making up to the convention itself, only time would tell if the convention, when seated, would use the vast power the legislature had bequeathed on it.[20]

Specific opposing ideals and opinions began to develop even during the weeklong session of the legislature, however. The house voted on three occasions to allow notable politicians to speak to the public in its chamber during the week, and Mississippi congressman L. Q. C. Lamar as well as William L. Harris and William Yerger all did so, one Jackson paper calling Lamar's speech a "profound, logical and eloquent presentation of the sectional issues which are now agitating the country." Lamar advocated secession in his speech to the legislature and in others he gave in surrounding areas. Yet he was evidently still torn between whether to act rashly and secede without any other slave states or whether to proceed cautiously. And Lamar's quandary was the crux of the issue. Few Mississippians were against the idea of secession; almost everyone believed it was the proper step for the state to take now that Lincoln had been elected. The only debate was whether Mississippi should secede by itself or wait for other Southern states.[21]

Even though Lamar and others had not made up their minds, the lines were beginning to be drawn. Some Mississippians advocated immediate separation to allow their economy to get on track and to prepare for war, while others counseled slave state cooperation as the best way to defend the South. In fact, at the end of Lamar's address, lawyer Fulton Anderson offered an opposing viewpoint, or what one secessionist paper described as "widely variant . . . , and to our belief fall[s] far short of the requirements of the crisis." The lines were often murky, however. For instance, Wiley Harris had to correct the position attributed to him in a Jackson paper to say that while he was not wedded to the necessity of cooperation with other seceding slaveholding states, as erroneously reported, such correlation would certainly make the move easier and not doing so would "greatly increase the difficulties of such a step."[22]

Despite such murkiness, there were already quasi-formed caucuses maneuvering in the legislature. The group becoming known as immediate or separate state secessionists, mostly Democrats, originally left the requirements to be a delegate open-ended concerning residence, hoping to "enable certain notable fire-eaters to get into the Convention" from less secessionist districts. Another group became known as cooperationists, mostly former Whigs. The major amendment to the bill, offered by a more cooperationist leaning legislator from Warren County, W. C. Smedes, required that delegates reside in the counties from which they were elected for at least four months, thus putting an end to any hope of the secessionists running the table during the election. Throughout the entire process, the labels were still vague and meant different things in different parts of the state. The *Jackson Weekly Mississippian* reported that "the term 'co-operation' is very vague and indefinite, and can have no practical application in contradistinction from immediate State action." In helping to clear the visibility, however, firmly secessionist *Mississippian* editor Ethelbert Barksdale did go on to say that "the term was doubtless assumed in many cases as a cloak for submission—unionism."[23]

While there was a split on how to proceed toward secession, there was almost continual agreement about the role of slavery in any separation. Several counties, such as Kemper, Hinds, and Bolivar, sent memorials to the legislature, and the two houses worked out a joint resolution of their own addressing the reasons for their actions. Citizens in Kemper County, for instance, asked the legislature to call the convention and arm the state. They mentioned the election of Lincoln as the major cause for their demands, referencing his and the North's opposition to "the institutions of the South." Elsewhere, they mentioned the South's "most cherished institutions and her social system." The joint legislature's resolutions used no such code words; an early draft openly described the slavery issue as the reason for secession, frequently using terms such as "domestic institutions of the slaveholding and non-slave-holding states," "African servitude," and "Abolitionism." The final resolutions stressed the state's sovereignty and such laws as the Fugitive Slave Act, using the familiar words "our property" and "our institutions," but also using some variation of the word "slavery" no less than nine times in the short document. There is no doubt that the legislature viewed the slavery issue as the main reason for secession.[24]

Despite the already forming battle lines, once the legislature acted, the floodgates opened and the canvass was on. Counties all across the state began to organize meetings to elect representatives to the convention. Most of these meetings took place in early December, well before Election Day on the 20th. Most were firmly immediate separationist in nature. In Jackson, for example, secessionists became known as "Minute Men" as they readied for a countywide convention to be held in Raymond on December 10. That "Southern Rights" convention ultimately nominated a slate of determined candidates, including the well-regarded Wiley Harris and lawyer Warren P. Anderson. The gatherings in other counties saw similar action. A debate in Canton between secessionist A. P. Hill and Judge C. C. Shakelford saw a response to Hill's secessionist speech, which an observer called "wild halloo and brutal noise." At Oxford in Lafayette County, the local paper declared that "the meeting of the 5th inst. By which our candidates for the State Convention were nominated, was very nearly unanimous. The Court room was densely crowded with people, and those who voted against the adoption of the [secessionist] report of the nominating committee scarcely exceeded a score in numbers." In Warren County, where cooperation sentiment was clearly in the majority, a secessionist convention nevertheless nominated William Henry Johnson and William H. McCardle, although the local cooperation papers took delight in describing the affair as "the most disorderly [meeting] which ever assembled in the county, and plainly shows that there is no spirit of harmony in the secession faction." Still, that group passed a resolution stating "that for the wrongs under which the South has suffered, there is but one remedy, that is secession."[25]

There were cooperationist conventions as well, including an attempted statewide meeting on November 29 at Vicksburg, but only four counties sent delegates. That lackluster turnout illustrated a weaker and less organized opposition effort. Still, cooperationists met in individual counties all across the state. In Madison County, what one anti-secession paper described as the "'bone and sinew' of the country . . . the 'solid men' of Madison," met at the Canton courthouse and passed resolutions condemning separate state secession and advocating a "Southern Convention." They also argued that any action should be referred to the people for a vote and that the state's congressmen should remain in Congress to work on a compromise. They insisted that "nine million of free white people, with three million of faithful slaves to provide for their necessities, should not be alarmed, by the mere inauguration of Lincoln." And despite the lack of organization, there was some confidence in the cooperationist ranks. The Yazoo County coopera-tionists nominated C. F. Hamer and Fred G. Smith and wrongly declared their election "is certain by a decisive majority."[26]

By far the most influential cooperationists were in Warren County, where friendly newspapers such as the *Vicksburg Whig* supported their stance. The cooperationists held local elections to determine delegates to a county con-vention on December 8. That convention, described by secessionist papers as a "submission meeting" and "Union-at-any-price" event, nominated for-mer U.S. senator Walker Brooke and lawyer Thomas A. Marshall as its can-didates. Local papers took up the cause and daily gave reports on the two candidates' speeches, activities, and attempts to usher in cooperation, urging everyone to attend speeches, "the ladies particularly." The cooperationists were so well organized in Warren County that events were held where other speakers addressed crowds at the same time that Marshall and Brooke were speaking in different portions of the county.[27]

Although the Vicksburg papers supported the cooperationist candidates, they did run opposing secessionist candidates' advertisements. But they lev-eled every accusation they could in doing so, pointing out how secessionist Johnson had been a member of the 1851 convention and had voted against a secessionist resolution. "Let the secessionists stick a pin there," decried the cooperationist *Vicksburg Whig* on December 14. The editor added, "if a con-servative should say such a thing, he would be charged at once with giving aid and comfort to Black Republicanism." Johnson and McCardle ignored the attacks and offered direct questions for Marshall and Brooke to answer, such as whether they supported a Southern convention, whether they sup-ported an ultimatum to the North, and whether they supported secession with all the slave states participating. In a heavily cooperationist county, however, Marshall's and Brooke's answers only solidified their support.[28]

Some counties opted for neither extreme, nominating relatively unop-posed tickets. In fact, the *Natchez Courier* reported that only a "little over half the counties . . . [are] contested." Another paper declared, "In Holly Springs, there is but one sentiment: resistance to Black Republicans and free negro." The people of Yalobusha County, "discarding all parties and party names," nominated two delegates apparently without other opposition, William R. Barksdale and Francis M. Aldridge. Their resolutions supported Mississippi separation, but only with other slave states and with the consent of the people of the state via a referendum. In Copiah County, the convention nominated a Breckinridge delegate and a Bell delegate without any opposition, but called in their resolutions for "immediate withdrawal of the State of Mississippi from the Union, without reference to the action of any other state."[29]

Historian Percy L. Rainwater has asserted that these counties produced "coalition" tickets, one secessionist and one cooperationist teaming together without opposition. Although many historians of Mississippi secession have followed his idea, they cite no other sources but Rainwater. Unfortunately, Rainwater cited only general newspapers and no specific articles. Nevertheless there is little evidence to support such an official compromise. The only press support for this idea comes from a *Natchez Courier* article in which the editor explained that "in a large number of counties, there was no contested candidates upon the one side or the other—for co-operation or for State secession—having been nominated by county meetings and elected without opposition." However, the account does not say anything about a coalition, just that there was no opposition. Adding to the doubt about a coalition in the nine counties Rainwater enumerated, the contemporary newspapers' effort to delineate the side of the elected delegates firmly placed each county's delegates as a whole into either the cooperationist or secessionist camp. Newspapers did not split any of the county candidates at the time, with the exception of Itawamba County, where three delegates were listed as secessionist and only Arthur Bullard was called a cooperationist. Yet even there, the split was not half and half, which was necessarily one of the tenets of coalition tickets.[30]

Surviving newspapers, which for these years are the best gauges of county-level elections, are rare for most of the allegedly coalition counties, but extant papers from two of them indicate that no coalition maneuvering took place. In Panola County, one of the supposed coalition ticket counties, the *Weekly Panola Star*, reported that the election "passed off very quietly. There being no opposition candidates, the people took but little interest in the matter. Scarcely one half the votes of the county were polled." The vote turned out 730 for Edward F. McGehee and 722 for John B. Fizer, with twenty votes scattered among seven others who were probably not official candidates but whose names were written in. Obviously there was no opposition to McGehee and Fizer, but nothing in the newspaper indicated that they were elected as a coalition, or that one was secessionist and one was cooperationist. In fact, the secessionist *Jackson Weekly Mississippian* labeled both McGehee and Fizer as cooperationists, while the cooperationist *Vicksburg Whig* labeled them both as immediate secessionists.[31]

The newspaper coverage of the canvass in Lafayette County provides more information on the matter of coalition. Thought to be a coalition ticket of Lamar, who had left Congress to return home and campaign for a seat in the convention (he was present at the opening of the 2nd Session of the 36th Congress on December 3 but left Washington by December 12), and Thomas D. Isom, the ticket was actually secessionist. The secessionists in the county pushed through Lamar and Isom in a meeting at the courthouse, and the *Oxford Intelligencer* reported, "the co-operation party of Lafayette County being dissatisfied with the nomination of Lamar and Isom as delegates to the State convention of the 7th of January, have agreed to run a conservative ticket and have nominated D. Robertson and J. S. Buford to represent them in said convention." The newspaper went on to state, "Yes, and the 'conservative ticket' has agreed that it won't run," adding in response to a question concerning whether there was even a cooperationist party in Lafayette, "Unquestionably we have. We do not assert that it is a large party, but large or small it is no more and no less than a party." In the final vote, Robertson and Buford polled 161 and 148 votes, respectively, which were nowhere near Isom's and Lamar's totals of 834 and 815, respectively, but still were significant. And this time, the Jackson and Vicksburg papers labeled both Isom and Lamar as secessionists. Obviously the two secessionist delegates from Lafayette County were not coalition candidates.[32]

Like the coalition ticket issue, only scraps of evidence remain concerning the actual county canvasses. A future delegate from Hinds County left perhaps the most detailed account of a convention canvass. Already one of the leading men in the state and destined to play a major role at the secession convention, Wiley P. Harris wrote in his autobiography that he was hesitant to even enter the race. He told supporters that secession "was one of those movements which if it meant anything would not end speedily, and that I was loath to embark upon it, because I did not clearly see where I was or where I was to land." Yet his supporters won him over, and he joined a secessionist ticket that also included William B. Smart and Warren P. Anderson. But the ticket had problems from the beginning; Harris recalled: "My colleague was not gifted with the faculty of speech-making and our opponents were the very ablest men in the State, William Yerger, and Fulton Anderson." Harris detailed some of the canvass process when he related, "they obtained the advantage in every debate, except the last, which was held at Jackson." Harris believed that last debate turned the tide for the secessionists, but readily admitted, "the audience was largely on my side at the beginning."[33]

In regard to issues, Yerger and Anderson "charged" Harris and the others with supporting secession even without cooperation from other slave states. For his part, Harris "conceded that one state could not maintain herself out of the Union, but that they must withdraw, each for herself and one must venture to take the step in advance." Harris had attended multistate conventions before and knew they were destined to do nothing. As a result, he charged the cooperationists with "a scheme which, whether so designed or not, was destined to fail of any result, through dilatory measures, conventions, conferences, debates and resolutions, all ending in no decisive act and that we would be covered with disgrace by it." Other immediate secessionists across the state echoed Harris. In Pontotoc County, Charles Fontaine wrote, "we should secede first and cooperate afterwards."[34]

The prospects of war were also debated, Harris wrongly insisting that no war would come. Anderson and Yerger argued there would be "a war of great stubbornness," and they thus desired that the border states be on board before such a step was taken. Harris countered that the "advice of these states would be to delay actions to try other methods," which would end in nothing being done. Harris won the debate and eventually the election, mainly because "the general sentiment was adverse to war, and there was a general desire to avoid it by thinking men." Harris had thus told them what they wanted to hear.[35]

John H. Aughey, although not a candidate but a pro-Union Presbyterian minister in Choctaw and Attala counties, also left a record of the local events during the secession canvass. Since he was later arrested for Unionism, fled north to Union territory, and published a book in 1863 about what he called the "iron furnace" of secession, he perhaps cannot be cited as an impartial observer. But his account contains two opposing speeches from the Choctaw County election, one given by the unsuccessful cooperationist R. C. Love. Asserting that secession meant war, Love counseled moderation by waiting until "Mr. Lincoln does something unconstitutional," and then securing concert of action with other states: "Would not Mississippi cut a sorry figure among the nations of the earth?" He concluded that Mississippi should "look before we leap." According to Aughey, the other unnamed speechmaker, obviously William F. Brantley, William H. Witty, or James H. Edwards, talked of "this accursed Union" and referenced good news out of

Tallahatchie County in which seven "tory-submissionists" were hanged and the cooperationists were not even canvassing the county. Making his account more believable, the secessionist candidate in Tallahatchie County eventually won by a landslide, 171–11.[36]

Aughey left a vivid account of his own voting, obviously in Choctaw County because Attala actually sent two cooperationist delegates to Jackson. He arrived at the polling place in his precinct, asked for a Union ticket, "and was informed that none had been printed, and that it would be advisable to vote the secession ticket." He "thought otherwise" and wrote out his own "Union ticket." He recalled he "voted it amidst the frowns and suppressed murmurs of the judges and bystanders." He went on to say he placed the only Union vote in that precinct, which is doubtful since the three cooperationist candidates in Choctaw each received over 500 votes. He added, "I knew of many who were in favor of the Union, who were intimidated by threats, and by the odium attending it from voting at all."[37]

There were numerous complaints of intimidation elsewhere as well, such as in Jefferson County, where the cooperationist *Fayette Times* complained its candidate was not able to get into the race until December 15, and then his campaign circulars did not appear until the next Monday, a mere three days before the election. The paper worried about shenanigans taking place, stating in italics that for "*some* unknown cause," his circulars were not widely distributed. The paper decided, "Had the people known it, we feel confident that he would have been elected." In Rankin County, the cooperationists leveled charges that secessionists used whiskey, demagoguism, and "promises of corn and meat" to gain support. R. F. Crenshaw wrote in mid-December that the people were so "convulsed here now in Miss. With Secession, that the man who does not give, not only <u>one day</u> but <u>all his time</u> to his Country is regarded at best a lukewarm patriot."[38]

Historians such as Christopher Olsen and particularly William L. Barney have examined the threats of violence and the use of fear in the secession canvass. Numerous manners of swaying the vote took place, with Pettus even beginning to whip up war support by buying arms to defend the state. The secessionists certainly pushed their beliefs with abundant banners and speeches; future Confederate general and Mississippi governor Benjamin Humphreys remembered that in Sunflower County, "secession banners were everywhere." Such patriotic fervor no doubt swayed some. William L. Barney has described a "triumvirate of paramilitary organizations" such as "Minute Men" associations, vigilance committees, and volunteer military companies that also worked hard for secession. Secessionists also used the

Mississippi Counties
1861

economic argument to good effect and played on many Mississippians' turmoil, such as worries about the recent drought in the central portion of the state. While Christopher Olsen agrees in part, he concludes that "secession was much more populist than manipulated, more instinctive than coerced." There is no doubt that some threat took place, but Mississippi would probably have voted a secessionist convention no matter how much coercion occurred. And there are accounts of the same trickery or underhandedness taking place on the other side. The secessionist *Jackson Mississippian* warned its readers to "beware of split tickets," saying they would be "as thick as blackberries in June." It went on: "Examine your ballot carefully, before you deposit it. Be sure you are all right and then go the whole figure."³⁹

Others used their status to gain votes. Most thought secession meant war, so several of the candidates, including Miles McGehee, Charles Clark, and Edward P. Jones, offered 100 bales of cotton as an "advance to purchase arms and munitions of war for our defense." A less well off Lamar offered $200. Lamar, Jones, and McGehee all won their elections, but Clark was defeated. Still, it must have been more than just mere campaigning; several noncandidates also offered the same, with H. C. Chambers giving 100 bales and Jefferson Davis offering $1,000.⁴⁰

With this mixture of elements common to all Mississippi elections of that day, the sixty counties in the state held their canvasses on December 20, 1860, the *Vicksburg Daily Whig* belting out a large headline, "Are You Ready?" Turnout was extremely low, only about 60 percent of those who had voted in the presidential election in November. Most observers admitted that the immediate secessionists had the election well in hand and that this belief may have accounted for the significantly low turnout. When the votes were counted, that intuition proved true.⁴¹

The county election returns in the secretary of state's files in the Mississippi Department of Archives and History indicate no major pattern except for an overall two-to-one majority for the secessionists. The votes were landslides in some counties, such as in Tallahatchie, where Alexander Pattison defeated his opponent J. C. Stark 171 to 11. In Marion County, Hamilton Mayson defeated William Barnes and Lemuel Lewis 90 to 4, and in Neshoba County, David Backstrom beat Ira N. Nash 601 to 58. Perhaps the biggest landslide was in Harrison County, where David C. Glenn defeated L. L. Davis 314 to 1.⁴²

The votes in other counties were much closer. In Wilkinson County, Alfred C. Holt won his election over Jones S. Hamilton 334 to 306, while in Washington County, Jacob S. Yerger defeated W. L. Nugent by only seven votes, 129 to 122. In Bolivar County, Miles H. McGehee defeated Charles Clark by twenty-three votes, 202 to 179. The closest race was in Issaquena County, where Albert C. Gibson defeated F. W. Moore by a mere two votes, 73 to 71.[43]

By early January 1861, then, Mississippians had invested their trust in the hands of 100 men who would decide their fate. The legislature had called for the convention, and the local elections had determined the membership of the state body. Although the wait for the opening of the convention now began, not all sat idle until January 7. Some joked about secession and union, R. F. Crenshaw reporting that the men were all for secession but the women were for union: "Union of hearts and a Union of hands," he said. Cordelia Scales similarly joked, "notwithstanding the great secession excitement here, some of the ladies seem to be in favor of 'Union to a man.'" There was also serious business to be done. Never one to remain inactive, Governor Pettus was busy during the interim period, corresponding with other governors and appointing the various commissioners to the individual slave states. Those commissioners were busy traveling and speaking, as were those from other states to Mississippi; the *Charleston Mercury* reportedly recommended the treatment for cooperationist commissioners from border states: "feed them—drench them in champagne and let them go." Pettus also invoked a higher power, asking that the citizens of Mississippi pause for a day of "fasting, humiliation, and prayer" on December 31, during which businesses would close and the people would gather at their respective churches "so that the united voice of a whole people may go up to Heaven for counsel and assistance."[44]

But it was primarily the delegates who were acting during the wait, mostly in the backrooms in undercover negotiations about the future nature of secession. As the weeks passed and January 7 loomed nearer, the delegates were already beginning to coalesce around fairly solid ideals that they would bring to the convention.

- 2 -

DELEGATES

January 1861

FOUR DECADES AFTER THE MEETING OF THE MISSISSIPPI SECESSION convention in 1861, the youngest member of that body, Thomas H. Woods, reflected on what had happened, how it had happened, and the men who had made it happen. He was in a nostalgic mood as he wrote; he was, after all, one of only a few members still alive at that point. Despite the disastrous results of the war the convention had helped bring on, Woods placed a chivalric halo around the convention, presenting the delegates as heroes of a lost cause and the elite of antebellum society. "It can be truthfully affirmed by the youngest and most inconspicuous member of our Secession Convention," Woods remembered, "that in learning, in ability, in patriotism, and in nobility of individual character no such body had ever before, or has ever since, been assembled within our borders." To Woods, looking back after nearly half a century, the convention delegates were the best Mississippi had to offer for making such a momentous decision.[1]

Woods's ideal of Southern manliness and honor was clearly a part of the Lost Cause myth then sweeping the South, and it readily became the accepted version of the convention. And other famous Mississippians supported Woods's thinking. Wiley Harris wrote that "the convention of the State of Mississippi was composed of the best men of the State," and J. F. H. Claiborne argued, "it was a convention of the ablest, the purest and the most opulent men in the State." Obviously Woods, Harris, and Claiborne were all writing years after the event when the time for unity had come. Only a few contemporaries offered any exception, and some jokingly, with Joel Berry remarking, "this Convention is for talent and ability—composed, as it is, of the most distinguished men in the State, with the exception of myself, and perhaps a few others." John L. Power, in detailing the most notable figures of the membership, added, "other great men were there by the score, and others then unknown to fame."[2]

But were the delegates the best Mississippi had to offer? Were they the cream of the social and political elite of Mississippi? To truly understand the convention, what happened, and why it happened, the delegates must be understood. A comprehensive analysis of who they were, what ideals they brought to the convention, and their backgrounds must be made to determine if delegate Woods was correct.

The statistical breakdown of the 100 delegates offers some surprising new pieces of information. Some of the statistical information has already been plowed by contemporary newspapers as well as such historians as Percy L. Rainwater and Robert Wooster, but there are other factors that still beg to be defined. Fortunately, there is a wealth of information on the members, starting with a descriptive roster of delegates compiled by the reporter of the convention, John L. Power. Although that list contains a wealth of statistical information, it is neither infallible nor complete. Cross-referencing the data with census records as well as biographical sketches not systematically mined previously provides historians with an abundance of data on the men of the Mississippi secession convention.[3]

Most of the delegates were younger rather than older. Thomas Woods correctly noted, "they were gentlemen in the full maturity of splendid young manhood, in the main." The average age of the Mississippi delegate was forty-two, with only ten delegates in their twenties. There were twenty-five delegates in their thirties, but the largest group was those in their forties; forty-six of the delegates were in that age range. Given the shorter life expectancy of the day, it is logical that only sixteen were in their fifties and only three in their sixties. The youngest member was Woods of Kemper County; he was a mere twenty-four at the time, unmarried, and fresh out of college. The oldest was Henry Vaughan of Yazoo County, who at age sixty was born just three months into the nineteenth century. While none of the delegates remembered the volatile times of the American Revolution, they were certainly reared on stories of those events. And fully 40 percent of them had been born prior to or during the War of 1812, the second American Revolution, as it was known.[4]

With most of the members born in the early days of America's existence and before major expansion westward occurred, it is not surprising that forty-six of the delegates were born in the original thirteen states, with twenty-three more born in Kentucky and Tennessee, states that had joined the

Union prior to 1800. South Carolina produced the most delegates, eighteen in all. While expansion took place laterally as families of the Deep South migrated westward with their institution of slavery while the settlers of the Midwest were mostly from the middle Northern states and New England, such prevailing lateral tracks produced common bonds of community and custom. Thus the vast majority of the members came from Southern families. Ninety-three of the 100 members were born in a slave state or territory, and those east of Mississippi produced fully 77 percent of them. While the relatively young state of Mississippi produced a surprising fourteen native sons for the convention, those states and territories to the west were obviously not key producers of delegates. Missouri produced one delegate, Samuel Benton of Marshall County, and Arkansas was the birthplace of another, the young Woods of Kemper.[5]

There was only a scattering of delegates from Northern free states, including Josiah Winchester born in Massachusetts, Henry T. Ellett from New Jersey, William Booth from New York, Harvey W. Walter from Ohio, James L. Alcorn from Illinois, and Jacob S. Yerger and William J. Douglas from Pennsylvania. As expected, the birthplace of each delegate had at least something to do with his views on secession. Three of the seven born in free states, 42 percent, opposed secession while only 32 percent of those born in Southern states took the same position. Ironically, in several cases, those Northern-born cooperationists came to the South in their childhoods, while most of the more secessionist Northern-born delegates grew to manhood in the North. In reality, while birthplace had an obvious effect on molding most of the delegates to Southern views, it was not determinative.[6]

The occupations of the various delegates were almost as varied as the men themselves, but there were several dominant groups. Delegate Woods asserted that "the Mississippi Secession Convention was adorned, inspired, and largely controlled by its lawyer members. Judge Wiley P. Harris, then and until his death the recognized and unchallenged leader of the bar in Mississippi, was pre-eminently influential in the work of that epoch-making assembly, and his voice was regarded as the voice of an oracle. . . . Beside Judge Harris, there were Lamar, George, Brooke, Marshall, Yerger, . . . Barry, . . . Alcorn, with many another,—all accounted luminaries of the first magnitude in the legal firmament." In all, some forty-five of the delegates had some type of law career. Most were outright lawyers, while some had more specific positions. Seven of the delegates were local judges; four delegates, James R. Chalmers, James S. Johnston, Samuel H. Terral, and Jehu A. Orr, had spent time as district attorneys; Alexander M. Clayton and

Samuel J. Gholson were federal judges; Clayton was a former member of the High Court of Errors and Appeals (the state's supreme court); David C. Glenn had been the state's attorney general; and James Z. George was the state supreme court's reporter.[7]

The other dominant group was the planter or farmer class, many of whom used the terms interchangeably. Fifty-one of the delegates listed some type of agricultural pursuit as their chief occupation or were heavily involved in that business prior to the convention, and that does not count other distinct agricultural jobs such as the two delegates who were saddlers. Of course, there was a wide variation in this group, from the small subsistence farmer all the way up to the large plantation owners with hundreds of slaves, which Woods described as "the lordly owners of immense landed estates, who lived the ample and opulent lives of country gentlemen."[8]

The delegates who fell into both of these dominant groups oftentimes switched back and forth and could rightfully claim to be members of both. And once they became self-sufficient and wealthy, they often dabbled in extracurricular activities of interest, most notably politics. Thus a large percentage of the delegates had some type of political experience when they came to Jackson in 1861, ranging from the U.S. Congress down to local town alderman. There was also a justice of the peace, a member of a county board of police, a tax assessor and collector, a court reporter, a supreme court member, two sheriffs, and two circuit clerks. Many of the delegates also held higher offices, such as a U.S. marshal, a U.S. consul to Havana, and a member of the Mississippi River levee board. Many of the delegates engaged in numerous other duties such as party convention delegates, candidates for governor, and 1851 constitutional convention delegates. Three—Samuel Gholson, Wiley Harris, and Alexander Clayton—had been elected by the legislature to represent the state in the April 1860 Atlanta convention that never occurred. Obviously the highest state officers were those members who were or had been members of the legislature. Thirty-eight delegates had represented their locales in Jackson, while four of the members had served in other state legislatures. George R. Clayton of Lowndes County and L. Q. C. Lamar of Lafayette County had served in the Georgia legislature, while Joel H. Berry of Tippah County had served in the South Carolina legislature and James L. Alcorn in the Kentucky assembly.[9]

The most renowned politicians were the delegates who had previously served in the U.S. Congress. William S. Barry, Wiley P. Harris, Daniel B. Wright, Henry T. Ellett, Samuel J. Gholson, and L. Q. C. Lamar had all served in Congress during the 1850s, with Lamar having just left his seat in December 1860. Walker Brooke had served in the U.S. Senate.[10]

In addition to the law, planting, and politics, the delegates collectively held other positions in a wide range of fields. Woods remarked, "the most casual observer would have been struck with the vigorous and intellectual appearance of the membership." Several had been schooled at the state university at Oxford, and others had attended such institutions as the University of North Carolina, the University of Virginia, Yale, and Princeton. Eleven delegates had some type of medical training and were physicians, five were editors or printers of newspapers, and two were teachers. Lamar was on the faculty at the University of Mississippi. Only two were ministers, causing Woods to remark on the "absolute divorce of church and state." There were also three mechanics and a stock raiser. William A. Sumner of Calhoun County listed his occupation simply as "varied."[11]

Given the martial nature of the antebellum South, surprisingly only three members were veterans of the Mexican War: James Z. George, John B. Deason, and Albert P. Hill. John J. Thornton was a militia officer in Rankin County, as were James R. Chalmers in DeSoto, John B. Deason in Hancock, and Samuel H. Terral in Clarke. Most delegates were married, but there were seven single men, including James M. Nelson of Pike County who did not consider himself single but a "Bachel'r." There were ten widowers and two sets of brothers: the McGehee brothers, Edward and Miles, and the Miller brothers, Andrew and Hugh. Perhaps most fascinating, one of Monroe County's delegates, Samuel Gholson, had earlier challenged the county's other delegate to a duel.[12]

Given the emphasis on slavery in the canvassing for delegate positions in December, the members' slave ownership was significant. The average number of slaves owned by each delegate for which there are records (four counties' censuses are missing) is around thirty-four. The number is heavily skewed by a few large owners such as Henry Vaughan, who owned 293 slaves, and the median number is probably more descriptive at 16. Furthermore, when each slave owner is broken down, despite incomplete slave schedules in the four counties, a very different picture emerges.[13]

Historians have traditionally posited that ownership of twenty slaves placed the individual into the planter class, probably due mostly to the later wartime limit created at that level for exemption from the Confederate army. More recently, historians have revised that number to fifty or more slaves, Ralph Wooster labeling such owners as "large planters." Either way, owners of numerous slaves did not dominate the convention, and were apparently little liked in society. Wiley Harris noted that planters were "without influence" and "deserved to be unpopular. The insufferable arrogance and ostentation of these people at home, and abroad, drew upon them actual antipathy everywhere." They "became a thorough . . . and a recognized nuisance," he said. In fact, sixteen of the members did not own a single slave, and an additional twenty-seven owned ten or fewer. Ten more owned between eleven and nineteen slaves, which put the total number of delegates considered to be out of the planter class at fifty-three, a slight majority. Twenty-one delegates owned between twenty and forty-nine slaves, which, if the threshold of fifty is used to designate elite status, meant that 74 percent of the delegates were not elite planters. On the other hand, there were a few large planters in the membership. Seventeen delegates owned between 50 and 100 slaves, one owned 140, and four were super planters with 200 or more. Walter Kiern of Holmes County owned 211 slaves, Miles McGehee of Bolivar owned 234, Alexander K. Farrar of Adams owned 238, and Henry Vaughan of Yazoo owned 293.[14]

Since most capital in the state was vested in land and slaves, the net worth of each delegate largely followed the number of slaves each owned. Almost always, the members with more slaves were better off. Five members had a net worth of zero, and they owned no slaves. Twenty-one of the delegates had a total net worth of $10,000 or less, which meant a full quarter of the delegates had a net worth of less than that amount. Only fourteen members had wealth higher than $100,000, with four being above $200,000 and only Alexander K. Farrar of Adams County having above $300,000. It is not surprising that Farrar was from the Natchez area, where historians have long noted the abundance of rich planters.[15]

Yet in actuality, political persuasion, not slaveholding status, seems to have proved more essential in determining how the members viewed their duty in Jackson. And the politics of geography made a big difference in the representation at the convention. The locations from which those cooperationist delegates hailed indicated where the majority of the opposition to secession lay, the same area that had supported Constitutional Union Party candidate John Bell. The twenty-three delegates who were listed as cooperationists came from Adams, Amite, Attala, Bolivar, Calhoun, Coahoma, Franklin, Jones, Pontotoc, Rankin, Tishomingo, Tunica, Warren, and Washington counties, six of which were large slaveholding counties along the Mississippi River. A Vicksburg paper aptly described these areas as "depositories of great wealth—and as no one of respectable intelligence will deny, largely interested in the institution of slavery." Two other anti-secession counties were situated adjacent to the plantation area of Adams County, and Rankin was one of the largest slave-owning counties in the state. The *Vicksburg Whig* declared the cooperationist victory in Rankin, which had earlier

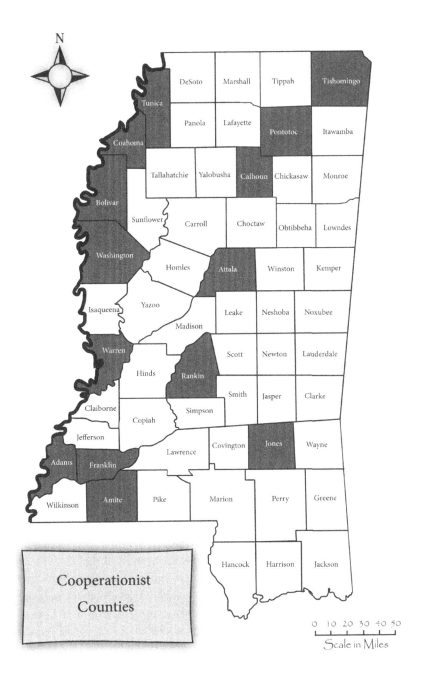

N

DeSoto
Marshall
Tippah
Tishomingo
Tunica
Panola
Lafayette
Pontotoc
Itawamba
Coahoma
Tallahatchie
Yalobusha
Calhoun
Chickasaw
Monroe
Bolivar
Sunflower
Carroll
Choctaw
Obtibbeha
Lowndes
Washington
Homles
Attala
Winston
Kemper
Isaqueena
Yazoo
Leake
Neshoba
Noxubee
Madison
Warren
Scott
Newton
Lauderdale
Hinds
Rankin
Smith
Jasper
Clarke
Claiborne
Simpson
Jefferson
Copiah
Covington
Jones
Wayne
Adams
Lawrence
Franklin
Wilkinson
Amite
Pike
Marion
Perry
Greene
Hancock
Harrison
Jackson

Cooperationist
Counties

0 10 20 30 40 50
Scale in Miles

voted for Breckinridge in the presidential election, as the "greatest victory of the age." Tishomingo County, in the extreme northeast hill country, contained comparatively fewer slaves, but was ironically the other large area of cooperationist sentiment. A Vicksburg cooperationist paper declared it "the banner county of patriotism and conservatism." Itawamba County later proved to be cooperationist as well, thus making the northeast hill country look even more favorable to cooperation. The cooperation sentiment was therefore strongest in the Mississippi River counties and the northeastern sector of Mississippi, with a few locales scattered among the rest.[16]

Conversely, the secessionists did best in the old Democratic areas of north-central Mississippi and the southern portions of the state. One newspaper reported that the southeast quadrant of the state "is all a fire with the Spirit of '76." Intelligence from north Mississippi, as reported in the *Jackson Mississippian*, similarly indicated that secessionism was "sweeping everything before it in that section of the State." A visitor from Panola County told the paper it was "seething hot" for secession.[17]

Old-line political party affiliation also played a major role in shaping the various caucuses about to form in Jackson. The largest number of delegates were Democrats and old Whigs. The violent decade of the 1850s and the election of 1860 had done major damage to both parties, putting the Whigs formally out of existence but allowing old Whigs to retain enough dedication to continue to use the name even in 1861. Still, the volatile 1860 election had split what was left of both political groups. Generally speaking, the Democrats were pro-secession while the Whigs favored cooperation. At least forty delegates listed some type of variation of Democrat, whether it be "Secession Democrat," "Southern Rights Democrat," "States Rights Democrat," or something else. In all, twenty-three members gave some variation of being a Whig, although some of them were in the secession camp as well. Many took generic labels based on what Ralph Wooster has called their "intense loyalty to the South." They called themselves "Southern," "Southern Rights," or "States Rights." Others listed strange labels such as "A Mississippian," "Disunionist per se," and "Opposed to Universal Suffrage."[18]

The religious affiliation of the members similarly provides hints into their views on slavery and secession. Not every delegate listed his religious preference, but those who did were mainly Baptists, Methodists, Episcopalians, and Presbyterians; those denominations accounted for 81 percent of the members at the convention. Sixteen listed the Baptist Church, and twenty-five, a full quarter of the delegates, listed the Methodist Church. Those two denominations had already split over the slavery issue, so most of their views can be readily discerned. The Presbyterians only split after the convention and during the war, thus accounting for some of the cooperationist feeling among them. In addition to those major denominations, thirteen delegates listed themselves as Episcopalians, with three Catholics. There were also variations of "Christian," "Friendly to All," and members who listed "Jesus Christ," "Free Will," or "Masonry." Some were more devout than others, so any indication of just how much any of the members' religions tempered their politics is a guess. It can be assumed, however, that Baptist minister William J. Denson of Rankin County and Cumberland Presbyterian minister Arthur B. Bullard of Itawamba County were perhaps the most religiously devoted.[19]

Combining all these characteristics results in significant insights. Most of the delegates were young to middle-aged, in their thirties or forties. Most were born east of Mississippi in slave states and then migrated westward as the new territories and states opened up. Most were Protestant, either lawyers or farmers, with many of them being both as they diversified their growing wealth. Many of them had thrown their hats into the political ring and had been elected to an assortment of mainly local and state offices. Most were not rich, having to work hard in the law or farming to keep revenue flowing to support their families. The majority owned slaves, but most owned only a few, below the magic number of twenty that differentiated between the subsistence farmer and the planter, and far below the revised elite number of fifty used today. The majority of the delegates were still working to become elite, large-scale slave-owning lords. While most were comfortable, there were no millionaires. The entire group as a whole seemed to be rather normal instead of extraordinary, representing well the state's population.[20]

A representative convention member was Charles D. Fontaine of Pontotoc County. Forty-three years old, he had been born in Virginia and had moved to Mississippi as a young adult. He had studied law under the famous Jacob Thompson, eventually opening his own practice in Pontotoc, where he developed local status. He was not rich, his net worth only $8,350 in 1860. He had, however, managed to buy four slaves, who were probably domestic servants rather than agricultural hands. With a prospering law career, Fontaine dabbled in politics, even running unsuccessfully for governor during the 1855 Know Nothing period in Mississippi. He was also sent to Jackson to represent Pontotoc County in the legislature. He was Episcopalian and listed his political persuasion as "Disunionst per se."[21]

Another average member was Methodist James B. Ramsey of Lauderdale County. He had been born in North Carolina and had moved with his family to Alabama, where he grew to manhood and obtained an education. He was a physician by profession, first practicing in Alabama before moving on westward to near Meridian. He was forty years old at the time of the convention and had obtained some status as a physician in the community. Ramsey dabbled in planting, owning thirty-three slaves in 1860, although he listed his net worth in 1860 as only $3,000. Obviously most of his money was tied up in land and slaves. He listed his politics as "Secession Democrat."[22]

An average member of the convention on the higher end of the scale was Stephen D. Johnston of Hernando in DeSoto County. Born in Georgia, he was forty-nine years old at the time of the convention and made his living in agriculture. He owned a large plantation and worked fifty-five slaves. His net worth in 1860 was $58,000. He also served on the local county board of police as well as in the state legislature. He was a Baptist and independent in political persuasion.[23]

An examination of these and other members of the convention thus indicates the proclivity of local lawyers, small farmers and laborers, limited slave owners (if at all), and moderate estate values, painting a picture of a fairly common set of men studded by a few elite. Indeed, only a mere handful of delegates to the 1861 convention, such as James L. Alcorn and Wiley P. Harris, had been members of the earlier 1851 convention. On the other hand, an investigation into who was not a member of the convention also yields important information. Despite delegate Woods's high-toned synopsis, its seems that many elite, able, patriotic, and noble Mississippians were not there for a myriad of reasons, including work elsewhere, lack of interest, or defeat in the December canvass. A look at who was not a member of the convention can tell us almost as much as examining who was there.[24]

The pool of potential convention members was obviously depleted due to several statesmen already holding political offices. Had John J. Pettus not been the governor and thus ineligible for the convention, he would have been an eager participant no doubt. Others in the executive branch of Mississippi's government were likewise disqualified because of their current jobs. Men such as Attorney General Thomas J. Wharton and State Auditor Erasmus R. Burt were well known among Mississippians and could have been elected were they not already ensconced in their political positions.[25]

The men in the judicial branch suffered a similar exclusion, specifically the judges on the state High Court of Errors and Appeals. Alexander H. Handy, Cotesworth Pinckney Smith, and William L. Harris were all stalwarts of the bar in Mississippi, with Harris having been offered a spot on the U.S. Supreme Court but turning it down. Several former members of the state supreme court, such as William L. Sharkey, were likewise well known but not a part of the convention. Alexander M. Clayton was the only former member involved.[26]

The members of the legislature were not precluded from becoming members of the convention, but most did not try to do both. Most likely, members of the legislature saw the convention as a separate and distinct body taking separate and distinct actions, and they thought the two should remain separate. That Governor Pettus was likely to call a special session of the legislature during the convention also determined legislators' thinking.[27]

Still, four members of the legislature were elected to the convention. Philip S. Catching was a senator from Copiah County, while Henry T. Ellett was a member from Claiborne County. Marshall M. Keith of Newton County and Edward P. Jones of Sunflower County were members of the house. But then there were a number of other well-known Mississippians in the legislature who were not members of the convention, among them Absalom M. West of Holmes County, W. C. Smedes of Warren County, Wirt Adams of Issaquena County, J. A. P. Campbell of Attala County, Charles Clark of Bolivar County, Charles E. Hooker of Hinds County, and William S. Wilson of Claiborne County. Three of these, Clark, Campbell, and West, ran for positions in the convention but were defeated.[28]

Mississippi's representatives in Washington were also extremely well known and considered to be the elite of politics and society, but only one of them became a member of the convention, Representative L. Q. C. Lamar. He had left his congressional seat in December 1860 to return home and canvass for the election. Neither of Mississippi's senators, Jefferson Davis and Albert Gallatin Brown, were candidates for the convention, but remained in Washington through the terrible ordeal of the secession winter. The other four representatives in the U.S. House of Representatives—Reuben Davis, William Barksdale, Otho R. Singleton, and former governor John J. McRae—likewise remained in the nation's capital.[29]

Then there were the commissioners Governor Pettus sent to other Southern states to carry the standard of Mississippi secession. Such luminaries as supreme court justices Alexander H. Handy and William L. Harris, Attorney General Thomas J. Wharton, and legislators Wirt Adams and Charles E. Hooker traveled the South seeking cooperation in secession. Only two of the eventual commissioners were defeated in the canvass for the convention, George S. Gaines of Wayne County and Fulton Anderson of Hinds County. Other well-known Mississippians who became commissioners were likewise not part of the government or the canvass, including the sitting secretary of the interior, Jacob Thompson, and former congressman Winfield S. Featherston.[30]

One of the major reasons fewer luminaries than expected were part of the convention was because many of them had been defeated in the election. The extant returns for the December 20 election list 217 names (including the delegates from the counties with no returns but not including several grouped together only under a "scattering" heading in several counties). Two future governors were not sent to Jackson, including Charles Clark, who lost a very close election in Bolivar County to Miles H. McGehee, and Benjamin Humphries, who lost by a landslide in Sunflower County to Edward P. Jones. Both would be Confederate generals, and Clark would be governor in just two years and Humphries in four; few governors rose from obscurity so fast, so they must have had at least some following in the years prior to their election. The sitting Speaker of the house, J. A. P. Campbell of Attala County, was denied a seat, as was state senator A. M. West of Holmes. Fulton Anderson of Hinds County, who Mississippi luminary James Z. George described in the 1850s as the "best lawyer in the State," was likewise denied. In Tishomingo County, defeated candidate Leroy B. Gaston was a college president in Corinth, and lawyer William M. Inge had attended the United States Military Academy at West Point. Newspaper editor William H. McCardle of Vicksburg was likewise not among the winners. Perhaps the most prominent Mississippian to be denied a seat was William Yerger of Hinds County, who was a former justice on the supreme court and a well-known lawyer.[31]

There were numerous other well-known Mississippians who chose to stay out of the process altogether, men such as Jackson newspaper editor Ethelbert Barksdale, former Choctaw chief Greenwood Leflore, and writer, geologist, and professor B. L. C. Wailes. Many called on historian and politician J. F. H. Claiborne to vie for a seat, but one newspaper reported, "he positively refused to be a candidate, as he has for the last twenty years declined to run for any office." The paper added that the men who had agreed to run "were ready to decline in his favor," but he wanted no part of it. The convention's membership thus lacked many of the most notable Mississippians of the time.[32]

Even if the elected delegates were not the cream of Mississippi's statesmen, how those who were elected lined up was crucial to the outcome of this movement of secession. Most counties did not require their delegates to vote any certain way (Greene County being an exception), but those elected generally represented the interests of the majority of the population in those counties, and they often made promises during the canvass to adhere to one side or the other. There were apparently any number of ways the counties themselves determined what tickets would be provided or what individual candidates ran on. The election returns rarely list any party or ideology on the results transmitted to the secretary of state's office in Jackson after the election, although a few offer glimpses into what the voters were looking at when they voted. For instance, the returns for Panola County list some candidates as cooperationists. The reporter for the Lauderdale County election was careful to note that the two winners were on the secessionist ticket while the losers were cooperationists. In Yazoo County, the winners were listed as "States Rights" while the defeated candidates were listed as cooperationists. Even more specific titles were given on the Hinds County election results. The winning ticket was labeled the "Southern Rights Ticket" while the losers were listed as the "Southern Cooperation Ticket."[33]

With the election decided in late December, the breakdown in secession and cooperationist delegates had coalesced to a point in early January that most could see who would dominate the convention. The *Jackson Weekly Mississippian* printed a running total of all known delegates' standing on secession or cooperation throughout the intervening weeks, and the *Vicksburg Whig* did likewise. By January 9 the *Natchez Courier* was able to state the position of ninety of the delegates: sixty-three being immediate secessionists and twenty-seven cooperationists, although it said that many of the secessionists were pledged to allow the people to vote on secession, which was a variation of the cooperationist argument. Although reminding readers that cooperation could be defined in many ways, the Jackson paper ultimately verified only sixteen cooperation candidates by early January. The *Whig* was able to determine seven more. On the other hand, the *Mississippian* was able to verify that sixty-six of the delegates elected in December were of the "immediate secessionist" mindset. To all onlookers, it certainly looked like secession was only a matter of time.[34]

Obviously their own affiliation played a role in how the papers determined delegate positions. The *Vicksburg Evening Citizen* went so far as to argue that the clause in the U.S. Constitution that forbade any state to enter into a treaty, alliance, or confederation made cooperation "directly violative of the letter of the Constitution." More pointedly, the various papers determined the candidates' sides when in doubt, such as when the *Vicksburg Whig* explained that the delegates from Yalobusha and Tippah counties were "claimed by the secessionists, but the platforms adopted at their nominations declared against separate State secession." On other occasions the papers claimed the candidates to be something different than other papers did, and in a few instances the papers even cited the wrong candidates as winners. Mostly, the cooperationist papers wrongly declared their candidates to be the winner, but in the case of Lawrence County, both sides mistakenly listed cooperationist Fleet T. Cooper as the winner over William Gwin. In the close and apparently disputed election, Gwin ultimately became the official delegate by a fifty-four vote margin.[35]

Like numerous elections before and since, the secession convention canvass resulted in two major disputed races, one in Adams County and the other in Warren. The genesis of the disputes lay in the formula used by the legislature to calculate how many delegates each county would have at the convention. The lawmakers derived a formula based on representation in the state legislature, where the cities of Natchez and Vicksburg were allotted their own representatives apart from the counties. When the legislature declared that each county would have representation in the secession convention based on county delegations, that left Natchez and Vicksburg without any representation.[36]

A heated debate resulted, particularly in Natchez and to a lesser degree in Warren County, over which candidates were actually the duly elected delegates to the secession convention. In Natchez, Edward M. Blackburn and George W. Marshall argued that they were the actual delegates despite the fact that they were handily beaten in the county election. They argued that they represented Natchez, not the county, and thus won the voting in Natchez. The same argument was made by W. H. McCarlde and W. H. Johnson in Vicksburg.[37]

There was such a commotion in Adams County that the "disunionists" held a meeting in Natchez on January 2, calling themselves the "State Rights Association of the City of Natchez and the County of Adams." The participants declared their candidates, Blackburn and Marshall, elected. Fiery speeches ensued arguing whether "individual rights" were to be a state, county, or city issue. In this case, it was the city of Natchez that exercised its right to be heard. The larger context of this issue was not lost on Judge Reuben Bullock, who in speaking to the association declared, "The violation of this principle has brought our common country to its present deplorable condition." Nothing ever came of the affair, however, mainly because Blackburn and Marshall chose not to continue the argument "although [they] were] legally elected." The cooperationist delegates, Farrar and Winchester, were thus seated at the convention and took full part in the proceedings.

The Warren County cooperationist delegates did likewise, although the demise of the controversy did not stop the *Vicksburg Whig* from taking swipes at the opposition: "A meeting was held . . . at which it was resolved that the badly beaten disunion candidates for the Convention in that county, were elected. We are not surprised at this, or at any thing else they may do. The rule or ruin party who have been robbing the government, certainly would not hesitate to rob the people of their elective franchise."[38]

Whether secessionist or cooperationist, lawyer or planter, slave owner or non–slave owner, these men were nevertheless dedicated to their state and its people, and were actually unified on most issues. One observer wrote in December how secession was a confirmed fact: "Our citizens seem almost unanimous for resistance to black Republican rule; they are only divided as to the best measures to be adopted in making a thorough resistance." And the delegates who represented that united people were more alike than different as well. One Northern reporter who later observed the convention described the members as an anthropologist might describe a newfound tribe of aborigines: "They first impress you by their pastoral aspect—the absence of urban costumes and positions. Their general bucolic appearance would assure you, if you did not know it before, that there are not many large cities in the State of Mississippi." But after such derogatory remarks, the reporter complimented them on their manhood: "Your next impression is one of wonder at their immense size and stature." He went on to describe "all around you are broad-shouldered, herculean-framed, well proportioned men, who look as if a laugh from them would bring this crazy old Capitol down about their ears; and a sneeze shake the great globe itself." He also added, "they have large, fine heads, and a profusion of straight, brown hair, though here and there you see a crown smooth, bald, and shining." The reporter ended by saying, "taken for all in all, they are fine specimens of physical development, with frank, genial, jovial faces."[39]

In the hands of these 100 herculean men, then, was Mississippi's fate in the looming convention as well as the effects of that action for decades to come. Yet Thomas H. Woods was caught up in the reminiscences of the past and let a few truly luminous members make the entire group seem more noteworthy than it was. In fact, the membership of the Mississippi secession convention seemed to be more common than elite. The fact that only three of the delegates (L. Q. C. Lamar, James Z. George, and James L. Alcorn) have had, or truly deserve, modern academic biographies is telling, and much of their fame was gained after the convention. Those of lesser status likewise won much of their limited fame after the war. Thus the group that gathered on January 7, 1861, at the statehouse in Jackson was, while competent, not the elite and flower of the state. The elite were already tied up elsewhere, chose not to take part, or were defeated in their attempt to be there. Perhaps fittingly, coming out of the Jacksonian "Age of Democracy," the fate of Mississippi was mostly in the hands of commoners.[40]

- 3 -

ORGANIZATION

January 7–8, 1861

JACKSON, MISSISSIPPI, WAS A COMPARATIVELY SMALL SEMIFRONTIER town in January 1861. With a population of only 3,191, the city was tiny compared to some of the more urban and cosmopolitan locales in the South such as New Orleans or Charleston. For an area that was only a generation or two removed from frontier status and even less from Native American possession, Jackson was nevertheless an important place for the citizens of Mississippi. It was the center of the state's society, politics, and economy, especially after the railroad boom brought two lines crossing there. One visitor noted that Jackson "was one of those delightful villages, calling themselves cities, of which the sunny South by no means enjoys a monopoly—where everybody knows everybody's business, and where, upon the advent of a stranger, the entire community resolves itself into a Committee of the Whole to learn who he is, where he came from, and what he wants." Secession convention delegate James Z. George wrote of the high society at a party in Jackson in the 1850s: "There are a great many gentlemen and fine looking ladies in attendance." To his family in tiny Carrollton, Mississippi, 100 miles to the north, George described the party as "a most bilious affair, as they say here." Still, the people were hardly awe-inspiring, George even remarking to his wife, "I find the great men down here are not so very great after all." He added, "They grow small as you approach them."[1]

Jackson was established in 1821 and named in honor of Andrew Jackson, the hero of the 1815 Battle of New Orleans. The legislature, meeting in various places like Washington, Columbia, and Natchez, desired a more central location, and the race was on among existing towns to claim the honor. The legislature instead decided to create an entirely new city in the recently opened Indian lands and sent a commission of three members northward to lay out streets and locate a suitable place for the capitol building. The legislature chose an area on high ground just west of the Pearl River, very near LeFleur's Bluff, one of the earliest settlements in Mississippi. The town itself sat on the bold bluffs overlooking the floodplain of the Pearl River. The area was a good choice, situated as it was where several transportation routes, most notably the Pearl River and the Natchez Trace, merged. The commission soon laid out streets and began a building program, including a statehouse "for the reception of the General Assembly."[2]

The commissioners and their hired architects and laborers went to work with a fury and soon had a modest statehouse erected in time for the legislature's meeting in January 1822. This marked the official opening of the state capitol, although the entire building had been constructed for a mere $3,000. Soon Jackson became the center of political, economic, and social activity in Mississippi, and it grew in population and status. Newspapers, hotels, churches, and industry all began moving into town, with the attendant social services. But it was not long before the government outgrew its original statehouse, necessitating the need for a new one.[3]

This second capitol building, the one in which the convention would meet, sat in a prominent location on the edge of the bluff itself. In 1833 the legislature appropriated $95,000 for the new building, and it opened to the government in 1839. The building sat in "a shaded square," one reporter noted during the convention, writing that it was a "faded, sober edifice, of the style in vogue years ago." The architect, William Nichols, built a large, beautiful, three-story structure with "an Iconic portico in front, and an immense dome upon the top." Atop the copper dome, the reporter continued, "is a miniature dome, like an infinitesimal parasol upon a gigantic umbrella." He added that "the whole is crowned by a small gilded pinnacle, which has relapsed from its original perpendicular to an angle of 45°, and looks like a little yellow jockey cap, cocked jauntily upon the head of a plethoric Quaker, imparting a rowdyish air, quite at variance with the general gravity." The less than stellar description ended with the reporter describing a first story of "faded, cracked free-stone, the front and end walls of stucco, and the rear of brick."[4]

The bottom floor housed offices, including the governor's, and residences for the building's keeper. A "spiral stairway" had to be traversed to ascend to the second floor, and another to reach the upper floor. In the vestibule beside the staircases sat "two musty cannon," perhaps indicative of the state's later military mentality in secession. The Northern reporter who was not impressed with the venue to begin with noticed "a little darkey sound asleep" on one of the cannons. He could not decide, he said insultingly, "whether he was watching the gun, or the gun was watching him." The second level was where most of the business occurred. Visitors could there walk around a "balustrade which surrounds the open space under the dome." Halls led by offices and smaller rooms to the left and right, at the end of which were the large legislative chambers, the senate on the southern end and the house of the northern side. Galleries for each hall occupied the third floor, while offices and rooms in the center of the building contained the state library, the High Court of Errors and Appeals courtroom, and other offices. The secession convention occupied the House of Representatives chamber, the largest room in the building.[5]

By 1860 the effects of the transportation, industrial, and communication revolutions were apparent in Jackson. The state's recently built rail system connected in town, where the north–south New Orleans, Jackson, and Great Northern Railroad crossed the Southern Railroad of Mississippi. River traffic was also increasing with more steam power on the waterways. The telegraph connected Jackson with the outside world, and industry and mechanization had reached the city, including several large factories in an

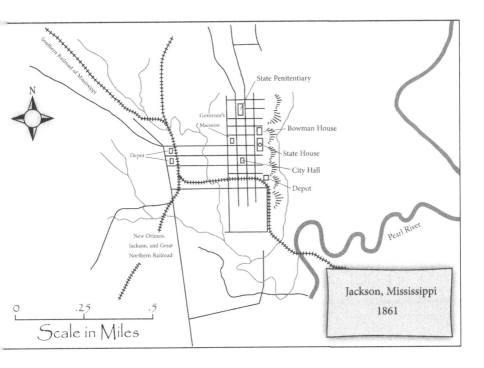

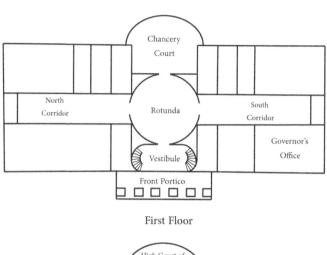

First Floor

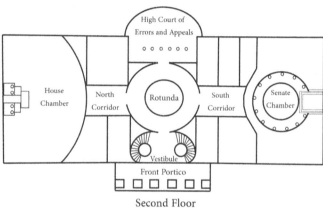

Second Floor

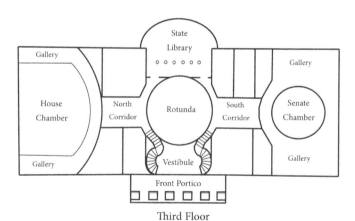

Third Floor

Mississippi State House - 1861

otherwise industry-deprived state. Restaurants and hotels cropped up to serve the needs of visitors and residents, the most famous being the Bowman House next door to the state capitol. There were also Masonic, concert, and lyceum halls. Other government venues were built in the same building spree, including a governor's mansion and penitentiary. The nearby Jackson city hall building was also a prominent structure. In all, Jackson was a thriving place for interior Mississippi.[6]

As 1861 rolled around, there was a lot of anticipation and excitement in Jackson. The delegates began to make their way into town in those early days of the year, some of them requiring long and tiring trips. The delegates from extreme north Mississippi or the Gulf Coast had to travel great distances, and the winter weather of early January made it all the more difficult, with as much as six inches of snow blanketing the eastern portion of the state on January 7. Fortunately, the newly minted railroad system proved a boon to the travelers.[7]

Yet there were several preparatory moves that had already taken place before the convention began on January 7. Several of the members, seasoned in politics, were already thinking, planning, and strategizing. One of them was L. Q. C. Lamar. A U.S. representative, Lamar had come to realize that nothing could be done politically in Washington to halt the crisis so he had left his seat and returned home to be elected to the convention. He took the liberty, even before he left the capitol, to draft an ordinance of secession, and he began to gather opinions on his draft. His first attempt was a long, sometimes rambling statement that included everything from the beginning of Mississippi's history as a state to its future. Lamar thought the ordinance itself should contain enough provisions to take care of Mississippi's needs. For instance, Mississippi should join together with the other fourteen slave states in a republic, and all treaties should remain on the books, all contracts would remain valid, and all officers in judicial and law enforcement roles would remain the same. All laws, as well as the U.S. Constitution, would remain the same as well. Lamar said nothing about slavery, but the institution was protected under the current laws of the United States, he believed. The only major issue was that the secession ordinance would not go into effect until nine of the other fourteen slave states (plus two territories) seceded as well.[8]

Lamar expounded on his feelings in a letter to a confidant:

It will be observed that the plan proposed aims at no change in our form of government, but seeks to protect existing forms from destruction. It proposes to give us our old glorious constitution in vigorous operation, strong enough to suppress domestic violence and repel foreign inva-sion, safe in the affections of our people from the attacks of fanaticism and sectionalism and black Republicanism and red Republicanism all combined. It gives us all the laws of the old Republic, and those grand decisions of the judiciary, which have grown up around the constitu-tion, as part of the fundamental law, and are almost as sacred as the constitution itself. It proclaims to the civilized world that as loyalty to the constitution is the law of our conduct at home, so will good faith and the observance of treaties regulate our intercourse abroad. It gives us the traditions and the historic wealth, colonial and revolutionary, of the glorious old Commonwealth of Virginia. In a word, it gives us the Union and constitution as the fathers made them, and separates us from the enemies to both, who themselves have seceded from the constitution, and are indeed rebels and traitors.[9]

Obviously Lamar was not thinking in revolutionary terms, seeing the proposed action taken by Mississippi and the other Southern states as a conservative counterrevolution to the real revolution begun by the North. Others were thinking the same thing. Wiley P. Harris wrote that "there was going on a silent revolution, irresistible in its inevitable tendency, which was to change the essential character of the Federal Union." Certainly Lamar's thoughts went through several revolutions themselves between December and his arrival in Jackson in January, and it is not known what state the ordinance was in when he arrived. But it was a start.[10]

There was also a behind-the-scenes movement closer to the actual con-vention's opening to caucus like-minded secessionists together and deter-mine their plan of action. Although shrouded in mystery because of a lack of sources, many of the die-hard secessionists, what the *Jackson Weekly Mississippian* called "a majority of the delegates," met on the morning of January 7. The ostensible reason for their meeting was to streamline the organizational process once the convention began. In reality, however, it was more to make sure enough secessionists were in lockstep to push their agenda through. They planned to establish a course of action, apparently in-cluding whom they would support for president (newspapers were already pushing their favorite candidates), how they would run the convention, and their goals for secession. Their plans also included making Lamar, who was not shy about touting his ordinance, the leader of the secession movement. Unfortunately, little is known about the caucus, but it did seem to catch the cooperationists off guard. Perhaps they were more naive politically, or they could have thought the opposition would act in good faith and let the convention run naturally. At any rate, the cooperationists apparently did not meet prior to the convention's opening, but soon did so, trying to make up for lost time.[11]

Despite the preliminary moves, there was immense excitement in the great hall on that clear morning of January 7, 1861. The delegates began to gather and milled around the floor or the hall leading to the chamber, smoking, renewing friendships, and no doubt talking over the chances of immediate separation or delay. The galleries were already crowded, mostly with women in their finest dresses intent on seeing the greatest show since Andrew Jackson was welcomed in that very building in 1840. The rest of the state and indeed the nation were watching as well, the editor of the *Vicksburg Evening Citizen*, J. M. Swords, editorializing that "this day, the 7th of January, 1861, is an important day in the State of Mississippi." Other papers such as the *Natchez Courier* kept informed by "telegraphic dispatches" and more complete mailings from Jackson. John L. Power, the *Mississippian* reporter covering the convention, summed up the feeling by stating simply, "no body of men ever assembled for more serious business." All eyes thus centered on the statehouse in Jackson where one by one, the delegates appeared that January day and the clock ticked on toward high noon.[12]

As the time for assembly came in the house chamber and the proceedings began, one can get a feeling of the scene from an eyewitness's description: "At the north end of the apartment sits the president, upon a high platform occupying a recess in the wall, with two Iconic columns upon each side of him. Before him is a little, old fashioned mahogany pulpit, concealing all but his head and shoulders from the vulgar gaze. In front of this, and three or four feet lower, at a long wooden desk painted in imitation of dark grained marble with white panels, sit two clerks, one of them smoking a cigar. Before them, and still lower, at a shorter desk, [is] an unhappy Celtic reporter, with dark shaggy hair and eye brows." He went on to describe: "Upon one of the columns at the president's right hangs a faded portrait of George Poindexter, once a senator from this State. Further to the right is an open fire-place, upon whose mantel stands a framed copy of the Declaration of Independence, now sadly faded and blurred, a lithographic view of the Medical College of Louisiana, and a pitcher and glass. On the hearth is a pair of ancient andirons, upon which a genial wood fire is burning."[13]

The other attributes of the chamber were not so glowingly described. The speakers delivered their speeches in front of the lowest desk from "a little table or stand, which looks as if it might have been called into existence by a very drunken carpenter on a very dark night, from the relics of a superannuated dry goods box." The reporter also jokingly described the "hypocritical plastering" that had peeled off some of the walls, "leaving bare the honest worn faces of the original bricks." The reporter noticed "there must be some peculiar nonadhesive influence which acts upon the plastering in Jackson," indicating that it had also "seceded" from the wall in his hotel room. He also related that Samuel Gholson, one of the members of the convention, had told him of a time in the old statehouse when "an acre or two" of plastering had fallen on Sergeant S. Prentiss while he was making a speech. Gholson added that it "quite overwhelm[ed] him for the time."[14]

The reporter went on to describe "a faded brass chandelier, with pendants of glass" suspended by a "rod tapestried with undisturbed cobwebs." He called it a "medieval relic [that] is purely ornamental, for the room is now lighted with gas." The high walls had "small windows, with faded blue curtains flowered and bordered with white, and each suspended from a triple bar of gilded Indian arrows." Around the periphery of the room were "a semi-circle of ten Ionic pillars, and beyond them a narrow, crescent shaped lobby." A gallery sat atop the pillars, extending around the three sides of the room away from the main desk.[15]

On the main floor, inside the columns, were the delegates' desks, which one reporter described as "stand[ing] in rows like the letter D, are of plain wood painted black. Their chairs are great, square, faded mahogany frames, stuffed and covered with hair-cloth." Other chairs were haphazardly arranged in the lobby and hall, giving "that variety which is the spice of life." At least to one observer the room smelled musty, which fit well with the same smell coming from a hoard of dogs that "is all prevalent about the building."[16]

Despite the shabbiness of the chamber, the official convention journals state that the meeting began precisely at noon on January 7, but at least one of the cooperationists, John W. Wood, claimed that the secessionists tricked the opposition and called the convention to order "more than thirty minutes before the usual time for such bodies to convene." Wood stated that he and several other Unionists had planned to call the meeting to order and "call a conservative member to the Chair." The secessionists, he declared, "anticipated" this move and jumped the gun. Whether such drama actually took place or Wood was later chafing at the domination of the secessionists is not known. Perhaps he and other cooperationists were a little embarrassed to find out the secessionists had already caucused together, something they had not thought to do.[17]

The delegates nevertheless soon took their seats, apparently divided by their opinions on secession itself; one cooperationist later made a comment about his colleagues offering amendments "from this side of the house." Wherever they sat, the convention soon came to order when what Wood called an "ultra Secessionist," Samuel J. Gholson of Monroe County, called the convention to order. Gholson was one of the most respected members present; he was a lawyer by trade, but was then a U.S. district judge. He had served in the state legislature as well as two terms in the U.S. Congress. He was also an elite planter and was very rich. Gholson was a man to listen to, and a fitting voice to call the meeting to order.[18]

Gholson quickly made a motion to appoint a temporary chairman to preside until a president could be elected. He nominated, and the secessionist-dominated convention approved, Henry T. Ellett of Claiborne County. Like Gholson, Ellett was a well-known politician, lawyer, and planter. He had served in the legislature as well as in Congress, and was a secessionist. Everything was going according to plan.[19]

When Ellett took the presiding chair, he suggested the convention open with prayer and called on Vicksburg Methodist and Episcopal South pastor Charles K. Marshall to do so. Contemporary Mississippi politician and historian J. F. H. Claiborne noted that "the Northern pulpit and priesthood had had so profound an influence in making this Convention necessary, it must be regarded as a high tribute to the Southern clergy, and a profound expression [of] your dependence on Providence, that it was deemed prudent to open this solemn convocation with prayer." Despite being from a cooperationist county, Marshall nevertheless offered a secessionist prayer. He asked God "to look down upon us in compassion and mercy, [and] vouchsafe to these Thy servants assembled in General Convention, the guidance and support of Thy Holy Spirit." He continued that the Northern states had for years "pursued the purpose of depriving us of our just rights and destroying in our midst the institution which Thy providence has solemnly bound us to uphold, defend and protect."[20]

After the prayer, the roll call of the counties was called, but not before it occurred to the delegates that they needed a secretary. Ellett appointed William H. H. Tison of Itawamba County, whom he had known as a state legislator during the 1850s. Tison began calling the list of counties alphabetically, and the delegates, one by one, came forward and registered their presence, starting with the disputed delegates from Adams County. When the roll call was completed, ninety-eight members had signed in, with only James S. Johnston of Jefferson County and Jacob S. Yerger of Washington County absent. With a quorum obviously in attendance, Gholson now moved to the major duty of the day—election of the convention president.[21]

It was here that a crack in the secessionist facade emerged. The caucus had decided earlier that morning that the president would be William S. Barry, the "silver tongued orator from Lowndes," as one witness called him. Barry was well known among the delegates as a large planter, lawyer, state legislator, and congressman. His experience as Speaker of the house as well as his impeccable secessionist and Democratic credentials made him an obvious choice to lead the secession convention. But Barry did not win hands down. When the vote was finished and the tellers appointed by Ellett (Warren Anderson of Hinds, Joel Berry of Tippah, and James Nelson of Pike County) tallied the votes, Barry fell well short of the majority he needed to become president. With ninety-seven delegates voting (Ellet as chair presumably being the missing vote in addition to the two missing members), the prevailing candidate needed forty-nine votes. Barry received only twenty-seven, which no doubt made several secessionists squirm in their chairs. Other votes for secessionists were scattered among other prominent members such as Gholson and Ellett, as well as Hugh Miller of Pontotoc, Alexander Clayton of Marshall, David Glenn of Harrison, and Wiley Harris of Hinds. Most troubling was the fact that cooperationist James L. Alcorn of Coahoma had received seventeen votes, just ten behind Barry. Yerger and other cooperationists received a few votes, but Alcorn was the obvious opposition candidate.[22]

The convention then moved to a second vote, and Barry increased his votes to forty-one, with the other secessionist nominees still holding some support. Alcorn went down to thirteen, but Barry still did not have the forty-nine he needed. On the third vote, however, he received fifty-eight, with Alcorn getting fourteen and Miller twelve. Barry was thus called to the chair, Ellett appointing Alcorn and Miller, the second- and third-highest vote getters, respectively, to accompany him. Once there, Barry addressed the convention with a short speech, during which he thanked the members for their confidence and immediately called for secession. "They were assembled under a consciousness of many multiplied wrongs," Barry stated, "assembled to devise measures of redress. To secure our rights in the Union appeared past all hope; to secure them outside is the duty devolving upon this Convention." He "hoped, looking to Heaven for guidance, that the action of the Convention would tend to the honor and glory of Mississippi." Clearly, there was no doubt where Barry stood, and there was no doubt that his position as president was fairly preordained, despite his needing three ballots to get elected.[23]

Barry's election as president sealed the fate of Mississippi; the convention's decision was a foregone conclusion. Thomas H. Woods later remembered, "The advocates of immediate and independent action were complete masters of the situation, and, from the first day's meeting of that superb body, it was manifest to the most superficial observer that the die had been cast." Even in his introductory prayer Reverend Marshall asked God: "may we never have occasion to regret the steps we are about to take in the great work that now lies before us."[24]

"In the prime of his physical and intellectual strength," one observer noted, Barry then led the convention through its further organization as the delegates made other appointments. Israel Welsh of Noxubee County made a motion to elect a permanent secretary, and L. Q. C. Lamar nominated one of his University of Mississippi students, Francis A. Pope of Holmes County. The *Vicksburg Whig* characterized him as a "young gentleman of talent, and fully competent to discharge the duties of the place." It took Pope two votes to get the requisite number for selection, but he became secretary, prompting one Pontotoc County delegate to write his son, then a student at the state university, "your acquaintance Pope was elected secretary and is getting along very well." An assistant was soon provided as well, one W. W. Humphries, a lawyer of Lowndes County and no doubt supported by Barry. Wiley Harris moved to elect a doorkeeper, and he nominated his friend Samuel Pool. He was likewise not elected over his opponents J. W. Clingan and W. M. Israel on the first ballot, but Henry Ellett moved that Pool be elected by acclamation, which he was. Similarly Israel Welsh of Noxubee County moved to elect a sergeant at arms and nominated the *Southern Broad-Axe* editor, W. Ivy Westbrook of Oktibbeha County. Others nominated a list of individuals such as J. J. Denson and E. Farrish, and, according to one paper, others put their own names forward, but Westbrook led the first ballot and was then elected by acclamation as well. One Northern reporter described Westbrook as dressed "in a gray coat, and without a neckerchief, [who] walks to and fro, with hands in his pockets." He added that he had a striking resemblance to Kansan James H. Lane, although he was sure "it is safe to infer that he cannot pour out the intense and bitter eloquence of that astonishing frontier orator."[25]

As the afternoon wore on, other parliamentary issues came up as the convention continued its organization. Ellett successfully made a motion that the "Rules of the House of Representatives of the State be adopted, so far as applicable, for the government of this Convention," and he also wanted to allow the president to appoint two pages. Other issues were dealt with throughout the afternoon, such as a motion by Welsh for the doorkeeper

Pool to provide each member of the convention with a copy of the House of Representatives rules and a motion by George Clayton of Lowndes County for a committee of three to be sent to the governor apprising him of the organization of the convention and asking for any pertinent correspondence the convention may need to be aware of. Barry appointed George Clayton, Alexander Clayton, and James L. Alcorn to be that delegation.[26]

The major action came that afternoon when Lamar rose to make a motion "that a committee of ___ be appointed by the President with instructions to prepare and report as speedily as possible, an ordinance providing for the withdrawal of the State of Mississippi from the present Federal Union, with a view to the establishment of a new Confederacy, to be composed of the seceding States." *Mississippian* reporter John L. Power remembered years later, "I have a vivid recollection of him as he arose in his place immediately after the organization of the convention." There was discussion about filling in the blank, and the members finally decided on fifteen and passed the motion.[27]

After all the organizational moves, the convention decided to adjourn for the rest of the day and begin its major work on Tuesday. But before doing so, William S. Barry, of all people, was asked to announce that "the friends of cooperation and united Southern action were requested to meet in the Senate Chamber tonight, at 7 ½ o'clock." Obviously the cooperationists had decided that it was time to organize. Indeed, they were far behind the secessionists in organization and results; the work of the day said as much. The only ones who had had any say thus far were the major secessionists, and of those the major political figures led. It is not surprising that the elite would dominate the organizational proceedings, but it is interesting that mainly Barry, Welsh, Ellett, Gholson, Lamar, and Harris had dominated the proceedings. All were well-known statesmen, and in fact all but Welsh had been in Congress. The lack of similar participation by Alcorn or Brooke was notable, and Yerger was not even there yet. Perhaps they were just glad to have their full complement in attendance; the *Natchez Courier* approvingly reported that their disputed cooperationist delegates from Adams and Warren counties "took their seats unmolested."[28]

Little is known of what transpired that night as the cooperationists met in the Senate chamber to discuss their options, but Alcorn was the acknowledged leader. Apparently there was more than one session that night and the next morning. "I was called to the Chair and the deliberations of the canvass were continued through many sessions," he later wrote. Several of the leading cooperationists made speeches, a now-arrived Yerger arguing that secession meant war, and war meant conscription "upon the non-slave-holding classes of the South." Alcorn similarly remembered, "I endeavored to give a picture of the South when the Northern soldier would tread her cotton fields, when the slave should be made *free* and the proud Southerner stricken to the dust in his presence!" Others talked of the folly of "taking the slave from under the protection of the Constitution and putting his freedom up to be fought for."[29]

Yet all could see clearly that secession was a reality; Alcorn wrote that the immediate secessionists "will listen to no reason" and predicted that "the Convention . . . [would grow] daily more and more intolerant." It thus became clear what the cooperationists had to do to stop or delay the movement: "We must appeal to the people!" Alcorn wrote. Secession was a reality. All the Unionists could do now was to slow down the secession movement, hopefully calming down their colleagues' enthusiasm for leaving the Union. Consequently, the plan changed from defeating secession to its delay, namely by a statewide referendum. And if that failed, the cooperationists also made plans to run a ticket in the upcoming fall 1861 state election to repeal the ordinance. The ticket, as worked out by the sullen cooperationists in caucus, included convention delegates Jacob Yerger for governor, James L. Alcorn for attorney general, and Miles McGehee for treasurer. "It was agreed that the ticket should be announced at an early day and the canvas [*sic*] be begun," Alcorn remembered, "the watchword to Repeal! Repeal!"[30]

The full convention met at the appointed time the next day, 10:00 A.M., again with the galleries filled to the brim. One newspaper reported, "the excitement is intense. The galleries of the Convention were crowded with ladies. The military paraded to-day, and went through the evolutions of mimic warfare. A flag with fifteen stars was displayed. The hotels are thronged with interesting citizens from abroad." Perhaps some of the excitement was due to growing anger in Washington; Senator Albert Gallatin Brown, watching the peace negotiations in the capital, had wired friend Daniel B. Wright the day before: "Hope is dead. Secede at once. To-day is the darkest yet." In addition, Jacob Thompson, secretary of the interior, resigned his office on this day, news of which no doubt thrilled the masses in Jackson. While the onlookers took in the festival atmosphere, the militia paraded, with Governor Pettus even calling for the artillery to prepare "ball cartridges." The main attraction, however, continued to be the convention, and those who could get inside the statehouse had a front-row seat to view the delegates, who began their more detailed work with a prayer by Reverend Whitfield Harrington, a local Southern Methodist Episcopal minister.[31]

Once again the cooperationists were fairly quiet; their plan of delay and later repeal was not noticeable on the warm second day of the convention, perhaps demonstrating that their caucus sessions may have continued on into that evening or even the morning of January 9. The secessionist delegates meanwhile began to offer several small and fairly inconsequential motions, such as James Chalmers of DeSoto asking that reporters and the press be allowed into the chamber, but with the understanding that the president could have them expelled at any time. Still smarting over the disputed delegates from Adams and Warren counties, Francis Rogers of Monroe County moved that a committee be appointed to examine all "certificates of membership" to the convention; Barry appointed the members, with Rogers heading the group. Alexander Clayton moved that commissioners from other states be allowed seats on the floor of the convention, which was likewise passed, as was the formation of a committee to inform those commissioners. Alternatively, a motion by Samuel J. Gholson to send an additional commissioner to "our sister State" Alabama was tabled when Josiah Clapp of Marshall County opposed it on the grounds that a commissioner was already assigned to Alabama. Other small and routine items were also dealt with swiftly throughout the day, including a report from the committee sent to confer with the governor, a motion to allow the state's judges seats on the floor, a motion to prepay any postage for members of the convention, as well as a motion by Wiley Harris that each member be given a copy of the local *Jackson Mississippian*, to which Vicksburg delegate Thomas A. Marshall unsuccessfully proposed an amendment that a copy of the opposing *Vicksburg Whig* be supplied as well. Obviously the lines were being drawn. Marshall, of course, wanted to support his hometown newspaper, but it was mainly because the *Mississippian* was a staunch secessionist paper while the *Whig* would have added a counterpoint and allowed the cooperationists to get their message out more fully to the delegates. Not surprisingly, the secessionist majority voted the amendment down.[32]

Also during the day, the two missing delegates, Johnston and Yerger, took their seats, giving the convention its full complement of 100 members. Their arrival marked the beginning of serious business. The two main issues on everyone's minds were the secession ordinance and the means to support an independent Mississippi. The convention soon delved into each one, with Barry, despite unofficial word the night before, officially announcing the membership of the secession ordinance committee.[33]

When Barry made his announcement, it was immediately clear that the committee was controlled by secessionists and was also heavily made up of elite statesmen. However, it also contained, as described by J. F. H. Claiborne, "representative men of different shades of politics." Lamar was made the chair, and Harris, Gholson, Ellett, Alexander Clayton, and other luminaries were members. Other lesser-known but emerging secessionists were also included, such as Alfred Holt of Wilkinson County and James Z. George of Carroll. There were also well-known cooperationists involved, who were extended an olive branch. Alcorn, Brooke, and lesser known cooperationists such as John A. Blair of Tishomingo, Elijah H. Sanders of Attala, and Benjamin King of Copiah were included. A couple of those who were middle-of-the-road delegates were also appointed, including Hugh Miller of Pontotoc and George Clayton of Lowndes. Yet the secessionists were firmly in control, as seen in the initial appointment of secessionist David Glenn and his withdrawal "privately" so that revered lawyer and Whig Orlando Davis of Tippah could take part. Glenn said that he desired the "true and able old line Whig" to be included, but as some historians have asserted, Glenn may have been angling for a bigger position. If there was any doubt, however, Barry would not have consented to replacing a staunch secessionist with a moderate.[34]

The other major concern was how to support the independent state once it had seceded. The secession delegates had already worked out a mechanism for doing so, but one member of the caucus, Harvey W. Walter of Marshall County, jumped the gun. He offered a preliminary motion that appointed a committee to prepare a constitutional amendment authorizing the state to borrow money for defense and to "pledge the faith of the State for the repayment of the loan." Daniel B. Wright of Tippah offered a minor amendment that recognized the "existing means for the defense of the State"; basically, Wright wanted the state militia to receive a part of any money allotted to the war. Obviously two issues were on Walter's mind; he was expecting a war and wanted to prepare for it as quickly as possible. But he was also very worried, as were others, that the convention would take too much power upon itself and basically become the de facto ruler of the state, supplanting the governor, legislature, and even the constitution. Walter wanted to make sure everything was done constitutionally.[35]

Unfortunately, the issue was a bit premature. Walker Brooke noted on the floor that "the contemplated withdrawal of Mississippi from the Union would authorize the committee to take other amendments into consideration." With that in mind, David Glenn stepped forward, as was evidently planned all along before Walter forced the issue, and offered a detailed and obviously prewritten substitute for Walter's motion that would establish a

series of six standing committees of seven members each. These committees would be tasked with almost everything that conceivably might face
the state in an independent existence or on a wartime footing, including
Walter's area of financial concern. There were committees on citizenship,
federal jurisdiction and property, postal affairs, the state constitution, military and naval affairs, and a Southern confederacy. Glenn's motion, with a
note that each would "inquire into the matters properly pertaining and to
report thereon by ordinance or otherwise," was an effort to stop a multitude
of small motions such as Walter's as well as place the decision-making process in the hands of committees appointed by the president. That, of course,
would guarantee that the secessionists controlled each committee. Politics
aside, Glenn's organizational structure also set in motion a remarkably
forward-looking process to deal with any issue before it became a major
problem.[36]

Despite withdrawing his resolution upon Glenn's proposal, Harvey Walter was still not satisfied and offered another motion that the committee
on the state constitution (not even appointed yet) should quickly report an
ordinance that would amend the constitution so that the state could borrow
money for its defense. It was essentially what he had offered earlier, but this
time he placed it in the context of Glenn's committees.[37]

Immediately James R. Chalmers of DeSoto County offered a counteram-
mendment changing Walter's state constitution motion to a convention ordinance, thus fully placing power over the constitution in the hands of the
convention. This set off a lively debate over who had the power to amend
the constitution. Alcorn himself, in the first major involvement of the cooperationists, argued that amending the constitution would bring up "certain difficulties" and admonished the delegates that no "real necessity" for
doing so existed and to not even "entertain the thought of proceeding to
amend our present Constitution." Others rallied to his standard, including
George Clayton of Lowndes, Samuel Benton of Marshall, and Albert P. Hill
of Madison County, who argued that the convention should confine itself to
its legislative mandate. Clayton reminded the members that the constitution
could only be changed by "the manner provided by the instrument itself"
and argued that if the convention tried to do so, it "would be in direct violation of the organic law." Just as many voiced their opposite belief that the
convention was indeed sovereign, even over the constitution. Judge Gholson declared the convention "omnipotent"; Israel Welsh thundered, "here
are the people"; Daniel Wright of Tippah insisted that the delegates were
"fresh from the people"; and Robert W. Flournoy of Pontotoc argued that

the convention "possessed sovereign and absolute power to amend, alter or abolish, the present constitution, as it might see proper." Such an imposing figure as Henry Ellett remarked that he "had no scruples about the power of the convention to amend the Constitution in any particular." Obviously a territorial battle within the convention was shaping up over the delegates' power.[38]

Seeing that a potential split was emerging, a few of the most respected delegates counseled caution. Obviously the last thing the secessionists wanted was a split in their caucus here on what was probably the eve of the secession vote. The highly regarded Wiley P. Harris thus declared that he had "no doubt" but that the delegates could amend the constitution, but counseled that they should "not touch it except in points necessary to advance the remedy, to which we are determined to resort, in the present emergency." He further stated that he thought the expenses would be taken care of with taxes, but stipulated that "he was disposed to remove all obstacles in the way of every resource at our command." And it was not just the secessionists who counseled caution. In a miraculous streak of self-denial, Alcorn also advised unanimity. He declared that this was not a money question; he would be in the lead in supporting the proposed confederacy, if it came to that. But he argued that while he thought it should not be done, the convention of the people had "plenary power—that its ordinances were above the Constitution." His unanimity had an effect, with Hill also deciding that it was not so bad for the convention to have some say in the constitution; he decided he would support Chalmers's amendment, but still stated that the convention should not have "illimitable power over the existing constitution." Similarly, David Glenn reminded everyone why they were there in the first place. He said that he did not agree with either side, but that he was willing to go along with either for the sake of unity, because "both looked to the prompt withdrawal of Mississippi from the Union." The galleries erupted in cheers at Glenn's proclamation, to which Barry responded that he "would not tolerate any further demonstrations in that quarter." When the vote was taken, Chalmers's amendment was voted down, but Walter's original resolution passed. Presumably Walter was satisfied, but there were no doubt serious concerns at the already visible lack of unity. And secession itself had not even come up yet.[39]

After the tension of the debate, most delegates' moods were lifted when a message from Georgia arrived stating there was "no doubt" about that state's immediate secession. The galleries burst into applause again, and Barry once more warned that he would clear the observers from the room if dignity was not restored. David Glenn took the floor and admitted that he had taken part in the "expression of exultation." The galleries rolled with laughter. One delegate noted that "the ladies in the gallery [were] looking smilingly in the direction of Mr. Glenn."[40]

With some order restored, both figuratively and literally, Samuel Gholson moved to adjourn for the day, even though it was only noon. He wished to allow the secession ordinance committee time to do its work. Before doing so, however, Wiley Harris took the floor once more to again try to heal any split that might have occurred over the amendment process. He reminded the delegates of the context of the issue, and declared that "there was no difference in the Committee on the main point, and he thought they would be prepared to report to-morrow morning."[41]

The convention had thus done its duty of putting itself "in a working condition," as David Glenn described it. It adjourned to meet again the next, fateful day, January 9. And for at least one delegate, the deed was as good as done. Despite the bickering, John W. Wood of Attala later wrote that by the end of the second day, "the proceedings . . . all indicated very clearly that the secession of Mississippi was already *fait accompli.*" The appointment of the secession ordinance committee, the examination of the cooperationist seats from Warren and Adams counties, the continual talk of defending the state after secession, and even the denial of the *Vicksburg Whig*'s distribution on the floor indicated to Wood that secession would happen. Consequently, he decided that if something did not change the next day, he would leave—for good.[42]

- 4 -

SECESSION

January 9, 1861

L. Q. C. LAMAR WAS THE MAN OF THE HOUR. HE WAS WELL KNOWN IN Mississippi, a planter, educator, and politician. He was one of Mississippi's congressmen, but he left Washington in mid-December to give his full attention to secession. He was elected to the convention from Lafayette County and had even begun working on a draft of a secession ordinance weeks ahead. Although his position on immediate secession had shifted since his election, as apparently had that of many delegates, he came to Jackson armed with his draft. Everything went like clockwork—from his calling for a committee to draft an ordinance to his being appointed chairman of that committee. Now he had free rein to manipulate, coerce, or lead, whichever was needed most.[1]

But Lamar soon ran into difficulty. Although he seemed to dominate the proceedings, he apparently was not all-powerful. He had received fewer votes in his home county, in fact, than had Thomas Isom, his fellow Lafayette County delegate, illustrating the fact that he was not universally liked even in his home county. One member of the convention even expressed his concern over Lamar's political ability, remarking that he "proved himself no parliamentarian and a very dangerous debater." The biggest affront to Lamar, however, came when the committee began to work on his ordinance.[2]

There is no record of the committee's deliberations, but we do know that they worked several long hours. The *New York Times* reported, "the Committee on the Ordinance of Secession is now in caucus." It also added, "the excitement and anxiety is intense." Apparently they worked throughout the evening of January 7, even though Barry did not officially announce the committee until the next day's session. Several newspapers reported the membership of the committee on January 7, and Wiley Harris reported on January 8 that the committee was making good progress. No doubt they worked throughout the afternoon of January 8, and probably into the night. What we do know is that the final result offered before the convention was very different from Lamar's original proposal.[3]

Whether Lamar made the major changes in his document himself or whether the committee made the changes is likewise not known, and it could have been both. Lamar later noted that there was "a great diversity of opinion among the members of the committee in regard to the manner of framing the ordinance," but that the work of the committee was done "with a spirit of justice and toleration." Thus the version submitted to the convention was a much more streamlined document than Lamar's original December draft. Lamar's original version was long and detailed and included not only secession but also contained such items as international treaties, postal affairs, constitutional issues, and confederation with other seceded states. The ordinance that came out of the committee was a shadow of the original. It was a mere four sections long, and significantly stripped down much of the broad powers attributed to the state in the original. The ordinance as presented simply repealed any "laws and ordinances" that Mississippi had made to become part of the United States, resumed sovereignty in the state, and absolved Mississippi from any obligations to the United States. It went on to absolve any officers from Mississippi of any oath they may have taken to the United States, kept any law "not incompatible with this Ordinance" on the books, and opened the state to a confederation with other seceding states. That was it. The ordinance said nothing about international treaties, postal issues, the state constitution, political governance, judicial matters, or contractual items. Most significant, in the rush toward immediate separation, the language requiring a certain number of other states to secede was deleted.[4]

Perhaps the committee thought the earlier draft was too far ranging, placed too much power upon the convention, or simply was overblown rhetoric. Or perhaps the committee realized that each of the issues except for secession would be dealt with by committees they themselves had voted to form on January 8. Perhaps the committee also thought that those issues were far too important to be dealt with in one large ordinance; they needed the full discussion, investigation, and research of individual committees for each. As a result, the secession committee members ignored issues that could be handled at a later time by other committees. Their main focus was secession, and their abbreviated ordinance took care of that effectively.[5]

The ordinance was ready by Wednesday morning, January 9, and La-mar prepared to offer it to the full convention when it assembled at 10:00 A.M. The people were ready, the *Oxford Intelligencer* reporting, "the city of Jackson this morning is in an intense and deep state of excitement. The city is full of persons from the surrounding counties, who are awaiting to almost breathless suspense the action of the Convention." The weather was unseasonably warm and cloudy, perhaps reflecting the mood inside the statehouse, where the atmosphere was likewise starting to simmer. "On that memorable morning," Alexander Clayton later remembered, "long be-fore the convention assembled every inch of space in the hall was densely packed, and profound silence prevailed. A deep sense of solemnity per-vaded the multitude." After a short delay of thirty minutes, the conven-tion finally came to order when Barry took his seat and asked Reverend W. C. Crane to open the day with prayer. Clayton remembered "the awful stillness was broken by sobs in every quarter of the apartment. Men and women were on their knees in prayer; tears streamed from many eyes, and every countenance evinced profound sorrow." After the prayer, a few small matters were quickly dispensed with, including the reading of the minutes of the day before, a report on correspondence from the governor, and the seating of Armistead Burt and Edmund W. Pettus, commissioners from South Carolina and Alabama, respectively. John L. Power reported that the convention turned its full attention to Burt and Pettus; they "were invited in, received by the President, and took their seats." Pettus was an obvious choice to be commissioner to Mississippi; his brother was John J. Pettus, governor of the state. Barry briefly welcomed the commissioners and then continued the proceedings. There was big business to attend to, and it was no time before Lamar took the floor and brought the secession ordinance up for consideration.[6]

Lamar spoke for a few minutes, informing the delegates that the com-mittee had "brought to this subject the most patient reflection and calm de-liberation," despite differences of opinion in the committee of fifteen, which he attributed to the fairness of the appointment process, which was done "with a view to the full expression of the various classes of opinions." In the ultimate conclusion, however, "none differed widely." He labeled the result-ing ordinance "perfect" and, he hoped, "stamped … by the hand of God." He added that now "the problem involving the safety of the State had passed from the hands of the committee." He also reminded the members that they were carrying out the will of the people who had elected a majority of seces-sionists. He asked that "the Convention would discharge the duties which they owed to the people by enforcing with unanimity the decree given from the ballot box."[7]

At 11:10 A.M. Lamar read the ordinance, and the delegates received their first full taste of what they would be discussing and voting on. "The People of the State of Mississippi, in Convention assembled, do ordain and declare, and it is hereby ordained and declared as follows," began the ordinance. Four sections then spelled out what was being done, including the first, which stated "that all the laws and ordinances by which the said State of Mississippi became a member of the Federal Union of the United States of America be, and the same are hereby repealed." The state, the delegates declared, "shall from henceforth be a free, sovereign and independent State." The second section "abrogated and annulled" any oaths taken by state government officials, while the third declared that all still-compatible rights, treaties, and laws made as a part of the United States were still in effect. The fourth section allowed Mississippi to form another "Federal Union" with states that had likewise seceded.[8]

After the full reading, Lamar summed up where the convention stood. He declared the issue in contention was "the safety of the South, the integrity of society, the inviobility of our hearth-stones, and the purity of our Anglo-Saxon race." He reminded the members again that the people of Mississippi had spoken at the ballot box by voting overwhelmingly for secession. At the end, Lamar asked if the minority had any amendments or suggestions, and declared that he would give them full and free time to debate. He said that he "would take no advantage of parliamentary stratagem," but would give them "ample opportunity for free discussion and the expression of every variety of opinion."[9]

The critical moment had come. If no one rose to oppose Lamar, the issue would pass surprisingly easily. But if the cooperationists protested, it would be much more difficult. At that point, as breathless silence must have dominated the room, Jacob Yerger stood and declared he had amendments to offer. All knew what that meant: secession would not be a simple matter. The cooperationists were going to fight, and despite their quietness since the beginning of the convention, it was now when they chose to erupt. In fact, the cooperationists on the committee of fifteen had already produced a "minority report." Now they began to discuss some of their objections and desired amendments as determined at the caucus the night before in the senate chamber. They did not have the power to defeat secession, and they knew it, but they did see a slight glimmer of opportunity to delay it. If they could delay, then perhaps they could woo over to their side some of the moderates. It was a fight worth fighting, and really the only one that had any chance of success. Thus, when Yerger announced that there were amendments to be offered, all hope of an easy passage vanished. Most observers still thought secession would ultimately prevail, but it would not be simple or easy.[10]

The fireworks began immediately. Alexander Clayton, one of the most revered members of the convention and a member of the committee, stood and declared that he had worked hard for the ordinance and stood by it. Obviously disenchanted with the idea of changing it or even considering amendments, he declared that "every word" in it was what it should be and "not one jot or tittle did he disapprove." Others joined in, and soon it looked like yesterday's rancor was welling up again. The last thing Lamar and the secessionists wanted was for a crack in their unity to emerge, much less be shown to a watching world. A decisive Lamar thus took control of the situation.[11]

Unfortunately for later historians, Lamar called on the delegates to go into secret session. He clearly did not want to allow any view of non-unity, and he further did not want the cooperationists, whom he correctly perceived would be the main delegates voicing their disdain, to make any headway with the public. Fissures in the secessionist caucus also emerged, however, even on the issue of the secret session. Henry Ellett, the revered statesman who had been the temporary chairman prior to the organization of the body, spoke against anything being done in secrecy. "There was nothing confidential in the character of the business before the Convention," he declared, and while admitting that such items as military policy or planning should be done in secret, "the people did not come up to the Capitol expecting to be excluded from the deliberation of the Convention." Lamar responded that "there might be facts developed the publication of which would be incompatible with the interest of the State at the present time." The *Mississippian* reported that Lamar, convinced of the necessity of secrecy, "with reluctance" then did "what he very seldom does": he moved the previous question and won the issue.[12]

The convention went into secret session at 11:30 A.M., "greatly to the disappointment of the assembled multitude," one delegate wrote. Barry relieved their disgust somewhat when he made plain that "when the debate was ended the doors would be opened." "The vote on the adoption of the ordinance will be made public," he promised. Thus there is very little record of what transpired during the next five hours in the secret session. Only glimpses are available, but the general picture is that the cooperationists

made several heartfelt speeches against secession. Logically, the secessionists remained mostly silent. Knowing they would change few minds, and
realizing that they did not really need to, they let the cooperationists vent
their anger and then moved on. Delegate Thomas Woods remembered that
the secessionists "did not choose to delay that action by any unnecessary
words."[13]

Little specific is known about what happened that afternoon. Thomas
Woods remembered that "the debates were brief; there were no set orations;
and there was absolute freedom from all acrimony." The only real glimpse
into the secret session came from delegate John W. Wood of Attala County.
A dedicated cooperationist, he made a fiery speech during the secret session. He later wrote, "Notwithstanding the unfavorable indications, and
outside pressure, I determined to make a last effort for the old Flag, more
as a protest than with the hope of defeating the passage of the ordinance."
And the only reason we have the speech, the only one from that afternoon's
secret session, is that Wood later printed it. He tried to get it included in the
official journal, but those compiling the records would not print it due to
the call for secrecy.[14]

Wood spoke at length, reminding his hearers that opposition to secession was not opposition to Mississippi or slavery, which apparently was on
everyone's minds. "My ancestors being large slave-holders, and always a
slave-holder myself—my family all native Mississippians, I challenge any
member of this body for greater devotion to the true interests of the South,"
he thundered. Yet he declared that a revolution cannot be successful if the
hearts of the people are not fully in it. He insisted that "the hearts of the
people of Mississippi are not in this revolution," and continued, "I know that
the hearts of my constituents are not, and I shall represent their will upon
this floor." He blamed the hasty decision for a convention on "the excitement of a presidential election [that] has not yet subsided."[15]

The cooperationist delegate from Attala County further gave the analogy
of the ship of state that, having been through many storms, could not be
broken. He promised to "stand upon the Old Ship as long as there is a plank
upon her decks, or an inch of canvass fluttering in the breeze." Denying the
right of secession, he viewed the act "about as reasonable as the right of a
part owner of a boat to destroy his part." He said the members had been
"lulled by the cry of peaceable secession; but, Sir, there is no such thing as
peaceable secession." Forecasting war, Wood pointed out that Mississippi
had no army, navy, or even government to defend the people; a taxation system did not even exist. Significantly, he declared, "this day, which has been

ushered in with so much enthusiasm, by the assembled thousands here, I fear, will prove the darkest day that ever broke upon the State."[16]

Wood then finished with a morbid prediction. Addressing Barry, he thundered:

> *Let me only warn you and this Convention, that if Secession is carried out, there will be nothing but ruin and desolation follow in its course— war, war, inevitable war, the depreciation of every species of property, stop laws, and bankrupt laws, the neglect of agricultural pursuits, the collection of large bodies of troops, the diseases which will necessarily spread among them; and before the last act in the great drama is closed, not only war, but "war, pestilence and famine" will spread over the land a scene of devastation, desolation and destruction. The last words I have to say are, that posterity will hold you Sir, and this Convention, responsible for the act which you this day commit.[17]*

During this harangue, Lamar and the secessionists bided their time, letting the cooperationists proclaim their rage and offer their arguments in secret, where they would have no effect on the people outside. Their obvious hope was that all the pent-up disgust and detestation would be spent inside the closed hall during the afternoon, and that the cooperationist delegates would be calmer when the open session leading to the actual vote occurred later in the afternoon.

This strategy worked. Barry called the convention back into open session at 4:30 P.M., and the galleries quickly filled as crowds wanted to witness the historic scene. Although the *Oxford Intelligencer* reported that "from nearly every man there comes a voice for immediate and unconditional secession from the Federal Union, and Mississippi's declaration of independence as a free and sovereign power," inside the hall the feeling was not quite so much jubilation. One delegate later remembered, "there were no brilliant orations, and there was an absence of all rhetorical display and elocutionary flourish. The tremendous responsibility pressing upon the Convention was seen on every countenance. From Judge Harris, solitary, silent, introspective, and Mr. Lamar, brooding, abstracted and melancholy, downward through all ranks and classes was an air of fixed solemnity."[18]

When the evening session opened with a motion to form yet another committee to deal with the governor, the cooperationists who had met in caucus to discuss their options began their work. Although the issue of secession was not in doubt, the cooperationists had formulated a series of amendments that could stall immediate and unconditional secession until a compromise could be worked out between the North and South. By placing time and contingency restraints on secession, the cooperationists hoped to bleed the convention's enthusiasm until the will of the people would come around to some sense of reality.[19]

Jacob S. Yerger of Washington County began the delaying process by of- fering a long substitute ordinance that would "provid[e] for the final adjust- ment of all difficulties between the free and slave States of the United States by securing further Congressional guarantees within the present Union." This was an attempt to halt secession based on compromises like those that had secured peace in 1820, 1833, and 1850. Even then several potential com- promises were in the works in Washington, D.C., and this one called for yet another convention of slave states to demand answers and promises. In essence, Yerger desired more time before taking such a monumental and potentially fatal step as immediate and unconditional secession.[20]

In writing the substitute, Yerger, though a cooperationist, firmly placed the genesis of the problem at hand on slavery. He declared, "for a series of years, a dominant majority in the non-slaveholding States have evinced, by a regular system of unconstitutional and unfriendly legislation, a fixed and determined hostility to the slaveholding States of this Union." He contin- ued, "the citizens of the Southern States have been denied an equal right with the people of the non-slaveholding States to enter upon and occupy with their property the common territory of the Union and to be protected in its enjoyment therein." He further spoke of the "conflict, irrepressible in character, [that] exists between free and slave labor, and have declared [the North] that agitation on the subject of slavery shall continue until slavery itself shall be abolished, and to that end have elected to the Presidency of the United States a man fully committed to these views, and who stands pledged to bring to bear all the influence and patronage of the Federal Gov- ernment to enforce and carry them into effect." He asserted that the "contin- ued agitation of the slavery question tends to the disquiet of the people of the slaveholding States." To remedy the slavery-related issues, Yerger called for a convention in Lexington, Kentucky, in February to "secure the rights of the slaveholding States in the Union, and to finally settle and adjust all questions relating to the subject of slavery in such manner as will relieve the South from the further agitation of that question."[21]

The delegates began voting immediately after Yerger offered his amend- ment. Because it was such an important ballot, the members voted individu- ally instead of by voice vote, as had been the case thus far. When the votes were tallied, despite what one secessionist member noted as "Judge Yerger's ... admirable paper[,] ... worthy of its eminent author," it was obvious the delegates were in no mood for delay. The amendment was voted down by a margin of seventy-eight to twenty-one, with one abstention, John W. Wood. Although John L. Power reported that Wood was absent "in consequence of serious indisposition," Wood himself later wrote, "seeing that the Convention had made up their minds to pass the Secession Ordinance I determined to take no further part in their proceedings." He remained in the capital several more days, but did not take part in any portion of the January convention thereafter. Wood's vote, of course, would have made twenty-two nays, but even with his vote it was a landslide for the secessionists. Even more significant, there also seemed to be a split developing in the cooperationist ranks. James L. Alcorn did not even vote for Yerger's amendment. Presumably Barry, Lamar, and the rest of the immediate secessionists breathed a sigh of relief after this first critical test of immediate and unconditional secession.[22]

But the cooperationists were not through. James L. Alcorn now offered a more conservative amendment to secession. His amendment stipulated that Mississippi's secession, which he viewed as a foregone conclusion, would not go into effect until Alabama, Georgia, Florida, and Louisiana had all left the Union and "resume[d] their sovereignty." Alcorn was hedging the state's bet on secession by making it contingent on the other states' actions—literal cooperation.[23]

With no patience for delay or contingency, the convention voted down Alcorn's amendment seventy-four to twenty-five. Although he lost four of the delegates who had voted for Yerger's amendment, Alcorn voted for his own and picked up seven others. In another significant development, however, Walker Brooke, one of the leading cooperationists, did not support Alcorn. Perhaps he did not like the contingency attribute, or he could have been repaying Alcorn's negative vote on Yerger's amendment. For whatever reason, the secessionists still had a solid majority, with the cooperationists continuing to split.[24]

Walker Brooke of Warren County offered the third delaying amendment, which continued the contingency and delay proposals: "This Ordinance shall not take effect until the same shall have been ratified by the qualified electors of the State and to this end an election shall be held ... on the second Monday of February 1861." This move would not only delay secession, but it would also ask the people of the state to approve the action. J. F. H. Claiborne rightly summed up the effort: it would give "time for deliberation while we stood on the brink of the dark abyss."[25]

The cooperationists knew this amendment was their only real chance of delaying secession, and it was not a given that it would be defeated. Alcorn later remembered that there had been much talk of such a compromise between the immediate secessionists and cooperationists, and many of the secessionists had agreed to platforms that called for such a statewide referendum in their county canvasses. "This proposition was at one time informally agreed to," Alcorn wrote, "but the Secession sentiment grew apace." Likely, when Barry, Lamar, and the other immediate secessionists realized they had enough votes to go straight through, they withdrew from the agreement and went directly to immediate secession.[26]

Once again the cooperationists gained a few votes, but they were defeated seventy to twenty-nine. This time, the cooperationists, perhaps thinking this was the best chance they had, closed ranks and voted all together, including the leaders Alcorn, Brooke, and Yerger. While losing three delegates who had voted for Alcorn's amendment, Brooke had gained seven others, four of whom had not voted for any of the amendments thus far. Nevertheless the cooperationists were out of amendments. Their tactics, while a long shot in the first place, had failed. Delegate Thomas Woods noted, "no further effort was made to stem the resistless tide."[27]

With all attempts by the cooperationists to delay or circumvent secession defeated, Lamar brought his original report, the ordinance of secession, to the floor for the final vote. By this time all in the chamber knew what the result would be, but tension still filled the assembly hall. "The President put the question without a surplus word," Alexander Clayton remembered, asking, "Shall the Ordinance now pass?" One by one the secretary began calling the roll, and one by one the delegates cast their lot, most in a "monosyllable," Clayton recalled. It was about dusk, around 5:30 P.M., the setting sun casting a solemn glow over the proceedings.[28]

"Over the entire Convention brooded a spirit of gravity and seriousness," one delegate remembered. Another onlooker reported that "the deliberations were calm, statesmanlike, manly and dignified, ... [done] more in sorrow than in anger." As the secretary of the convention called each delegate to vote, the tone became especially somber. "As each member responded in tones vibrant with intense feeling suppressed, the murmur of conversation and the rustle of movement ceased, and a stillness as of death held the great assembly," one writer reported. Edmund Pettus, Alabama's commissioner, wrote that "there was no symptom of applause or other disorder to disturb the solemnity of the scene." Secessionist after secessionist voted aye as the roll call went on, and even a few of the ardent cooperationists voted for the measure. Several of them took the opportunity to explain their votes, since they had been elected as cooperationist candidates and had to explain to their constituents why they were not voting the cooperationist line.[29]

The most anticipated votes were those by the leading cooperationists. Alcorn was the first of the major anti-secession members to cast his vote, and indeed the first in the entire convention. He was fully aware of his position, writing his wife, "I am one who is rushed to for work, I have been assigned some very responsible positions." All eyes were glued to see how he would vote, one witness describing how "his vote was awaited with intense interest." When his name was called, Alcorn addressed the convention with "unaffected emotion," John L. Power reported:

> Mr. President: I have thought that a different course in regard to the settlement of this great controversy should have been adopted, and to that end I have labored and spoken. But the die is cast—the Rubicon is crossed—and I enlist myself with the army that marches on Rome. I vote for the ordinance.

"My speech on voting for the ordinance was received by the convention and in the galleries with long and loud applause," Alcorn wrote his wife, "the ladies waved their handkerchiefs and a most profound sensation ensued." No doubt the applause was from a great sense of relief as Alcorn made his somewhat surprising stand with secession.[30]

When Walker Brooke's name was called later in the process, he similarly addressed the convention:

> Mr. President: I was elected by a large majority as what is known as a co-operationist, which means, as I understand it, one who was in favor of united Southern action for the purpose of demanding further guaranties from the North, or failing in that, the formation of a Southern Confederacy. I have, to the best of my ability, endeavored to carry out the views of my constituents in these respects. I have acted in good faith and with no desire to make factious opposition. I have failed. . . . Influenced by considerations of this character, which I now cannot more fully express, I feel it my duty, painful as it may be, to part from those with whom I have hitherto acted, to assume the responsibility of casting at least one of the votes of Warren County for the passage of the ordinance as reported. I vote aye.

A member of the convention remembered that Brooke's soliloquy was given "in a tone of infinite sadness, and with bowed head." He also remembered "this thrilling scene . . . the wave of relief and joy that swept over the Convention and [that it] broke into involuntary applause upon that momentous occasion."[31]

More and more cooperationists voted for the ordinance as the roll of names was called, and each explained his reasoning. Marcus Stephens declared that "the question was now reduced to submission or secession, and he was for secession, and should therefore vote for the Ordinance." William Sumner stated that "he had felt bound to perform certain duties to his constituents," but "could now best serve the interests of the State by voting for the Ordinance." John B. Herring stated that he had voted for all three amendments and had "attempted to fulfill the duty imposed on him by his constituents." He had pledged himself in the canvass to support only cooperation among at least eight slave states, but he only had the opportunity to vote for Alcorn's amendment for cooperation among five states. Yet that was enough for him to have fulfilled his duty as he saw it, and, Herring stated, he "saw no further use for apparent division among the people of Mississippi, but on the contrary, great necessity for union." Robert Flournoy similarly argued that with war inevitable, it would be treason to take up arms without seceding, and that he "would never, by any act . . . , place any citizen of Mississippi in that condition." William Tison also made the point that in voting for Alcorn's amendment he was not voting his personal feelings but that he had "felt in honor bound to carry out the wish of his constituents." In effect, Alcorn summed up their feelings that a show of unity was needed: "I and others agreeing with me determined to seize the wild and maddened steed by the mane and run with him *for a time*. We voted for secession and signed the ordinance."[32]

Two members who voted against the ordinance also spoke. Alcorn described them and the other staunch cooperationists who voted against secession as determined "to make no bargain with secession, to be guilty of no stultification, and stand firmly by their flag though struck to the earth under its folds!" Arthur Bullard of Itawamba noted that he knew of only "two secessionists in his county" and that he had to vote as his constituents wished. However, he assured the people of Mississippi that Itawamba County would do its part in providing troops to defend the state. Similarly, John Blair of Tishomingo also declared he would vote as his constituents wished, arguing that "the highest duty of a delegate [is] to remain faithful, in every contingency, to the people whom he may represent." He then clarified his actual stance, however: "I am for resistance—not submission to Black Republicanism rule: only differing somewhat in the form and time in which that resistance should be made." But he, like Bullard, promised all the support Tishomingo County could give to undergird the state in the decision of the convention. "In opposing, to the last honorable extent, the declared voice of the State," he was nevertheless "recording myself against that which so soon should command my obedience."[33]

As the vote continued on, everyone in the assembly hall began to realize that secession was a foregone conclusion. "The galleries and the floor of the Hall were crowded with spectators of the solemn scene," one writer noted, and "as the roll call made it manifest that the result would be largely in favor of the adoption of the ordinance, tears gathered into the eyes of nearly every actor and spectator." In the end, the final vote was eighty-four to fifteen, with the most die-hard cooperationists still opposing the move. All fifteen who voted against secession had voted for the Yerger and Brook amendments, and all but two delegates had voted for Alcorn's. Wood of Attala was the only delegate who did not vote.[34]

When the final vote was stated, "a profound silence for some time prevailed." Then President Barry called Reverend Harrington to pray once more, this time "on behalf of the new-born Republic." The minister began, "Almighty God, We the people of the State of Mississippi, in convention assembled in the exercise of that sovereignty with which thou hast ordained us, have in this Solemn hour, reserved to ourselves the power delegated to the Federal Union." He asked God's blessing on the new republic. "It was a scene of moral grandeur," recalled Commissioner Pettus, "the doing of a brave deed by a gallant people, trusting in God."[35]

With secession accomplished, the delegates quickly began to finish their business so they could, most of them, celebrate their independence. Indeed, people inside and outside of the statehouse were already celebrating. "The result was received with the most vociferous cheering," the *Oxford Intelligencer* reported. "The enthusiasm was intense. The ladies waved their handkerchiefs, and some joined in the chorus, and many a fair face ... [had] tears of joy." Before adjournment, however, Charles Fontaine of Pontotoc moved that the ordinance be "written on parchment and appropriately arranged for the signature of the members." Warren Anderson of Hind County made a motion that the president send telegraphic news to the slave states.[36]

Then there occurred one of the most dramatic moments of the entire convention. "Just as twilight fell over the statehouse," C. R. Dickson "entered the Hall," the *Jackson Weekly Mississippian* reported, "bearing a beautiful silk banner, with a single star in the center, which he handed to the President of the Convention as a present from Mrs. H. H. Smyth, of Jackson." One onlooker described it as a "little blue flag with its single red star in the center." Another eyewitness remembered that "the members saluted it by rising, the vast audience uniting in a shout of applause." Barry took the banner and, according to Power, "with a tear in his eye and tremor in his voice," remarked to the convention that it was "the first banner unfurled as the emblem of the young Republic." As one, the delegates and observers in the galleries "joined in prolonged applause," the *Mississippian* reporter wrote, while another wrote that "strong men bowed their heads and wept." He concluded, "I shall never cease to recall this, the most solemnly impressive scene I have ever witnessed."[37]

As the convention itself adjourned "amid the plaudits of the multitudes," the news began to travel fast throughout the town. Delegate Wood, brooding in his self-imposed exile away from the statehouse, described the celebrations: "The passage of the Ordinance was announced by the roar of artillery. The old Flag, which had been so long in the Capitol, was taken down, and a new one, with one star, placed in its stead, amid the shouts of the multitude and applause of the members." Indeed, the people of Jackson were in a festive mood. Fire bells first announced the vote, and they were soon joined by the booming of cannons, fireworks, the tolling of other bells, and the shrieks of steam engines. Illuminations glowed in the now dark city streets, one newspaper describing the "prominent places brilliantly illuminated." Large crowds began to gather around the statehouse and immediate area, celebrating independence.[38]

The flag unfurled in the statehouse that evening was the banner that would become known as the Bonnie Blue Flag, inspiring the song that was sung for the first time that night during the celebrations in Jackson. Although others later claimed to have written the song, the best evidence gives credit for the authorship to a young Irishman named Harry McCarthy, "a well known actor and comedian." Even those who later claimed authorship admitted that the tune was "an old Irish chord" McCarthy had been performing in Jackson that week. In fact, though, none other than Wiley Harris was the instigator of the song. He had met McCarthy on the street earlier in the day and told him, "Mac, the convention will adopt the ordinance of secession sometime this afternoon and you will have a large audience this evening. Permit me to offer a suggestion: Give us a patriotic song—one which, perhaps, will be universally received as a national air—something soul stirring and patriotic, that may become as immortal as the ordinance itself." A few hours later McCarthy penned the famous song, singing it over and over that night to "a house crowded to its utmost capacity" at Spengler's Hall, a theater on Capitol Street very near the statehouse. The author sang the song while a pianist accompanied him, and he "promenaded the stage back and forth, waving his flag," while the excited crowd hurled gold and silver coins onto the stage. "He was encored again and again, twelve or fifteen times at least, until he became hoarse from singing and the audience almost exhausted from applauding," a newspaper reported. John L. Power put the song in type, and a Civil War icon was born.[39]

People all across the state likewise began to react to the news as it spread from Jackson. The *Vicksburg Whig* and the *Natchez Courier*, both openly cooperationist, printed the names of the delegates elected as cooperationists who voted for secession, hinting that they had been traitors. The Natchez paper made special mention of John Blair and his cooperationist stand to represent his constituents. It also stated that "the people of Jefferson county will, we take it, have an account to settle with Mr. Johnston, their delegate to the Convention, in voting against submitting the secession ordinance to the people; he having been voted for upon the distinct understanding that he was pledged to such a course." The Natchez paper also noted that delegate J. H. Powell had been burned in effigy in Jones County for voting for secession. Most Mississippians celebrated as the news arrived, however. The *Weekly Panola Star* and the *Oxford Intelligencer* both reported that they stopped the presses to include news of the action. "We stop the press at 8 P.M. to announce that a dispatch has just been received from Jackson, announcing that Mississippi has formally seceded from the Union," the Oxford paper reported. All across the state the news caused massive celebrations. "Oxford is brilliantly illuminated," the paper continued, "bells are ringing, and guns are being fired. Three cheers for our gallant State!!" Reuben Davis, one of Mississippi's returning congressmen, heard the news on his trip home. "At Corinth I met the tidings that the ordinance of secession had been adopted by the convention," he remembered. As he continued home, he noted, "I was scarcely out of the sound of cannon all the way." He described how "at those stations where cannon could not be procured, anvils were brought into requisition, and were managed with so much skill as to produce an equal uproar." Even Mississippi's Episcopal bishop, William Mercer Green, issued a circular to his clergy telling them to replace prayers for the president with those for the governor, the state legislature for the Congress, and the state for the nation.[40]

Despite the celebration, there was still no getting around that fact that there was significant opposition to immediate secession that might not bode well for the future. In fact, the cooperationist sentiment displayed unsuccessfully at the convention should have forewarned all observant watchers of an issue that would come up again and again during the later war, that of Unionism in Mississippi and the will of the people to fight. Obviously the final vote was not a complete representation of cooperationist sentiment in the convention. A more accurate count of those numbers was the Brooke amendment (twenty-nine supporters) to allow the people of the state to ratify the ordinance of secession. Had that amendment succeeded, it would have been interesting to see exactly how much Unionist sentiment was contained within the larger population. Presumably there would have been a higher turnout than for the convention election. Percy L. Rainwater, the foremost expert on Mississippi secession, predicted that the secession referendum would have passed the state, but with only a small majority.[41]

Total cooperationist numbers can be safely set at one-third of the members of the convention, which Alabama commissioner Edmund Pettus described as a "respectable minority." Thirty-three members (including Wood) voted for at least one of the delaying amendments or against secession. While 33 percent is relative, high in some cases such as inflation or unemployment and low in terms of vote counts or wins and losses, in this instance it seems remarkably high. That 33 percent of Mississippi delegates to the convention were for delaying or putting contingencies on secession seems fairly large.[42]

Of those thirty-three delegates, their statistics can also help define the difference in cooperationism and secessionism. The average age of the secession opponents was older than that of the average convention delegate, their average net worth was lower than the convention average, and a much larger percentage owned less than twenty slaves than convention-wide. Thus the average cooperationist was older, poorer, and less involved in slavery than his secessionist counterparts. The opposite was true of the secessionists; they were younger, richer, and had more slaves, interestingly indicating that slavery had a lot to do with their ideals.[43]

The counties from which the cooperationists came told a similar story. The largest percentage of the cooperationists, 45 percent, came from the northeast section of the state, from the counties of Tishomingo, Itawamba, Pontotoc, Calhoun, Yalobusha, and Lafayette. Another 27 percent came from the Mississippi River and Delta counties, with the rest scattered throughout the more central counties. Just as with the convention canvass and the breakdown of cooperationists and secessionists, the final tally of cooperationists followed the same pattern—most hailing from the northeast hill country that was fairly poor and somewhat less endowed with slavery and

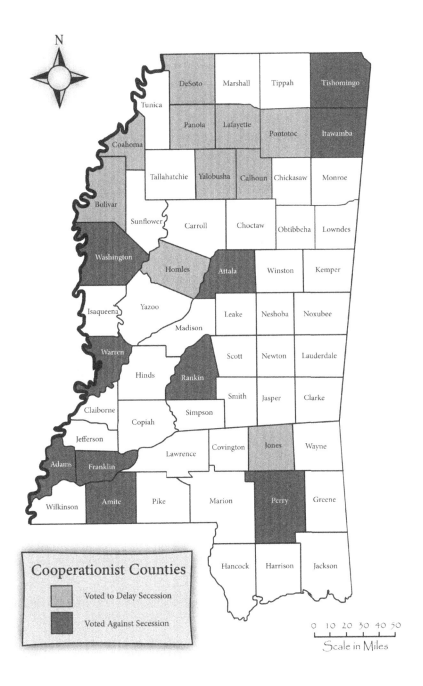

N

Cooperationist Counties

Voted to Delay Secession

Voted Against Secession

0 10 20 30 40 50
Scale in Miles

the large plantation–rich slave counties along the Mississippi River. Certainly politics made strange bedfellows.[44]

But the deed was done, and now the delegates, after the revelries of the night, had to convene the next morning at 10:00 A.M. and continue their work, which, in many ways, was just beginning. The easy part had been done; now came the huge task of making Mississippi truly sovereign in economics, politics, and defense.[45]

Significantly another change also took place that night as the focus began to change to the future. Most cooperationists, bent on delaying or hopefully even defeating secession, seemingly blended with the secessionists into one caucus after the vote. Their effort at opposition was over; now they were seceded Mississippians who were dedicated to working for the best for their independent state. Cooperationist leader James L. Alcorn summed it up well. Although some historians doubt his sincerity, describing him as hoping rather to be on the side of power, he later remarked that "division in the Convention, it was feared by all of us, would encourage Federal aggression. The show of a united and unbroken front might stay the hand of bloody war." Whether sincere or not, Alcorn no doubt swayed others to that point of view. The *Oxford Intelligencer* printed a similar editorial, stating, "almost an entire unanimity prevails among the heretofore cooperation party to present a united front, undivided by party or personal dissensions. The individual members are opposed to anything which savors of submission to the rule of Black Republican Jacobin functionaries." Alcorn's change is thus illustrative of the switch made by several of his followers. A mostly united Mississippi would thus either live or die by the decision made that fateful day of January 9.[46]

- 5 -

COMMITTEES

January 10–12, 1861

AFTER THE ORDINANCE OF SECESSION WAS PASSED ON JANUARY 9 AND the nightlong celebration was completed, a new day dawned in Mississippi. The weather changed from warm and muggy to cool and clear, and so did the attitude of the delegates. Secession was the major aim of the convention, and it had been on that basis that the delegates had heretofore aligned themselves. Party loyalty, declining in Mississippi anyway, was not an absolute issue on secession. As a general rule, more Democrats were secessionists and more former Whigs were cooperationists, but those brands did not hold altogether firm during the election canvass or during the first three days of the convention. Obviously many Whigs voted for secession, and more than a few Democrats supported the delaying amendments; three Democrats voted against secession itself. The fight over immediate secession had caused the national party political cards to be reshuffled in Mississippi.[1]

Yet once the divisive issue of secession was over and done, the political balances reshuffled again in what became the second phase of the convention. Now the issue was what action to take to make sure Mississippi was able to take care of itself, whether alone or in a new confederacy. The ninety-nine delegates thus began to shift their thoughts on January 10 to politics, economics, law, and society, and the old alliances of the previous day were gone, with new ones forming. Most Mississippians, even those severely opposed to secession, now supported an independent Mississippi and eventually the new Confederacy. Thomas B. Webber of Marshall County spoke for many when he wrote in his diary: "As much as I have opposed secession and separate state action, as my State has now seceded I must sustain that position or be a traitor to the State of my adoption."[2]

Within this context, which was certainly not altogether clear at the time, the somewhat politically disoriented delegates, perhaps still reeling from the excitement and celebration of their secession the day before or wondering where to go from here, began to plod through the massive amount of business at hand. There had been an effort to organize the work into committees with jurisdiction over certain areas, but for the rest of the week, the delegates trudged seemingly blindly forward. It would take a few days for the organization and tidiness so evident in the handling of the secession business to return.

During this change of focus, most of the members roomed at hotels and boardinghouses, most notably the Bowman House in the next block north of the statehouse. So many delegates as well as observers were in town that rooms were at a premium, and almost everyone had to double up. The crowded situation became even worse the next week when the legislature assembled, bringing even more people. One visitor in Jackson left a less that stellar account of his stay: "Mournfully metropolitan was Jackson in one respect—the price of board at its leading hotel." Still, the visitor groaned, "the accommodations were execrable." And those rooms were crowded with working men. Several left accounts of how busy they were during the convention, working as they were in session six days a week with committee work and other items on the agenda. James L. Alcorn wrote his wife, "I have been dear Amelia very busy since my arrival." Charles Fontaine similarly wrote his wife, "I am in good health, but have no leisure or amusement." He later described how "my whole time has been occupied with my duties of delegate to the Convention. We are making important changes in our organic Law." Many members performed their work often in detriment to their own personal lives. Hugh R. Miller wrote one of his sons during the convention that "I was so much occupied for weeks before I left home" that he did not see to his affairs. He now admitted, "I have been so much absorbed in the questions of the day that I have neglected my domestic affairs." Some of the delegates even worked through sickness. "Your Uncle Andrew is a delegate from Tunica, and is able to attend to his duties, though he suffers a good deal from rheumatism," Hugh Miller wrote his son. Only James L. Alcorn spoke of any frolicking, telling his wife that he hosted a "handsome supper" for the commissioners from Alabama and South Carolina. He reported, "speeches were made and a pleasant time generally [was had]." In presenting a "handsome bouquet" to Burt of South Carolina, Alcorn made a short speech, which, he said, was "loudly applauded."[3]

Despite the issues that plagued him as well, President Barry had much of the responsibility for getting the convention back on track. While he sought to organize the convention into various areas of domain when the delegates met on Thursday morning, January 10, he was also responsible for publicizing the secession ordinance. He did that by sending notes to the various Southern governors and dealing with larger entities such as Mississippi's congressional delegation. Senator Jefferson Davis sent a telegram on January 10 asking, "is it intended we shall withdraw immediately, or shall we wait for the official ordinance?" Most of the congressmen were not this hesitant and resigned two days later, on January 12. The five representatives, including Lamar who had left in December and Reuben Davis who had left on January 5, informed the House of Representatives of Mississippi's action and "announce[d] that we are no longer members of this body." They regretted having to resign, but said that the state's action met their approval, and "we shall return to her bosom to share her fortunes, whatever they may be." Senator Brown similarly informed the U.S. Senate that Mississippi's action "no longer permits us to take an active part in the proceedings of this body, either by speaking or voting." Brown informed the Senate that his colleague Jefferson Davis was sick at his home but that he shared this view. By the start of the second week of the convention, therefore, all members of the state's congressional delegation had personally informed their respective house that they were no longer members.[4]

Back in the convention itself on this January 10, Barry waded through the normal administrative items of a prayer by Reverend John Hunter and the reading of the previous day's minutes. In an effort to get the work of the convention organized quickly, he then announced the memberships of the various committees agreed upon two days previously. For instance, Barry placed several well-known legal minds on the Committee on Citizenship, including Walker Brooke of Warren County and George Clayton of Lowndes. Also included were Jehu Orr of Chickasaw, Edward McGehee of Panola, Albert Hill of Madison, James Dyer of Holmes, and Oswell Neely of Kemper. Brooke, Orr, and Clayton were very respected lawyers, and McGehee and Neely were large plantation owners. Three of the members—Brooke, McGehee, and Dyer—had voted for delayed secession the day before, but that did not preclude Barry from making Brooke the chairman of this committee. The old secession lines of battle were indeed breaking down.[5]

The Committee on Federal Jurisdiction and Property was made up of more secessionists. Wiley Harris of Hinds, Harvey Walter of Marshall,

James Z. George of Carroll, George Wilkinson of Yazoo, and Daniel Wright of Tippah were all solid secessionists and were well-known lawyers and planters, Wright and Harris having served in Congress previously. Thomas Marshall of Warren and M. D. L. Stephens of Calhoun were the only cooperationists. Wiley Harris was the chairman, a good choice for almost any position in the convention. As it was routinely expected that there might be some confrontation over federal property in the state, Harris's wise leadership would be needed.[6]

The Committee on Postal, Financial and Commercial Affairs was chaired by Jeremiah Clapp of Marshall County, with Gholson of Monroe, Edward Jones of Sunflower, Walter Kiern of Holmes, and Benjamin King of Copiah all firm secessionists as well. Miles McGehee of Bolivar and Arthur Bullard of Itawamba were the only committed cooperationists. As the economy and commerce would be critical to the newly independent state as well as any confederated nation, it was logical to place some of the richest planters on the committee, men such as Kiern, who owned 211 slaves, and Miles McGehee, who owned 234. Gholson and Jones were also wealthy planters, and Clapp was an elite but smaller planter as well. Obviously Barry was thinking in terms of cotton being the state's major asset in its finances and commerce.[7]

The Committee on the State Constitution had some of the brightest political minds in the convention and was chaired by Hugh Miller of Pontotoc County. Among the members were Henry Ellett of Claiborne and cooperationist Jacob Yerger of Washington, both well-respected politicians and planters. Also on the committee were planter Cyrus Baldwin of Chickasaw, William Bolling of Winston, Russell Beene of Itawamba, and John Herring of Pontotoc. Ellett had been in Congress, and the rest, except for William Bolling, had served in the state legislature. Beene, Herring, and Yerger had been for cooperation in the voting the day before.[8]

The Committee on Military and Naval Affairs was chaired by James Chalmers of DeSoto, who was on the state militia's governing military board and was a militia company captain, with other members including William Brantley of Choctaw, Israel Welsh of Noxubee, Charles Fontaine of Pontotoc, William Smart of Hinds, John Fizer of Panola, and William Tison of Itawamba. While few of them had any real military experience, they would mostly rise to high status in the war that would follow, including two Confederate generals and other high-ranking officers. Interestingly, none of the Mexican War veterans were on this committee, nor were militia officers John J. Thornton, John B. Deason, or Samuel H. Terral, the last of whom was on the governor's military staff. Only Tison had voted for any of the delaying amendments the day before.[9]

Perhaps the foremost committee was the Committee on the Southern Confederacy. In fact, David Glenn of Harrison County had probably opted out of a seat on the secession committee of fifteen hoping to gain the chairmanship of this committee, which he reported was "regarded as the most important in the list." He did so. Also on the committee was Lamar. Other members were David Hurst of Amite, Francis Aldridge of Yalobusha, William Douglas of Simpson, James Johnston of Jefferson, and Alfred Lewis of Jackson. Only Hurst and Aldridge had voted even remotely cooperationist the day before.[10]

In appointing these committees, Barry was obviously still mostly thinking in terms of secessionist and cooperationist partisan lines. Most committees were firmly in the hands of dedicated secessionists such as Harris, Glenn, Chalmers, and Clapp, and each one had a majority of secessionists on them. However, there is some indication of a thawing in Barry's mind. Brooke's chairmanship of the citizenship committee was significant, although it may have been a reward for ultimately voting for secession the day before. Likewise, the placement of dedicated cooperationists on each committee demonstrated Barry's more progressive stance, but then he had done the same thing on the secession ordinance committee itself. Still, only four of the fifteen who had voted against secession found their way onto a committee. The rest, like the other fifty-seven delegates, were not on any major committee as yet. Most notably, James Alcorn and Alexander Clayton were included in this group.[11]

Yet no sooner had Barry appointed the committees than the delegates began to offer their own resolutions apart from any committee's oversight. For example, it took a motion to invite South Carolina commissioner Armstead Burt and Alabama commissioner Edmund W. Pettus to speak to the convention (even that faced a substitute resolution by Jehu Orr, which passed) and then a new committee to take care of the details of whether they wanted to address the members in secret session or not. More troubling, delegate Israel Welsh offered a resolution that called on the legislature to pass an act to "effectually prevent the introduction of slaves into this State" unless the owner came too, and with the express purpose of becoming a citizen of Mississippi. Welsh spoke in favor of his resolution, insisting that it should go to the federal relations committee. Benjamin King of Copiah countered that it should go to the property committee. Others spoke for or against certain committees, including Daniel Wright, who wanted a special committee. Samuel Benton of Marshall opposed the resolution, stating that the state was in "troublous times" and that they should do nothing "that might seem inimicable [sic] to the rest of the slaveholding States." Daniel Wright of Tippah added that he had talked with others and feared that such a move would sever any relations between the Deep South cotton states and the border states, who, his sources in Washington, D.C., told him, were even then contemplating "a Middle Confederacy." Henry Ellett agreed, reminding the convention that the very law was before the state legislature just now. He saw no reason, after the fiery debate a couple of days ago, "to put the Legislature and Convention at antagonism on a point like this"; besides, he added, passing it now would adversely affect the border states. "To adopt that policy now would only afford them [border states] a pretext for delay," he concluded. Hugh Miller spoke most bluntly, arguing that "we had enough to do without entering on questions of such a character." Benjamin King of Copiah County offered a substitute for Welsh's resolution, insisting that Miller's committee on the state constitution should "take into consideration the subject of the inter-State slave trade." Although he consented to withdraw his reference to the resolution going to a special committee, which President Barry warned might not contain members favorable to it, Welsh stood his ground "with great reluctance," he said, and pressed on, remarking that "if it is a matter of irritation, be it so." To many delegates' relief, the convention finally tabled the measure.[12]

James Dyer of Holmes County similarly offered a resolution that Chalmers's Military and Naval Affairs Committee be instructed to look into "erecting batteries at Vicksburg, Natchez," and other sites on the Mississippi River. It was also to report the resolution to Governor Pettus for implementation. Various members immediately began to amend the original resolution, Daniel Wright adding Mississippi City on the coast and James L. Alcorn adding Friar's Point and Prentiss, which he deemed vulnerable points. They were also near his plantation. There was even a substitute resolution, which Dyer refused to accept. Like Welsh's proposal, the delegates once again believed that they were getting too far ahead of themselves and tabled both the original resolution as well as a substitute.[13]

On and on it went for the next several days. Delegates offered their own resolutions, telling the committees what to deal with rather than the committees formulating legislation to send to the convention. Yet only one resolution had ample weight behind it to pass. Wiley Harris offered a substitute resolution to Dyer's military language, this time to instruct the Military and Naval Affairs Committee to form a "Military Board" and also to amend the

constitution to allow for the organization of volunteer companies into higher military units such as brigades and divisions. Harris acknowledged that
he was doing this "at the request of some military gentlemen," and it later
came out that Governor Pettus was behind this resolution, which passed.[14]

As Thursday wore on the delegates became increasingly agitated at the
individualistic chaos. Jeremiah Clapp stated that the delegates were "talking
about matters now that should perhaps be more appropriately discussed in
secret session." He also said that some "discretion" should be allowed to the
committees, a theme taken up by David Glenn: "when we have standing
committees it was wrong to bind them absolutely to vote by instructions."
Glenn was clearly worried about any restrictions that might be placed on
his own committee dealing with the Southern Confederacy, about which
he had definite ideas. Others chimed in, however, William B. Smart alerting
the members that such action was "premature." More forcefully, Henry Ellett
cautioned that "we were traveling too fast." In particular, the convention was
"issuing here, as a convention, military orders" better left to the state's commander in chief, Governor Pettus.[15]

All the while there were also mundane matters. Burt, the South Carolina
commissioner, would certainly be seated in the convention, and a seat was
also offered to U.S. Army major Earl Van Dorn, as well as, curiously, to two
Louisiana convention delegates who were from Mississippi, L. P. Conner
and John Perkins. Albert C. Gibson of Issaquena County offered the resolution to seat the two Louisianans, who represented parishes directly across
the Mississippi River from his county. Samuel Gholson also read a letter he
had written to President James Buchanan resigning his federal judgeship.
"On the 9th day of January, A.D., 1861," he wrote, "the sovereign State of
Mississippi, by her Ordinance, dissolved her connexion with the late Federal Union, and annihilated all Federal jurisdiction and authority within her
limits. Consequently, it is proper for me to inform you that upon this dissolution of the Union, my function and authority as District Judge ceased,
and became utterly extinct from and after that date."[16]

Yet when the convention turned to a really significant issue, a resolution
offered by James Chalmers that would raise money "for the purpose of arm-
ing, equipping, and placing the State of Mississippi in a condition to defend
herself," several delegates, including Alcorn, Ellett, Walter, and Chalmers,
debated the issue before several members requested, and Gholson made
the motion, that the convention go into secret session and stop debating in
public. Before doing so, however, Gholson noted, "we were now entering on
the [real] work of the convention."[17]

Little is known about the workings of this or other secret sessions. Hugh Miller told his son that "a great deal is done in secret session which does not appear in the papers." In this case, the delegates lifted secrecy on only two small issues. One was to request federal postal workers "to continue to discharge their duties until otherwise ordered by this Convention." The other was a simple resolution stating that Mississippi recognized South Carolina as a "sovereign and independent" nation and would "correspond and treat with her as such."[18]

That afternoon and evening, after the convention had adjourned, the committees finally began their work. Realizing that immediate issues such as postal efforts would instantly impact the people on a daily basis, that committee worked especially hard that evening to prepare an ordinance. Several of the members also began to think about how to rein in the independent delegates and their many individual resolutions. And those concerns readily appeared when the delegates met for their fifth full day at 10:00 A.M. on Friday, January 11. First was an opening prayer by Reverend Thomas W. Caskey, in which he asked that Mississippi "be permitted peacefully to withdraw. . . . But should the dark cloud of war hover over us, and dangers gather along our path, give us true hearts to pursue the right." Next came the reading of the minutes, but then the convention seemed to return right back to divisive and almost irrelevant issues. For instance, there was some discussion and eventually a committee appointed for "engrossing and enrolling," and one for the enrollment of the secession ordinance, which caused a delay in the signing of the document.[19]

There was also a dispute over a resolution to appoint a committee to find a different location for the convention to meet when the legislature convened on January 15. Walker Brooke offered a motion to find a different place for the convention, but that motion was voted down. Some discussion ensued, with Barry and others looking to see exactly where the governor stipulated the called session of the legislature should meet and with Samuel Gholson retorting that the act of the legislature calling the convention stated they would meet at the statehouse as well. Hugh Miller argued that it was fine with him to "abrogate" the legislation, and offered a resolution calling for the convention to meet at the capitol and the governor to find the legislature somewhere else to meet. Samuel Benton noted that the legislature "consists of two bodies—this only one," and Warren Anderson stated that the decision should be left to the governor, who after all had called two separate bodies to meet at the same place. Alfred Holt of Wilkinson County cautioned that the debate was "placing ourselves in an undignified position" and recommended yielding to the legislature. William Tison then offered a substitute for Miller's resolution that called for the convention to meet elsewhere, and James B. Ramsey of Lauderdale County motioned to table both. That failed, and Tison's amendment passed, although Brooke's earlier one saying about the same thing had failed. The delegates were going around in circles.[20]

The chaos did not end there, and delegates continued to present their own resolutions apart from committee action. The fracturing of committee sovereignty in favor of the overall convention became so strong that when Barry informed the convention that he had a very important message in regards to the military situation and would refer it to that committee, Hugh Miller of Pontotoc offered a mild protest against "referring any matter to a committee before first being considered by the Convention." Miller quickly dropped his protest and agreed to Barry's action, but he illustrated the lack of parliamentary order among many members of the convention.[21]

Sensing the gathering spiraling out of control, several delegates called for the convention to look at the big picture and rein in all the individual motions and resolutions. Cyrus Baldwin of Chickasaw County offered a resolution that all ordinances be read three times before passage and that they go through one of the committees, to which would be added a "Committee of Reference." He cautioned that he "did not believe that the intellect of a Webster could keep pace with the purport of ordinances by being merely read once at the desk." His motion failed after some debate, in which James Chalmers reminded the convention that the rules of the House of Representatives, which they were using, contained that very provision, but it was nevertheless a start at getting control of the situation.[22]

Josiah Winchester asked to address the convention on the same problem, although he would soon get at the crux of the new ideological and political caucuses forming even then in this second phase of the convention. Illustrating the growing breakup of what there was of cooperationist solidarity, William Tison, who had voted along with Winchester on most of the delaying amendments, now raised a point of order against his address. Showing an unlikely coalition, President Barry, who had voted directly opposite of Winchester on each vote, declared that Winchester was in order and allowed him to speak.[23]

Winchester spoke about the need to "settle definitively the powers of the delegates here." Could the convention make decisions normally left to the governor or legislature, and could the delegates speak for the people themselves? The initial skirmish on this subject had been in dealing with amending the state constitution, and then another dealt with referring the ordinance of secession to the people in a referendum. Winchester noted that "there was a great difference of opinion" and argued that the current "American system of conventions" dictated a "limited" representation of the people. Otherwise there would be public fear of the convention "establish[ing] a monarchy, a despotism or an oligarchy." He reminded the convention that the government was made up of three branches, and it took all three of them to function in a republican manner. After voting secession and providing a means of defense, he ended, "our powers and duties were at an end," and "our work could be ended in an hour so far as setting the organic law of Mississippi was concerned."[24]

No doubt several members wished their work would be done within the next hour, but that obviously was not to be. Nevertheless Winchester had provided a firm check on the convention, and it seemed to help. In addition to Winchester's restraint, the work of the committees also began to appear on the floor, and this structured the proceedings as well. Jeremiah Clapp reminded the delegates to respect the committee system, illustrating the "necessity of moving with great caution and deliberation, . . . that no ordinance or resolutions contemplating action on the part of this body, should . . . be adopted until every facility was offered for scrutinizing and criticizing it thoroughly." And to ensure that this happened, President Barry announced the appointment of another major committee: Ways and Means. On this committee he placed some of the best minds in the convention, including Alcorn, Wright, Benton, Warren Anderson of Hinds, Philip Catching of Copiah, Albert C. Gibson of Issaquena, and William Denson of Rankin. Alcorn was convinced this committee was the most important of all; he described it to his wife as the committee "whose duty it is to provide for the war, the most responsible of all positions."[25]

A structured procedure of committee work soon became even more apparent. Jeremiah Clapp, head of the Committee on Postal, Financial and Commercial Affairs, offered a resolution to keep the mails running in the state. While admitting that the issue was a "very complicated and comprehensive one," his committee's ordinance acknowledged the need "to avoid, as far as practicable, any disturbance of existing arrangements and contracts for carrying and distributing the mail." In a partisan slap at the limited powers faction growing in the convention, the committee stated "the people of Mississippi in convention assembled" declared that all former U.S. postal workers, laws, regulations, and contracts should continue "in full force and effect." Clapp reminded the delegates that a convention of seceded states would meet in a few weeks and would form a national government that would probably make national decisions concerning the mail. He thus argued that "as we look . . . forward to a new confederation at an early day, . . . all that is now necessary . . . [is] to make a provisional and temporary arrangement." Clapp asked that 200 copies of the ordinance be printed and that it be taken up for debate at a specific time. He also spoke "at some length" on the ordinance, reporting that he desired full and free debate on all ordinances, but that this was simply a temporary patch to keep the mails running until a more permanent government was in place. He argued that if Mississippi intended to remain independent, then the legislature would have to devise an entire series of laws and funding. Most expected Mississippi to become a part of a confederacy, however, which would obviously take over the federal oversight. His committee had followed South Carolina's lead, Clapp reported, although it had "gone a step further" and included a mechanism to enforce the laws.[26]

Other small but important work also went forward as the convention awaited a speech from South Carolina commissioner Burt, scheduled for that Friday afternoon at three o'clock. The convention assigned a committee the task of making sure the engrossed ordinance of secession was correct and ready for the delegates' signatures. Alexander Clayton indicated that it was "a true and perfect transcript of the original." Conversely, in an effort to strengthen ties that were already forming in the post-secession political makeup of the convention, James Z. George of Carroll County offered a resolution to allow a seat at the proceedings, in addition to members of the state high court, to "all persons who have heretofore held that office or the office of Justice of the Old Supreme Court of this State." Historian William L. Barney has commented that this action "had an air of nonpartisan magnanimity and exhibited proper respect for the courts, the institution most venerated by the [cooperationists]."[27]

The time then arrived for Burt's address, so all other business ceased and President Barry introduced the South Carolina commissioner. Armistead Burt was a native South Carolinian who was a lawyer and politician, having served in the state legislature as well as several terms in the U.S. House of Representatives, where he chaired the Military and Naval Affairs Committee. At the Mississippi convention he spoke to galleries packed to overflowing. He reported on South Carolina's action, calling that state Mississippi's "elder sister," stating the reasons for secession, and illustrating a bit of the action and unanimity of the South Carolina convention. Then he congratulated Mississippi on its action, and called the delegates to participate in the

South Carolina–called convention at Montgomery in February. Burt ended with a call for unanimity, thundering that with "the South united, no power on earth can conquer it." He added, "Our enemies may burn down every house, and kill every man and the very women will defend it." Burt was "frequently and loudly applauded," the *Mississippian* reported, and the delegates, on such a unified and high note, adjourned the convention to meet again the next morning. Conversely, Alabama's commissioner Edmund Pettus chose not to address the convention, reporting to his governor that his task had been completed when Mississippi seceded.[28]

Saturday, January 12, was the final day of the first week of the convention, and the previous five days had been taxing both physically as well as emotionally. Obviously wishing to get on with the business at hand, there was little time taken off on the weekend, although the convention would observe the Sunday day of rest throughout the session. After a prayer by Revered D. A. Snow and the reading of the minutes for the day before, the convention began its work at 10:00 A.M. Once again individual members offered their own resolutions to the convention and even ordinances for referral to the committees. By Saturday, however, the work of the individual committees began to take precedence. The committees had been hard at work, both in the evenings and particularly in the mornings. David Glenn asserted that his own "experience was that the morning after breakfast" was the best time for committees to meet.[29]

Many of the members had been fretting over monetary issues, fully realizing that Mississippi was now on its own financially. If war came, as many expected, it would cost a huge sum of money to defend the state, whether by itself or within a confederacy. Raising revenue was thus on everyone's mind, even by such narrow constructionists as Josiah Winchester. Much like the immediate concern for postal affairs, the monetary situation was a major, immediate issue. Thus James M. Dyer of Holmes County, a member of the Citizenship Committee, immediately offered a resolution for the Ways and Means Committee to raise revenue. Arguing that war was "reasonably expected," he stated that "we must appeal to the patriotism of the people." Dyer called for the selling of bonds "in sums ranging from one hundred to one thousand dollars" at 8 percent annual interest, to be paid back in the future as cash or in taxes. The money raised was "to be expended in the military defense of the State." The resolution also allowed the committee to switch to treasury notes if they were preferred over bonds. Dyer spoke on his resolution, arguing that this was no time to raise revenue with taxation. He called a rise in taxes "onerous," and there would be a delay until they could be collected. He also argued against using the banks for loans, an issue pushed by Alcorn, remarking that banks were primarily useful to commercial economies. Dyer argued that Mississippians were "strictly an agricultural people." After Dyer concluded his remarks, the resolution went to the Ways and Means Committee, and the convention moved on.[30]

The raising of revenue for military defense, as important as it was, was but one of the immediate issues on the delegates' minds, however. Another was the military on the ground. The Military and Naval Affairs Committee had worked hard in the few days since its appointment and presented two reports on this Saturday. The hurry was probably so the delegates could spend the weekend perusing the recommendations and be ready to debate and amend them as necessary when the convention reassembled the next week. The first report came from committee chair James Chalmers, who offered "An Ordinance to regulate the Military System of the State of Mississippi." This major piece of legislation, which one newspaper predicted was "likely to prove a fire brand in the midst of the citizen soldiery, and cause a general flare up," called for a division of volunteer troops to be broken down into four brigades of two regiments each. The regiments would contain companies of infantry and cavalry, and these volunteers would be trained periodically but be allowed to remain at their homes until called for in an emergency. A brigadier general was to command each brigade, with the division itself commanded by a major general. Each of the five generals, to be elected by the convention itself, would, along with the governor, constitute a "Military Board," which would oversee the state's military assets. Chalmers asked that the ordinance be printed and tabled for the time being, with debate on the topic set for the next week. Interestingly, within the ordinance there was one potentially controversial item that would probably bring a swift rebuttal from those who deemed the convention as already taking on too much power. Section 7 of the ordinance stated that "all parts of the Constitution, all acts and laws of this State in conflict with this ordinance be, and the same are hereby, abrogated and annulled."[31]

William Brantley, also on the Military and Naval Affairs Committee, offered another ordinance, this one "An Ordinance to provide for surveys and fortification of military sites within the State of Mississippi." The ordinance simply called for the Military Board set up in Chalmers's ordinance to have the state's military sites surveyed and to report to the board the costs for their fortification. This ordinance was likewise printed and laid on the table for future debate.[32]

Yet there was dissension even in the military ranks. William Smart, also on the Military and Naval Affairs Committee, brought a third ordinance to the convention, although it came from him individually, not the committee.

He argued that at least part of the division set up in the initial ordinance would be needed in the field quickly. Mississippi would need "at least a few well-disciplined troops" to meet an invasion, he said. He itemized the cost of everything from arms, equipment, clothing, and ammunition for 2,000 infantry, 510 cavalry, and a battery of artillery. He believed the total to be $1,100,000. Chalmers, chairman of the Military and Naval Affairs Committee, replied that he was "opposed to raising a regular standing army" and would not deal with the ordinance unless the convention referred it to his committee. But he asked that it be printed and a time set for its debate the next week as well. Thus even with the committees beginning to take charge of the flow of business, all those committees were not on the same page. The *Mississippi Free Trader* was correct that the military bill would cause problems, and the militia interests in the state had not even registered their opposition as yet.[33]

More examples of individual action followed. Charles Fontaine of Pontotoc offered an ordinance stating that "the Chickasaw, Choctaw, Creek and Cherokee Nations respectively be invited to appoint delegates to the Convention of the slave-holding States to assemble at Montgomery, Alabama, on the first Monday in February next, to share in its deliberations in organizing a government for a Southern Confederation; and that said nations be severally invited to enter into a confederation on equal footing with the other slave-holding States." He also wanted state commissioners to be sent to those tribes. The idea was referred to Glenn's Southern Confederacy Committee. Warren Anderson of Hinds motioned that a committee be created to "draft an address setting forth the causes why Mississippi seceded from the Federal Union." David Glenn, chairman of the Southern Confederacy committee, said his members were already looking at that very idea.[34]

Perhaps most significant, Alexander Clayton offered a resolution to amend the state constitution, obviously fueling the fears of those who thought the convention was going too far. The issue had cropped up a couple of times that week, but Winchester's pleading that the convention not go too far quieted it somewhat the day before. Now Clayton asked that the constitution, which required action by "two successive Legislatures" to raise money, be changed "until the difficulties now existing between this State and other foreign States or Governments are adjusted." It was only a matter of time before this issue boiled up into a major controversy.[35]

Other small and mundane issues came and went throughout the day as well, matters such as a resolution by Ellett to have all the ordinances enrolled and deposited with the secretary of state, bickering over the permanency of

COMMITTEES: JANUARY 10–12, 1861 | 95

the "temporary Executive Council," and a call for the state auditor to provide the convention, when it dealt with monetary matters, data concerning taxable land, slaves, property, sales, and loans in the state. More significant, in one of the mundane actions, Walker Brooke asked for explanatory language to be appended to the bottom of the ordinance of secession, explaining why those who signed it had done so. It stated simply that signing the document was "in testimony of the passage." Thus Brooke told the convention in a call for unity that all members should be able to sign whether they were for secession or not. He thought every member should sign and that the added language allowed all to "consistently and conscientiously do so." Time would tell if he was right, but that Brooke's recommendation passed the convention unanimously was a good sign. Ellett also called for the signing to be put off until the following week, presumably to affix the extra language and to wait for the legislature to observe the act.[36]

By Saturday afternoon the convention moved to pending business on the postal ordinance Jeremiah Clapp had offered on the preceding day. That business, as well as a secret session, finished the convention's work for the week. Clapp made a motion that the convention go into the "Committee of the whole" for debate on the ordinance, which was a well-known tactic that allowed freer and easier dealings with legislation; Congress and the legislatures frequently took that route, and even the Constitutional Convention in 1787 had done so, George Washington himself stepping aside for another presiding officer. President Barry stepped aside when the convention went into committee, with Pontotoc County delegate Hugh Miller taking the presiding chair.[37]

Opposition emerged immediately. Robert Flournoy of Pontotoc County argued that the postal bill was not firm enough, or in his words "did not come up to the requirements of the Convention." He argued that keeping the current system was worthless, that it took a month to get his papers, and that they were frequently damaged. He argued that the state could devise a much better system rather than continuing a broken process. He recommended a superintendent, but Clapp responded that it was not the convention's duty to revise the system but to allow the mail to keep running. He argued that the legislature should take up Flournoy's complaints, offering a biting reference to the heated debates earlier that "the Legislature has all legislative power not withheld from it by this Convention." No doubt several of the strict constitutionalists squirmed in their seats at his statement. Harvey Walter of Marshall County went so far as to say that the ordinance was not compatible with the ordinance of secession. With the lines drawn, several of the delegates continued the debate on the ordinance. Alcorn, Gholson, Ellett, and George Clayton all participated and also discussed a new issue that emerged: what to do about the U.S. postal service still operating in Mississippi, since the federal government did not recognize Mississippi's independence. Walter stated that he would not pay U.S. postage, but Clapp posited that just accepting U.S. laws did not put them under federal jurisdiction: he "did not deem it incompatible to adopt the laws of the Medes and Persians—it would be no reason why we should adopt their jurisdiction also." In the midst of it all, Wiley Harris offered an amendment "with a view to brevity, clearness and legal accuracy," he said, to keep the delegates on track: it was basically a compromise that allowed the convention or the legislature to make postal changes. Although his amendment was passed, when Miller reported the ordinance back to the house with the recommendation of changes, Harris's amendment was curiously defeated. It seemed that even Harris could be bucked in the convention, but more important, that the delegates were still somewhat going in circles. The full convention then debated the ordinance again, with amendments by William Bolling and Henry Ellett. Several delegates argued that it was perhaps best to just keep the current system until further events required action. Running out of time, the convention voted to print the bill and take it up the next Monday.[38]

When debate on the postal ordinance ended, the convention went into secret session by motion of L. Q. C. Lamar, presumably for militarily significant issues. The only motion voted on without secrecy was another wise amendment by Wiley Harris stating that "the people of Mississippi recognize the right of the free navigation of the Mississippi River, for commercial purposes, in time of peace, by all States occupying its banks, and that they are willing to enter into proper stipulations to secure the enjoyment of that right." The *Mississippian* noted that the resolution was unanimously adopted. Even as it debated Mississippi's military needs, the convention signaled that it did not want a war.[39]

When the delegates adjourned after the secret session, the first week of the convention was over. It had been a momentous week to say the least, highlighted by the actual act of secession. But the momentum of the week came to a crashing halt as the members began sorting out the rest of their monumental business. With the delegates intending to make the way calm and smooth through the use of standing committees, the first days after secession proved anything but that. The delegates offered individual motions, resolutions, and ordinances, hardly working through the committee system emplaced so hopefully just a few days earlier. In doing so, the members violated a wise caution from Wiley P. Harris a few days previously. He warned that important issues "should be matured in committee [and] when matured there it would be reported as an ordinance of the convention." Making the chaos more acute, the political lines drawn over secession were broken, and new alliances were already forming. And the delegates were also beginning to grate on each other's nerves as well. William R. Barksdale wrote a friend, "I do not expect to speak any more during the sitting of this convention." He explained, "there is as much danger of a man speaking too much as too little. Some men in the convention have already lost their influence and do not even get the respectful attention of the house while speaking because they have spoken so much."[40]

Yet by the end of the week, the committee system was beginning to work, with the postal and military committees already reporting ordinances. While that did not stop independent-minded delegates from continuing their calls for their own pet ordinances, the process was nevertheless beginning to smooth out. No doubt all hoped the next few weeks of Mississippi sovereignty would run more smoothly than these first days. Only time would tell.

- 6 -

CEREMONY

January 14–15, 1861

WHEN THE MISSISSIPPI SECESSION DELEGATES RECONVENED AT 10:00
A.M. on a showery and windy Monday, January 14, the easy and most glamorous part of their work had been done. In one week they had organized
themselves, seceded from the Union, and then begun the process of committee work that would govern the remainder of their deliberations. How
much of a break the delegates took on Sunday is unknown, and it probably
varied with each delegate according to his religious dedication, committee
assignments, and work ethic. Some members representing counties close
to Jackson went home, the *Vicksburg Evening Citizen* reporting on Monday
that "both of the delegates from Warren were in town yesterday." What is
known, however, is that when the convention met the next Monday, it began
work on the various committees' draft ordinances. By the end of the week,
all six of the initial standing committees as well as the later-added Ways
and Means Committee would have reports or ordinances ready for the convention. And as the delegates waded through the work, a new paradigm,
hinted at in the latter part of the previous week, began to solidly emerge,
one that would recast the battle lines over secession into a new political
construct that would form the nucleus of the political opposition throughout the coming war in Mississippi. Wiley Harris recognized the change
immediately, addressing the convention on Monday perhaps both literally
and figuratively about "the new order of things initiated by the ordinance
of secession."[1]

What was occurring in January 1861 in Mississippi, as well as in other
states, was not altogether unlike that which had occurred in U.S. history at
the formation of the constitutional government in the early 1790s as well as

the emergence from the so-called Era of Good Feelings in the mid-1820s. It took a few years after the creation of the modern American government for political parties to emerge. But form they did, patterned after the ideologies of two dominant statesmen, Alexander Hamilton and Thomas Jefferson. The common enemy of the 1770s as well as the common divisiveness of the state-level arguments under the Articles of Confederation had diminished with the newly ordained Constitution. Hamilton's Federalists, bent on industrialization and a strong central government run by the elite, battled Jefferson's Republicans, vying for agriculture, states' rights, and the common man. Similarly, the emergence of a second party system in the 1820s and 1830s developed from a unified political hegemony where a common enemy, again the British, once more brought the two political sides together in a nationalistic venture. Like the split in the 1790s, this second split also developed around central figures, Andrew Jackson and a host of opponents against him, including John Quincy Adams, John C. Calhoun, Henry Clay, and Daniel Webster.[2]

The new wave of politics in Mississippi began to fully emerge in this second week of the convention. The common political enemy of the state, perceived U.S.-backed abolitionism, was removed after the January 9 act of secession. At that time the issues of immediate separation or cooperation with other states or cooperation within the Union were all but gone, and a new set of issues developed. The delegates began to fall into similar lines that had recast opposing ideologies before. Issues such as state sovereignty or central governance, the participation of the common man in government, and the role of the government in society emerged again, this time at the convention. Former secessionists and cooperationists banded together on each side of the issues, and, as before, these major issues would coalesce around major figures.[3]

Unlike the recasting of the political spectrum in the 1790s and the 1820s, however, Mississippi's Confederate politics never reached the maturity of generations of political parties in the United States; indeed, political parties never developed within Mississippi or the Confederacy. The divisiveness seen in other Confederate states both within the states as well as between the state governments and the Confederate central government likewise never affected Mississippi to the degree it did Tennessee, Georgia, or North Carolina. But the split was nevertheless there in Mississippi, emerging already in the convention itself as major leaders began to line up behind differing ideologies on how this newly independent state of Mississippi should be governed.[4]

This new construct developed as the various committees offered their resolutions and ordinances during this second week of the convention. In fact, three of the committees did so on the first day of that week, Monday, January 14. After the normal administrative tasks (interestingly not includ-ing an opening prayer) such as reading the previous meeting's journal and President Barry reading an official telegram announcing the "formal with-drawal" of the Mississippi House delegation in Washington, D.C., the con-vention turned to the postal ordinance, which had been offered the previous Friday and heavily debated on Saturday. After an unsuccessful attempt by William S. Bolling of Winston County to amend it with a section dealing with the assumption of U.S. government contracts, despite the fact that he assured the convention that he was not trying to "embarrass the action of the Committee" and that he had been "induced to submit this proposition from a conference with many members," the convention passed the original ordinance easily, "by an almost unanimous vote" announced the *Vicksburg Whig*. In essence, the ordinance declared that all "laws, contracts and regula-tions" for carrying and protecting the mail in effect prior to secession would be continued "so far as they are not incompatible with the terms and intent of said ordinance."[5]

The postal ordinance was minor compared to the reports of the other committees, however. Wiley Harris reported an ordinance from his Federal Jurisdiction and Property Committee, stating that jurisdiction of all federal property in Mississippi on January 9 would be "resumed and vested in the State of Mississippi." It also defined the power of the legislature as well as fed-eral courts. To allow the members time to digest what was in it, the ordinance was tabled and ordered to be printed. The convention set a special time to deal with the issue on Wednesday at 11:00 A.M., but Harris felt the need to ad-dress the convention immediately. Again fearing an outbreak of state versus central authority in the form of legislative versus convention power, Har-ris told the convention that the committee thought it necessary to bring up this issue outlining the legislature's power after the convention adjourned. In reference to overstepping the state constitution, he argued that the conven-tion was "supreme," yet counseled that the "disturbing hand of indiscriminate innovation shall not be employed on the State constitution." He wanted the convention to exhibit "a sense of duty which will confine our action within the narrowest limits compatible with the necessities springing out of the change of relations with the government of the United States." He admitted, however, that the "sense of duty" he spoke of "cannot be assumed as the limit of their power." He also identified loftier goals, such as hearkening back to the words of the Declaration of Independence when he paraphrased "the protection of life, liberty and property." He added, in hopes of stemming any renewed controversy, that "it is important that no doubt shall exist," and that "our object has been not to legislate, but to remove all doubt of the power of the Legislature over the subjects embraced in the ordinance."[6]

Harris calmed the gathering, and the convention moved on, turning to the military ordinance already on the table. James Chalmers's committee had worked long hours to compose an ordinance that would fill the needs of the state. As such, he worked not only with his convention committee but also with the state's sitting military board, which governed the volunteer state militia. Chalmers was also on that board, which Pettus had summoned on January 5, along with other such Mississippi military luminaries as Christopher Mott, Charles Clark, Carnot Posey, and Richard Griffith. That committee was meeting at the same time the convention was in session, with Chalmers performing double duty, sometimes chairing the militia military board. This body appointed a committee to confer with the convention's Military and Naval Affairs Committee, and the major issue at stake was who would elect the proposed generals on the convention-established military board overseeing volunteer units. The *Natchez Courier* said that the militia board members left one meeting in "dignified disgust." Finally, the sitting military board hesitatingly agreed to allow the convention to elect the generals, but there were other points of contention as well, and Chalmers had a fine line to walk.[7]

As chairman of the convention committee, Chalmers requested the members to go into a committee of the whole, which was done, with Samuel Gholson in the presiding officer's chair. The convention had dealt with the committee's report amid the massive chaos of the end of the previous week, with William Brantley and William Smart offering their own ordinances as well, and Chalmers going on record that he did not condone Smart's. The committee of the whole thus went into a lengthy debate and reported numerous detailed amendments to the ordinance, but voted down even more. Chalmers argued for a militia-type force of some "good men who should be left at their respective homes until the necessity arises of calling them into actual service." Chalmers was basing his ideas on the "French system," in which babies were enrolled when born. One onlooker remembered that Chalmers "spoke in eulogizing terms of the discipline and bravery of French soldiers, as manifested in the late contests in Europe."[8]

Not everyone was as enthused as Chalmers about the French or the haste with which the convention was moving on the military bill. Warren P.

Anderson called for postponement, noting "there is no actual war now." He added that "there was a great ignorance with reference to its details," arguing that even with his "little military education, he could point out several deficiencies in the bill." Anderson further argued that "we were all groping in the dark—we needed a pilot and that pilot would soon be at hand," namely Jefferson Davis. Francis Rogers voiced his support for waiting, and even Charles Fontaine of the military committee said that "the members ought to have time for investigation." Several other members objected to delay, however, and thought they should send the boldest possible message to the North. Samuel Benton argued that the North was watching, even describing a New York newspaper reporting their action on January 7. Mississippi should show the North "that we are in earnest." Benton, who had voted a straight secessionist line on January 9, was supported in his sentiments by none other than James L. Alcorn, illustrating the blurring of the old lines of secessionist and cooperationists in a new paradigm of politics. Alcorn, probably looking to make himself famous as a general, desired, he said, "to leap into this contest with an elastic bound." Chalmers stated that he and Anderson agreed, that "though traveling different roads, they both aimed to the perfection of the bill." Anderson reiterated that postponement would keep the convention "from active legislative ignorance." Anderson's motion to delay was defeated, however, and Chalmers, who was in charge, notified the members they would "progress as far as possible to-day."[9]

Other motions were defeated as well, with one by Cyrus Baldwin even ruled out of order. The convention accepted many changes as Chalmers went through the ordinance section by section. The most heated debate raged when some delegates thought the regulations were too similar to U.S. regulations, which Edward P. Jones argued was an entity "with which the State of Mississippi has just dissolved her connection." Chalmers agreed to a point, stating, "there was a great deal of force in the gentleman's remarks." Israel Welch, on the other hand, argued that "we should adopt what has proven a good system." Afterward, the debate turned to monthly wages, with a call to see exactly what the United States paid its officers and men. Hugh Miller called for more data, supported by Daniel Wright, who argued that "we should first see our longitude and latitude before we take our departure." After what the *Vicksburg Whig* described as a "lengthy debate," all saw that the committee of the whole would not finish the bill that day and so reported its work back to the convention. When the full convention reconvened and agreed to the committee's report, they set a special order period on Thursday at noon to deal with the military bill.[10]

The convention's desire for a firm military policy was the result of the widespread belief that war was very likely. Despite assertions from historian Percy L. Rainwater that most delegates did not believe a war was possible, surviving contemporary correspondence indicates a widespread feeling that war was indeed feared. Hugh Miller wrote a son that "we are going forward to arm the state and prepare for defense with men and money," and later warned his two sons studying at the University of Mississippi, "you and Edwin must apply yourselves closely to your studies, as we may have troublesome times and you may not have an opportunity to finish your college course." Charles Fontaine flatly stated, "I think we are bound to have a war; perhaps on a large scale and bloody cost." James L. Alcorn predicted, "if war ensues of which I have no doubt, I think I will be elected a Brigadier General." Thomas Woods later concluded, "on the floor of the Convention and in its committee rooms the earnest note of preparation for war was heard."[11]

The need for a military policy was partly evident because of the volunteer organization and movement of military companies throughout the state. Even during the convention's sessions, citizens throughout Mississippi organized themselves for the war most thought was coming. Infantry companies were organized, one in Lowndes County raising $4,000 for their equipage. At times, some units were jealous that Governor Pettus had called others into action. Ivy Westbrook, the convention's sergeant at arms, wrote Pettus on January 14 that he had heard Pettus was calling up militia companies and asked that his local company, the "West Point Grays," be called too. Many of the units traveled to Vicksburg in January, including an infantry company from Edwards as well as an artillery battery named the Quitman Artillery. Numerous guns "of heavy calibre" also arrived at Vicksburg onboard the steamer *Charmer*, the gift of Louisiana governor Thomas O. Moore to Pettus and his Mississippians. On a lighter note, Absalom Dantzler, one of the legislators in town for the special session, wrote home, "I saw some little boy soldiers marching about yesterday. They had little guns, a fife, and a drum, uniforms and caps. . . . They . . . paraded about like they understood their duty well."[12]

Two events at Vicksburg during this time were no kids' play, however. On January 13 a Northern boat named the *A. O. Tyler* steamed south on the river and approached Vicksburg around the great bend in the river. The artillery and infantry at Fort Hill hailed the vessel, but the *Tyler*, "not understanding the meaning of the signal," moved on past and came to at the wharfboat at Vicksburg itself. The *Vicksburg Evening Citizen* reported "had it not been for another boat the 'City of Louisiana' coming in between her and the shore, she would no doubt have been fired into." A much more frightening episode took place the next day when a rumor erupted that the steamer *Silver Ware* was approaching Vicksburg loaded with hordes of invading Northern troops. The vessel ultimately landed with nothing more than its normal load, but the population had been whipped to a frenzy.[13]

Despite the long, tedious hours on the military bill, the rest of Monday was taken up with the appointment of a committee to deal with the House of Representatives, set to assemble the next day in the same room. There was some talk of equipping the nearby unfinished concert hall, to be renamed "Independence Hall," but Chalmers, Glenn, and Baldwin all objected, citing the cost of preparing it. Baldwin argued that an entire military company could be raised for the cost, and Chalmers noted that the building was open and unfinished and worried that the delegates may be "risking our lives" in the wet January weather. President Barry appointed Edward P. Jones, Orlando Davis, and Thomas P. Young to work out a solution with the House of Representatives, preferably allowing the convention to occupy the hall after 2:00 P.M. each day the legislature was in session. David Glenn noted that he had talked to many members of the house and the split would work; after all, the morning was the best time for committees to meet anyway. A secret session then filled the remainder of the day, the only known action being a resolution that the postmaster in Jackson be furnished with enough copies of the postal ordinance to send one to every postmaster in the state.[14]

After the first long day of the second week of the convention, the delegates had surely realized that their seemingly glamorous task was not all glory and acclaim. In fact, the work was grinding down into mundane and boring legislative work, fittingly mirroring the turn in the weather from clear and chilly the week before to a little warmer but still dark, windy, and rainy almost the entire second week. But at least the chaos of the previous week had died down, and by the end of Monday's session the convention was running more smoothly. Then Tuesday, January 15, saw everyone receive a boost of adrenaline. Tuesday was the day set aside to sign the secession ordinance. The event had been delayed, but today was the day. Also adding a flavor of difference was that Governor Pettus had once again called the state legislature to a special session, the date of assembly Tuesday, January 15. Thus, as the convention began its work that day, so also did the legislature, which caused the already crowded hotels, restaurants, and bars to become even fuller. Because of the overcrowding, the *Vicksburg Evening Citizen* called on the convention to move to Vicksburg, citing its major accommodations, easy access, cheaper cost, and communication ability. It also declared that Vicksburg was now "the seat of war, and it would be no more than proper for the Convention to hold its session in this place." The idea of Vicksburg being the seat of war was preposterous at the time, but it unknowingly foreshadowed the war's later reality.[15]

Unfortunately for the legislative agenda, there was a quorum in neither the house nor the senate on Tuesday, due mainly to a major storm delaying the rail transportation of legislators to Jackson over the weekend. The *Mississippi Free Trader* reported a "serious obstruction . . . caused by heavy rains" on both the Mississippi Central as well as the Southern Railroad between Jackson and Vicksburg. Mail and telegraph lines were also affected. Of course several of the convention delegates were also members of the legislature and were already in town, Henry Ellett fulfilling the role of temporary president in the absence of senate president James Drane when the legislature finally came to order.[16]

A quorum appeared the next day, but though the legislature met in the succeeding days, little of note occurred. The *Natchez Courier* observed, "there was really nothing for them to do." That sentiment was shared by Absalom F. Dantzler, a member of the House of Representatives from Jasper County, who wrote his wife on January 17, "the legislature has done nothing of consequence as yet." He worried that the legislature might stay in session for weeks doing nothing, waiting on the convention to decide what it would do. But he was patriotic about it all: "the circumstances which cause us to be called here are of an extraordinary nature, and the events which are crowding upon us are of grave importance."[17]

Dantzler remained worried about two legislative bodies meeting at the same time, however, and like others was wary of the convention taking authority from the legislature. Several in the convention itself were already questioning how much power the delegates were taking, and Dantzler felt the same way. "The convention will doubtless make many changes in the Constitution," he wrote, "so as to adapt it to the new position which Mississippi has assumed as an independent republic." He added that the legislature would have to follow along and provide "much and varied legislation to accommodate the laws of the state to the exigencies of the times," especially if war came, as he expected. He noted, "there looms up a dark and portentous cloud, whether behind it is a star of hope and promise, or the lightening [*sic*] of ruin and disaster I know not." It all depended on the will of the convention: "If the convention decides to take upon itself the responsibility of going into a general system of legislation, why there will be no use for the Legislature here and we will go home, but if it confines itself to what I think is its legitimate sphere of action, which is to make only such changes in the Constitution or organic law of the State as to adapt it to the new position which the state has assumed as an independent republic then there will be much for the legislature to do." Dantzler's views of the convention mirrored those of many other observers at the time. Some thought the convention was taking too much power, the *Natchez Courier* mockingly stating in reference to the governor, "we believe the Convention has not altered his title yet."[18]

And that very debate was occurring with greater frequency in the convention itself, which continued the offering of ordinances on this Tuesday. On Tuesday morning, David Glenn offered the Southern Confederacy Committee's ordinance with a short address, which he described as a "brief but emphatic report with resolutions" outlining the committee's basic ideas of sending seven delegates to the convention in Montgomery and accepting the South Carolina proposal of each state having one vote. The ordinance also proposed that whatever government was set up in Montgomery, whether provisional or permanent, it should be referred back to the Mississippi convention "for our ratification or rejection."[19]

Glenn later indicated how the committee arrived at its decision, the only real insight there is into the workings of the various committees or caucuses. And even Glenn's account is not very helpful, mainly because either in reality or in Glenn's mind, he was the major actor in committee deliberations. "I gave nearly all my time to this most important subject," he later wrote, "and the whole work devolved upon me." He later recalled, "I had no aid save Lamar who proved himself no parliamentarian and a very dangerous debater." With the work done and presented, the convention, in order to give time to study the language, ordered the ordinance printed and made it the special order of business for Wednesday at 11:00 A.M.[20]

As required by the mandate of the previous week, the convention then turned to William Smart's minority ordinance to the Military and Naval Affairs Committee's report. Smart later remarked that he was fully aware of the danger of making such a move because this "bill [was] liable to ruin a delegate's record more than all others, should he make a mistake." But he insisted that he "had no regard to popularity." Essentially, the resolution created an immediate standing army consisting of a brigade of two regiments of infantry, three squadrons of cavalry, and a battery of artillery. The convention dealt quickly with the plan, however, voting it down easily, and then went on to take care of other mundane business such as offering seats in the convention to the Speaker of the house and the president of the senate. President Barry also appointed a new Committee on Indian Affairs.

Logically, all the members were from the north or central sections of the state, the area most recently taken from the Native Americans. The major committee ordinances also continued to be presented amid the mundane work, Walker Brooke next offering an ordinance from the Citizenship Committee. Like the others, it was printed and would be dealt with later.[21]

In the midst of the mundane ordinances, however, something offered an exciting change from the monotonous legislative action of the previous several days. By late morning, Alexander Clayton moved to begin the process of signing the ordinance of secession. This action was slated for 11:00 A.M. The convention had planned to sign the document as early as Friday of the previous week, but had delayed it until Saturday before finally moving the time to 11:00 A.M. on Tuesday, January 15. Most likely, the delay was to wait until the legislature was in session so the legislators could witness the event. In fact, Clayton offered a resolution, and the convention approved inviting the governor and legislators to witness the signing ceremony. Clayton also formulated the process of the signing, with the president and secretary first affixing their signatures and then the remaining delegates doing so when their counties were called in alphabetical order. With the process worked out, Barry appointed William Booth, William Brantley, and William Tison to inform the governor that the convention delegates were ready to sign. Only with Pettus, the house and senate, and the High Court of Errors and Appeals "having been announced" did the ceremony begin.[22]

One by one, as their counties were called in alphabetical order, the delegates came forward and signed with a gold pen brought in specifically for that purpose from the Treasury Department. James R. Chalmers used a separate pen, "which he intended to transmit to some of his posterity," he stated, and others apparently did the same, a newspaper reporting that members "in many instances, intend keeping the pens with which they signed the ordinance as a sacred testimonial of their devotion to Mississippi." The *Vicksburg Whig* declared the ceremony an "act of the Convention and of the people in whose name the solemn edict was registered." The signing lasted from 11:20 in the morning, when Adams County delegates Josiah Winchester and Alexander Farrar signed, until 12:45 P.M., when Henry Vaughan and George B. Wilkinson of Yazoo County were the last signees. The mood was serious. One newspaper reported the crowd of onlookers was "cool and undemonstrative, yet the play of the facial muscles indicated gladness of heart as the predominant feeling." Apparently only when Jacob Yerger, the spirited cooperationist leader who had refused to vote for secession, signed "with a magnanimity and patriotism beyond all praise," in the words of delegate Thomas Woods, did the crowd offer up a "suppressed murmur of applause." Alexander Clayton gave a small idea of the emotion, later writing, "I have stood by the death beds of my best beloved—of darling children and devoted friends, and felt the agony of those terrible moments; I have passed through many scenes of acute suffering and sorrow, but never have I witnessed one that wrenched the heartstrings like this."[23]

Although a Vicksburg paper called it a "unanimous act," only ninety-six delegates signed the ordinance that day. Realizing that secession was a reality, most cooperationists took Alcorn's lead and signed the document. Only two flatly refused, including John W. Wood of Attala County, who had been absent since before the actual vote on secession. However, John J. Thornton of Rankin County had attended the other sessions and purposefully remained absent from the convention on January 15 so he could not sign the document. Power noted that he "positively refused to sign." One member of the convention remembered Thornton "was constrained thereto by an immovable determination to do no act which might contribute to the secession of the State." Two other members were absent on Tuesday, James H. Edwards of Choctaw County and Alexander Pattison of Tallahatchie, but they came forward later and signed the document. The *Vicksburg Whig* was obviously in error when it stated that it had "no doubt Messrs Thornton and Wood will sign it on their return to Jackson." Nevertheless the *Memphis Daily Appeal* asserted that such unity "put the action of Mississippi beyond all cavil and dispute." It was correct.[24]

With the deed done, the convention tasked Secretary of State C. A. Brougher to have the ordinance "suitably framed for its better preservation in his office." He did so, affixing his seal two days later to a copy, keeping the original on file. Lamar also offered a resolution providing a copy of the ordinance to each of the commissioners in the different states for use in their work, and later the convention gave exclusive right to Secretary Pope and T. S. Hardee, who had written the official version on parchment, to make copies for sale. The convention also approved a motion from David Glenn that his committee look into selecting a commissioner or commissioners "whose duty it shall be to visit the City of Washington, and lay before the President of the United States [Buchanan] an authentic copy of the ordinance of secession passed by the Convention, and confer with him upon the future relations and intercourse of that Government, and Government of the State of Mississippi."[25]

Despite this ceremonial interlude, the convention returned that afternoon to recognize Florida and Alabama, whose conventions had formally notified Pettus of their secession, as "sovereign and independent nation[s], and will correspond and treat with [them] as such." In an act of formality, Daniel Wright of the Ways and Means Committee also offered its ordinance on Tuesday afternoon, which, like the others, was printed and made available for debate at a later time. The report allowed the governor to issue up to $5 million worth of treasury notes or bonds. Interestingly, showing a growing split within the new political factions of the convention and state, James L. Alcorn also presented a "Minority report" that called for "an institution of credit and finance under the title of the 'Bank of the Commonwealth of Mississippi.'" Alcorn's minority report was also printed to be discussed later.[26]

The disagreement in the finance committee over how to proceed was illustrative of the growing split in the convention itself. And that emerging split would only grow wider as the convention trudged on. Now that the ceremonial actions of passing and then signing the secession ordinance were over, there was nothing left but mundane yet important work. The *Mississippi Free Trader*, in fact, reported on the change even then taking place: "the frenzy of excitement has passed, and given place to a sober determination to sustain, with life, fortune, and sacred honor, the independent State of Mississippi." Yet the mixture of unexciting debate coupled with growing splits among the delegates was a formula for volatility. All was not settled yet.[27]

- 7 -

DIVERGENCE

January 16–19, 1861

AS THE DELEGATES RETURNED TO THEIR ROOMS AND BOARDINGHOUSES after the ceremonial but mostly unified signing of the secession ordinance that Tuesday, January 15, none could have known what lay ahead on the next day, a raw and cloudy Wednesday. But the growing fissures in the delegates' presecession coalitions soon worsened, and there were delegates who seemed to revel in increasing the growing divide. And to almost everyone's surprise, it began immediately when the delegates reassembled the next morning.[1]

The budding organization and unity seen the day before in the signing of the secession ordinance took a dreadful turn as work on the ordinances continued on Wednesday as the convention met at 9:30 A.M. The first jolt was a series of resolutions offered immediately by George Clayton concerning "the powers and duties of this Convention." Agitating the issue Harris had tried so hard to dampen on Monday, Clayton argued that the convention needed resolutions "for the purpose of defining the duties and power of the Convention to prevent confusion hereafter, and also to save the State from a precedent which might endanger the liberties of the people." As described in the *Vicksburg Whig*, Clayton's resolutions declared "that legislative acts passed by the Convention would be inoperative and void, because the Convention was called for a specific purpose, and that not for purposes of legislation." The issue was larger than just the convention, however; prominent citizens and several papers throughout the state were already beginning to editorialize on the gross accumulation of power in Jackson. B. L. C. Wailes complained in his diary that the convention was meeting in "permanent and chiefly Secret session—and little is known of their doings." The *Natchez Daily Courier* noted that "a great strife, it seems, exists as to whether the Convention was limited to the question . . . [of secession], or whether its members were sent there to do what they pleased; in short, whether their object was a special one or whether we are now living under an oligarchy of Ninety-Nine." And the editor went even further, hinting at a revolution amid the counterrevolution: "The truth of the business is, we are in the midst of a revolution and at present are governed by an oligarchy of Ninety-Nine. What they will do or how far they will go remains to be seen."[2]

Clayton certainly agreed with the Natchez paper. In denying that the convention was "absolute and unlimited over the persons and property of the citizen" and that they "possessed no inherent power, but only derivative," he argued that the convention "was called by the people for a specific purpose, to-wit: the secession of the State from the Federal Union, and the formation of a Southern Confederacy." He even cited Greek mythology about taking care to miss both Scylla as well as Charybdis, or a rock and a hard place. In all, Clayton offered four resolutions that stated that the convention was merely called to secede and set up a new government, that setting up a new government was "the extent of its power," that the convention should not tamper in legislative areas which by extension could also lead to other areas of government such as the judiciary, and finally that the convention only amend the constitution to allow for secession and the creation of a new government. In short, Clayton said that the convention should leave all other items to constitutional mechanisms already in place and thus not to "uproot . . . the very foundations of the government."[3]

Clayton was no doubt sincere, but the convention was in no mood for controversy just when things had begun to flow smoothly. Surprisingly, the delegates promptly tabled the resolutions and ordered them printed for future deliberation. Desiring to move on with actual business, they then turned to more work for the Military and Naval Affairs Committee. Now that Smart's resolution had been voted down on Tuesday morning, David Glenn recommended that the committee look into defending the coastal region of the state, where he was from of course, charging that Pettus had "neglected" the area. More important, Wiley Harris brought up the Federal Jurisdiction and Property Committee's resolution, which had been slated for debate at 11:00 A.M. The convention went into the committee of the whole, with Samuel Gholson in the chair, and the delegates in committee offered three amendments and reported the ordinance back to the convention, which made it the special order for the next day at 11:00 A.M. The convention then took up Glenn's Southern Confederacy ordinance, again going into the committee of the whole with Alexander Clayton in the chair. The members debated the issue all afternoon, breaking for a short secret session but returning for an open evening session at seven o'clock. Evidently, little of real secrecy was debated in the afternoon session, because an irritated Warren Anderson made a motion that only genuinely secret matters should be debated in secret session and that "all other matters be ruled out of order by the President."[4]

Despite all the disagreements and secrecy, the delegates were making progress, especially on the confederacy issue, which almost all agreed was within their realm. In the debates over what the Southern Confederacy would look like, several issues came up. By far the most contentious topic was the issue termed "reconstruction," not to be confused with the more famous postwar Reconstruction, but whether to allow nonslaveholding states into the new Confederacy. When the debate erupted, Glenn admitted that his committee had not considered the question, and even Wiley Harris admitted that he had not given much thought to it. Both Samuel Gholson and Charles Fontaine offered amendments that only slaveholding states would be allowed into the future Confederacy. Numerous delegates expressed opposition, thus pitting die-hard secessionists against each other. Jeremiah Clapp was adamant that a middle-of-the-road policy was needed. Certainly, he argued, "there was an irreconcilable antagonism of opinion between the two sections," but he posited that "whilst we prepare for war, we should do nothing to produce unnecessary exasperation, but extend to them the olive branch." In fact, citing "the illustrious Calhoun" as a mentor, Clapp noted that Mississippi and the South should stand firm on the basic idea to "preserve our government and institutions separate and distinct." Still, he argued, they may need positive relations after the war with a variety of states, so nothing should be done to burn bridges.[5]

Alexander Clayton echoed Clapp, going so far as to state, "we shall be obliged to have treaties with them. We cannot live without them in peace." He also cited the historic example of the French trying to maintain connections throughout the Mississippi Valley, noting that their efforts came to naught in two battles fought in Mississippi, one in Pontotoc County and the other in Monroe. Clayton also reminded the convention that denying slaveholding states entry into the Confederacy would limit the South's westward expansion; "the gold mines of California may be potent auxiliaries to the cotton fields of the South," he noted. In summarizing his moderation, Clayton advised that it would be best now not to "drive some of the Southern

States from consultation with us" and that "as yet we have no evidence that these States will ever desire to unite with us. In my opinion, it is unsafe to say beforehand what we will do in that event. We may best decide when the time comes."[6]

James Chalmers offered a substitute to Fontaine's resolution, emphasizing "our willingness to unite with any State or territory" that "by its laws, recognize and protect, within its proper limits, property in slaves." Basically Chalmers opted to join with anyone, even nonslaveholding states, as long as they recognized the right to slavery. Chalmers was so forceful that Fontaine offered to withdraw his amendment, which Chalmers responded to "with pleasure," changing his substitute to Gholson's amendment instead of Fontaine's. Chalmers echoed President Barry's sentiments that perhaps some of the southern portions of Indiana, Illinois, and Ohio might join with the Confederacy, settled as they were by immigrants from slaveholding areas of Virginia and tied as they were to the Ohio River and the eventual use of the great Mississippi River, which, Chalmers advised, "percolates through the whole great vallies of the West, like veins through the human system." Chalmers also advised that delegates to Montgomery "represent the views of the Convention, and not their individual sentiments" on this issue. By the time Clapp, Clayton, Chalmers, and a host of others such as James Z. George and even President Barry himself had spoken and the delay of the unneeded secret session used up more time, the convention decided to delay its further debate on the Southern Confederacy amendment. The delegates adjourned until Thursday afternoon at two o'clock, the time worked out with the legislature for a joint occupation of the hall. The *Natchez Courier* was so perturbed at this turn of events that its editor reported, "so many amendments had been introduced and acted upon, that it is almost out of place to publish the plan as originally reported."[7]

Despite the obvious hold the Southern Confederacy issue had over the members, the convention resumed debate on the military bill when it met Thursday afternoon, once again going into the committee of the whole, with Gholson presiding. After a long debate and several amendments, the convention returned to normal format on the motion of Jehu Orr, who advised the delegates that there were still more amendments to be offered from "several members [who] were absent." Then in stark difference to the unending debate on the military bill, Harris called the Federal Jurisdiction Committee's ordinance to the floor after the enrolling committee reported it was correctly printed. Under Harris's leadership, it passed unanimously, thus becoming the third major ordinance passed by the convention.[8]

When the convention again turned to Glenn's Southern Confederacy Committee's ordinance, however, the new splits in the political order became more vivid and continued on for the next few days. The debate and votes illustrated how former secessionists and cooperationists, once split on the issue of secession, were now partners on each side of the new issues facing the state. In the committee of the whole, with Gholson presiding, the convention made several amendments to the ordinance through the afternoon and into an evening session at seven o'clock, but debate centered around two main parts: the process of the election of delegates to the Montgomery convention and whether convention delegates could be elected to go to Montgomery.[9]

At stake again in both issues was the power of the convention in relation to the state legislature and even the people. William R. Barksdale offered an amendment that provided one delegate to Montgomery for each congressional district as well as two at-large delegates. "Each district possessed a man of sufficient integrity and ability," Barksdale argued. The young Barksdale, just twenty-six years old, was proud of his amendment, privately writing a friend, "the amendment which I offered and spoke in favor of was to one of the most important committee reports that has been made or will be made during the sitting of the convention." He went on to explain how "my speech was highly complimented by all the big men of the convention, especially Judge Wiley P. Harris . . . and many others too numerous to mention." Barksdale was so proud of his work that he "sent to different persons of my acquaintance 32 copies of the morning paper containing the proceedings of that day." Several delegates such as James Dyer, William Tison, William Bolling, and William Smart agreed, with Harvey Walter of Marshall voicing his expectation that he and his district "certainly expected to be represented in the proposed Convention."[10]

Not everyone was as enthused with Barksdale's amendment as he was. Glenn had no major objection, but tended to think that the members "should be untrammeled in the selection of delegates." Others agreed, but by far the most vocal opposition came from Edward P. Jones of Sunflower County, who argued that one district may have more than one of the best men in the state while other districts had none. "In order to secure the highest talent," he advocated an open election, and then he went on to make one of the longest speeches in the convention. Saying that "he could not, without doing violence to his impulses and convictions, refrain from expressing his repugnance to it," he desired to throw off all illusion to "the late Federal authority." He argued forcefully that voting by former congressional districts would spur "petty sectional rivalships and internal State dissentions," and explained how, conceivably, four of the seven delegates to Montgomery could come from the same township and, even more probable, all seven could come from one side of the state or the other. Despite Jones's adamancy, in the end the convention approved Barksdale's amendment, temporarily at least.[11]

Jones's speech led to a larger issue: could convention members elect themselves to the Montgomery convention or to any other major post. Jones argued that no member should be "eligible or elected to any position of honor, profit or trust, which position was created by action of this Convention." "The Convention, like Caesar's wife," he noted, "should be above suspicion." Citing a rule that prohibited legislators from taking jobs they had created, Jones insisted that "nothing would be more likely to engender discontent and disaffection in the minds of the people towards this convention than the distribution among themselves, by its members, of the honors and positions which they had breathed into existence." He warned that any move to go that route "would be opposed."[12]

Although the convention quickly dispensed with Jones's concern about congressional districts, his argument about their right to take positions they had created touched off a firestorm of debate in which delegates lined up on each side. All soon saw that the 7:00 P.M. time set aside for the election of Montgomery delegates was not possible. Warren Anderson advised that "we were progressing too rapidly" and that they were about to elect delegates for offices not even created yet (the ordinance still had not passed). Gholson agreed that "the Ordinance should be perfected before we proceed to the election of delegates." Thus the debate was allowed to continue, with Gholson offering an amendment prohibiting any of the delegates from being allowed to go to Montgomery. David Glenn admitted that friends said they wanted him to represent his district, but he approved Gholson's idea, joking that it could be construed as a "death bed repentance." Jehu Orr and young Thomas Woods joined in the debate on Gholson's, Jones's, and Glenn's side, opposing any member of the convention from becoming a delegate to Montgomery, while Brooke, who stated that "there were gentlemen in the Convention whom he would be proud to see represent Mississippi," led the fight for no restrictions. Harvey Walter and Samuel Benton, both total secessionists on January 9, sided with the major cooperationist leader Brooke. Benton argued that the people had spoken in the convention by electing the delegates and that "the members of it should not be disfranchised."[13]

The vote taken on Gholson's amendment was the first recorded roll call vote since the secession vote a week and a day earlier, and thus is the first indication of how political lines had changed. On this vote, ninety-three members cast a ballot. Of the fifteen who voted against secession, three were absent, but the other twelve were split equally down the middle, with six voting for the amendment and six against. Of the thirty-two delegates who voted either against secession or for one of the delaying amendments, six were absent, but of the other twenty-six, nine voted for the amendment while seventeen voted against it. The split was about the same on the secessionist side, with secessionist leaders such as Glenn, Gholson, and Wright voting for it while delegates like Clayton, Harris, and Lamar voted against it. In the end, the amendment failed on a sixty-one to thirty-two vote. Clearly, the previous factions had broken into new lines of contention, mainly over the power of the convention.[14]

After a break to calm frayed nerves, the members returned for an evening session at seven o'clock and continued debate on the issue. This time the main question was another part of the Southern Confederacy ordinance: whether the constitution established at Montgomery should be ratified by the convention, a new convention, or the people of the state. In short, the power of the convention was again the major point of contention. Glenn considered all the other preliminary issues of congressional districts and convention jobs as minor compared to this one, which he described as "the great question of the body." Once again Gholson was the chief instigator of the major debate when he offered an amendment that the Confederate constitution as passed at Montgomery should be submitted to another convention of delegates for approval. Wiley Harris came to Gholson's side, arguing that it would take months for a new government to be set up and that the present convention should not sit that long. Jacob Yerger, Francis Rogers, and others supported the idea as well.[15]

On the opposing side was David Glenn, who, almost alone, carried the fight for the dominance of the convention. "It was my opinion," he later wrote, "that we had the power and right to act that duty, experience, and the crisis demanded we should act." He argued that the convention "should see the work to its consummation before they laid down their commissions." When Glenn took up the fight, he later recalled, it "elicited all its [the convention's] talent and much of its violence." In fact, Glenn described how "I was furiously assaulted by Wiley Harris Judges Yerger Gholson and Rogers and many others which led to one of the fiercest debates which ever occurred." Glenn argued that it was "useless to refer the Constitution back to

the people or another Convention." Asserting again his supreme convention stance, Glenn argued that "this body was clothed by the people with
full power to act as they pleased." Orr backed Glenn in the debate, as did
Brooke, who stated, "we should stand by until the last stone was put in the
building" and that his "baggage was checked all the way through." But Gholson feared the convention becoming "a Provisional Government or a 'Rump
Parliament.'" On and on, Glenn, Harris, and Gholson continued the "lively
triangular discussion," the *Vicksburg Whig* calling the debate "an exciting
passage of arms . . . in which satire and ridicule were strongly blended with
the weight of logic and argument." Gholson went so far as to label Glenn
"too much excited" over the issue. Glenn shot back that "the gentleman from
Monroe should be the last to accuse him of becoming excited," and went on
to explain: "He had heard his clarion note sounding in his ear on all subjects
great and small that had come before the Convention." Glenn even added
a backhanded compliment, intimating that while Gholson was full of hot
air, "as to going with him to the field of battle, he would not want a better
compeer, though he might want a better looking one." Although the debate
became heated at times, the *Whig* noted that "each gentleman sustained the
high reputation for forensic display which each had gained in other fields."
Tiring of the vitriol so late in the evening, L. Q. C. Lamar suggested that
the different views were not all that different and that they "could be made
to harmonize." Yet he wanted to do so on a fresh day and moved that the
ordinance be sent back to the committee for more work. Voting to do so, the
convention adjourned for the day, but not before assigning the soon-to-be-
elected delegates to Montgomery "prefer[ed]" instructions to confine their
task to nation building, not governing. In other words, the delegates would
be sent to Montgomery with specific instructions to set up a government,
not to become that government themselves.[16]

Despite a night of rest and reflection, Friday's session, beginning at 2:00
P.M., continued the divergence. After James Chalmers asked that the military ordinance be returned to his committee for further work and a short
secret session, the convention turned into the committee of the whole, with
Orr in the presiding chair, and moved to consider the Ways and Means
Committee's bill to provide money for the defense of the state. This issue
had been thoroughly divisive already, with the committee itself producing
a majority and a minority report, and with a substitute for both also called
for on the floor. Once again new splits emerged as Samuel Benton, Wiley
Harris, Warren Anderson, and Daniel Wright led the fight for a tax on land,
slaves, and capital, while a mixture of secessionists and cooperationists

railed against it. Pure secessionist Cyrus Baldwin, who offered an amendment to tax slaves, land, and loaned money, backed the ordinance in debate, and secessionist Warren Anderson gave numbers to the equation, stating that a tax of a quarter of a percent would raise nearly $2 million in three months. "If the people haven't got the patriotism to bear direct taxation, they won't have the patriotism to buy your bonds," he added. Cooperationists such as Robert Flournoy, Thomas Marshall, and James L. Alcorn agreed in principle, but argued that the ordinance as it stood would force "the rich alone . . . to bear the burden." Alcorn called Baldwin's amendment "class legislation," arguing that it would "strike with consternation the property holders of the State." He added that under it "slavery would be as safe in the hands of the abolitionists." "The poor should bear their portion," he insisted. But the opposition ranks were not totally harmonious. Alcorn also opposed a direct tax, supporting an ad valorem tax instead. Debate raged throughout the afternoon and into an evening session meeting at seven o'clock, with Alcorn doing a great deal of speaking. He ruled out bonds that would hurt international credit but supported a "judicious and well regulated banking system controlled by directors of known financial ability." He was pushing his central bank idea again. Perhaps the old opposing lines of Andrew Jackson and Henry Clay were actually emerging.[17]

Although Pontotoc's Flournoy vocally supported the idea, numerous delegates quickly lined up against Alcorn's bank policy, including Daniel Wright, who "replied . . . attacking his position," the *Vicksburg Whig* recorded. Wright argued that "capitalists and patriots" would buy bonds rather than bank notes, adding that the central government about to be instituted would eventually assume all state debt anyway. No doubt a few pure states' rights advocates squirmed in their seats at this comment, and Wiley Harris offered his vocal opposition while Warren Anderson replied that bonds would merely be "waste paper in the hands of the Governor." The bitter taste of the proposed bank was still on Alexander Clayton's lips when he later stated flatly, "I object to any union of Bank and State. It converts the bank into a political machine, and turns it away from the proper objects and purposes of a bank." Clayton continued, "agricultural communities . . . [particularly] should have great fear of its appropriateness." James Dyer agreed that banks were fine for "commercial communities," but the agricultural South had no need of them. Previous attempts in Mississippi to charter a bank proved to be what Dyer called "the most disastrous [episode] known to any people." He also argued that banks in Tennessee and other states would attempt to drive down a Mississippi bank's credit in competition. He stated flatly, "into such institutions the breath of life should not be breathed."[18]

The convention was thus stalled. Eventually the members left the ordinance for the night in response to Thomas Marshall's call that the military committee and auditor provide more data on economics, taxes, and the needs of the troops in the field. The convention, needing a break to calm the further fractured nerves, adjourned until the data could be obtained.[19]

The hopefully rested and presumably calmer delegates met again on Saturday at 3:00 P.M. and immediately heard Barry read a dispatch from Mississippi's commissioner to Missouri, Daniel R. Russell, stating that a convention bill had passed the legislature there "with great unanimity." After James H. Edwards and Alexander Pattison came forward to sign the secession ordinance and a special committee was formed to write an address to planters in the state urging them to plant food crops instead of cotton in case war erupted, the convention proceeded to consider Walker Brooke's ordinance from the Citizenship Committee. Going into a committee of the whole again, with J. W. Clapp presiding, the delegates then engaged in a serious debate over the meaning of Mississippi citizenship.[20]

The main issue at stake was whether noncitizens could move into Mississippi and become citizens. The ordinance fell on the side of leaving the way open for new people to come in, with Brooke leading the fight for openness. At one point Brooke asserted that a "Chinese wall should not at once be built between this State and the Northern States." In fact, he said that "many capitalists and manufacturers of the North" were planning to move into Mississippi, which would only aid the growing independent state. James M. Dyer also weighed in on the side of openness, arguing that little should be changed until "a Southern Confederacy should be formed, when a general system could be adopted." To bolster his point, Dyer pointed out that "there is now here a gallant Mississippian, who has been, for upwards of twenty year[s], absent from the State, in the military service of the United States, but like a true son, when difficulties surround it, he has come back and tendered his sword to his native State." Dyer was evidently talking about Earl Van Dorn, who had been tendered a seat at the convention. Dyer argued that "no oath of fidelity should be exacted" from people like Van Dorn. While admitting that foreigners would need "a course of pupilage to fit them for citizenship," Dyer nevertheless agreed with Brooke that any change in the law would deflect "Northern capitalists"; "their money will seek other channels for investment." One of Brooke's other main allies on this issue was Wiley Harris; the most well regarded cooperationist and secessionist thus teamed together on this issue.[21]

Just such an astonishing coalition emerged on the opposing side as well. William Barry, now a regular member of the committee of the whole, railed against the idea of allowing new citizens in "without the formality of an oath" until a new central Southern government decided the issue. He specifically warned about spies who might infiltrate the state. James Dyer dismissed that concern, saying, "an oath will not restrain them. If they are base enough to come here and act the part of spies, they will not hesitate, to commit perjury." Brooke agreed: "a mere oath would not be sufficient guard against such characters." Coming to Barry's support was none other than James L. Alcorn, who responded to Brooke's line about a Chinese wall by saying, "a wall similar to that built by the Britons" would suffice. He argued that "Yankees and Abolitionists" would rush in and perhaps take over the government.[22]

At such an impasse, the convention turned that afternoon back to the Ways and Means Committee's bill to raise revenue, with Joel Berry once more offering an amendment to tax slaves, which again brought a heated debate to the floor. Warren Anderson offered a plan to raise $500,000 through loans, which, he said, would "not conflict with any other plan before the convention." Francis Aldridge also submitted a plan for raising money for the state. Seeing the revenue debate also spiraling out of control, Chalmers motioned for the debate to be postponed and resumed the next week, presumably when the committee could retake control.[23]

After the acrimonious debates, the final committee to report to the convention that week did so in an anticlimactic fashion. Hugh Miller's State Constitution Committee dealt with two issues, but Miller and his fellow committee members gave two negative reports requiring no further action. One regarded the task of preparing a coat of arms and flag for the state, which Miller reported they had looked into and asked to be "discharged from the further consideration thereof." The task would be better handled in a special committee of five. The other issue involved the appointment of ambassadors, consuls, and ministers to foreign nations, and again Miller stated that the committee members thought that it "is neither expedient nor necessary to take any action thereon at the present time." They asked to be relieved of that duty, too. Both requests passed.[24]

Following the major debates of the day, and at times in between, the convention also tended to minor business such as a farewell letter from South Carolina commissioner Armistead Burt, who reported his task completed and congratulated the convention on its work. The convention then passed congratulatory resolutions in his honor. Other small issues were also voted on, such as a motion by Warren Anderson to appoint a committee to look into procuring a fireproof building to be used as a powder magazine; the convention voted it down. Wiley Harris's motion for federal court clerks to make copies of all records passed easily, and William Witty, William Gwin, Porter Myers, Thomas Catching, and James Nelson received leaves of absence presumably to get a head start on returning home over the Sunday break. The convention elected Henry Ellett as the convention's president pro tem because President Barry would be late in arriving back in Jackson Monday morning. The convention also confirmed the appointment of commissioners to the other states. The most notable motion came from Henry Ellett, who called on the convention assembling the next Monday, January 21, to do so at the concert hall. This passed, but then the delegates changed their minds later that evening and decided to meet at the local Masonic Hall. A three-hour secret session also took place that evening at seven o'clock, during which mostly mundane issues were discussed, except for Wiley Harris's call to allow the governor to borrow money to sustain the troops then in the field. The exhausted delegates then left the statehouse around 10:00 P.M., no doubt ready for the Sunday break.[25]

Thus ended the second week of the slowly plodding convention. The *Vicksburg Whig* correctly reported that "the time of the Convention for the past two or three days has been spent in debating the various ordinances and resolutions reported by the different committees." Such a lackluster explanation was perfect for the lackluster work. Delegate Charles Fontaine fully agreed, writing his wife, "nothing has occurred that can interest you much." Still, the long hours of the convention passed with important if not glorious work. Fontaine confided to a friend, "we are getting along slowly with our ordinances, but it is well that we should 'hasten slowly' in the important organic changes we are making to adapt our . . . Republic to the new order of things." Fortunately, the signing of the ordinance of secession on Tuesday had offered some excitement amid the mundane work, but the members were nevertheless losing patience with the process and each other. William R. Barksdale almost apologized for offering an amendment at one point, citing "the signs of impatience which have already shown in regard to the discussion of amendments to these resolutions."[26]

Unfortunately, the convention's counterpart was doing no better, and was in fact seemingly getting in the way. When the legislature finally met on Wednesday, it had little to do. "Both houses of the legislature met today," reported the *Vicksburg Whig*, but added, "nothing of interest transpired in either branch." In fact, almost all saw the convention as the main decision-making body, with the anti-secessionist *Whig* even declaring, "it is thought that as the power of the Convention is supreme that the legislature will adjourn and leave the Convention to transact all business pertaining to the proper equipment and position of the State." Almost as if begging for equal status, the House of Representatives merely passed resolutions inviting the convention delegates to seats within their sessions, but few took the opportunity. In fact, the legislature was more of a bother than an ally by causing the convention to move elsewhere. On Friday the convention even passed a resolution to send a committee to discuss "the course which the two bodies propose to adopt. . . and also as to the propriety of the adjournment of one of said bodies to a future day."[27]

Nevertheless despite competition with the legislature and the depressing weather that a nearby newspaper called either "drizzly wet, or damp and cold," the convention had made great progress in working through all the major committees' ordinances. As the delegates prepared to relax over the Sunday break or return to their homes, most thought that the next week would see the passage of those bills and their work would be done. Whether it could be done that quickly was debatable; there were still a lot of decisions to be made. But the increasingly homesick delegates could hope.[28]

- 8 -

VOTES

January 21–23, 1861

BY THE TIME THE DELEGATES TO THE MISSISSIPPI SECESSION CONVEN-
tion returned to work on the rainy and disagreeable Monday, January 21,
several things had changed. Mississippi's remaining member of Congress,
Senator Jefferson Davis, left Congress that day. In a long, sad, and affec-
tionate speech, Davis threw his lot in with his state and bid his colleagues
"a final adieu." Closer to home, the convention was in a new venue, meeting for the first time in the Masonic Hall on the second story of Jackson's
city hall. Having planned to meet at first in the unfinished concert hall and
even spending $76 to get it into shape for the convention, the delegates had
changed their minds at the last minute on Saturday night and opted for the
Masonic Hall instead. The members voted $50 to the "Masonic fraternity"
for its use and another $15 for its "fitting up." It was all very troubling, how-
ever, Charles Fontaine writing a friend, "I am in the bustle and confusion
incident to a change of our place of holding the Convention." Yet the largest issue on everyone's minds was timing. As the delegates assembled that
Monday morning, most realized they were moving very slowly, especially
on some of the larger issues such as the ordinances dealing with the formation of the Southern Confederacy and the military committee's bills. The
Natchez Courier noted that it was "unable to present to our readers any very
clear idea on to what it is doing." Absalom Dantzler, one of the legislators,
similarly complained to his wife, "the convention has not done much since
it passed the Ordinance of Secession, more than to discuss and in some
measure to mature plans for raising money to place the republic of Mississippi in a state of defense." And the more they debated and amended those
ordinances, with some being sent back to committee for another start, the

longer they would drag out the proceedings. Many of the delegates were obviously missing their families and wanted to get their work done and return home.[1]

Yet there was more to it than missing their loved ones. The delegates were actually under the gun. Mississippi was "in the midst of revolution," Samuel Benton had declared as early at January 14. Whether that was technically true or not was debatable, but most delegates saw the need to hurry and get a military ordinance passed and a military board established so it could organize itself to arm and defend the state. An even more important issue was the Southern Confederacy Committee's ordinance in which the delegates would spell out their participation in that new government, especially the state's delegation to the convention set to begin in Montgomery on February 4. That was a mere two weeks to the day from the beginning of this third week of the convention, and the members had yet to even determine what their official status was and who their representatives to Montgomery would be. Time was running out. It would take time to pass an ordinance, elect the state's delegates to Montgomery, and then have them travel to Alabama. Certainly the state's delegation did not want to be late and miss any appointments. Another factor was that some of the state delegates could possibly be members of the convention itself. If so chosen, these individuals would be torn as to whether to miss part of the convention in Jackson or go to Montgomery. The best idea, some thought, was to accelerate the work and get it done, letting the basic structure established in the convention begin to work, and letting the entities such as the military board, delegates to Montgomery, and even the state legislature work amid the broad lines established in the convention. But to do so, the members would have to work hard in the next few days, perhaps even to adjourn for good by the end of the week.[2]

The delegates thus filtered in, excluding the Adams County members Farrar and Winchester, who made a "flying visit" home on Saturday and did not return until Tuesday. The convention delegates thus began to wade into their unfinished ordinances when they met at 10:00 A.M. on Monday, January 21, at the Masonic Hall. After dealing with some preliminary motions such as providing the legislature with copies of resolutions that required their action, allowing the secessionist *Jackson Mississippian* reporter John L. Power a seat in secret sessions (proposed by cooperationist Alcorn no less), and moving through a secret session, the members soon heard from the various committees that previously had ordinances referred back to them. Glenn, for example, reported his ordinance from the Southern Confederacy

Committee, and later in the day Chalmers reported his ordinance back to the convention from the Military and Naval Affairs Committee. But those issues would be dealt with later; Monday was dedicated to the Ways and Means Committee's ordinance.[3]

Daniel Wright of that committee brought this ordinance to the floor, and the convention spent the remainder of the afternoon debating and amending it before taking a break and returning at 3:00 P.M., spending some of that time in the committee of the whole. Yet not all were happy with the progress; it fell to Henry Ellett to recommend that the committee start over and send to the floor an ordinance "providing for the collection of a special State tax of 50 per centum on the present State tax," and also to issue "treasury notes or certificates of loan" up to a total of $1 million at 10 percent interest. The motion also included a future tax to pay for the loans. Not everyone agreed with Ellett on this issue, as the previous week's debate had illustrated, and the secessionists certainly did not flock together. Alexander Clayton challenged his secessionist ally with a substitute motion. He called for the original ordinance to be recommitted to the committee, and advised that the committee work on the treasury note idea as well as an ad valorem tax on all taxable property, including a seventy-five cent tax on slaves. Clayton argued, "in the last hundred years, no nation had undertaken to raise by immediate, direct taxation, the funds necessary to carry on war. The most absolute despot in Europe would as soon think of abdicating his throne as to resort to such a course." Firmly stating that he had no "wish to inaugurate a system of class legislation," he nevertheless supported a higher ad valorem tax on slaves, arguing that "taxation is the price which property pays for protection; and that price should be commensurate to the value." And to make sure this tax was absolutely fair, he advocated the use of treasury notes "of so small an amount that even the humblest of her citizens can aid in the movement." Not satisfied, Joel Berry offered an amendment to Clayton's substitute amendment, which required that the committee should work within the "present revenue system of this State" for any taxation, in other words not to invent new taxes. If anyone had hoped to move quickly through the ordinances, Monday's revenue debate did little to fortify such feelings.[4]

With so many proposed amendments on the floor, the convention began to work through them methodically. The pending bill was Berry's amendment to the substitute amendment, which the convention voted down. Next was Clayton's substitute, which was also voted down. Then the question returned to Ellett's original motion, which called on the committee to start over, and this passed. In the end the convention basically voted to tell the committee to start over. Several members were despondent at all the maneuvering, William R. Barksdale writing a friend that "the fact is the only simple, honest and direct way to raise the money is to tax the people and raise it. . . . If the people have not got patriotism enough to bear such a tax as this then they have not got enough to sustain this movement of secession." Warren Anderson had earlier uttered the same basic argument on the floor.[5]

But it was even more complicated than that. Cyrus Baldwin argued that all polls should be exempt from taxation, but the delegates voted that down. James Z. George brought up an even more important issue when he recommended that the committee include in its forthcoming ordinance a tax on slaves at a dollar a head instead of the "fifty per centum on the present state tax." George argued that "they had brot on the war and must pay for it," and he wanted to make slaves a special category for additional taxation over and above what Ellett's recommendation entailed. The time nearing 6:00 P.M., and having spent nearly all day in debate, the delegates were simply in no mood to deal with George's recommendation and voted to table it before adjourning for the night.[6]

Because of the lack of progress the day before, the members arrived at the Masonic Hall on Tuesday with a full day ahead of them, and they would indeed put in several very long hours. Immediately when the convention opened at 10:00 A.M., Gholson took the convention back to the Ways and Means Committee's bill, suggesting that the delegates instruct the committee to include an additional tax on slaves, over and above what George had recommended the night before. The total would be $2 per slave, a major increase from Clayton's seventy-five cents before and even George's $1. His motion also included taxing out-of-state bonds or deposits by Mississippians. The motion surprisingly passed, again pitting secessionists such as Chalmers and Harris against others such as Glenn, Gholson, and Lamar.[7]

With instructions sent back to the finance committee, the members then turned to other matters, including sending the Citizenship Committee's ordinance back to that committee as well. The bulk of the morning and early afternoon, however, was used up when the convention turned to the military bill. The committee had been dealing with changes along with the state's militia military board, and Chalmers went through the revised ordinance in sections, with numerous amendments being considered. Some were superficial, such as those offered to move certain counties into or out of certain regiments' domains. Other amendments by Hugh Miller, Francis Rogers, Benjamin King, Alfred Holt, James Dyer, William Brantley, and Chalmers himself were passed that changed wordage. One particular amendment made compensation available to any soldier injured and the same for any widow. But several motions offered by Cyrus Baldwin, James Z. George, James Nelson, William Barksdale, Charles Fontaine, and Samuel Gholson were defeated. An amendment to allow the governor to appoint men to vacancies on the board also failed. When George offered an amendment to change officer pay, however, the convention tabled the motion for later debate. One wonders how many men in that room planned to be officers in the coming war.[8]

The most significant issue concerned the pay of privates. James Z. George offered another amendment that raised a private's pay to $12 a month. George, a former private in Jefferson Davis's regiment during the Mexican War, explained that "they were the persons who did the drudgery work and the hard fighting. Their duties were more onerous than those of the officers. It was no desirable position to be a private in the army." George stated that he had talked to military men on the militia board such as Richard Griffith, who agreed with his proposal. Fellow secessionist Israel Welch countered that "this was no time to be making military experiments" and favored the current system. Others chimed in, but Gholson moved to amend George's amendment by setting the pay at $20 a month, arguing that this would allow poor farmers "to obtain something like a compensation which they could receive at home." He also reminded his opponents that Mexican War privates had had the opportunity to gain new lands as bounties and such was not available in 1861. Warren Anderson countered that the ranks would easily be filled with "young and unmarried men," and Robert Flournoy added that there needed to be a major distinction between officers and enlisted men in every way, pay included. He argued that "the responsibility of an officer was great," and that the U.S. Army already had the highest pay in the world; he did not want Mississippi's to go even higher.[9]

Gholson eventually withdrew his motion, but George stood firm with his, arguing that "Mississippi at this time wanted the services of every son" and that in an army of citizen soldiers, "a private should receive as much to support his family as an officer." The committee chairman Chalmers as well as Charles Fontaine pointed out that with the benefits of clothing, food, and other items, currently the "compensation" was actually $22 a month. Eventually George's amendment was tabled, but Cyrus Baldwin called for $15 a month before Chalmers offered a substitute that put officers' pay (which was still on the table in the form of the other amendment by George) at the same rate as the Federal army and raised a private's pay to $16 a month. This passed. George's two issues were thus resolved to his liking. His bills had not been passed, but he had agitated sufficiently for similar action to be taken.[10]

After the grueling session in which Wright also reported the Ways and Means Committee's bill from committee, the members fortunately learned a bit of good news: the legislature had adjourned for good, and the convention could again utilize the House of Representatives hall. The larger impact of the legislature adjourning was not lost on the people of the state. The *Vicksburg Whig* noted, "the Convention will now take the entire charge of all changes in the Constitution, levy all taxes, &c."[11]

When the convention met at 3:30 that afternoon back at the statehouse, the members heard a note from the South Carolina governor urging Mississippi to send delegates to Montgomery. That was exactly the thought on everyone's minds, and Glenn thus brought up the Southern Confederacy ordinance again. He argued that the question was one of "power, principle and duty": that "if we were incompetent to ratify the action of the Montgomery convention, we were incapable of passing the Ordinance of Secession." Amendments once again came and went, with narrow votes illustrating the new changes to the political thinking. Edward Jones again brought up his ideas on electing delegates by congressional districts and also allowing members of the convention to be delegates. Glenn simply responded that those issues had been decided by "two distinct votes on previous occasions." Jones kept insisting until another vote was taken on eliminating the district limitations, and it passed by a forty-three to thirty-six vote.[12]

Given the testy debate of the previous week, the main arguments not surprisingly came over ratification amendments by Francis Rogers, Alexander Clayton, and Charles Fontaine. Much of the debate centered around the convention's ability to ratify a permanent or provisional Confederate government. Rogers argued that the provisional Confederate constitution should be referred to the people of the state in another convention. Clayton offered a substitute for Roger's amendment, which stated that a convention of all Confederate states should ratify the constitution. Clayton lost his argument, and, after another break in the evening after which the members gathered again at 7:00 P.M., Fontaine offered another substitute that stated that the people of Mississippi would ratify the constitution in a convention called by the Montgomery delegates or the governor, but not the legislature. Rogers withdrew his motion, and the convention passed Fontaine's instead. Yet when the official vote on it was taken, Fontaine's amendment was defeated in a forty-three to forty-nine vote. No doubt the delegates were tiring. W. B. Smart asked permission to change his vote on Fontaine's amendment because with so many amendments, he "found it difficult to understand them properly."[13]

Then the argument returned to whether the constitution should be voted on by the people of the state. Lamar, relatively quiet after his work on secession, now argued in support of Glenn that the people were fully speaking through their delegates and that they had expected "when dissolved from one confederacy to be transported to another." Francis Rogers then changed his target from Glenn to Lamar and took issue with him, citing confusion in the ordinance and advocating a popular referendum: "He [Lamar] says they might reject. Then, sir, I do not want a government that the Southern people would reject." Smart likewise stated, at the acknowledged risk of being unpopular, that he could not "bind a free people to any form of government without their acquiescence or consent." Others took issue with the delegates in Montgomery forming a permanent instead of a provisional government. Walker Brooke said he did not care whether a provisional government constitution was referred to the people, but the people should be consulted about the formation of a permanent government. He explained that it took years for a permanent government to be created after the revolution, and argued that Mississippi was "in a state of revolution—the flames [are] burning around us, and the smoke [is] upon our garments." He opted for a provisional government to "last us through the war," and then he would support a more permanent regime. Brooke went so far as to offer an amendment that removed an entire section of the ordinance dealing with a permanent government, but it failed. James Nelson of Pike County also spoke up in support of a provisional government, arguing that creating a permanent one so quickly "savored of monarchial tendencies." Gholson agreed, but President Barry disagreed, arguing against the people having a say in a referendum and stating the convention could adjourn temporarily and gather again after the Montgomery convention. Basically, he advised against "too many elections." He also broached a new subject, that of who would appoint or elect Mississippi's representatives to a new Confederate congress. Chalmers also added that he did not wish to limit the delegates in what they could do: "If the delegates from Mississippi were not clothed with the same power as the delegates from the other states, they could have little or no influence."[14]

Vote after vote took place before Glenn finally put the entire ordinance to a vote. It passed, the *Vicksburg Whig* noted, surprisingly "by a large majority." It contained most of what Glenn had wanted, including ratification by this convention, and he felt no small joy in what he described as his "complete triumph over their combined forces." Glenn was still bitter years later when he wrote how "throughout the contest Clayton of Marshall Clayton of Lowndes Brooke . . . Clapp were either actively or privately against me." But he had prevailed: "I carried my whole programme at last tho often defeated." With the process now set up, Glenn recommended that the delegates start voting for members of the delegation to Montgomery the next day at 11:00 A.M.[15]

The ordinance itself stated that Mississippi would send seven delegates to Montgomery, that being the number of senators and representatives it had in the U.S. Congress. The task of this convention was to organize a provisional national government. It stipulated, moreover, that a permanent government would need to be ratified by the convention then seated or by the people themselves if the convention had adjourned. There was some admittedly blurry reasoning in the ordinance, perhaps purposefully, but the clear work before the convention was to elect the Montgomery delegates.[16]

The Mississippi convention turned to that task quickly after assembling on Wednesday and disposing of a few minor issues, including the appointment of committees to prepare a flag and coat of arms as well as a committee to prepare an address to the state's planters. Not surprisingly, Barry appointed the huge planters of the convention on the latter committee, including Henry Vaughan, Miles McGehee, and Walter Kiern, along with lawyer George Clayton and physician Willis Lea, both smaller slave owners. Another motion granted seats to the current Mississippi congressional delegation. Glenn offered a resolution instructing his committee to investigate and return an ordinance for electing or appointing members of a new congress, the exact issue Barry had broached the night before. Alexander Clayton then offered an ordinance stating that any part of the state's constitution at odds with what the convention did would be "abrogated and annulled to the extent of such conflict but no further." This divisive bill was sent to the State Constitution Committee for work.[17]

As decided the night before, the convention then moved to the election of delegates promptly at 11:00 A.M., although a few other preliminary actions took place before the actual voting began. The most notable resolution passed was offered by Elijah Sanders, which required the convention to adjourn by Saturday at 2:00 P.M.; the delegates were now officially under the gun. Getting back to the voting, Barry appointed Chalmers (he was the one who wanted secret ballots), Gholson, and Arthur Reynolds to act as tellers. The convention also decided the rules: no nominations would be made, and a winning delegate would have to have a majority of those voting.[18]

On the big issues of the vote, Edward Jones's persistence had partially paid off. Still, members from the various congressional districts had already met and nominated candidates from their areas. James L. Alcorn had been nominated in his district, telling his wife, "I think the convention looks to me with great confidence—my speeches are listened to with great respect. I have been offered a seat in the Southern Congress to assemble in Montgomery, Alabama." Ultimately, however, all the work done in the district caucus was for naught, as the convention opted to take all seven delegates from across the state with no reference to districts. But Jones was only partially successful; the convention still allowed its own members to be elected, and that issue was obviously on many minds. Immediately prior to the voting, two members removed names from contention. Henry Ellett notified the convention that David Glenn would not be a candidate, obviously because it was his committee overseeing the vote. Similarly, *Jackson Mississippian* editor Ethelbert Barksdale had asked James Dyer to notify the convention that he would not be a delegate, prompting even the rival *Vicksburg Whig* to "regret" the decision, noting the "presence of editors is particularly needed." Barksdale asked that his name should be "*unconditionally* withdrawn," and Glenn asserted through Ellett that "it was impossible . . . to accept the position, if conferred on him."[19]

With the preliminaries out of the way, the convention turned to the vote. Sixty-five men received at least one vote, but only one name was listed by a majority of delegates on this initial ballot: Wiley P. Harris. His election was not surprising, he being the calm but steady hand in the convention. He received a total of fifty votes out of ninety-two cast. The closest candidates to him were Walker Brooke with thirty-eight, Alexander Clayton with thirty-five, nonmember William S. Wilson with thirty-four, and President Barry with thirty-one. The others received votes anywhere from in the twenties down to many who garnered only one. Not surprisingly, Glenn and Ethelbert Barksdale received twenty-six and twenty-four, respectively. The sentiment for Barksdale was especially vocal, with young William R. Barksdale writing, "I think him the soul of patriotism and bravery."[20]

With Harris elected, the members turned to a second ballot. But first several other members came forward and removed their names. Lamar, who had received twenty-two votes, stated publicly that he had privately repeated to his friends that he would not serve and wished to remove his name for reasons "purely private and personal, but such as would be satisfactory to the Convention if he felt at liberty to state them." Francis Aldridge, who received nine votes, withdrew his name in favor of older men who "from their age and experience, were more competent to represent the State." In like manner, Ellett, Jacob Yerger, and Alcorn also removed their names, Ellett doing so "gracefully, but positively." Alcorn wrote his wife that he "told my friends that I had rather be placed in the army, to the battle field my dear wife I must go." James Dyer once again rose and repeated editor Barksdale's "unconditional" wish not to be included.[21]

The second ballot saw fifty-six men receive votes, including thirty-four for men who had removed their names from contention. On the ninety-one ballots, however, only two received a majority, Brooke with fifty-nine and Wilson with forty-nine. A third vote of ninety-two members saw only Alexander Clayton win with fifty-three votes, although Barry and Jeremiah Clapp were close with votes in the high thirties. A fourth vote saw no one receive a majority, with the highest being Barry, Francis Rogers, and J. A. P. Campbell. After this vote, Clapp likewise removed his name from candidacy "in a few choice words that did his modesty and his manhood great credit," delegate Thomas Woods remembered.[22]

With the voting at a standstill, the convention recessed, the delegates due back at 3:30 that afternoon. Presumably backroom deals would be reached in the interim, and the voting would go more quickly when the delegates returned. Unfortunately, when the convention reassembled, a fifth vote resulted in no one pulling ahead. Barry, Rogers, and Campbell remained in the lead, with James T. Harrison pulling up to them and Hugh Miller making some progress. The sixth ballot, however, decided the state's representation when Barry, Campbell, and Harrison received forty-seven votes each, one more than needed, out of a pool of twenty-one who received votes. With the voting done, Glenn quickly offered one more resolution providing for the appointment of two senators by the governor and the special election of representatives to the new congress about to be established.[23]

The seven delegates prepared to head to Montgomery as soon as the state convention adjourned. Obviously Harris and Brooke were known commodities who were highly respected. The *Vicksburg Whig* applauded their selection, stating that they were "among the ablest lawyers and best citizens of this section of the State." Their selection also illustrated the breakdown of old secession lines within the convention, with Harris and Brooke being polar opposites when it came to that issue. Clayton and Barry, both members of the convention, were also widely known if not quite as respected as Harris and Brooke. Clayton had served on the state's highest court and as U.S. consul to Havana, and Barry was president of the convention and a former Speaker of the Mississippi house. Although not a member of the convention, being defeated in the canvass, J. A. P. Campbell of Attala County was also well known; he was the current Speaker of the house. William S. Wilson of Claiborne County was not as well known, being a younger man, but he was in the state legislature. The *Vicksburg Whig* described him as "a young man of rare powers and of conservative but firm views." Of all seven, lawyer James T. Harrison of Lowndes County was the least known, the *Whig* nevertheless reporting that he was "said to be fully up to the requirements of the station which he has been selected to fill."[24]

With Glenn's time-conscious work now done, Chalmers stepped forward and brought the military bill to the floor, hopefully for passage and then a continuation of the voting for members of the military board. The ordinance's history had included work by the convention committee as well as the sitting militia board. The militia board was not totally supportive, and in fact a recommendation to the convention's Military and Naval Affairs Committee to proceed to a vote succeeded only by a "bare majority." The opposition was so great that a minority report to the convention accompanied the proposed ordinance, and many hoped the minority report would produce a substitute ordinance. Yet with so much debate the day before, most members were satisfied with the ordinance as it stood and realized they had to move on. The convention thus voted for it by a large majority.[25]

This fifth official ordinance set up the "Military System" of the state. It called for the raising of eight regiments of volunteer infantry, to be completely separate from the militia, with additional cavalry and artillery as well. Each regiment was assigned counties within districts covered by that particular regiment. The regiments would be formed into two-regiment brigades, which would make up a four-brigade division. Four brigadier generals were to command the brigades, with one major general to command the division. Together, the brigadier generals, the major general, and the governor made up a "Military Board," which would "make all needful rules and regulations not contrary to law" and have "entire control over all the arms and military property of the State." The troops were organized into companies and regiments, but would "be considered as on furlough, subject however to be drilled at such times and places within their respective counties as their company officers may order, until called out for drill or actual service by their Major General." The ordinance also dealt with pay, rank, exemptions, and disabilities.[26]

With the ordinance passed, the convention turned to electing the Military Board. This time, nominations would be permitted, and Gholson, Anderson, and Russell Beene acted as tellers. Not surprisingly, only one vote was required for the major general position, with Jefferson Davis receiving eighty-eight votes and Reuben Davis and Earl Van Dorn receiving one each. It was no question that Davis wanted this position, although talk had already begun that he might be pushed for president of the entire Confederacy at the Montgomery convention. The *Vicksburg Whig* went so far as to report his election was "in accordance with the expectation and desire of the people," and remarked that he had no "superior" in military prowess. Nominations were then taken for the brigadier general positions, with various members nominating such men as Van Dorn, Charles Clark, W. C. Faulkner, Richard Griffith, W. C. Falconer, J. L. McManus, C. H. Albert, J. C. Russell, C. H. Shot, Thomas W. Harris, C. W. Mott, H. H. Miller, Joseph R. Davis, W. F. Gaines, John H. Miller, Daniel R. Russell, and convention delegate James L. Alcorn. No one won on the first ballot, although Van Dorn, Clark, and Alcorn led. A second vote likewise decided nothing, with the same three still ahead. A third ballot saw Van Dorn win with sixty-one votes. A fourth ballot elected no one, and the convention adjourned until an evening session at 7:30. That night a fifth ballot elected Clark to the second position, and Alcorn won on the sixth ballot. A seventh was not decisive, but after numerous members spoke in support of their candidates, Mott won on the eighth after Glenn pushed his candidacy "in eulogizing terms again." The grueling work of voting was now complete, and as late as it was when the delegates finished voting at 9:00 P.M., the convention adjourned to meet the next day.[27]

Major General Jefferson Davis was obviously a well-known military man in Mississippi. He had won fame in Mexico as colonel of the famous "Mississippi Rifles," being wounded at Buena Vista. Since then, he had served as secretary of war under Franklin Pierce and as a U.S. senator. There was probably no man in Mississippi, or even perhaps the South, more familiar with the military than Davis. There was less enthusiasm for the brigadiers, the *Vicksburg Whig* reporting only that the lower generals were "generally well known." But they were a capable bunch. Clark had been colonel of the Second Mississippi Infantry in Mexico, was a huge planter in the Delta, and was in the state legislature. Van Dorn was a recently resigned major in the U.S. Army, a West Point graduate, and a veteran of the Indian wars out west. Mott was the youngest, but was a Mexican War veteran, a lawyer, and commander of his local militia company. The *Whig* labeled Alcorn "eminently a civilian," but promised that he "will make an excellent soldier."[28]

This military board began meeting even during the sitting of the convention, overseeing the growing body of troops within the state. New companies were being raised in all corners, with other local organizations emerging as well. The main backbone of the defense of the state was thus the new volunteer division as well as the old militia; newspapers such as the *Vicksburg Whig* were quick to point out that the new military board "*does not* repeal the militia system." Indeed, the state already had troops aiding Florida at Fort Pickens; one newspaper bragged that "we can take Fort Pickens at any time, but a political question behind this at present delays the assault." And more and more troops were emerging. The *Vicksburg Whig* reported that so many Mississippians were leaving Bethel College in McLemoresville, Tennessee, that it had "seriously affected" the instruction.[29]

The marathon day on Wednesday took a lot out of the delegates with all the voting, behind-the-scenes politicking, and the give and take of compromise. Yet the members could see progress emerging out of the long days spent in the statehouse. They had passed several ordinances, including arguably the two most important ones. But there was still a need for haste in terms of sending the newly elected delegates off, hopefully with the convention itself adjourned. Failure to do so would cause problems, particularly with the president himself slated to go to Montgomery. If the convention tarried long, Barry would either have to hand over power to a replacement or perhaps miss some important business in Montgomery. The best remedy all the way around was to adjourn so that Barry could fulfill his duties at both places. Of course the same was true for the others such as Harris and Brooke, although their leadership roles were not as important as Barry's. The other major ordinance was the military affairs bill, and now that it was passed and a board elected, the board, too, could begin work building up the state's defense. Thus even as the days ran long, tempers flared, and emotions ran even higher, progress was being made, and the delegates, by midweek of this third week in session, were beginning to see positive results.

- 9 -

ADJOURNMENT

January 24–26, 1861

JUST BECAUSE THE DELEGATES HAD MADE MAJOR PROGRESS DURING the first days of the third week of the convention, this did not mean that their work was anywhere nearing completion. Although they had passed five ordinances, including arguably the most important ones, there were many more still in committee and awaiting action on the floor. These would prove to be divisive as well, ensuring long and vociferous debate. And the members were digging themselves into a hole by continually delaying action on so many of the ordinances, and they would continue to do so for the next several days. Thus, by the end of the week, they would be faced with either taking the needed time to thoroughly debate and pass all the awaiting ordinances or simply opt for speed and pass all of them with little more thought.

Meanwhile, the weather turned clear but cold, perhaps a fitting rendition of the mood in the house chamber itself. The members were obviously beginning to tire of the process. One observer noted a typical day at the convention: "Some [members] are sitting with their chairs tilted against the wall, some upon stools, and two are slowly vibrating to and fro in pre-Raphaelite rocking-chairs." He noted that it looked "quite the appearance of an interior Kentucky bar-room on a Winter evening." He continued on, describing "two or three of the members are eating apples, three or four smoking cigars, and a dozen in their seats with their feet resting upon the desk before them." Unless one of the extraordinary members was speaking or a particularly volatile subject was before them, many delegates seemed to ignore the proceedings. "Fifteen or twenty of the members are reading this morning's *Mississippian* or the *N.O. Picayune* or *Delta*, and the rest are listening to the one who is on his feet," he noted.[1]

After the long twelve-hour sessions of the past two days, the delegates abbreviated their work on Thursday. They had obviously passed the most critical legislation that was time conscious—the Montgomery delegate and military bills. Now those elected under that legislation could begin their work while the convention continued with its business. Yet there was still a lot of work to be done, and the most important piece still remaining was the Ways and Means Committee's bill raising revenue to support the military in the field. Thus, when the delegates reassembled on Thursday, that debate took up most of the day, the *Natchez Courier* calling it "the most unpleasant debate that has occurred since the assembling of the Convention."[2]

The members met at 10:00 A.M. and covered several items quickly: dealing with communications from the governor and former federal officials inquiring about how to proceed in their work. In more important actions, Jeremiah Clapp offered an additional postal ordinance from that committee, and Jehu Orr offered a resolution that would delay legal and economic action for twelve months. Glenn brought up newly pending resolutions from his Southern Confederacy Committee, but Ellett offered a substitute, and the two discussed their different stances before the convention decided to send the resolutions back to the committee and set the debate for the next day. There was even time for a short secret session, but the members discussed the need not to "go late." They thus turned to the major effort of this day, the revenue bill.[3]

The convention went into the committee of the whole, with Jehu Orr presiding and debate occurring between Ellett, Chalmers, Joel Berry, and Harvey Walter. No changes in the ordinance resulted. Then the convention dealt with the ordinance by section. The major debate occurred when James Z. George again offered an amendment to tax slaves separately from other property, at $1.25 per slave. George, noting himself a slave owner, addressed the convention, arguing that "this question of slavery was the cause, to a great extent, of the present troubles, and if there was any species of property that should pay its due, it should be the slaves." He calculated that the money the original ordinance would raise would be a "pitiful sum" that would make the new Confederacy, if that was Mississippi's part, "a splendid pauperism." Berry once again supported George's effort, it being basically the same thing he had recommended unsuccessfully the week before. Berry assured the convention that he was not antislavery or pushing "class legislation," but was in fact following John C. Calhoun's logic of slavery being "a blessing to both the white and black races." But he reminded his hearers that his constituents were primarily nonslaveholders, and he thought the burden should be carried "in proportion to what he is worth." Yet he flatly stated that his constituents would be "found in the front rank and in the thickest of the fight" if war over slavery came. Still, several members balked at the amendment. Both Alcorn and Harris went on record against George's idea, and Chalmers countered with an amendment putting restrictions on George's proposal. He lowered the rate on slaves to the rate on land, and Daniel Wright then moved that both proposals be tabled, much like George's amendments in days past. Chalmers's amendment was tabled, but the convention refused to do so with George's. After a break until 3:00 P.M., the convention returned to the Ways and Means Committee's ordinance and dealt with several small issues, such as John Herring of Pontotoc changing his vote and amendments from William Eckford and Harvey Walter about inmates at the state penitentiary producing goods for the war effort. There was as usual a substitute amendment offered to one of these, and both were referred to the Military and Naval Affairs Committee before the convention again took up the pending question of George's slave tax amendment. Henry Ellett and James Chalmers next offered amendments to George's amendment that literally took the wind out of George's taxation purpose, making the tax not per head as George wanted, but setting a rate at twenty cents per $100 of value in slaves.[4]

The convention then enthusiastically debated George's amendment. Gholson and James B. Ramsey spoke in favor of the amendment, and Aldridge and Marshall spoke against it, with Clapp calling George's and Ellett's amendments "equally monstrous" and arguing that this issue was "peculiarly within the province of the Legislature." Aldridge said that no average value could be put on a slave as "their value is constantly in fluctuation," but countered that the delegates should not "be trammeled by any precedents. . . . We act for ourselves, and not for the Legislature." He went on to describe their actions as "class legislation." When Chalmers moved to vote, however, the absence of a quorum was noted, and the roll call showed fifteen members missing from the convention. Some time was taken to bring a number of them back, and the votes were then taken. Ellett's amendment passed by a narrow forty-five to forty-three vote, but George's amended amendment then failed by a large majority, George himself voting against his now changed amendment. And he was not the only one. David Glenn thought it necessary to explain to the committee why he had voted not to table George's amendment and then voted against it.[5]

Despite his focus on the Southern Confederacy ordinance, David Glenn had become heavily involved in the debate. He was not a supporter of George's amendment, calling it "low and dangerous demagoguery," but he was concerned about a larger issue involving the legislature. He admitted that he was "not familiar with the principles or details of measures of revenue," but what he had learned from the committee and the debate on the floor left him "not greatly enlightened." In fact, he related that the opposing side "have been as sparing of facts, figures and argument for their cause as those who maintain it. Thus members are left to be guided by their own reflections." At issue for Glenn was the surprising news to him that slaves in Mississippi were taxed at a far lower rate than other property. If slaves were taxed on an average at the same rate as land, each would have a tax of $1.25, which is where George and the others came up with their figure. At present, Glenn was surprised to learn that slaves were only being taxed at seventy-five cents per slave. He was outraged at this "gross inequality" and wondered why the legislature had for so many years been able to keep it a secret to him and presumably to others. "Why has it not been pointed out and corrected before?" he asked. Glenn argued that the legislature's action "raises a powerful presumption against it," but then again, perhaps this was a legislative issue, and certainly not one to be contended with at a convention during a time of potential war. Glenn seemed unsure what to do. If such a stalwart as Glenn was indecisive, what were the rest of the members thinking?[6]

Several members then discussed an amendment taxing money loaned out of state. Benjamin King offered an amendment with a blank at the percentage amount, and Alcorn filled it at thirty cents on every $100. King pronounced it "not high enough." He remarked that he himself was "disposed to bleed freely" and wished it to be higher. Henry Ellett chimed in that he was against taxing out-of-state money altogether, saying that "legislation upon money had already forced the money of citizens from the State" and that to add more tax would be suicidal. James Dyer added that taxing money in other states could be "a two edged sword"; other states could do it back to Mississippi. Realizing this was opening another huge debate, the delegates obviously felt frustrated with so many votes that literally changed nothing, and they adjourned for the day.[7]

A cold and cloudy Friday dawned the next day, and there was little progress, except in pushing the various ordinances forward toward a final vote. When the delegates met at 9:00 A.M., the wear on everyone was obvious. In fact, not enough members appeared on Friday morning to make a quorum, and Barry had to send Ivy Westbrook, the sergeant at arms, to "bring in the absentees." A quorum soon materialized, and the convention proceeded, amazingly handling an unusually large amount of minor business. One motion called for the appointment of a committee to go over the records of the convention for publication. Another, from Alfred Holt, asked the governor to send northwestern governors copies of the secession ordinance with the promise of "our determination not to obstruct in any manner the peaceable navigation of the Mississippi River within our limits." Walker Brooke offered a resolution that the legislature could pass no laws involving debts, mortgages, deeds, or other such items except by a three-fourths vote of each house. That motion was referred to the State Constitution Committee, as was an offering from William Bolling that dealt with amending the constitution to allow the legislature to make certain economic laws. There was also a naval ordinance considered, but debate on it was "indefinitely postponed."[8]

By this time the delegates could see that the last major item remaining before the convention was economic in nature. The delegates had passed the secession ordinance and then set up the mechanism to join the Confederacy and to defend itself. Smaller issues such as postal affairs were also handled. The big item left was to raise money for the state's defense, as many of the delegates openly assumed war was coming. Jacob Yerger argued that "so much depend[s] upon the accumulation of revenue sufficient to arm and equip an efficient body of citizen soldiers." James Dyer echoed his sentiments, stating, "a hostile collision with the North must be reasonably expected." Consequently the convention turned again to the Ways and Means Committee's ordinance, and as had been the practice throughout the convention, members began to amend it in various ways. A determined James Z. George once again offered an amendment that taxed slaves directly, this time at $1.20; his amendment actually passed this time by a narrow margin, as did another amendment of his dealing with local sheriffs' duties in the taxation process. Benjamin King, President Barry, and James L. Alcorn also offered successful amendments, King's resolution to tax out-of-state money causing additional debate but also vocal support from Brooke, Yerger, Alcorn, and Walter. Walter stated that he was "in favor of taxing all money loaned in Wall Street as heavily as if loaned at home." Yerger even went so far as to argue that "if any exemption is to be made, it should be in favor of the citizen who loans his money within the State, thus adding to its capital and means of development." The tax was finally set at 0.3 percent. Conversely, Alexander Clayton failed in his attempt to alter the payment of interest on treasury notes, and Edward Jones failed in his effort to allow tax deductions for out-of-state money.[9]

Realizing other business was backing up, the convention made further financial debate the special order for the next day. It then moved to consider other items on the agenda, such as a supplemental ordinance from Harris's Federal Jurisdiction and Property Committee. The convention made this another special order for the next day. After an afternoon break and returning at 3:00 P.M., it did the same with a "military fund" bill. The members were clearly putting off controversial issues until Saturday, the day of their scheduled adjournment.[10]

Upon returning from the break, the big issue was Glenn's new Southern Confederacy ordinance concerning representatives and senators for the new Confederate congress. The convention had earlier made it clear that it did not want its initial delegates to support turning themselves into a congress at Montgomery. Henry Ellett and Glenn had sparred the day before over how to elect those representatives, with each offering competing plans. Ellett won out, offering a successful amendment that allowed the current set of senators and representatives to remain in office until a new election could be held. The convention delayed further work, however, and then turned to assuring resigned U.S. officers the same pay in the state service as they had earned in the federal army. It also heard an additional postal ordinance from Clapp's committee, which was returned to the committee with two other resolutions, and it approved the formation of a "Governor's Council" to advise Governor Pettus after the convention adjourned. There was also a "test vote" on excluding nonslaveholding states from the future Confederacy, which failed by a large margin. The members also provided themselves "the same compensation and mileage" as the state legislators received.[11]

The delegates had functioned in a structured and organized manner after that first week's chaos. With the deadline for ending the convention looming on Saturday afternoon, however, that chaos was beginning to reappear. Members began once again offering their own resolutions outside the committee structure, and worse, they kept delaying their final votes on several important ordinances until Saturday. Whether that was a tactical calculation or just procrastination is not known, but it set up a hectic day for Saturday. Perhaps a major change in the weather also excited the delegates as snow began to blanket the area late in the day on Friday. Whatever the reality, the convention would hopefully be over the next day, and the members could return to their homes or, as some were already doing, would be going off to war.[12]

The big day arrived, a cold and white Saturday, January 26, and the members assembled at 9:00 A.M. The snow the previous evening had blanketed the entire area, and the temperature remained below freezing well into the morning despite a bright sunshine that made the snow glimmer. Intent on adjourning that day, however, the delegates had a pile of work to plow through. They had, for better or for worse, postponed final action until this day. Now little time was left for debate. It was time to act.[13]

The delegates wasted little time. After offering more leaves of absence for members who were leaving, the dwindling convention moved to Brooke's Citizenship Committee's ordinance. The bill stated that all U.S. citizens domiciled in Mississippi on January 9 would be citizens of the state and laid out the process of naturalization. The old laws would hold except that the oath would be taken to Mississippi instead of the United States. This ordinance also allowed Confederate naturalization laws to take precedent once they had been enacted. Brooke succeeded in getting this ordinance passed easily, and the convention moved on.[14]

The next issue, dealing with the African slave trade, was handled in a short secret session. Alfred Holt made a motion that declared the convention's intent that the state not reopen the slave trade. Hugh Miller moved to table the resolution, which failed, and then the original resolution passed by a large majority. There was a small cadre of opponents to the resolution, led by James Z. George, who felt so strongly that they asked to include a protest that stated the international slave trade issue was out of the convention's authority and it was thus usurping power from the legislature. In fact, the legislature had already acted. George and eleven others signed the protest, among them Hugh Miller, William Brantley, and Oliver Dease.[15]

The members then tackled the process of reassembling to vote on joining the Confederacy. Fearing some type of negative parliamentary maneuver that would prohibit the convention from reassembling and thus causing the state's population to ratify the Confederate constitution, Glenn made a motion that the convention could be recalled under action of President Barry or a committee to act in his stead if he was incapacitated. This could be done prior to June 1, 1861, at which time the convention would be adjourned sine die. One amendment from Jacob Yerger failed to stipulate a permanent adjournment, while another succeeded in changing the date to October 1. With Orlando Davis and Gholson vocally supporting it, the amendment and ordinance passed, Glenn taking pride in defeating one last attempt to put the constitution to a vote of the people: "I checkmated them and carried a resolution to adjourn subject to call from our President," he crowed. The motion also called for a committee to act in case of the death or resignation of the president, and Barry appointed Philip Catching, A. P. Hill, and Warren Anderson as the committee. Thereafter other issues were dealt with, such as the idea of not including free states in the confederation to be established, which was tabled, and passage of a fortifications and military sites ordinance that dealt with surveying and erecting fortifications to defend the state.[16]

By this time the 2:00 P.M. deadline for adjournment had come, but the members "rescinded" the motion and continued on. The delegates then amended and passed the supplemental ordinance from the Federal Jurisdiction and Property Committee that dealt with "waste and unappropriated lands," which was the issue brought up when land agents in Columbus asked how to carry on their duty. Basically, the ordinance continued the same work in the state's name rather than the United States.[17]

Finally, the convention confronted the biggest issue of all, the Ways and Means Committee's bill to raise revenue for the defense of the state. This time the ordinance passed easily, with only one more amendment. It put in place the direct taxes as well as the ad valorem tax on property and slaves. The money as well as $1 million in treasury notes to be issued were to go into a "military fund." Building on the momentum, the delegates then passed a supplemental postal ordinance that set up the office of the postmaster general and defined his duties, and they also passed the State Constitution Committee's ordinance that removed the term "United States" in the document, but also included a statement that anything in the constitution that was different from the ordinances of the convention would be annulled. The delegates also passed an ordinance to select representatives to congress, and that ordinance allowed the sitting senators and congressmen to take their seats in the new Confederate government.[18]

Other smaller items passed, such as printing copies of the ordinance of secession for the various county sheriffs to use; publication of the convention's journal; aiding the city hospital in Vicksburg in preparation for war; thanking the Mobile and Ohio Railroad for offering its services to the state during war; establishing a flag and coat of arms for the state; allowing the governor to borrow money to keep the troops in the field equipped; establishing an executive council of Warren P. Anderson, Madison McAfee, and T. C. Tupper to advise the governor; paying the expenses of the convention; and having auditors to audit the books. In fear of letting something fall through the cracks, the members even discussed a special committee "to ascertain if anything had been neglected that should be attended to before adjournment." Walker Brooke countered that there may need to be one to "also inquire whether anything had been done which ought not to have been done." Cyrus Baldwin, who made the original motion, decided that the idea would "impose too much labor" and withdrew the resolution.[19]

The most momentous action that day, however, was passage of a motion by Warren Anderson that a committee of five produce a document setting forth the reasons for Mississippi's secession. Barry appointed a group of convention leaders to the committee, including Alcorn, Lamar, Alexander Clayton, Anderson, and Glenn. After an hour break, the committee returned with "A Declaration of the Immediate Causes Which Induce and Justify the Secession of the State of Mississippi from the Federal Union." The document, apparently written by Clayton, "declare[d] the prominent reasons which have induced our course," and was centered firmly on slavery. "Our position is thoroughly identified with the institution of slavery," the document read, "the greatest material interest in the world. . . . [A] blow has long been aimed at the institution, and was at the point of reaching its consummation. There was no choice left us but submission to the mandates of abolition, or a dissolution of the Union, whose principles had been subverted to work out our ruin." This committee continued: "We must either submit to degradation, and to the loss of property worth four billions of money, or we must secede from the Union framed by our fathers, to secure this as well as every other species of property. For far less cause than this, our fathers separated from the Crown of England." This statement leaves no doubt that Mississippi seceded and went to war to protect slavery.[20]

With its work completed, the convention tendered its thanks to Barry for his "dignified and impartial manner in which he has discharged the duties of President." Gholson moved that the convention adjourn, but Barry first took the liberty to address the delegates. Set to travel to Montgomery with Harris and the others, he gave a brief closing address. After reminding his hearers that more work would come for the convention, namely the ratification of a future Confederate constitution, Barry congratulated the delegates on "the work of destruction." He then called them to greater efforts. "More is required of the future than has been in the past. . . . What lies before us will test the heroism, the higher, the nobler qualities of our race, inherited from revolutionary sires." He probably had no idea how right he was.[21]

The convention thus adjourned that afternoon at 5:30, having completed its work of setting Mississippi on the path toward independence and war. The delegates were now free to return to their homes, pick up their lives once again, and prepare for the future. Obviously the delegates would meet again at some point to ratify the Confederate constitution, but for now most went back to their lives. Some began to raise military units. Some prepared their own finances and homes for war, and five of them prepared to travel to Montgomery for the all-important convention that they hoped would create a nation.[22]

The delegates thus leaving Jackson for Montgomery, their homes, the army, or any other duties and concerns had nevertheless left a major impression on the history of Mississippi. A state for some forty-four years, Mississippi had taken the momentous step of revoking statehood and casting out on its own, theoretically, at least, until it joined other like-minded slave states in a national government to be formed shortly. And it was no small feat. Talked about, hinted at, and dreamed of in some cases since the formation of the nation back in 1787, the split was now reality, and Mississippi had played a key role in the process. While other states were preparing to do so, and would do so shortly, Mississippi was the second state to leave the Union. South Carolina, after all, had tried to confront the federal government before, but it backed down when no other states came to its side. Now Mississippi at least had joined the South Carolinians, and the act symbolically opened the floodgates for even more states to follow, which they did.

And Mississippi had seemingly seceded without its first rank of leaders. While there were notables in the convention such as Harris, Alcorn, Lamar, and Brooke, the vast majority of the delegates were midlevel statesman, and not a few were lower-level county politicians at best. Nowhere in the halls of the convention were found the Davises, Thompsons, Browns, or Claibornes of Mississippi. Rather, the leaders of the movement, who were obviously the most vocal on either side of the issue, were men such as Alexander Clayton, David Glenn, Samuel Gholson, Samuel Benton, James Chalmers, and Henry Ellett, all of sufficient historical importance but not necessarily the cream of Mississippi society or statesmanship.

Despite the delegates being middle-of-the-road statesmen, a Northern reporter who saw incivility in everything from the statehouse to the members' dress complimented their speaking. It had been "generally good," he said, adding that the delegates spoke "fluently, and with grammatical correctness." He did note, however, that the delegates' "inability to articulate the letter r—his 'mo's,' and 'befo's,' and 'hea'a'—convey reminiscences of the negress who nursed him in infancy and the slaves with whom he played in childhood." In further describing the members' oratory, the reporter noticed that almost all delegates were respectful and that there was "little bandiage or satire, a good deal of directness and coming right to the point, qualified by the strong Southern tendency to 'pile up' the adjectives." He also noted that the delegates were "great mutual admirationists," adding that "every speaker has the most profound respect for the honest motives, the pure patriotism, and the transcendent abilities of the honorable gentleman upon the other side. He is free to say that it excites his regret and self-distrust to differ from such an array of learning and eloquence; and nothing could compel him to do so but a high sense of duty." A slightly less impartial observer, Alabama's commissioner to Mississippi, Edmund W. Pettus, wholeheartedly agreed, reporting to his governor that the convention's "deliberations were conducted with the order, dignity, and solemnity fitting the deliberations of a sovereign people changing their form of government."[23]

The decisions that these unsophisticated yet capable men made were collectively more important than the decision-makers' statuses indicate. In these men's hands were the issues of loyalty, independence, or treason, and it turned out that while they had their differences, the convention produced only one real Unionist, John W. Wood. Thus there seemed to be little real difference between the secessionists and cooperationists in terms of support for Mississippi itself, as almost all the cooperationists left their former ideals and morphed with the secessionists into a supporting role for Mississippi (and eventually, by extension, the Confederacy itself). Beyond that one issue of secession, however, the delegates also made numerous other decisions that would have an effect on literally every other Mississippian then living in the state, and in many cases on generations of Mississippians for decades thereafter. The decisions these men made in terms of government, the state's relationship to a central authority, and primarily the state's finances were extremely significant. In the social realm, their decisions would affect how Mississippians worked; how they related to foreigners, Northerners, and even immigrants; and most important, the relationship between the races.

It was perhaps in the racial realm that their decisions would have the most effect, because their convention would eventually lead to war and a complete turnover in the economic and social aspects of slavery, and would begin the long process of equalization of the races that is still going on today. A few realized as much, such as when the die-hard cooperationists argued that slavery would be better protected in the Union that little by little took some of that freedom rather than putting it up for a quick and painful death in a war. Still, despite some long-held and erroneous modern arguments about slavery's minuscule role in secession, the delegates obviously had slavery on their minds in almost every decision that they made, and it was on their tongues more than most Mississippians realize today.[24]

The major debates over slavery in the convention attest to its stature, from the argument over renewing the Atlantic slave trade and the attending protest inserted into the journal to the debates over taxation of slaves. Each attests to how central the institution was to what the delegates were doing and thinking. Alexander M. Clayton could not have put it more bluntly when he remarked, "We are in the midst of a great work. This movement was inaugurated to protect the institution of slavery, and to preserve it from destruction." And if that were not plain enough, the declaration of causes passed on the last day of the January session spelled out what the delegates thought was the main issue causing their action. Slavery was that main issue, causing the secession of Mississippi, the effort to build a nation, and eventually the war that secession sparked. Probably any delegate, were he asked during January 1861 why Mississippi was leaving the Union, would have answered simply slavery or white supremacy. While the economic and social theses of Christopher Olsen and William Barney make sense in retrospect, none of the delegates realized that their action was a masculine response budding from an antiparty political culture that emphasized community on the precinct and county level; they just knew slavery and white supremacy were threatened, and they had to respond.[25]

The causes of the war had many nuances other than slavery, of course, and was admittedly and initially over the Southern states' right to secede (which nevertheless was brought on by slavery). Initially, war was being waged by the North to preserve the Union and deny those states the right to secede. Quickly, however, the Federals realized that the Union could not be preserved unless slavery was destroyed. This debate literally altered the course of U.S. history, not to mention the history of Mississippi. The delegates leaving Jackson that January 1861 truly believed they had acted correctly, although no doubt some harbored strong reservations. But it was done, and all that was left was to play out the hand that they had dealt themselves.

Thus all realized that a new day was dawning in Mississippi. The state had declared its independence and was probably about to join the Confederacy. Most thought a war was imminent. The most perceptible observers, however, could also see a new dynamic in the state's politics, a change in the old secessionist/cooperationist lines that hearkened back to the old opposition between Whigs and Democrats. Big changes were taking place, and those who recognized them could only wonder where they would lead Mississippi.

INTERIM

February–March, 1861

WHEN THE DELEGATES LEFT JACKSON IN LATE JANUARY, THEIR WORK was not over. The members and the many other entities they set up in the January session of the convention remained hard at work on everything from the growing military activity to their own personal and public finances. All knew they would eventually be called back together in session at the statehouse. They also knew in a larger context that many of them would be involved in the war effort, which was already heating up. Perhaps some even thought of their possessions, slaves, and land and wondered what effect the seemingly irrepressible war would have on them.

The individual delegates returned to their homes and took care of business that had piled up while they had spent three weeks in Jackson. The lawyers returned to their cases, some of a high profile. James Chalmers wrote Governor Pettus during the interim asking for leniency for a criminal in Marshall County: "he has suffered enough for the offense." Similarly, John B. Fizer of Panola County wrote the governor asking for a pardon for a local man convicted of "assault and battery with intent to kill." Fizer reported that he was a friend of the man and that the entire population of Tallahatchie County would look on a pardon with great applause. Oliver C. Dease of Jasper County wrote the governor asking that a friend be appointed as a land agent since the regular officials had resigned, and "there are no persons authorized to take charge of the office." The delegates were clearly using their status and recent acquaintance with the governor and the state powers to their advantage.[1]

Others were involved in embryonic military activities. Charles D. Fontaine wrote Pettus in late February tendering the services of the "Pontotoc

Dragoons" to the Military Board, calling it "one of the very best drilled, and most efficient Militia Companies in the State." Hugh Miller similarly advised the governor that his militia company, the "Pontotoc Minute Men," were ready for service but needed arms: "we are without arms and very desirous to get them of a good quality." Miller stated that "if none better can be supplied we would be content, <u>for the present</u>, with the percussion musket," and asked Pettus to send them either to Oxford on the Mississippi Central Railroad or Tupelo on the Mobile and Ohio. For his part, Pettus corresponded with convention president William Barry in Montgomery on a number of issues that should probably come before the next meeting of the convention.[2]

The governor also had to deal with a growing number of memorials from Northern states reacting to Mississippi's secession. Several legislatures sent resolutions to Pettus and other governors confirming their loyalty to the Union and their willingness to fight to keep it together. Some states sent memorials agreeing to send delegates to compromise conventions, but most were of a confrontational manner, especially those from Wisconsin, Ohio, and Minnesota. Minnesota's "Joint Resolutions on the State of the Union," for example, declared that since several states were "at this time in open rebellion against the Government," it resolved that "the Government of the United States is supreme," that Minnesota "hereby pledges and tenders to the General Government all its military power and industrial resources," and that "concessions and compromise are not to be entertained or offered to traitors." Most of these resolutions were passed in the various legislatures even as the Mississippi delegates sat in convention in Jackson, but they probably did not arrive on the governor's desk until after the convention's adjournment. The attempt to cater to the northwestern states by assuring them free navigation of the Mississippi River was clearly not working.[3]

Pettus obviously cared less about the reaction of Northern governors than he did about those from the other Southern states, particularly the border states, which even then were teetering between secession or loyalty to the Union. Pettus and other governors had operatives in each of those areas working to sway them toward secession. These "commissioners," as they were called, were sent to urge secession and united action on the part of the slave states. According to historian William Barney, they also helped take some political heat off the secessionists from cooperationists who counseled waiting for unified action; indeed, Pettus actually appointed a few cooperationists among the commissioners. While unwilling to wait to secede, the fire-eaters could nevertheless point to the commissioners as an attempt at cooperation among the slave states. And there was a lot of thought put into the significant position of commissioner; when he could, Pettus appointed men who were native to the state to which they were sent. Thomas Wharton, for example, was sent to his native Tennessee, while Charles Hooker traveled to his native South Carolina and William L. Harris went to his native Georgia.[4]

The commissioners John J. Pettus appointed were a busy set before, during, and after the convention itself. In fact, some were still busy as late as mid-February, while the Confederate Montgomery convention was meeting and wooing border states to join the Confederacy. The commissioners to the Deep South states encountered few problems and were greeted and pampered by the respective states much as Edmund Pettus and Armistead Burt had been in Jackson. William L. Harris and Wirt Adams in Milledgeville, Georgia, and Baton Rouge, Louisiana, respectively, performed their work to willing audiences as early as December 1860, while former Mississippi governor Joseph W. Matthews and Charles Hooker addressed the Alabama and South Carolina conventions, respectively, in mid-January, even while their own state's convention was seated. There is no record of H. H. Miller or G. S. Gaines addressing the conventions in Texas and Florida.[5]

People in the Upper South states that seceded later in the spring and summer of 1861 were a different set of hearers. George Fall in Arkansas and Jacob Thompson in North Carolina delivered their messages in December, although never addressing the legislatures or any conventions. Thomas Wharton addressed the legislature in Tennessee during Mississippi's convention, and Fulton Anderson in Virginia, in February, was the last to act. Eventually, all those states joined the Confederacy, but only after the firing on Fort Sumter.[6]

The commissioners with the least amount of success were those sent to the most northern of the border states. Daniel Russell sent a promising telegram during the Mississippi convention, which was read before the delegates, that Missouri had passed a convention bill and surely would follow the rest of the South. Given the discord and even military actions in that state, that was not to be. Winfield Scott Featherston reported he delivered his message to Kentucky's officials in December, and they acted on it after he left, but not to the point of actually leaving the Union. Alexander H. Handy in Maryland called on the governor, but the chief executive refused to call the legislature to deal with the issue. Handy then delivered his address at multiple points in the state in "a lucid and elaborate manner," but it likewise failed to convince Marylanders to join the Confederacy. The most militant state against a Mississippi commissioner was Delaware, where Henry Dickinson addressed that legislature in early January, but it then voted its official "disapproval" of secession.[7]

Each commissioner obviously faced different circumstances and different reactions, with different results. The speeches they gave, however, were not necessarily different. For instance, each of the six extant speeches given by commissioners, as found in the appendix to the printed journal of the convention's proceedings, contain similar elements of the need for secession; the importance of states' rights; the North's offensive against the South's rights; statements of the original intent of the U.S. Constitution, which had been deformed by the North; and, as pointed out by Charles Dew, a firm commitment to the institution of slavery and a belief that slavery and racism were the driving forces behind the admonition of states' rights and secession. Many of the commissioners reflected on Lincoln's election and used the term "Black Republican" freely. Coupled with the major emphasis on slavery in the convention itself, especially the declaration of causes for secession, the commissioners' speeches leave no doubt that slavery was the key issue in the secession of Mississippi.[8]

But the central theme in each of the commissioners' addresses was not necessarily slavery, abolitionism, or even states' rights, although each of those was presented as reasons for Mississippi's actions. The key theme, indeed the reason each commissioner was sent to his respective state, was a call for cooperation between the Southern states. Each of the six speeches centered on this idea: "I come to commune with you in reference to the fearful political crisis which has befallen our common country, in the hope that the co-operation of Tennessee may be secured," Thomas Wharton declared in Nashville; Charles Hooker spoke of "soliciting their co-operation in the position which Mississippi has taken" in South Carolina; Wirt Adams declared he came to Baton Rouge "to express the earnest hope of Mississippi that Louisiana will co-operate with her in the adoption of efficient measures for their common defense and safety"; William L. Harris represented Mississippi in Milledgeville, Georgia, "to ask for her the sympathy and co-operation she seeks for the common good"; and Fulton Anderson in Richmond, Virginia, extended "to you the invitation of my State and people, to unite and co-operate with your Southern sisters who are already in the field, in defense of their rights."[9]

Yet even as the commissioners crisscrossed the South in their cooperationist effort, others were hard at work as well. Another group toiling almost endlessly during and after the convention adjourned was the military board established and elected on January 23. With Jefferson Davis as the major general and Van Dorn, Clark, Alcorn, and Mott commanding brigades, the board met with Pettus in late January, when Davis arrived from Washington, D.C. They began to appoint staff officers such as adjutant general Richard Griffith, chief of ordnance Samuel G. French, and the recently resigned congressman William Barksdale as quartermaster. They also hammered out a set of procedures, *Orders of the Military Board of the State of Mississippi*, going into great detail in the process.[10]

A massive turnover in the board's personnel soon began, however, severely preventing continuity and probably also effectiveness. The most notable resignation came in early February when Jefferson Davis left the board to become the provisional president of the Confederacy. Earl Van Dorn advanced to Davis's position, but he also soon left to become a Confederate general, as did Clark, who replaced Van Dorn. Mott also left to raise a regiment. With the convention adjourned, Pettus appointed new men to fill these positions, such as Richard Griffith, Absalom M. West, and William Barksdale. Griffith and Barksdale also left to raise regiments, however, and Pettus finally settled for John W. O'Ferrall and Charles G. Dahlgren as the new brigadiers. As major general, after some political bickering between Pettus and his cooperationist enemy Alcorn, who was next in line for the position, Pettus finally settled on former congressman Reuben Davis. This other Davis was certainly a better choice than the civilian Alcorn, having been colonel of the Second Mississippi Infantry during the Mexican War, but Alcorn was supposed to get the position by law. "For Alcorn Governor Pettus entertained bitter dislike," Davis remembered, but Davis made it plain that he could not take the position over Alcorn. "Governor Pettus promptly refused this, and insisted that I must take his first offer," Davis continued. "You may as well accept now, for I will never promote Alcorn," Pettus thundered. Alcorn eventually agreed to remain on the board and allow Davis the major generalship. By then, however, the board's usefulness was dwindling as more and more state units went into the Confederate army. In fact, meetings of the board became more and more infrequent later in 1861, and between the meetings Davis boasted, "my authority became absolute. The convention had made no provisions for controlling my action."[11]

By far, however, the group that had the most lasting impact on Mississippi and its citizens during this interim was the small delegation elected to represent the state in Montgomery. The four members of the convention barely finished their work in Jackson before leaving for the Alabama capital.

In fact, they had to take an extended route because of the bad weather's effect on transportation between Jackson and Montgomery. Because of this, the delegation traveled as small groups, with Harris, Brooke, and Wilson going 900 miles through Corinth, Chattanooga, and Atlanta before arriving in Montgomery from the east. It had taken much longer to get to Montgomery than it should have given the relative nearness of Jackson. Such a miserable development should have told these nation builders about the sad state of their transportation system, at the least. Still, when these men arrived in Atlanta, they rode the same train as some of the more famous delegates from the east, including Robert Barnwell Rhett of South Carolina.[12]

Others arrived as the days passed, and the convention came to order. Harrison, in fact, appeared immediately prior to the opening of the proceedings at noon on February 4, but Clayton and Campbell were still missing, and Campbell would not arrive during this opening session. Clayton would eventually appear, and when he did, he would bring major news with him that would affect the convention and the future of the Confederacy.[13]

The delegation that eventually assembled at Montgomery, with Campbell absent, was an interesting lot. There was even a family reunion of sorts, with Barry's father-in-law, Thomas Fearn, being a delegate from Alabama. There had been a conscious effort on the part of the convention to elect the best and brightest of Mississippi, with Edward Jones then remarking in his single-handed quest for justice, "Let us, then, unite in the selection of the best men. Let us choose them by moral and intellectual test alone. Let them be statesmen—firm of purpose, sagacious in council, brave in resolve, and invincible in fortitude." Statesman they may have been, but others looked on most of the Mississippians as second-rate. Although Harris routinely impressed all in the convention and the lone cooperationist Brooke did as well, despite suspicion about his commitment to the Confederacy, the rest were not roundly admired. One observer, in fact, wrote that the Mississippians were "the most braggartish" of all the delegations. Others routinely described the Mississippi delegates as wordy and not especially of statesmen material.[14]

Yet for several reasons, the Mississippi delegation was a force to be reckoned with. First of all, the delegation had not split like many of the other states' legations, most notably Georgia and South Carolina. Delegates of those two states particularly hated each other, having been old enemies before the Confederacy was even dreamed of, and they brought those animosities with them to Montgomery. At Montgomery, they saw the future of the Confederacy and the leadership that was needed through very different prisms, adding to the embedded angst. The animosity was so great that many votes among the state delegations (each state had one vote in the convention, based on how the majority of the state delegation voted) were split, causing their strong positions to be fatally weakened, especially in asserting Georgians and South Carolinians for leadership positions. Indeed, many of the delegates from both states wanted to be president, and they maneuvered behind the scenes, causing even more trouble. Conversely, the Mississippians were solid and steadfast on most issues, sticking together and forming a powerful bloc that had to be taken into consideration. The behind-the-scenes political maneuvering rarely involved them, most schemers realizing it would do no good to try.[15]

The main reason the Mississippians had a lot of clout in Montgomery, however, was that they had perhaps the major Southern leader backing them, Jefferson Davis. Almost everyone in the convention realized Davis's ability, statesmanship, and availability. Everyone knew Davis would be a factor in the new government, although where he would land was very much debated. Some thought of him as president, while others had hopes that he would become the South's commanding general. He was, after all, the South's most notable military hero from his days in the Mexican War. Although Davis's job was yet to be determined, it was a given that he would be a high-ranking official. Since the Confederacy needed Davis and he was from Mississippi, the convention realized the less than stellar Mississippi delegation had to be reconciled with.[16]

The Mississippi delegation mainly pushed several big issues. One was a demand from their state convention that the Montgomery delegates should only erect a future provisional government. The Mississippi convention simply did not conceive of their delegation turning into their state's congressional membership. The convention, in fact, had already selected their slate of congressmen and senators for the new government.[17]

The Mississippians thus pushed the idea of a provisional government founded entirely on the old U.S. Constitution, with only a few corrections to ensure that the South's rights would be protected. In doing so, Mississippians served notice that they viewed the Confederacy not as a new nation and the new constitution not as a revolutionary document, but that the members were participating in a conservative movement whose idea it was to retake control of the original Constitution and reform it into what it was originally intended to be. The North, the argument went, had defiled the document and changed it into something it was not, and the whole idea of this counterrevolution was to bring it back to its origins. James McPherson's thesis of a conservative counterrevolution in the face of the Northern industrial and abolitionist revolution is particularly adept at explaining the idea in vogue among the Mississippians at Montgomery.[18]

But the Mississippians faced brutal opposition every time they argued for the delayed government, as they often did. Beginning in hotel lobby conversations and continuing on the floor of the convention, the Mississippians repeatedly pushed this idea, as they were instructed to by their convention. Others argued that if the present convention was not to become the provisional congress, leaving the states to later send representatives and senators, this would constitute perhaps a fatal delay in setting up the government. Most all the other states' delegations were interested in speed of action and opted to make their convention a one-house provisional congress. Without much support, the Mississippi delegation finally yielded. So much for the Mississippi convention's elected senators and representatives.[19]

A committee formulated a provisional constitution, and Mississippi's representatives on that committee were Harris and Barry. As the members met on February 5 and the next morning and evening, they began to observe one another more closely, with one member stating that Harris rarely spoke, but when he did it was "a ball that seldom fails to have effect." Others thought Barry spoke too often and too long. As the committee of twelve members began to formulate their provisional constitution, Barry and Harris began to push again for delay. Few of the members were willing to wait, and the constitution they produced in a couple of evenings was an almost verbatim copy of the U.S. Constitution. The major difference was that the congress would be unicameral, and the sitting convention would be it. As William C. Davis has noted, it was "hardly perfect, but sufficient until a permanent constitution could be framed."[20]

The Mississippians would not bend on the second major issue, however. They wanted their favorite son Jefferson Davis to be the president of the Confederacy, although many of them had just elected him as their state's major general. They saw full well that Davis, with his reputation, would do more good on the national level than as one state's commanding general. Harris and company quickly and forcefully began to push Davis for president, causing some of the other delegates, mainly those who wanted the position for themselves, to complain. Robert Barnwell Rhett, for instance, wrote, "Jefferson Davis and Mississippi have acted very meanly." He continued, "Instead of being here to give all their weight to the proceedings of the Convention, they cook up offices for themselves, and send tools here to carry out their selfish policy."[21]

Georgia and South Carolina had many claimants for the position, and the fact that Davis desired a military command over a political position muddied the waters. It even caused minor confusion among the Mississippi delegation. It took the arrival of Alexander Clayton on February 8 to clear up the matter. Delayed due to bad weather and high water, he arrived at exactly the right time with a letter from Davis saying he would not decline the presidency if offered. Yet the question of general or president still lingered until someone noted that Davis as president and commander in chief could actually take the field at any time. That settled the matter.[22]

Davis was elected unanimously on February 9, and he quickly made his way to Montgomery after a short time in Jackson to see to his duties as Mississippi's major general. James Harrison wrote to his wife of the excitement as the Mississippian became the first Confederate chief executive: "the president arrived here last night and will be inaugurated on tomorrow. . . . We will have quite a parade." He went on to say, "I am very glad he has arrived, for it is all important that we should have an efficient military and executive head to our Provisional Government." But Davis's efficiency would be very much questioned over the next weeks, months, and years, and is still debated today.[23]

The Mississippi delegation was also involved in other issues during the long and at times tedious debate in the now provisional congress. The state's delegates were not always able to accomplish all the state convention had tasked them to do, such as establishing a military academy along the lines of the federal institution at West Point. They were not successful, and hardly even tried amid so much other important work. Several times they wrote Governor Pettus for advice, such as on how the congress should fund the new government, especially the already increasing military defense budget. Barry wrote more than one letter urging Pettus to allow the Confederate government to take the million dollars in treasury notes the state convention had intended to use to fund Mississippi's military defense. The convention president reminded Pettus that "the government of the Confederate States will take charge of that subject, [and] the interest of the State will thereby suffer no detriment." Barry added that he would be glad to hear "the state of things at home," and that he and "our whole delegation" especially wished to hear about Pettus's views on the notes.[24]

While the other ninety-six Mississippi convention delegates went about their duties at home, the Mississippians in Montgomery were burdened with a variety of other tasks as well. They served on the numerous committees formed in congress, Brooke on the committee to organize the executive branch and patents committee, Harris on the judiciary and public lands committees, Barry on finance, Clayton on judiciary, Wilson also on patents, and Harrison on postal affairs. Harrison was also Mississippi's delegate to the congressional committee tasked with devising a new flag and seal, and so many prototypes were suggested that the committee worked long hours and soon became the butt of jokes at the seemingly trivial aspect of their work. Others had much more serious business, such as Davis when he arrived in Montgomery and began setting up his executive branch. Knowing the outcry would be fatal if he gave a major cabinet office to a Mississippian, the president opted to allot the almost insignificant and dreaded position of postmaster general to the state. Few other states would object to that, especially since they had gotten the coveted positions such as secretary of state, secretary of war, and attorney general. Davis had a hard time finding a man for the position and finally appointed friend Henry T. Ellett, a member of the state convention. The Confederate congress approved the nomination, but it did so before Davis had received word of Ellett's acceptance. Ellett turned the thankless and almost impossible job down, whereupon Davis finally settled on John Reagan of Texas. He turned out to be a wise choice; Reagan did a spectacular job.[25]

Despite the level of work, morale remained high. Harrison related to his wife, "we are all in good spirits and firm in our faith. There will be no halting or backing down—no attempt at re-construction." He added, "our proceedings thus far have given great satisfaction, and will, I think, continue to do so." Harrison and others felt self-confident in what they had done and looked for other states to join and only make that which they had established stronger. The border states, he declared, would have to choose: "As for miserable Tennessee, Kentucky, Virginia, &c they will have to choose between the two governments and will soon come to our side in spite of themselves." Yet even if they did not join the Confederacy, Harrison was confident the states that had already seceded were sufficient for success: "the cement has not been discovered that can make whole the broken vase of the Union."[26]

The congressional debates continued through February and into March, with the Mississippians playing an active part in amending bills, casting votes, and involving themselves in other functions of the legislative body. They generally stuck together, often voting as a bloc. At times, when recorded votes were taken, their voting patterns were discernable. Although they voted together most of the time, at other times there was some division, and the temptation would be great to take the old secession lines as a beginning point. But only once did Brooke cast a ballot totally at odds with the other Mississippi congressman. In fact, Barry cast more opposing votes than Brooke. The secessionist lines seemed to have broken down even in Montgomery, just as they had in Jackson earlier in January.[27]

The biggest job the congress had was to construct a permanent Confederate constitution, and the Montgomery delegates, now congressmen, were determined to do so before they adjourned so that the members could return home and push for ratification within their states. The constitution had to be in place so that the government could begin to fully function, the states could begin to send money to the national government, and the Confederacy could begin to defend itself. The deliberations on the new constitution were thus extremely important. The committee members tasked with developing a permanent constitution, including Alexander Clayton and again Wiley Harris, began their task on February 11 and worked hard on a permanent version, spending far more time on this one than they had on the provisional document—a total of sixteen days, although much of their time was also taken up in congressional deliberations. The document was completed by February 26, when the committee notified the congress that it was ready for debate. And debate it they did, for several agonizing days. It was finally accepted on March 11, passing easily, with congress adjourning quickly thereafter.[28]

Generally, the new constitution was very similar to the U.S Constitution, with the congress going back to a two-house legislature. Other differences emerged such as allowing cabinet officers a seat on the floor of congress, giving the president a single six-year term and a line-item veto, outlawing internal improvements, and leaning toward civil service regulations and free trade. The biggest issue was ensuring the right to own slaves and to spread the institution into new territories. Most members believed it was just a further refining of a very good document to begin with.[29]

When Barry realized that the completion of the constitution was near, he informed Governor Pettus about the delegation's return home and the next session of the state convention. "We are hard at work upon the constitution," Barry wrote in early March, "and will probably finish it this week. As soon as it is complete I propose to call the state convention together to meet say in two weeks from the time the call is issued." When the convention passed the constitution on March 11, Barry immediately wrote Pettus: "The constitution has just passed unanimously. Please issue a proclamation in my name for the assembling of the convention on Monday the 25th." Barry and his colleagues would hurry home and proceed to the business of Mississippi joining the Confederacy.[30]

Thus did the Confederacy gain a new constitution, much like the U.S. Constitution, but with significant explanations and assurances about slavery and its spread. Wiley Harris, for one, was happy with the result. He later noted, "in no other country, nor amongst any other people could this compact and complete organization have been formed in so short a time, fraught as it was, with such momentous consequences."[31]

By early March, then, the new constitution had passed through congress and went to the individual states for ratification. Passage would come quickly, the Mississippi delegates hoped, and Mississippi would take its place as one of the new states within the Confederate States of America. But as had been the case since secession, it would not be easy.

- 11 -

RATIFICATION

March 25–30, 1861

AS SOON AS THE CONFEDERATE CONGRESS ADOPTED A CONSTITUTION, all eyes in Mississippi turned to the state convention to see whether it would make Mississippi a part of the Confederate States of America. In reality, there was little doubt that Mississippi would join the other seceded states. Yet despite David Glenn's forceful leadership at the first session of the convention, it was still not a given that the sitting convention would be able to make that decision. Nevertheless William Barry put out the call even before he left Montgomery and hurried home to prepare for the assembly that was to meet on Monday, March 25.[1]

Not all the members appeared for the March session, however. Thomas Woods later recalled that "many of its members had already gone into the army then being mobilized for southern defense." In the martial atmosphere then existing, Mississippians felt that war was inevitable, especially after President Davis's initial call for 1,500 troops from Mississippi. In fact, four delegates had already joined military companies in February, an action that further portended war. Samuel Benton, Harvey W. Walter, and James R. Chalmers were officers in companies that would become the Ninth Mississippi Infantry, while Israel Welsh had joined as a private in a company that would become part of the Eleventh Mississippi Infantry. The convention, in fact, took the interesting step of paying their mileage and per diem, as if they had been in Jackson, because of "their response to the call of the State Executive for volunteer troops, to be placed at the disposal of the Government of the Confederate States." The resolution first only mentioned Chalmers, Benton, and Walter, but Samuel Gholson reminded the members that Welsh had "gone off as a high private" and should be included, which he was. In order to keep the military committee full with the departure of Chalmers and Welsh, Barry soon appointed Jehu Orr and Josiah Winchester. Other delegates were also a part of the growing army, but they had not yet left and could still perform their duties in Jackson.[2]

Other members were missing as well. James L. Alcorn wrote Barry from his plantation in Coahoma County: "I regret that serious indisposition, whereby I have been confined to my room for the past four days, denies me the pleasure and privilege of attending the called session of the convention." James S. Johnston similarly wrote from Jefferson County that he was not able to attend "in consequence of the severe and continued illness of my wife," adding that there was "no prospect of any such early or material improvement in the condition of my wife's health as would justify me in leaving home for any length of time." He thus resigned his seat. In addition, Henry Ellett, Porter J. Myers, James B. Ramsey, and Tyra J. Roberts apparently never attended the second session either, although none of them ever indicated why. One member who surprisingly chose to attend was John W. Wood, who had sulked after speaking against secession in January. He obviously hoped to do something about the travesty he perceived was in the making.[3]

Although the other ninety delegates would all take part in the March session, only fifty-nine members answered the call when the clerk read the roll on Monday at noon. But that was enough for a quorum, and Barry opened the convention to deal with the momentous issue of ratification of the Confederate constitution. This time, however, the convention and its work were old news. Citizens and onlookers who had been enthralled with the convention's work in January had experienced many more interesting events since that time, including the Montgomery convention, Davis's election, and his inauguration. More recently, Davis's initial round of military officer appointments garnered more attention than the state convention; long lists of appointments took valuable space in the newspapers. And because war fever was sweeping Mississippi, few papers in the state covered the second session in the same detail they had in January. In fact, most papers would not print a complete daily journal of the parliamentary action, simply printing the Confederate constitution in whole and noting there was a debate and vote on the document. Likewise, the galleries were rarely full. Most of the time they were nearly empty, one reporter mentioning on the last day that the galleries were "inhabited just now by two ladies in mourning."[4]

After Barry called the convention to order and the delegates took their seats, there were only a few minor issues to deal with before the fireworks began. The convention's secretary, F. A. Pope, had informed Barry that he was sick and could not fulfill his duties. Scrambling to find a new secretary this Monday afternoon, William Tison nominated Pope's assistant, W. W. Humphreys. He was a logical choice, but Walker Brooke nominated E. P. Russell of Jackson as well, which made the position contested, thus requiring a vote. Perhaps hoping to avoid a lengthy vote with the Confederate constitution awaiting their attention, James Dyer motioned that the clerk's position be tabled and handled the next day. Humphreys, the assistant, was tasked with the duties until a permanent replacement could be found. With that, the convention moved to the central issue, indeed the one David Glenn remarked somewhat exaggeratingly as "the only one thought of."[5]

That issue was not necessarily whether the Confederate constitution should be ratified, but how. "There is no opposition to the Constitution just adopted at Montgomery," the *Vicksburg Whig* declared. "There is, however, quite a diversity of opinion on the question of submitting it to the people." To get started, Barry presented to the members a letter from the Montgomery convention's president, Howell Cobb of Georgia. In the short note, Cobb explained that he was sending a "certified" copy for the convention's approval, explaining only that it was primarily patterned after the U.S. Constitution and only departed from that document "to guard against the evils and dangers which led to the dissolution of the late Union." The constitution was then presented to the convention.[6]

Wiley Harris began the process of ratification. He had, after all, been the driving force in the convention's proceedings in January. Then he had gone to Montgomery and played a major role in the creation of both the provisional and the permanent constitutions. Surprisingly, Harris had had a change of heart while in the national spotlight. He had been a supporter of slow and methodical progress and had opposed, to David Glenn's utter aggravation, the sitting state convention ratifying the document. Now Harris admitted that he thought the convention should ratify it and move on. War was obviously on the way. Glenn was pleased, noting, "I expected time had made changes." In fact, Glenn remembered how "Harris Barry Clayton and Clapp all came over to me. Harris openly avowed his change and declared I was right from the start." Harris later explained his movement: "When we brought back from Montgomery the Constitution which had been formed then, I opposed its submission to the people, because it involved delay and imperiled the whole undertaking. I felt that the defection of one state would be fatal." As many who are presented a different prism often do, Harris changed his mind and now sided with Glenn on the need for haste and quick ratification. He could only hope that many others had changed their minds as well, and David Glenn thought the same thing; Glenn certainly did not want to refight the battles he had fought, and barely won, in January.[7]

Harris thus offered a resolution that the constitution be printed and referred to a select committee of five, who would then offer an ordinance for its ratification. The convention agreed, and Barry appointed a powerful committee, including Glenn, Jacob Yerger, James Z. George, Edward Jones, and Orlando Davis. If Harris was the soul of the convention, Glenn was the chief tactician and orator of quick ratification, one newspaper calling him the issue's "champion," adding "certainly the talking champion." He later noted, "I was at once and on all hands, by friends and foes recognized as the Leader of the Ratifiers." Glenn was obviously all for haste. George could also be counted on; he was still not all that important of a delegate, but he had asserted himself quite strongly in the latter stages of the January convention after remaining very quiet in the first weeks. George had been particularly vocal about military pay, taxation of slaves, and especially the opening of the African slave trade. Orlando Davis and Edward Jones could also be trusted to follow Glenn's leadership, although the independent Jones, who had led the fight against having the delegates to Montgomery be chosen according to congressional district, could at times prove individualistic and quirky. On the other hand, Yerger could be counted on to lead the opposition to convention ratification, wanting as he did a direct vote by the people. Yerger had led the fight against secession in much the same delaying way, and whether this was a continuation of an opposition to secession itself or a more contextual effort to ensure that Mississippi was not being run by a limited cadre of statesman is not known, although the newly divergent political lines that developed after secession in January pointed to the latter. For whatever reason, however, Yerger would again be in opposition.[8]

Others besides Harris made the switch as well. Alfred Holt explained his change of position in a long speech. To Glenn's utter delight, Barry clearly changed his attitude as well; otherwise he would not have appointed so many Glenn stalwarts to the committee. Barry went so far as to advise ratification on the floor of the convention. Yet none of the changes stopped the opposition from making their case. After a couple of military-related issues (including what one newspaper reported as "an animated discussion" instigated by William Smart about allowing the Military Board to transfer units to the Confederate government as well as an approved motion by Francis Rogers—Smart's was referred to the military committee—for

Quartermaster William Barksdale to pay the volunteers then at Pensacola), George offered a resolution that the committee of five be instructed to present an ordinance by ten o'clock the next morning for ratification of the constitution "by this body on behalf of the State of Mississippi."[9]

The opposition responded harshly, and Glenn blamed newspapers, including surprisingly the secessionist *Mississippian* (again illustrating the breakdown of secessionist political lines), for such an attitude. He later wrote that the papers "had frightened many small men and what we gained in talent we lost in numbers." Glenn went so far as to state that "in fact, [ratification] was near falling victim to this 'dumb eloquence.'" Immediately chief federalist George Clayton offered a substitute resolution that provided "for the election of delegates by the people of the State of Mississippi, to ratify in Convention a Constitution for a permanent government of the Confederate States of America." Not satisfied, Yerger offered a different ordinance "as a substitute for the substitute offered by Mr. Clayton." His ordinance called "for the ratification or rejection of the Permanent Constitution by the people at the ballot box." Glenn fought back, offering an ordinance to substitute for George's, Clayton's, and Yerger's motions, obviously to allow for ratification by the sitting convention. Then out of the blue Walker Brooke steered the debate back away from Glenn's motion to that of a vote by the people at the ballot box, to be held within ten days, arguing that there was a definite idea in the "public mind" that the Montgomery convention had usurped legislative authority and that his constituents desired a public referendum. For his part, Brooke explained that he regarded ratification as "a fixed fact," and further stated that he "didn't care a straw how that might be accomplished," but he would nevertheless look out for the interests and desires of his constituents. Such a move was interesting to say the least, as Brooke had been a member of the Montgomery convention that had unanimously passed the constitution. Obviously his constituents' Whiggish and cooperationist ideals were more important to him. In Yerger's case, however, it is difficult to determine whether his actions were related to the old secession issue or were more in line with the new opposition to a strong central power. After all, it was not that far from cooperationism to liberalism in terms of federalism or opposition to a central ruling authority.[10]

The lines were certainly drawn, and hope of a speedy resolution quickly faded amid what the *Vicksburg Whig* described as the "brief but lively debate." At a point in the deliberations Barry wired President Davis in Montgomery: "we are in trouble." But the chance of passage of the constitution by this convention was not totally lost, and Orlando Davis, the revered judge,

ended the actions that were quickly growing out of control by making a motion that all the "various propositions" be referred to the committee of five.
Hopefully, that would end the piling on of ideas as well as put the decision-
making process in a group firmly dominated by supporters of convention
ratification.[11]

As during the January session when the convention had adjourned early
to allow Lamar and his committee time to work up a secession ordinance,
the convention delegates saw that there was little else they could do until
they heard from the committee. Thus the only other action that day was
Yerger's recommendation that the vote to refer Smart's resolution to the
committee be reconsidered so that he could offer an amendment that re-
leased all troops transferred to the Confederate army from any control of
the Military Board. Perhaps Yerger was again attacking a central authority
he loathed, but for whatever reason, he was certainly making himself a factor. One wonders if he missed Alcorn.[12]

The convention then adjourned, to meet at 10:00 A.M. on Tuesday.
When the delegates reassembled, there was more conflict over the new political attitudes, particularly by those who favored less central control over
Mississippi's affairs. An obviously agitated Walker Brooke had by this time
regained the opposing edge he had somewhat lost in the shuffle of Montgomery and Confederatism, but he certainly made his thoughts known on
the ratification issue the day before and continued his onslaught on Tuesday. Before the convention could turn to ratification, Brooke offered ordinances to repeal both the military board and defense ordinances passed in
January. Those ordinances, of course, put the sole power of the defense of
the state, both militarily and economically, in the hands of the convention
and the military board. Brooke, perhaps hoping like Yerger the day before
that the delegates would agree that the board was no longer necessary since
most troops would be going to the Confederacy anyway, began the day on
a note of opposition, foreshadowing what was to come on the ratification
issue. After "considerable debate" in which Brooke, George, Clapp, Gholson,
King, and several others spoke on opposing sides, the convention tabled
Brooke's ordinances and ordered them printed. He had made his point
nonetheless.[13]

The convention then moved to the pending business, ironically Brooke's
previous motion to have a statewide referendum on the constitution. Glenn
immediately introduced a motion to table the ordinance, but it failed by
a very narrow vote, forty to thirty-seven, with numerous old secessionists
voting not to table and at least flirt with the idea of allowing the voters to

decide. Newspapers called this a "test vote" on the issue, and it had been voted down. Glenn had his work cut out for him.[14]

Glenn later tried to put a positive spin on this vote, writing that "to get a showing of hands I moved to lay a Resolution of Brooke's on the table and was beaten by 3 votes!" He remarked, "our friends thought we were gone," but added, "I knew better. We had had no debate." Then his opposition unwittingly aided him. After winning the crucial test vote, the opponents overextended themselves and stanched the progress they had made. George Clayton could not resist making his pet theory an issue, calling for a new convention to ratify the constitution. When Clayton offered his motion as a substitute to Brooke's, Glenn was able to have it placed on the table by a vote of forty-five to thirty. The opposition would have been wiser to consolidate on the earlier success, but Clayton's actions showed a lack of cooperation among them, which led to a quick defeat and loss of ground Brooke had only recently won.[15]

Glenn was quick to capitalize on this turn of events, picking this time to offer the report of his committee of five, which would obviously bring the debate back to immediate convention ratification. He later wrote how "before they comprehended my object, I asked leave to report from my committee—granted—I asked leave to be heard—granted—I spoke three hours!" No wonder the *Vicksburg Whig* called Glenn the "talking champion."[16]

Yet even that was not easy, and Glenn later remembered "the struggle opened." Several delegates opposed Glenn, and he had to prevail by a vote of the convention. He succeeded in gaining the floor and offering his report, indicating a groundswell of support beginning to emerge. Glenn told the convention that the committee had asked him to "report an Ordinance providing for the adoption and ratification by the State of Mississippi, acting in its sovereign and independent character, the Constitution adopted by the Congress at Montgomery, in the State of Alabama, in the year of our Lord, 1861, and to recommend its passage." He hammered on the theme at length. Not to be outdone, Yerger took the floor and offered a "minority report," he being a minority of one on the committee, which called again for a statewide referendum "at the ballot-box." Yerger himself gave what the *Vicksburg Whig* described as "a powerful and able argument in favor of the right of the people to pass upon their fundamental law." The convention seemed again to be going in circles.[17]

Then John Wood spoke up, despite the fact that he had not even been present for most of the January session. For whatever reason, Wood decided at this point to become active, and he did so in a curious manner. He was brooding that "conspicuous among the advocates for a ratification by the Convention, were the delegates to the Montgomery convention, including the President of the State Convention." Still, he took the floor and made a motion to receive the majority report, the one favoring this convention's ratification. Everyone knew he was opposed to secession, convention ratification, and probably anything else the majority wanted, but his odd stance soon became more clear. Once Glenn's ordinance was on the floor, Wood was able to offer his own substitute to it. Obviously this was his plan all along, but he had to have Glenn's words on the floor to do so. Wood's substitute said about the same thing as Yerger's and Brooke's, calling for a ballot-box vote. Although Wood's motion then became the pending topic and would remain so for a couple of days, one wonders if his colleagues fighting Glenn and company resented this interloper who had not even remained in the convention in January appearing and taking such a prominent role now. If so, it only illustrated the lack of collaboration among the opposition.[18]

Under such a torrent of ordinances and substitutes and substitutes to substitutes, the convention broke that afternoon to reassemble at 3:00 P.M. When they did so, the members accepted the clerk Pope's official resignation and elected E. P. Russell as the new clerk. Russell would also have an assistant, Robert C. Miller. Brooke then called his items regarding the military and means ordinances from the table, but Alfred Holt was able to get them referred to the military committee. The convention then turned to its signature issue again, the Wood substitute. Rancorous debate that afternoon solved little, and the convention adjourned to meet the next day at 10:00 A.M. Wood admitted that "the debate was marked with a degree of ability and interest far exceeding any other debate in the Convention," but grumbled that "the influence of outsiders was brought to bear very heavily upon the result."[19]

A clear and pleasant Wednesday saw no progress whatsoever on the ratification issue, and actually witnessed digression. After some intermediary issues such as Glenn offering an ordinance regarding donating all waste and unappropriated lands to the Confederacy and passing (Glenn's was referred to a special committee) an ordinance by Brooke dealing with "Foreign Insurance companies," the convention then turned again to Wood's substitute for Glenn's majority report. Charles Fontaine brought the convention back to the new convention idea, however, offering that afternoon, after a break, a substitute for Wood's substitute, which called for the election of a new ratifying convention. In the midst of long speeches and major debate on the issues, which were only broken by another break and a reassembling of the convention at 8:00 P.M., as well as other small issues such as a report by the engrossing committee and a call to have Barry raise a Confederate flag, the convention continued to wade through the various facets of the debate. The delegates eventually adjourned late in the night, to meet Thursday at 9:00 A.M. But at least now they could see an end coming. In between the speeches on the issue, Robert Flournoy had proposed and succeeded in having a resolution passed that the debate would "be closed at one o'clock, to-morrow, and that the Convention then proceed to take a vote."[20]

Such a timetable proved utterly impossible to maintain, however, as became agonizingly evident when the debate began again that rainy Thursday morning. All saw that the debate would end no time soon, and Jeremiah Clapp called for the order of yesterday ending the debate at 1:00 P.M. to be "hereby rescinded." Another day of long debate thus transpired, with a 3:00 P.M. session and another one at 8:00 P.M. that lasted deep into the night. The delegates were seemingly debating the ratification issue to death.[21]

Even worse, the convention found it difficult to stay on task. Throughout the day numerous members took the liberty to bring up additional issues, no doubt causing rumblings among members already impatient to get through with their work and go home. For instance, Glenn brought the waste and unappropriated lands ordinance from his committee to the floor, where it easily passed. He also brought a motion to deal with the land agents in Jasper County, which was promptly tabled. Arthur Bullard offered resolutions providing "the highest commendation" for "the prompt response of the gallant Mississippi Volunteers to the call of the President of the Confederate States," as well as assuring them that "Mississippi will promptly attach herself to the Confederacy." Obviously almost everyone, except John Wood, agreed that Mississippi should join the new Confederacy; the question was only how. At the rate the delegates were going, the war would be over before they decided how to do it.[22]

Other issues also took the delegates' attention away from the main task. John B. Deason made a motion that a committee be formed to look into assuaging the drought-stricken counties in central Mississippi with corn provided for the poor. Glenn offered a resolution that would have suspended "tribunals as to the trial civil and chancery cases in court" (but not criminal cases) because so many lawyers and claimants had left to join the army; the issue was tabled and printed. James Z. George offered a similar resolution dealing with federal cases and records; it, too, was tabled. Charles Fontaine, who had taken over as head of the military committee with Chalmers's absence, reported back that the committee recommended that the delegates not pass Brooke's resolutions repealing the board and revenue ordinances. There was even a motion that required the convention to adjourn permanently on Saturday at 6:00 P.M. That, too, was laid on the table.[23]

Obviously tiring of the extended debate as well as the other more minor issues getting in the way, Edward P. Jones, never one to shy away from taking a stand, made a motion that debate on the ratification issue be ended and a vote taken at 10:00 A.M. the next day, Friday. He added significantly that "no further postponement be allowed." That passed the convention, which once again had a firm time period in which to work. The vote would be taken, for better or worse, on Friday morning. It was time to act one way or the other.[24]

The debate continued long and contentious, with the notables of the convention leading the way: Yerger, Harris, Gholson, Barry, Rogers, "the two Claytons," Winchester, Wright, Fontaine, Clapp, and Hugh Miller. They made numerous arguments such as the need for haste, the power of the convention to take such action, and the fact that delay and submission to another convention or the people were simply a guise for "reconstruction," or hoping to return to the Union. Others such as Harris made arguments about economics and foreign recognition, all of which required prompt action.[25]

Opponents of immediate ratification tried every way they could to dissuade the convention from taking such drastic action. At least one Northern reporter left a vivid if unflattering portrayal of one of the speeches, by ratification opponent Daniel B. Wright. The reporter was convinced Wright "conceived himself to be an orator," but decided he "spread himself very thin." He reported that Wright "quote[d] more Scripture incorrectly, irreverently, and irrelevantly" than anyone he had ever heard, and complained that he "understood him to allude to Samson as killing Goliath." He noticed that "other members listened courteously, though betraying a lurking suspicion that he was a bore."[26]

Most of the opponents of convention ratification dwelled on several key issues. One was an agreement that the convention had the power to ratify, but that fact did not make it right. The people still deserved the right to choose. Similarly, many opponents explained their position that, while personally ambivalent, they had made certain promises in their respective canvasses to refer the constitution back to the people. Charles Fontaine noted "a pledge distinctly given to my constituents prior to my election." More important, the opponents continuously fought the idea that in opposing convention ratification, they were somehow reconstructionists. Stung by accusations of disloyalty, to a man they disavowed that idea. Even John Wood thundered his approval of the Confederacy and the constitution, but warned that ratification by this convention would "raise a shout of indignation" among the people. In the end, it was a brilliant political maneuver to associate opponents of ratification with reconstruction, because the opponents spent more time denying reconstruction than they did fighting against ratification. Glenn let them rant (one was even noted in the journal as having "grumbled"), but at the end he gave another three-hour speech, what Glenn called "the best I ever made and probably will ever make again." A tired group of delegates thus adjourned well after ten o'clock that night.[27]

With a firm and unchangeable timetable in place, the convention met on a cloudy and warm Friday morning for what would be the ultimate showdown on ratification. Interestingly, however, even with such a deadline in place, the members first turned to other matters. One was a communication from Governor Pettus asking for help for drought-stricken counties, the very issue raised the day before by John B. Deason. Pettus also wanted other items passed, such as military funding for the troops at Pensacola, an issue also considered by the convention earlier. Pettus, it seemed, treated the convention as he would the legislature, which no doubt made many of the federalists in the membership very nervous. At any rate, the convention referred the letter to the committee formed the day before, but then turned to the passage of a supplemental ordinance to the one passed in January dealing with means to defend the state. Quickly suspending the rules and passing it, the convention then proceeded to the major topic.[28]

By then the 10:00 A.M. deadline had passed and debate was ended. The voting thus began, but a few more issues were still worked out behind the scenes before the vote took place. David Hurst and Daniel Parker, both of whom had voted against secession in January, were now on opposing sides and notified the convention that they were pairing off and thus would not vote on any ordinances short of the final vote. The commonly used technique of pairing and thus canceling each other's votes illustrated the division and weakening of the old secession/cooperationist blocs. Additionally, delegates such as William Sumner, Malachi Cummings, and Thomas Marshall explained why they would hold out against ratification. Despite the interruptions, the voting then began. The pending piece of legislation was Fontaine's substitute to Wood's substitute to Glenn's majority report. In a fifty-seven to twenty-eight vote, the convention voted down Fontaine's motion for a new convention to ratify the constitution. Continuing the blurring of the old secessionist lines that had begun in January, many of the secessionists and cooperationists split on the issue, with Gholson and others voting for Fontaine's amendment and Blair, Bullard, Farrar, and Winchester all voting against it. Curiously, even Walker Brooke voted in the negative.[29]

With Fontaine's amendment defeated, Wood's substitute for a public referendum then became the pending bill, but Samuel Gholson offered a stronger substitute that called for the ratification by the people, specifically laying out the process of voters placing tickets labeled "For Ratification" or "No Ratification." This move had obviously been worked out ahead of time and was palpable to the old cooperationists, with Brooke, Farrar, Winchester, and Blair all supporting it this time. In clear violation of the spirit of the deadline, Gholson's substitute was nevertheless allowed, but it too failed on a fifty-three to thirty-two vote. Now Wood's original substitute became the pending question, but when the vote was taken, it also failed on a fifty-six to twenty-three vote, with Brooke again curiously siding with the opponents of the substitute. Only one final impediment lay before ratification, and that was when Yerger "re-offered" his minority report as a substitute for the majority one. This effort failed on an even greater split in the vote, sixty-six to thirteen, with only the most stalwart opposition members voting for it.[30]

Francis Rogers then offered another substitute for the majority report, saying the convention would ratify the constitution, but it would not take effect until the people voted on it. This amendment was quickly laid on the table, Jehu Clapp arguing that it was "of the same batch already voted down by the Convention." That left Glenn's report as the pending legislation, but before the vote was taken, Samuel Gholson took the floor and urged "those who had acted with him in opposition to the Ordinance, to come forward and unanimously ratify the Permanent Constitution." Miller and Wright agreed, and Glenn knew he had won, although it would not be unanimous, as Marshall and Stephens took the floor to explain their upcoming vote against the ordinance. The convention thus accepted Glenn's report, and then moved to passage of the ordinance, the major vote of the session. In the end, the ordinance passed by a wide margin, seventy-eight to seven. Considering the dwindling support for delay each previous vote had illustrated, this vote was not surprising. Glenn was nevertheless ecstatic, remarking, "every member voted for it but 7!" Only the most stalwart opponents voted against ratification, including Wood and Yerger. The latter had fought a gallant fight but had lost. He quickly asked for a leave of absence and went home.[31]

Mississippi was now part of "a new Confederacy," and the convention adjourned until 3:00 P.M. News of the ratification rushed throughout the state and region, with Barry telegraphing the news to Davis in Montgomery. The news also went to the Mississippi troops at Pensacola, with General Charles Clark returning his receipt and notifying the convention that the news would be read in front of the troops. Several others mentioned various entities that should also have telegrams sent to them, and Brooke responded, "Yes, telegraph it to the whole world!"[32]

When the convention reassembled that Friday afternoon in an anticlimactic session, it once again waded through minor issues, and actually continued to do so during the next day as well. The delegates, only a fraction of whom remained after a mass exodus following the major vote, dealt with issues of the indigent, Indian lands, paying the new clerk, and even defeating Glenn's ordinance for a suspension of court proceedings. The next day, which proved to be a warm and comfortable ending to the convention, the members hoped to deal with every issue and be able to finish up on Saturday without returning for another week. Many delegates were already leaving, however, with some votes on Saturday garnering no more than fifty-seven total votes, barely half the membership. Most just left, but a few formally requested leaves of absence. Arthur Bullard, the *Vicksburg Whig* reported, "desired to leave for Pensacola."[33]

Those who remained fiercely debated and passed several ordinances, working around a break at noon to go to the governor's mansion, to which Pettus had invited them. Some of the debate dealt with amending the state constitution, correcting ordinances passed in January (such as the Federal Jurisdiction and Property Committee's bill), defining the power of the legislature, and providing for the indigent. There were also many minor items such as printing journals, providing for a state flag and coat of arms, making minor appropriations to cover expenses incurred during the week, and other similarly small details. Some of the most important work was providing electors for the upcoming presidential election, revising Mississippi's delegation to the Confederate congress, and filling the congressional position resigned by William S. Wilson, who informed the convention he could no longer attend to his duties. In a special election, Jehu Orr defeated David Glenn by only a few votes; the *Vicksburg Whig* reported, "the result not only seemed to astonish himself, but everybody else."[34]

One very interesting discussion took place around a proposal by John Deason that "when the Convention adjourns it resolve itself into a military company." There was apparently some serious discussion of the matter, with Jehu Orr adding an amendment that officers in this company "from Captain to Fifth Corporal" be appointed by the governor. The members voted on tabling the motion, which lost, and then they refused to refer it to the Military and Naval Affairs Committee. Then they decided better of the idea and defeated the resolution "by a small majority."[35]

The end eventually came, however, and the delegates took the time to offer their thanks to the clerks as well as to President Barry. Upon a motion by Albert Gibson to adjourn sine die, Barry gave a short but eloquent address thanking the members for their work and alerting them that "no man here need blush to the latest moment of his life." With that, Barry declared the convention adjourned forever.[36]

It was now time for the delegates to go and defend what they had done.

- 12 -

WAR

1861–1865

MISSISSIPPI CONGRESSMEN JAMES T. HARRISON COULD CLEARLY SEE
trouble ahead early in 1861. Almost in prophetic terms, he declared, "The
danger is in the United States Government attempting to collect the revenue
and keeping the forts now in their possession." And Harrison was not alone,
at least in Mississippi and at least in regard to the coming of war. Numerous
delegates had expounded on their idea that war was inevitable, with several
even giving Northern abolitionist and now Lincoln's secretary of state William Seward credit for his "irrepressible conflict" idea. It was widely known
that even President Davis was convinced war was a reality.[1]

But the people were ready and began to flock to the Confederate standard even before the firing on Fort Sumter and the official opening of hostilities in April 1861. The *Mississippi Free Trader* declared in late January
1861, "No one wears a gloomy countenance. Men, women and children are
influenced by the spirit of war. The plume and the epaulette, and the saber,
are now familiar things, and every one feels himself destined to fight." The
paper went on to conclude, somewhat prematurely as it turned out, "Indeed,
we would all be disappointed did the 'weak piping days of peace' come back
before the glorious clash of arms of a free people told the world that the
days of chivalry were not gone."[2]

That same sentiment ran through the convention delegates. Although
they had decided not to constitute themselves into a military company,
most of them who were of military age, and many who were not, were soon
among the ranks of the young men making up the Confederate army. One
member, Thomas Woods, later remembered, "soon after its adjournment the
mass of its members were to be found in the field."[3]

In all, 69 of the 100 delegates served Mississippi or the Confederacy in some capacity, the vast majority in the army. A few held a less militaristic position, serving in the state troops, in the state legislature, in the Confederate congress, as Confederate judges, or in some other capacity, but serve they did. Of the forty-one delegates who did not actually serve in a military unit, all were above the thirty-five-year age mark set as the upper reach of military age. Yet even among those, most were ardently supportive of the Confederacy, giving money to equip companies, serving in political or judicial offices, or sending sons to the war effort. That said, of the fifty-nine men who served in some capacity in a military unit, thirty-seven were over the age of thirty-five, or the accepted military age. The vast majority of those over thirty-five who served in the military were in their thirties and forties, while most of those over thirty-five who did not serve were in their upper forties, fifties, and sixties. Each individual's health also played a prominent role in whether he joined the army.[4]

The ages can be analyzed further to illustrate the delegates' commitment to the Confederate cause. When the Confederate congress passed its second conscription act in October 1862 and it went into effect in July 1863, extending the age for military service to forty-five, there was only one man under forty-five who did not serve in the military: John Wood, who had fought secession and ratification and had eventually moved to occupied Memphis, Tennessee, to become a vocal Unionist. And some of the older members tried to join up, despite their age. Wiley P. Harris suffered from an "infirmity of sight." Nevertheless he later remembered that he had "joined an artillery company but was laughed at, and without my agency, detailed for duties which I could perform."[5]

Interestingly, support for secession, or the lack thereof, had nothing to do with support for the Confederacy. Of the thirty-three delegates who were in some way cooperationists, nineteen served in the military and four were members of the legislature or congress, or held some other Confederate position. That left only ten who did not serve, and one well-off member of the latter group outfitted a company. Of the ten, nine were in their upper forties, fifties, or sixties, far older than military age. That left John Wood as the only cooperationist of military age who did not serve in the Confederate ranks.[6]

Of the fifteen delegates who voted outright against secession, eight went into the army, two held Confederate political positions, and five were too old (Wood, of course, did not vote against secession as he was absent from the convention). Of the most dedicated anti-secessionists, Yerger sent four sons to the Confederate army, Alcorn became a state militia brigadier general, Brooke served in the Confederate congress, and John J. Thornton, who refused to sign the ordinance, became colonel of the Sixth Mississippi Infantry.[7]

Further illustrating their zeal, the men who joined the Confederacy did so mostly early in the war. Most of the fifty-nine delegates who served in a military unit did so in the lower-numbered Mississippi regiments, illustrating the fact that they were in the initial wave of volunteers in the spring of 1861. A few others served in higher-numbered regiments, but most of them had performed other jobs earlier in the war. William Barry is an illustrative example. He served in the Confederate congress early in the war, but organized and led the Thirty-Fifth Mississippi Infantry in 1862.[8]

In these regiments, the delegates to the convention were, with only one exception, officers. Only Israel Welsh, who did not attend the convention in March because he had already joined a unit, served for a few months as a private in the Eleventh Mississippi before being discharged and entering the Confederate congress in Richmond. Most served in the infantry, although five held cavalry commands and several served in both the infantry and cavalry. Only Albert C. Gibson was an artilleryman. Of the delegates, four would become Confederate brigadier generals (Chalmers, Brantley, Benton, and Gholson), while two reached that rank in the state troops or militia (George and Alcorn). Nineteen of them became Confederate or militia colonels, many of them, such as Barry, Colbert, and Reynolds, often leading brigades in which they were the senior colonel while the general was absent. The rest held ranks from lieutenant colonel down to lieutenants, with a few holding staff positions such as adjutant general and judge advocate. In such offices, they served many of the most famous generals of the war, such as Harvey Walter on Braxton Bragg's staff, George Wilkinson on John C. Pemberton's, Lamar and Glenn both as judges in A. P. Hill's corps of the Army of Northern Virginia, Albert P. Hill as a judge in James Longstreet's corps, and Daniel B. Wright as a judge in Nathan Bedford Forrest's cavalry corps. Some held other positions: nine served in the state legislature during the war (Ellett, Dyer, Edwards, Cumming, Catching, Semmes, Neely, Jones, and Bonds), and David Hurst sat on the state supreme court during the conflict. Davis, Ramsey, Isom, and Holt all served as surgeons during the war.[9]

In all, the delegates seemed to be everywhere in the fighting, with the vast majority not surprisingly serving in the western theater between the Appalachian Mountains and the Mississippi River, a good number of them serving in Mississippi itself. Only fourteen served in Virginia under Robert

E. Lee. And they were not just confined to one unit or theater throughout the war. Many served in multiple units in multiple branches, often resigning to take a better commission or leaving their unit to raise another regiment. For example, James Z. George served first as a captain in the Twentieth Mississippi Infantry, then as a state brigadier general, and finally as colonel of the Fifth Mississippi Cavalry. Others, as noted, mixed military positions with political appointments.[10]

Despite the support the delegates provided for the Confederate war effort, the conflict turned out to be a heart-wrenching ordeal for most. Many of the members suffered wounds, spent much of the war in prison camps, or had plantations and possessions destroyed. All, of course, lost their slaves. Most sadly, thirteen of the delegates did not live to see the end of the war. Yet in an ironic twist, it was not war but natural causes that claimed the first delegate's life. Warren P. Anderson did not live to see the end of 1861, dying in Bladen Springs, Alabama, on September 9. His death marked the first of a string of deaths for the delegates during the war, but few would be as nonviolent as his.[11]

As the members fanned out in both theaters early in the war, it was not surprising that they met death and suffering. A few of the regiments endured the initial battles such as First Manassas and Ball's Bluff in Virginia before a harsh winter took a toll on their health. John A. Blair of the Second Mississippi, who had voted against secession, became the first delegate to be wounded, at First Manassas. Albert P. Hill of the Eighteenth Mississippi Infantry was wounded a few months later at Ball's Bluff. But the first real action came out west when five of the members were caught inside Fort Donelson, including George, Gibson, Reynolds, Sumner (who was also wounded), and Francis Marion Rogers, a captain in the Fourteenth Mississippi Infantry who was killed in the Confederate attack on February 15. He was the first of the delegates to die as a result of the war. Yet the carnage continued. Ten of the members were at Shiloh shortly thereafter, with John J. Thornton, who had refused to sign the secession ordinance, William F. Brantley, and Edward F. McGehee being wounded, and Francis Marion Aldridge, a captain in the Fifteenth Mississippi Infantry, being killed at the Peach Orchard.[12]

After that initial first shock that was Shiloh, with its nearly 24,000 casualties, Americans of both sides endured more and more of those horrendous battle tolls. The convention delegates and their families did the same. William J. Eckford, a captain in the Thirteenth Mississippi Infantry, was killed at Malvern Hill on July 1, 1862, but others' deaths were not just on the battlefield. Both Daniel H. Parker, a captain in the Seventh Mississippi, and Cyrus B. Baldwin, a lieutenant in the Thirty-First Mississippi, died of disease that spring and summer, respectively. On the home front, forty-eight-year-old Wright W. Bonds, who had joined the Second Mississippi but was not mustered apparently for health reasons, died at home. He was a member of the state legislature and would have a son killed at Gettysburg as well. Several of the members were also wounded in 1862, including Sumner at Fort Donelson; McGehee, Brantley, and Thornton at Shiloh; David Hurst, Samuel Gholson, and Walter Keirn at Corinth; Daniel Wright at Perryville; and William Witty at Stones River. Wright was taken prisoner at Perryville in addition to being wounded.[13]

The year 1863 was not as fatal to the delegates, but it still saw the death of fifty-year-old Stephen D. Johnston, who died because of a fall from his horse while fleeing Federal troops in DeSoto County. Hugh R. Miller, who was colonel of the Forty-Second Mississippi Infantry, was mortally wounded near the famous railroad cut at Gettysburg and died eighteen days later. Edward Jones received a wound at a small cavalry fight near Franklin, Tennessee, and Thomas Woods was hit near Fredericksburg in May 1863. Two members, Bruce Colbert and President Barry himself, were captured inside Vicksburg, while Edward Jones became a prisoner after being wounded near Franklin. Similarly, William Witty became a prisoner at Lookout Mountain, and John A. Blair was captured at Gettysburg.[14]

The next year saw two especially sad deaths. Andrew Miller, whose brother Hugh had been mortally wounded at Gettysburg the year before, died of natural causes in his sixties. That year also saw the death of one of Mississippi's generals, Samuel Benton. As colonel of the Thirty-Fourth Mississippi Infantry during the Atlanta Campaign, he led his brigade in the absence of its general. In that duty, he was mortally wounded in the Battle of Atlanta on July 22, 1864, and died six days later. His commission as a brigadier general only became official two days before his death. The year also saw a flurry of delegates wounded. Samuel Gholson was hit at Egypt in Mississippi, Alexander Reynolds and John Blair at Weldon's Railroad, and President Barry at Allatoona. William Tison was hit three times that year, yet somehow survived. Colbert, Barksdale, Tison, and Stephens were all wounded at Franklin. In addition, Thomas Bookter fell prisoner during the Meridian Campaign.[15]

By 1865 almost everyone recognized that the Confederacy's chances of winning were gone, yet the delegates and thousands of other Mississippians fought on. Two deaths occurred that year, Miles McGehee in his fifties at home and, perhaps saddest of all, Bruce Colbert, colonel of the Fortieth Mississippi Infantry, at Bentonville in mid-March 1865, just a few weeks prior to the end of the war. John B. Herring was wounded during the fighting near Petersburg, and John Blair was taken prisoner at Hatcher's Run near Petersburg on April 2, 1865, just seven days prior to Robert E. Lee's surrender. President Barry was captured near Mobile on April 9.[16]

In addition to the thirteen delegates who did not survive the war, at least ten members served time as prisoners of war: three captured at Fort Donelson, two at Vicksburg, and others at Perryville, Lookout Mountain, Mobile, and Gettysburg. A few were captured twice, including John A. Blair (who had opposed secession) captured at Gettysburg and then Hatcher's Run in Virginia. President Barry was captured at Vicksburg and then again at the end of the war at Mobile. James Z. George was captured at Fort Donelson and then again at a small cavalry action at Collierville, Tennessee. In all, George would spend more time in prison at Johnson's Island than he would in the Confederate ranks, over half the war. While these delegates experienced a myriad of Union prison camps, from Johnson's Island to Camp Chase to Fort Delaware, most served time at Johnson's Island.[17]

Far more delegates were wounded during the war. In all, some nineteen members suffered wounds, a third of those who were in the ranks. And where they were injured ran the length of the war, beginning with John Blair's wound at First Manassas. A few suffered more than one wound, such as Blair being hit at First Manassas and then again at Weldon's Railroad. Samuel Gholson was wounded at Corinth and then again at Egypt, the latter as a brigadier general. William Tison was hit a total of three times, at Resaca, Atlanta, and then Franklin. The desperate charge at Franklin took an especially heavy toll on the members, with Colbert, Barksdale, Tison, and Stephens all hurt there. Even worse, some of the wounded also fell into enemy hands. At times, the wounds were so severe that they ended the member's military career. Edward McGehee's foot was so terribly mangled at Shiloh that he was unable to walk. David Hurst at Corinth was so badly injured by a fall from his horse that he had to leave the army. John J. Thornton's wound at Shiloh also ended his career.[18]

The economic impact of the war caused the delegates major suffering as well. Many, especially the older ones who remained home, were confronted by devastation and destructive soldiers on both sides. Families of those in the ranks also suffered in the same manner. While the rich planters no doubt suffered, not all felt their plight, as Wiley Harris later noted: "I have felt that the disappearance of this type [planters] is not amongst the calamities of the South." Fewer indicators of such suffering exist in comparison to individual soldier's records, but one source is a comparison of the monetary values listed in the 1860 and 1870 censuses. Although the 1870 census is very incomplete (and many of the delegates had died by then), a representative idea of the economic cost of secession and war can be attained by studying it. Most delegates saw their value both in real estate as well as personal value cut in half. While these 1870 figures are representative and take many variables into account, most notably five years to recover from the losses of war after 1865, they nevertheless paint a grim picture. Examples include planter Edward F. McGehee, who was not only crippled at Shiloh, but also saw his real estate value go from $70,000 to $30,000 and his personal value go from $80,000 to $1,000. Harvey Walter saw his personal worth drop from $130,000 to $10,000. The most stark example was Thomas P. Young, who saw his personal worth go from $45,000 to $20. A few increases occurred, mostly in land value, probably the result of taking advantage of land liquidation resulting from the change in Reconstruction-era tax policies. Even when that occurred, however, most personal worth still went down. James L. Alcorn experienced the greatest increase in real estate value, going from $140,000 to $250,000, but then by 1870 he was governor of the state.[19]

Yet at the same time that many of the secession convention delegates were fighting and giving their lives and homes for the Confederate cause, there were a few who were becoming Unionists. Many realized the potential for trouble from Unionists, delegate William R. Barksdale speaking during the convention itself about the "croaking and disappointed demagogues [who] will seize upon this to stir up groundless opposition to that new constitution." In fact, some of the convention delegates in addition to John Wood came very close to Unionism, if they did not cross the line. Newspaperman John L. Power, who had covered the convention and had already printed his "neat pamphlet" and sold it for "only a dollar," reported, "there were others who were very loud for war, but who were very quiet when the time came for business, and who, if they enlisted, sought bomb-proof positions, and suddenly discovered physical disabilities that they had not before dreamed of." William Bolling of Winston County had been extremely vocal about his support for the Confederacy, how he would fund a defense of his home and would fight the enemy. "His voice was heard on nearly all occasions," one history records, "rallying the patriotic and chivalrous sons of Winston County, to arms. He proclaimed with vehement asseverations that he would be with them in their marches and drink all the blood that was spilt and pay for all the powder that was burnt." But when Benjamin

Grierson's famous raid in April 1863 went through Louisville, residents found that the vocal Bolling was the first man out of town. Bolling had "fled . . . and hid himself among the rocks in the mountains of Alabama," a county historian explained. Similarly, Robert Flournoy of Pontotoc County had always been suspected of Unionism, but residents thought they knew for sure once he joined the Twenty-First Mississippi Infantry. He soon resigned due, he said, to illness. Many thought, however, and he later admitted it, that he just could not bring himself to fight against the United States.[20]

Despite some isolated Unionism among the delegates, the vast majority were on the Confederate bandwagon, especially at first. When Unionism began to appear in Mississippi in late 1862 and grew throughout 1863 and 1864 to monumental proportions, the convention cooperationists were not part of that movement. They remained loyal to the Confederacy once they sided with the secessionists. The cooperationist leaders Brooke, Alcorn, and Yerger were not found among those who actively sought "reconstruction" as early as 1863, talking with Federal generals about the possibility of rejoining the Union. William T. Sherman wrote in July 1863 how "Judge Sharkey, Dr. Poindexter, and Mr. Yerger, with many other very intelligent and influential men, have consulted me as to moving in the matter of organizing the State to submit to the lawful authority of the United States. They admit themselves beaten, subdued, and charge their rulers and agitators with bringing ruin and misery on the State." None of these men had been delegates in the convention, the Yerger mentioned being William Yerger. The example of Thomas A. Marshall, cooperationist delegate from Warren County, is instructive. Union officials targeted cooperationists after the fall of Vicksburg and even went so far as to ask to meet with them. William T. Sherman wanted to meet with Marshall and did so. It was a futile attempt, though; Marshall made it clear that he would not turn against Mississippi. At the time, Marshall had a son and a brother in the Confederate army.[21]

As the most illustrative example of continued cooperationist support for the Confederacy, the agitation and contempt the cooperationists caucus felt for the secessionists immediately before secession quickly dwindled to nothing. The state ticket devised in those caucuses, which was planned to be offered in the fall 1861 election, never ran. The cooperationists had set their ticket as Jacob Yerger for governor, James L. Alcorn for attorney general, S. H. Reynolds for auditor, Miles McGehee for treasurer, and Thomas Catchings for secretary of state. "It was agreed that the ticket should be announced at an early day and the canvas [sic] be begun," Alcorn remembered, "the watchword to Repeal! Repeal!" Yet by the time the fall 1861 elections rolled around, Yerger had sons in the Confederate army, Alcorn was a state brigadier general, and Miles McGehee had equipped a company of the Twentieth Mississippi Infantry and was serving as quartermaster general of all state forces. The 1861 gubernatorial election thus came down to a contest among variations of secessionists, not secessionists versus cooperationists or Unionists. The 1861 election saw Pettus run against one of his own secession commissioners, former secretary of the interior Jacob Thompson. In the 1863 election, Clark won handily over Absalom M. West and Reuben Davis, both of them former military board members. Although West was less secessionist than Davis, Clark's election still left little argument about where Mississippi stood. Clark, after all, was a former Confederate general.[22]

Yet it was from this new, single Confederacy-supporting caucus that the post-secession political culture fractured. Out of the unity against an outside threat, quasi-parties emerged among the delegates during the remainder of the convention. This development set the stage for the rest of the war and in many cases afterward. The political lines, if not parties in a fiercely antiparty state, soon coalesced around the issues of centralism versus federalism. While firmly supporting Jefferson Davis and his new government, many of the states' rights advocates in Mississippi who supported secession soon nevertheless turned their focus again to states' rights, but this time not toward the central U.S. government but to the central Confederate States government. The new lines were drawn (like elsewhere) if not heartily contested (unlike elsewhere).[23]

During both sessions of the convention, the delegates' voting and debate illustrated the concern over how much power the convention, and by extension the Confederacy, would have over state functions, including the authority of the governor and particularly the state legislature. Many delegates railed against the convention having more of a say in government than the legislature, a belief that the debates over the delegation to Montgomery, the actions of those delegates while there, and then ratification of the Confederate constitution illustrated. Members of the convention who opposed such centralism—particularly Jacob Yerger, Josiah Winchester, George Clayton, James Alcorn, Francis Rogers, Charles Fontaine, Alexander Clayton, and Samuel Gholson—spoke freely and voraciously against the convention and Confederate government taking too much power from the state. That most of those who opposed centralism, particularly the most vocal leaders such as George Clayton, Samuel Gholson, and Alexander Clayton, were firm secessionists differing from their secessionist colleagues Glenn, George, Harris, and Lamar, and siding with cooperationists Yerger, Winchester, and

Alcorn, demonstrated the fact that the old secession/cooperationist political lines had vanished.[24]

Still, the growing split in Mississippi politics during the Civil War, both in the state as well as within the larger Confederacy, was fairly tame, especially when compared to the volatile situations in states such as Tennessee, Georgia, and North Carolina. In Mississippi's neighbor to the north, Governor Isham G. Harris presided over an occupied state for most of the war, generally not even upon his own soil. In Georgia and North Carolina, fiercely states' rights and anti-Davis governors fought the Confederate government in Richmond about as hard as they fought the enemy. Dual governments in Missouri and Kentucky, especially early in the war, only added to the fascinating political events in Civil War slave states.[25]

Mississippi was never that volatile or contested. While there is no comprehensive study of Mississippi's wartime politics, the likely reasons for relative calm lay in a multitude of factors. One possible reason was the firm if slightly disjointed leadership of Governor Pettus. He was reelected in 1861 and firmly led Mississippi through its crisis period early in the war. Several other states changed leadership early in the war, thus preventing the consistency seen in Mississippi. A second reason lies in Pettus's successor, another war-supporting if calmer and more dependable governor, Charles Clark. A major Mississippi statesman, he commanded the Second Mississippi Infantry in Mexico, served in the legislature, and had been defeated for a seat in the secession convention. As a Confederate general, Clark had been wounded at Shiloh and then crippled at Baton Rouge. Healthy enough to run for office in 1863, Clark continued Mississippi's support for the war.[26]

Perhaps the biggest reason Mississippi never saw the rancor of a Georgia or North Carolina, however, was because President Jefferson Davis was a Mississippian, and Pettus and Clark, as well as the lower statesmen and citizens, would not turn on their own. While Joseph Brown of Georgia and Zebulon Vance of North Carolina made life miserable for Davis, Pettus and Clark were always firmly in his corner. Mississippi's congressmen in Montgomery and then Richmond were also firmly behind the president, one example being Davis's veto of a bill involving the Atlantic slave trade. In the vote to override the veto in congress, which failed, all of Mississippi's representatives voted as a bloc to uphold the veto. Perhaps Mississippi historian John K. Bettersworth summed up the states' rights impact best: "at least where Mississippi is concerned, beware of exaggerating the work of this evil genius in bringing about the ultimate collapse."[27]

Another potential reason for Mississippi's rather benign political culture during the war came from the Confederate unity produced in the convention itself. Beginning as a sharply divided group along secessionist or cooperationist lines, those attitudes seemed to melt away quickly after January 9. Commissioner Edmund Pettus perceived the change, writing in the midst of the January session, "as the minority of delegates made no factious opposition, so the minority of the people are not inclined to make a seditious resistance to the sovereignty of the state. Those who were opposed to changing the form of government are now, with a patriotism worthy of all honor, determined to conquer or die in defense of the rights and sovereignty of their State." It seemed that almost every Mississippian (except perhaps Flournoy and Wood) accepted the Confederacy. The landslide vote on secession in the convention and the even greater support for signing the document helped the cause.[28]

Mississippi thus remained firmly in the Confederate column, with even those opposed to secession at the beginning now firmly supporting the state's new adherence to the Confederacy, both militarily and politically. That change had been wrought in the secession convention itself, when the arguments over secession vanished and new opposing attitudes took over, forming what there was of embryonic parties in the state during the war. And those differing caucuses had secessionists and cooperationists alike on each side, further illustrating the demise of earlier sentiments.

Yet there was one other sentiment that began to take hold of the delegates as well. As the war wore on and on, they watched their state crumble around them and certainly felt a major responsibility for what was happening. Mississippians could blame the poor leadership by Northern-born generals such as John Pemberton or acutely important deaths of major commanders such as Albert Sidney Johnston, or even claim that they were being overwhelmed by Northern hordes. They quickly argued such lines of thought, those ideas collectively becoming known as the "Lost Cause" myth after the war. But there is evidence that at least some of the delegates began to look back at their own actions in shock, deciding that they had perhaps moved too fast, too far, too adamantly. Delegate Thomas Woods later recalled, "was the great prize fought for worth the unspeakable cost and loss sustained and endured by the Southern people? Looking at the practical and immediate results, the answer must be in the negative."[29]

It was perhaps Wiley Harris who was in the best position to speak for the delegates; after all, he had been the governing spirit of the convention. Reflecting on his participation in the gathering, he later noted that secession had been "fraught with the most important consequences." He went on to explain: "We overlooked the vast superiority of the North in the very resources needed in war. I should say, moreover, that we had persuaded ourselves that England and France would not tolerate a blockade." And Harris was man enough to "candidly admit that many weighty considerations were entirely disregarded or overlooked by me in an absorbing anxiety lest the movement should fail in its early stages." The result was unmistakable: Harris called secession "that most disastrous experiment."[30]

Then he went further: "After the fear that the movement would break down had subsided, I began to look more attentively at the consequences which it involved." He went on: "When the Federal forces, naval and land forces, took possession [of] the Mississippi river, from its mouth to its source, it became apparent to me that we could never have the strength to recover it, and that it would never be surrendered to us . . . without it independence was simply impossible." Harris then concluded: "the conviction came over me," he admitted, "that we had made a sad mistake."[31]

By the end of the war in 1865, the effects of that "sad mistake" were evident across the breadth of the state. All across Mississippi was devastation, broken rail lines, almost nonexistent agriculture, shattered and torn dwellings, and a nonfunctioning state government. The governor was in Federal custody, Union troops had broken up the legislature, and the courts were all but nonexistent. On top of all that, the state was occupied by the enemy, who would determine the nature of life in Mississippi for the foreseeable future.[32]

Perhaps most symbolic of the devastation and change wrought in Mississippi was the fate of the original ordinance of secession as well as the various copies made at the time of its signing. Fortunately, the original ordinance was kept safe from looting; it was, after all, a supremely important historical document. When the Federals appeared at Jackson's doorstep in May 1863 and the state government fled eastward, the secretary of state's wife, Mrs. C. A. Brougher, thought to remove the ordinance from her husband's office. She put it in her trunk for safe keeping, and quietly held on to it for nearly a decade.[33]

The other copies made for various reasons were not so fortunate. Several examples exist of Union soldiers finding them across the state as they entered Mississippi and at times marched at will across the landscape. One can well imagine the reaction when a Union soldier found a copy of the very document of secession that had started all the trouble. An Illinois soldier operating around the state capital found "a tattered, blood stained document." The soldier wrote on it: "A record of treason captured near Jackson, Mississippi." In another instance, another copy read, "This document was captured by the 7th Kansas Cavalry in Oxford, Miss., on the 10th day of August 1864." It was signed, "Compliments of Maj. Malone of the 7th Kans. Cavalry."[34]

Perhaps the latter document was L. Q. C. Lamar's personal copy of the ordinance of secession that he himself had helped craft. If so, it had symbolically come to an inglorious end, much like the state's experiment as a whole. But the effects would be far more lasting.

- Epilogue -

CONSEQUENCES

1865–1921

WHILE DEBATING THE SOUTHERN CONFEDERACY ORDINANCE IN MID-
January 1861, Jeremiah Clapp said perhaps more than he knew when he
argued for the importance of the decision about to be made. "We are now
touching chords that will vibrate throughout the world, and for coming
years," he noted, "vitally affecting not only the interests of our State and of
the South, but of this continent and the world." While the decisions made at
the Mississippi secession convention indeed had a stark effect on the state
as well as the nation, those effects continued long after the war, and in some
cases are still having an effect even today.[1]

The immediate effect of secession was a horrible war that left Mississippi
a torn and wasted land in 1865. Many of its most promising sons were gone
forever, and destruction and turmoil would define a generation. Yet Mississippians quickly began to rebuild, led into renewal in part by the very men
who had led the state into secession. Aided by a very lenient initial policy
of Reconstruction, these secession leaders quickly took pardons and began
to rebuild their lives and the state along the same racially slanted societal
construct in effect before the war. Wiley Harris told of his pardon process:
"Judge Gholson's example, a very good one, decided me to apply for a pardon." No doubt with leaders such as Gholson, Harris, James Z. George, and
others applying for pardons, many of the others followed their lead.[2]

Over the following decades, most of these secession leaders grew to
love the United States again, taking their part in its government and society. But it took time for most. While men such as John Wood, Robert
Flournoy, and James Alcorn quickly disclaimed secession and turned to the
Republican Party, the vast majority who remained Democrats felt regret

not for secession but for the results of secession. John L. Power reported, "Mr. Lamar never regretted that action, but he did more than perhaps any other member of that body to restore the ties thus temporarily severed. His memorable expression at Sumner's bier, 'If we knew each other better, we would love each other more,' was the oil that afterwards helped to smooth the troubled waters between the sections." Lamar had indeed struck a chord when, as a congressman after the war, he offered a reconciliationist eulogy at abolitionist senator Charles Sumner's funeral. For others, however, it took more time. James Z. George congratulated Lamar on his "splendid appeal for an oblivion of the past," but admitted that he had "not outlived the prejudices of the past." Even George eventually came around, however, later telling a U.S. Senate colleague, "Sir, we acknowledge no inferiority; we confess no crime; we profess no repentance; we ask no forgiveness. But we acknowledge our defeat." His stance softened even more later, when he eloquently told the Senate:

> *The world moves and we must move with it, keeping abreast with all the practical questions which may arise and seeking their solution for the interest and welfare of the people. I will not pass my life in a dreamy contemplation of the beauty and excellencies of obsolete theories, now mere abstractions, and in picturing the benefits and glories which would have come from their observance. It is enough to know that they are no longer potent for the good or evil of the Union. They are gone, gone forever, and while I may indulge a tear over the tomb in which they are reposed, I will not pass my life in erecting altars to them or in ministering at altars erected by others.*[3]

As the leaders of the secession convention returned to their leadership positions in the state, were removed under the auspices of the federal government, and then retook those positions all within the ebb and flow of Reconstruction, it is instructive to examine the continued split of later politics into various wings of the dominant Confederate/Democratic Party in Mississippi. Obviously the split between the centralists and federalists that emerged in the convention itself continued on after the war. As noted, the political fighting that occurred in the state during the war was no longer between cooperationist and secessionists, but between almost all of them combined as Confederates. While a slight few cooperationists reasserted their stances in Republican-controlled Reconstruction in the late 1860s and early 1870s, most notably Governor Alcorn and Robert Flournoy, the

Democrats again took over the state in 1875 and continued to run its affairs almost uncontested for more than a century. The divisions among the power brokers in Mississippi after 1875 were thus within the Democratic Party, most notably the "Bourbon" and "Liberal" tags applied in the late nineteenth century. Although it is difficult to define those labels and confusion reigns as to who was in what group, it is a fact that former secessionists such as Lamar, George, and Harris split with other former avid secessionists such as fellow delegate James Chalmers, secessionist newspaperman Ethelbert Barksdale, and secessionist prewar U.S. and Confederate congressman Reuben Davis. The realigning of political thought brought about in the convention continued into the postwar years.[4]

During those chaotic and racially and economically volatile years after the war, many of the delegates continued to be leaders in the state, although some simply faded off into oblivion. One even wooed the daughter of a fellow delegate; William R. Barksdale became James Z. George's son-in-law after the war. Many of the members revisited their law practices or farms and plantations, while others returned to their native states or set out westward, a few going to Texas. Wiley Harris and James Z. George partnered together and formed the state's foremost law firm in the 1870s. Several of the lawyers became judges, with David Hurst, James Z. George, and Henry Ellett serving on the state's supreme court. Others served in the state legislature, while Albert Gibson served in the Louisiana legislature and Jeremiah Clapp served in Tennessee's. Edward P. Jones made a name for himself as an inventor of farming implements and lived for a time in London. More ominously, Charles Fontaine became a major organizer of the Ku Klux Klan in Pontotoc County.[5]

A small few left a major mark on Mississippi and even the nation. Alcorn became the Republican governor of the state in the 1860s and 1870s, turning many white Democratic Mississippians against him. He also served in the U.S. Senate. Lamar went on to serve in the U.S. House and then the Senate, became Grover Cleveland's secretary of the interior, and then finished his career as a justice on the U.S. Supreme Court. James Z. George led the Democratic "redemption" of Mississippi from Republican rule in 1875, served as chief justice of the state supreme court, and then became the state's longest-serving U.S. senator to that time. Others also held prominent positions, such as James Chalmers as a U.S. representative. Many others, Harris included, returned to their law practices and plantations. Six of the delegates were members of the state's 1890 constitutional convention, including John A. Blair, Walter L. Keirn, Thomas D. Isom, Wiley P. Harris, James L. Alcorn, and

James Z. George. There, they continued to keep Mississippi segregated and African Americans in a lower class of society.[6]

Yet there were far fewer delegates alive in 1890 as age and other maladies took their toll on the membership. In fact, while thirteen of the members did not survive the war, another fourteen did not survive the 1860s. President Barry died in 1868, the results of being broken by the hardship of war: his capture at Vicksburg and wound at Allatoona. Similarly, David Glenn, Jacob Yerger, and Israel Welsh all died during the second half of the 1860s. Sadly, Walker Brooke died in 1869 by choking on an oyster at a party. The next two decades were equally fatal, with some forty-four more members dying prior to 1890. Twenty-two passed away in the 1870s, including Confederate general William Brantley, who was murdered in 1870 near Winona, and John Wood, who opposed the memory of the Confederacy and secession until he died in 1878. Reverend William Denson died in a buggy accident in 1873, immediately after preaching his last sermon before retirement. Twenty more died in the 1880s, including Alexander Clayton, Samuel Gholson, John Thornton, and Henry Ellett, the sad and eerie circumstances of Ellet's death being unparalleled. He had just given a speech introducing President Grover Cleveland in Memphis, Tennessee, and remained on the podium while Cleveland was speaking, refusing to sit down. He suddenly had an "apoplectic fit," one observer noted, "rapidly turned deathly pale, [and] dropped heavily into the chair." Ellett "gave a few gasps," but was dead within minutes. More ominously, William Tison, who rose to become Speaker of the Mississippi House of Representatives after the war, was murdered in 1882.[7]

Thus only around thirty original members were still alive when Alcorn, George, Harris, and the others reassembled at the same statehouse in 1890 for a new constitutional convention. But the 1890s saw most of them pass away as well. Harris died in 1891, Lamar in 1893, Alcorn in 1894, George in 1897, and Chalmers in 1898. Several more died in the early years of the 1900s, and Thomas Woods wrote that only Samuel Terral, Jehu Orr, Marcus Stephens, William Sumner, and himself were still alive when he wrote his history of the convention in 1902. He had actually missed Thomas Isom and Absalom Powell, but the point was taken that the delegates were thinning rapidly. In fact, only Woods, Stephens, and Orr lasted into the second decade of the century, and only Orr lived into the 1920s, dying at the age of ninety-two on March 9, 1921.[8]

Orr was the last of the members, and with him passed Mississippi's personal connection with the secession convention. Yet the original ordinance of secession lived on, thanks to the efforts of Mrs. Brougher, the

1863 secretary of state's wife. She hid the document for ten years, until the Democrats retook control of the state in 1875. At that time, she turned it over to the new secretary of state, but it was amazingly piled up with other documents and seemingly lost for decades. Only in the last years of the nineteenth century did the secretary of state find the document "in a heterogeneous mass of rubbish against the old Capitol wall, under a record cupboard." It was fortunate that the sitting secretary of state was none other than John L. Power, the reporter who had covered the convention in 1861. He obviously knew what he had found and took special care to preserve the famous piece of history. It was soon turned over to Dunbar Rowland of the new Mississippi Department of Archives and History, where it has been housed throughout Mississippi's continual attempt to climb out of the pit the document itself had dug for the state. It remains there to this day.[9]

Unfortunately, the negative racial, economic, and societal effects of "that most disastrous experiment" are still very much in residence in Mississippi as well.[10]

Most of the secession convention occurred at the Mississippi statehouse, although conflict with the meeting of the legislature caused the convention to move to the Masonic Hall at city hall for a short period. This is a postwar view of the building. (Library of Congress)

The only known rendition of the secession convention illustrates the essence of the proceedings. An undercover Northern newspaper correspondent, Albert D. Richardson, created the drawing. (Richardso *The Secret Service, the Field, the Dungeon, and the Escape*)

Jefferson Davis was a sitting U.S. senator when the convention began but resigned upon news of Mississippi's secession. He returned to his home state and was tasked by the convention to lead the state's military prior to his election as president of the Confederate States of America. (Library of Congress)

State politician and planter William S. Barry led the convention as president, wielding vast power in appointing committees and governing the proceedi He was elected a delegate to Montgomery as well, ar later served as a colonel in the Confederate army. (L Bree, *The Confederate Soldier in the Civil War*)

The face of secession, L. Q. C. Lamar was still a member of Congress when he was elected to the convention. He arrived in Jackson with a draft secession ordinance and led the process successfully. Rather quiet through the rest of the convention, he went on to become a notable politician after the war as well, serving as a senator, as a cabinet officer, and finally as a U.S. Supreme Court justice. (Library of Congress)

s L. Alcorn, the puted leader of the erationists, fought sion mainly by trying lay it, but once it was a in thing he offered his ort in a show of unity. rved the Confederacy tate militia general, but many Mississippians's ire he turned Republican the war, serving as a nstruction governor and tor. (Library of Congress)

One of the most frequent speakers at the convention, Samuel Gholson was a federal judge who brought a great deal of legal knowledge to the convention. He resigned his judgeship and eventually became a Confederate general, losing an arm in the war. (Hooker, *Confederate Military History*)

James Z. George served in several major posts during the convention, fighting continually for the common man in everything from taxes to higher military pay for privates. He later served various high-level roles in the Civil War and became a major politician afterward, leading the effort to reinstate Democratic control in the state in 1875 and as a U.S. senator. (*Memorial Addresses on the Life and Character of James Z. George*)

James R. Chalmers brought a unique background to the convention as a lawyer, planter, and militia officer. He led the convention's Military and Naval Affairs Committee and also served on the contemporary militia board that was not always in agreement with the convention's actions, Chalmers being the negotiator between the two. He served as a general in the Confederate army and was a notable politician after the war as well. (Library of Congress)

lower-level convention delegates
on to make names for themselves,
am F. Brantley serving in the
federate army and rising to the rank
igadier general during the war.
ker, *Confederate Military History*)

Samuel Benton also became a
Confederate general, but unfortunately
perished at the Battle of Atlanta in
July 1864. He was one of many who
figuratively signed their death warrants
at the convention. (Hooker, *Confederate
Military History*)

Jacob Thompson was a well-known politician prior to the war, serving as a cabinet secretary in the 1850s. Governor Pettus thus tasked him to serve as one of the important secess commissioners spreading all over th South seeking cooperation among the slave states. Thompson was the commissioner to North Carolina. (Library of Congress)

Albert D. Richardson was an undercover correspondent for the *New York Tribune* who talked his way to a seat on the very floor of the convention. He studied the delegates and later wrote a less-than-flattering account of the convention. (Richardson, *The Secret Service, the Field, the Dungeon, and the Escape*)

APPENDIX 1.
ROSTER OF DELEGATES TO THE MISSISSIPPI
SECESSION CONVENTION

ALCORN, JAMES LUSK—One of the most prominent cooperationists in the secession convention, Alcorn was born on November 4, 1816, in Illinois. He was raised in Kentucky and worked in Arkansas before moving to Coahoma County, Mississippi, where he eventually owned a plantation near Friar's Point. He had a successful career as a lawyer and politician before the Civil War, serving in the state legislature as well as on the state's levee board. By 1860 Alcorn was a very wealthy man, owning seventy-seven slaves. He represented Coahoma County in the secession convention, where he avidly fought against secession before ultimately voting for the ordinance in a show of unity. Although he was sick during the March deliberations, he later served as a brigadier general in the state militia. After the war, he served as a Republican in several political offices such as the state legislature, governor, and U.S. senator. He was also a member of the 1890 Mississippi constitutional convention. Alcorn died on December 20, 1894.[1]

ALDRIDGE, FRANCIS MARION—A native of Alabama, Aldridge was born on August 9, 1823. He later moved to Yalobusha County, Mississippi, where he became a lawyer in Coffeeville. He served in the state legislature before the Civil War, but by 1860 he had gained only modest wealth, owning five slaves. Elected as a delegate to the secession convention from Yalobusha County, Aldridge voted for one of the delaying amendments, but ultimately voted for secession. He quickly joined the Confederate army, serving as a captain in the Fifteenth Mississippi Infantry. It was in this position that he was killed on April 6, 1862, at the Battle of Shiloh.[2]

ANDERSON, WARREN P.—Anderson was born in Tennessee around 1820. He later moved to Jackson, Mississippi, where he became a noted lawyer. He served in the state legislature in the antebellum years, and became a man of modest means, owning eight slaves in 1860. As a delegate to the secession convention from Hinds County, he was a strict secessionist. Anderson was too old to join the Confederate army, yet he became the first member of the convention to die, passing from an illness on September 12, 1861, in Bladen Springs, Alabama.[3]

BACKSTROM, DAVID M.—A native of South Carolina, Backstrom was born on April 20, 1812. He eventually settled in Neshoba County, Mississippi, working a farm around Philadelphia with sixteen slaves in 1860. He represented Neshoba County in the secession convention, where he was a staunch secessionist. He was too old to fight in the Civil War, but continued farming after the war. He died at his home on September 24, 1876.[4]

BALDWIN, CYRUS BRISCOE—Baldwin was a native of Virginia, having been born on March 3, 1821. He was a newspaper editor in Staunton and Lexington before moving to similar posts in Tuscaloosa and Livingston, Alabama. Eventually he settled in Houston, Mississippi, where he practiced law. Baldwin also served in the Mississippi legislature. He was a wealthy individual, owning fifty-six slaves in 1860. Representing Chickasaw County at the secession convention, he was a staunch secessionist and joined the Confederate army, serving as a lieutenant in the Thirty-First Mississippi Infantry. He did not survive the war, however, dying of disease on June 26, 1862, near Okolona, Mississippi.[5]

BARKSDALE, WILLIAM RUSSELL—A native of Alabama, Barksdale was born on April 26, 1834. As an infant, he moved with his parents to Yalobusha County, Mississippi, where he grew up. He graduated from the University of Mississippi and also obtained a law license. He later practiced law in Grenada. Barksdale owned no slaves, and representing Yalobusha County in the secession convention, he voted for one of the delaying amendments to secession, although he later voted for the ordinance itself. During the Civil War, he served in the Confederate army, primarily as a staff officer to Winfield S. Featherston and Edward C. Walthall. He was wounded in action at Franklin, Tennessee, in November 1864. After the war, Barksdale returned to law, serving as a district attorney as well as in the Mississippi state legislature. He married fellow convention delegate James Z. George's daughter, but died on January 10, 1877, in Grenada.[6]

BARRY, WILLIAM TAYLOR SULLIVAN—Born in Columbus, Mississippi, on December 10, 1821, Barry was educated at Yale University and returned to

Lowndes County, Mississippi, to practice law and farm. By 1860 he owned only seven slaves, but had made a name for himself in politics, having served numerous terms in the state legislature and rising to the position of Speaker of the house. He also served in the U.S. Congress prior to the war. Representing Lowndes County in the secession convention, Barry became its president. He was a staunch supporter of secession and the Confederacy, later serving as one of Mississippi's delegates to the Montgomery convention in February 1861 and being elected to serve in the Confederate congress. He resigned that position and joined the Confederate army, serving first as a staff officer for Charles Clark and then raising the Thirty-Fifth Mississippi Infantry. He led it, and at times the brigade to which it was assigned, through the war, and was captured at Vicksburg in July 1863, wounded at Allatoona in October 1864, and captured again near Mobile in the final days of the war. The war broke Barry's health, and he was sick for the next few years, dying on January 29, 1868.[7]

BEENE, RUSSELL O.—Born about 1816 in Tennessee, Beene eventually moved to Itawamba County, Mississippi, settling near Baldwin. He practiced law, served in the state legislature, and also dabbled in planting, owning eight slaves in 1860. Representing Itawamba County in the secession convention, Beene favored a delay in secession, voting for two of the delaying amendments. In the end, he voted for secession. Too old to serve in the Confederate army, Beene practiced law after the war. He apparently died in the 1870s.[8]

BENTON, SAMUEL—A nephew of Senator Thomas Hart Benton and native of Missouri, Benton was born on October 18, 1820. He later moved to Holly Springs, Mississippi, where he taught and practiced law. He also entered politics, representing Marshall County in the state legislature and the secession convention. He owned no slaves and had only modest wealth, but soon became a high-ranking Confederate officer. Benton missed the March session of the convention because he had joined the army. He served in the Ninth Mississippi Infantry before becoming colonel of the Thirty-Fourth Mississippi Infantry. He led a Mississippi brigade in the Atlanta campaign, and was mortally wounded at the Battle of Atlanta on July 22, 1864. He died on July 28, having been confirmed as a Confederate brigadier general two days earlier.[9]

BERRY, JOEL HALBERT—Born in South Carolina in 1808, Berry grew to manhood in that state, serving in the state legislature. In 1843 he migrated to

Tippah County, Mississippi, near Claysville, where he became a planter with twenty-six slaves in 1860. He also served in the Mississippi legislature, both in the house and senate. As a delegate to the secession convention from Tippah County, Berry was a strong secessionist and supporter of the Confederacy, but he was too old to serve in the military. He engaged in planting after the war before dying on March 22, 1875.[10]

BLAIR, JOHN ALAN—Born in Tennessee on August 23, 1835, Blair moved as a boy with his parents to Tippah County, Mississippi. He attended the University of Mississippi, graduating in 1860, and became a lawyer at Jacinto in Tishomingo County immediately preceding the Civil War. He had little time to make a fortune or dabble in slave owning before the war, but he was still prominent enough to be elected to represent the county in the secession convention. There, he was a staunch cooperationist. He voted to delay secession and then against the ordinance itself. Nevertheless he joined the Confederate army when Mississippi left the Union. He rose to the rank of lieutenant colonel in the Second Mississippi Infantry, often commanding the regiment in battle. He was wounded at First Manassas and Weldon Railroad. He was also taken prisoner of war twice, the first time at Gettysburg in the famous railroad cut. He spent his prison time at Johnson's Island before being exchanged, but was captured again at the end of the war at Hatcher's Run. After the war, he became a prominent political leader, serving as a lawyer, as district attorney, as a state legislator, and in the 1890 Mississippi constitutional convention. He died at Tupelo on November 1, 1898.[11]

BOLLING, WILLIAM S.—Born in Virginia around 1805, Bolling later migrated to Winston County, Mississippi, where he practiced law in Louisville. He apparently focused entirely on the law because he owned no slaves in 1860. He represented Winston County in the secession convention, and voted strictly secessionist. Too old to join the Confederate ranks, Bolling nevertheless supported the cause and collected guns for the army. After the war, he served as mayor of Louisville. He apparently died before 1870.[12]

BONDS, WRIGHT W.—Born in Tennessee around 1814, Bonds later moved to Tishomingo County, Mississippi, where he served in county government, most notably as circuit clerk at Jacinto. He held only modest wealth and no slaves, but represented the county in the secession convention in 1861. He was an avid cooperationist, voting for all the delaying amendments and against secession itself. When war came, he signed up for service in the Second Mississippi Infantry despite his age of forty-seven. Apparently, though, he never mustered fully into service. He gave a son to the war effort, however, killed at Gettysburg. Bonds served in the state legislature during the war, but died on August 20, 1862.[13]

BOOKTER, THOMAS C.—Born in South Carolina around 1835, Bookter migrated westward to Oktibbeha County, Mississippi. He was a small planter near Starkville, owning nineteen slaves in 1860. Representing Oktibbeha County in the secession convention, Bookter consistently voted secessionist. He soon joined the Confederate army, serving as a captain of Bookter's independent cavalry company, which later became part of the Eleventh Mississippi Cavalry. He was captured in February 1864 during the Meridian campaign and imprisoned at Fort Delaware. After the war, he moved to Tunica County, where he continued his agricultural pursuits. He apparently died in the 1870s.[14]

BOOTH, WILLIAM—Born on January 17, 1803, in New York, Booth moved as a child to Mississippi. He lived in various places, including Port Gibson and in Madison County before settling in Carroll County in 1835. Booth was a well-known politician in Carroll County, serving as sheriff as well as in the state senate. He also owned immense plantations with ninety-two slaves in 1860. He represented Carroll County at the secession convention, where he voted at all times for immediate secession. Too old to serve in the military, Booth continued his agricultural pursuits after the war, dying on May 8, 1875.[15]

BRANTLEY, WILLIAM FELIX—Born in Alabama on March 12, 1830, Brantley moved to Choctaw County, Mississippi, as a child. He practiced law in Greensboro before the Civil War, and also dabbled in planting, owning twenty-one slaves in 1860. He represented Choctaw County in the secession convention, and was a firm supporter of leaving the Union. He quickly entered the Confederate service, becoming a captain in the Fifteenth Mississippi Infantry and then colonel of the Twenty-Ninth Mississippi Infantry, serving in fellow secession convention delegate Samuel Benton's brigade in the Army of Tennessee. Upon Benton's death at Atlanta, Brantley became a brigadier general and fought the remainder of the war. After the war, he returned to his law practice in Greensboro, but was murdered near Winona, Mississippi, on November 2, 1870.[16]

BROOKE, WALKER—One of the most prominent anti-secessionists in the convention, Brooke was born in Virginia on December 25, 1813. He graduated from the University of Virginia in 1835 and taught school in Kentucky before moving to Lexington, Mississippi, to practice law. An avid Whig, he served in both houses of the state legislature as well as in the U.S. Senate before the Civil War. By 1860 he owned five slaves and lived in Vicksburg, representing Warren County in the secession convention. He was one of the most outspoken cooperationists, offering the amendment to delay secession by requiring it pass a popular vote, but ultimately voted for secession in a show of unity. Although he was too old to fight for the Confederacy, he was one of Mississippi's delegates to the Montgomery convention in February 1861. He served a year as a provisional member of the Confederate congress, but was defeated for a regular Confederate senate seat by James Phelan. Thereafter he was a part of the Confederate judicial system. After the war, Brooke returned to his law practice, but died at Vicksburg shortly thereafter on February 19, 1869, from accidentally choking on an oyster.[17]

BULLARD, ARTHUR B.—Born in Tennessee around 1822, Bullard later moved to Fulton in Itawamba County, Mississippi. There, he served as a Cumberland Presbyterian minister. He also owned land and eleven slaves, and gathered a modest wealth before the war. As a delegate to the secession convention from Itawamba County, Bullard was a staunch cooperationist and voted for all delaying amendments and against secession. Although too old to serve in the Confederate army, he nevertheless outfitted a local company and was appointed by Jefferson Davis, and confirmed by the Confederate senate, as an assistant quartermaster with the rank of captain. Bullard continued his ministry throughout and after the war, but died soon after the close of hostilities, in 1867.[18]

CATCHING, PHILIP S.—Born in Mississippi on November 14, 1816, Catching was a prominent antebellum official in Copiah County. He also worked a plantation near Georgetown, owning forty-four slaves in 1860. Prior to the Civil War, he served in the Mississippi senate, a position he also held during the secession convention of 1861, in which he represented Copiah County. He was an avid secessionist at the convention, and continued to serve in the legislature during the war. He served as the quartermaster for a camp of instruction at Brookhaven early in the war. After the war, he continued his planting operations before dying on March 30, 1874.[19]

CHALMERS, JAMES RONALD—Born in Virginia on January 11, 1831, Chalmers would become the most famous Confederate general to have served in the Mississippi secession convention. He attended college in South Carolina before beginning a law practice in Holly Springs, Mississippi, where he also served as district attorney. He also engaged in planting in DeSoto County near Hernando, and he owned forty-four slaves in 1860. Chalmers was a firm supporter of secession as a delegate from DeSoto County, and was such a supporter of the Confederacy that he skipped the March session of the convention because he was already in the army. He soon became colonel of the Ninth Mississippi Infantry, and became a brigadier general in February 1862. He led an infantry brigade at Shiloh and the other 1862 battles before taking command of cavalry in his native Mississippi. After the war, Chalmers made a name for himself in politics, serving in the Mississippi senate and as a representative from Mississippi in the U.S. Congress. He also practiced law in Memphis, Tennessee, until his death on April 9, 1898.[20]

CLAPP, JEREMIAH WATKINS—Born in Virginia on September 24, 1814, Clapp joined the Virginia bar but moved to Mississippi in 1841, taking up law practice and planting ventures in Holly Springs. He became rich in both, owning thirty-four slaves in 1860. Prior to the Civil War, he served in the Mississippi legislature, and represented Marshall County at the secession convention, where he was a firm secessionist. Too old to join the Confederate military, Clapp served in the Confederate congress and later as a government cotton agent. After the war, he moved to Memphis, Tennessee, where he practiced law. He also served in the Tennessee legislature. Clapp died at Memphis on September 5, 1898.[21]

CLAYTON, ALEXANDER MOSBY—Perhaps the most accomplished legal mind of the convention, Clayton was born in Virginia on January 15, 1801. He joined the Virginia bar at Fredericksburg and practiced law in Virginia, Tennessee, and Arkansas, where he was a federal judge, before moving to Mississippi in 1837. He practiced law in Holly Springs and owned a nearby plantation at Lamar, ultimately acquiring 140 slaves by 1860. Clayton rose to the top of the legal profession in Mississippi, ultimately taking a seat on the state's supreme court, known then as the High Court of Errors and Appeals. Later, he was the United States' consul to Havana, at the appointment of President Franklin Pierce. Clayton was a strict secessionist, having been part of the earlier 1850–1851 secession movement as well as a Democratic delegate to the stormy 1860 conventions. Representing Marshall County in the secession convention, Clayton was very pro-secession and authored the explanation of causes for secession passed by the convention. Clayton was far too old to take the field, but he was one of Mississippi's delegates to the Montgomery convention. He later served as a Confederate judge, which caused some resentment from his fellow convention delegate Samuel J. Gholson, who had been a sitting U.S. federal judge before the war. After the war, Clayton served as a circuit judge as well as the president of the board of trustees for the University of Mississippi. After retirement, he lived at his plantation near Lamar until he died on September 30, 1889.[22]

CLAYTON, GEORGE R.—Born on October 6, 1808, in Georgia, Clayton grew to manhood there, graduating from the University of Georgia and beginning a law practice and serving in the Georgia legislature. He moved to Columbus, Mississippi, in 1836, and practiced law and engaged in planting, owning thirteen slaves by 1860. He was a firm supporter of secession at the 1861 convention, representing Lowndes County. Too old to participate in the war, Clayton returned to his law career after the war but died in Athens, Georgia, on April 23, 1867.[23]

COLBERT, WALLACE BRUCE—Born on November 17, 1834, in Mississippi, Colbert became a lawyer and farmer near Carthage in Leake County. He owned no slaves and had little personal wealth, but he was an avid secessionist and Confederate supporter. He represented Leake County in the convention and then went directly to war, climbing the ranks in the Twenty-Seventh Mississippi Infantry before becoming colonel of the Fortieth Mississippi Infantry in May 1862. Colbert often led the brigade to which he was assigned, and was captured at Vicksburg in July 1863 and wounded at Franklin, Tennessee, in November 1864. He returned from his wound in time to take part in the Battle of Bentonville in North Carolina on March 21, 1865, during which he was killed in action.[24]

CUMMINGS, MALACHAI CRAWFORD—Born in Alabama on August 17, 1810, Cummings migrated to Itawamba County, Mississippi, settling near Fulton. He became a prominent judge and planter, owning fifty-eight slaves in 1860. He also served in the state legislature before the war. Cummings was a dedicated cooperationist as a delegate to the secession convention from Itawamba County, voting for all three amendments to delay secession and then against the final ordinance. He nevertheless supported the Confederate cause, despite his age, by equipping what became Company F of the Twenty-Fourth Mississippi Infantry. He also served in the state legislature during the war. After the conflict ended, he returned to planting, dying on April 28, 1895.[25]

DAVIS, JAMES SHELTON—Born in Alabama on March 24, 1819, Davis lived in several Alabama communities, working in stores and doctors' offices preliminary to graduating from the Jefferson Medical College in Philadelphia, Pennsylvania. He eventually moved to Marshall County and then to Salem in Tippah County, Mississippi, where he practiced medicine. He gained a modest wealth, owning only two slaves by 1860, but was nevertheless a solid part of the community. He was elected to represent Tippah County at the secession convention, where he was a firm supporter of leaving the Union. During the war, Davis served the Confederacy as a surgeon. After the war, he moved to Iuka, Mississippi, where he edited the *Iuka Springs Gazette*. He died at Iuka on November 29, 1879.[27]

DAVIS, ORLANDO—Born on September 13, 1813, in Tennessee, Davis later moved to Ripley in Tippah County, Mississippi, where he became a prominent lawyer and planter, owning thirteen slaves in 1860. He represented Tippah County in the secession convention, where he was an eager supporter of secession. Davis was too old to serve in the Confederate army, but nevertheless supported the Confederacy. After the war, he returned to the law, this time in Holly Springs, serving as a judge for many years. He had one of the best law libraries in the state and was for many years president of the Bank of Holly Springs. He died on August 4, 1898.[26]

DEASE, OLIVER C.—Born in Mississippi around 1806, Dease became a prominent newspaper editor at Paulding. He also served in the state legislature prior to the Civil War, and dabbled in farming, owning five slaves in 1860. Representing Jasper County in the secession convention, Dease voted consistently secessionist. Too old to join the war effort, he continued his farming operations after the conflict ended. He apparently died prior to 1900.[28]

DEASON, JOHN B.—Born in Kentucky on July 1, 1824, Deason moved to the Mississippi Gulf Coast and became a lawyer in Hancock County at Gainesville. He served in the state militia as well as in the Mexican War, at the rank of captain, in the Second Mississippi Infantry. Deason represented Hancock

County in the secession convention in 1861, where he was a die-hard secessionist. He quickly entered the Confederate army, serving first as a captain in and then as colonel of the Third Mississippi Infantry until its reorganization in March 1862, at which time he was not reelected. He later served in the state militia, in the Third Battalion Mississippi Cavalry Reserves. After the war, Deason returned to his law practice, serving as a district attorney and judge in Brookhaven. He was also a member of the state legislature. Deason died in Hattiesburg, Mississippi, on March 29, 1900.[29]

DENSON, WILLIAM—Born on August 9, 1800, in Tennessee, Denson later moved to Alabama before migrating to Rankin County, Mississippi, settling at Denson Landing on the Pearl River in 1828. There, he served as a Baptist minister and state legislator. He also had some agricultural pursuits, owning a farm near Sand Hill and owning seven slaves in 1860. Denson represented Rankin County in the secession convention, where he voted twice to delay secession but ultimately voted in support of Mississippi leaving the Union. Far too old to serve in the Confederate military, Denson continued his ministry throughout and after the war. He lived on the path of William T. Sherman's march to Meridian in 1864 and painted a Masonic symbol on his door, and he was not bothered. He died in a buggy accident on October 8, 1873, immediately after preaching his last sermon before retirement.[30]

DOUGLAS, WILLIAM J.—Born in Pennsylvania around 1823, Douglas later moved to Simpson County, Mississippi, working as a mechanic and saddler at West Point. He also dabbled in farming, owning three slaves in 1860. Douglas represented Simpson County in the secession convention and voted consistently secessionist. He soon joined the Confederate army, first serving as a lieutenant in the Sixteenth Mississippi Infantry until he was relieved of his command in the reorganization in April 1862. He later served as a private in the Thirty-Ninth Mississippi Infantry as well. Douglas apparently died prior to 1870.[31]

DYER, JAMES M.—Born in Tennessee on February 17, 1816, Dyer later moved to Holmes County, Mississippi, where he practiced law at Lexington. He also had some farming pursuits despite owning no slaves. The people of Holmes County elected him to represent them at the secession convention, where he voted for one of the delaying amendments before voting for secession itself. Although not in the Confederate military, Dyer served in the state legislature during the Civil War, and afterward returned to his planting and law practice. He died on March 31, 1871.[32]

ECKFORD, WILLIAM J.—Born in Alabama around 1831, Eckford later moved to Wayne County, Mississippi, and became a planter near Waynesboro. He represented Wayne County in the secession convention, where he voted strictly secessionist. Afterward he joined the Confederate army, and rose to the rank of captain in the Thirteenth Mississippi Infantry, which served in Virginia. He was killed in action on July 1, 1862, at the Battle of Malvern Hill.[33]

EDWARDS, JAMES H.—Born on February 21, 1817, in Alabama, Edwards later moved to Choctaw County, Mississippi, settling near the Oktibbeha County line. He owned a plantation that worked twenty-five slaves in 1860 and gained him some wealth. Edwards represented Choctaw County in the secession convention, where he was a dedicated secessionist. Past military age, Edwards served in the Mississippi legislature during the war, and continued his agricultural pursuits afterward. He died on January 3, 1885.[34]

ELLETT, HENRY THOMAS—Ellett was born in New Jersey on March 8, 1812, where he attended Princeton University and began a law career. He moved to Port Gibson, Mississippi, in 1837 and opened a law practice there. Ellett won a special election in 1846 to fill the U.S. House of Representatives seat vacated by Jefferson Davis, and served the remainder of the term. He did not run for reelection, but returned to his law practice. Ellett also served in the state legislature, and ran a plantation, which worked seventeen slaves in 1860. Representing Claiborne County in the secession convention, he was a die-hard secessionist, although he missed the March session of the convention. Upon the creation of the Confederate government, Jefferson Davis offered him the Confederate postmaster position, but he declined. Too old to serve in the ranks, he continued serving in the legislature during the war. After the fighting ended, Ellett continued his law practice, and served several years on the state's highest court, the High Court of Errors and Appeals. He then moved to Memphis, Tennessee, in 1868 and practiced law there, also serving in low-level political positions. He died on October 15, 1887, in Memphis immediately after giving a welcoming speech for President Grover Cleveland.[35]

FARRAR, ALEXANDER KING—Born in Mississippi on December 2, 1814, Farrar was one of the largest plantation owners in the secession convention in which he represented Adams County. His huge estate in Adams County, near Natchez, worked 238 slaves in 1860 and made him extremely wealthy. In addition to planting, Farrar also served in both houses of the state legislature prior to the Civil War. Realizing that war would disrupt his planting operations and the trade markets, he voted across the board as a cooperationist. He nevertheless supported the Confederacy, serving as the Confederate provost marshal of Natchez during the war. After the war, Farrar returned to planting, and died on May 29, 1878.[36]

FIZER, JOHN B.—Born in Tennessee on January 21, 1806, Fizer moved to Panola County, Mississippi, by way of Dyersburg, Tennessee. He became a well-known planter in the area, working thirty-six slaves in 1860 and gaining a substantial fortune. Representing Panola County in the secession convention, Fizer was a strict secessionist, and while too old to serve the Confederacy, he sent his nephew, whom he had raised, Confederate colonel and presumed general John C. Fizer. After the war, Fizer returned to his roots in Robertson County, Tennessee, where he died on August 15, 1871.[37]

FLOURNOY, ROBERT W.—Born in Georgia around 1812, Flournoy later settled in Pontotoc County, Mississippi, near New Albany. He was a lawyer by trade but also farmed, owning sixty-six slaves in 1860 and possessing some wealth. He represented Pontotoc County in the secession convention, and voted twice to delay secession and then against the actual ordinance. However, he changed his vote for the sake of unanimity. Flournoy joined the Confederate army and became a captain in the Twenty-First Mississippi infantry, but resigned in July 1861 due to infirmity. Other sources indicate that he decided he could not fight against the Union. After the war, Flournoy practiced law and edited a newspaper, but received the most attention for becoming a Republican in a thoroughly white Democratic state. That put him at great odds with most former Confederates, and helps explain the cooperationist stand he took at the convention and in the war. He died on October 24, 1894.[38]

FONTAINE, CHARLES D.—A great-grandson of Patrick Henry, Fontaine was born in Virginia on December 28, 1817. He moved to Pontotoc County, Mississippi, as a young adult and began the practice of law after studying under Jacob Thompson, later secretary of the interior. He also became involved in politics, serving in the state legislature before the Civil War and was an unsuccessful candidate for governor in 1855, being defeated by John J. McRae by a mere 5,000 votes. He also dabbled in farming, owning four slaves. Fontaine represented Pontotoc County in the secession convention and was a strict secessionist. During the war, he became a lieutenant in the Second

Mississippi Infantry before resigning due to sickness in October 1861. For the rest of the war, he served as a recruiting officer. Afterward, he continued his law practice and became a well-known member of the Ku Klux Klan. He died in Pontotoc in August 1871.[39]

GEORGE, JAMES ZACHARIAH—Born in Georgia on October 20, 1826, George would later become one of the most prominent alumni of the Mississippi secession convention. He moved to Mississippi with his mother and stepfather in 1834, first to Noxubee County and then on to Carroll County, where he grew to manhood. He fought in Jefferson Davis's Mexican War regiment and later joined the bar, studying under Carrollton lawyer William Cothran. Before the Civil War, George became a noted lawyer as well as court reporter for the High Court of Errors and Appeals, the state's highest court, in Jackson. He also owned a great deal of land and worked sixty-five slaves in 1860. Representing Carroll County in the convention, George was an avid secessionist, and quickly joined the Confederate army when the war began. He served as a captain in the Twentieth Mississippi Infantry in Virginia and at Fort Donelson, where he was captured in February 1862. Upon his exchange from custody at Johnson's Island, George served as a brigadier general of Mississippi militia, and then organized and became colonel of the Fifth Mississippi Cavalry. He was again captured in the regiment's first battle, at Collierville, Tennessee, in November 1863. He spent the rest of the war at Johnson's Island. After the war, George returned to his law practice, but became involved in politics, leading the effort to overthrow Republican rule in Mississippi in 1875. He was rewarded with a position on the state's supreme court, where he became chief justice, and later was elected to the U.S. Senate in 1880. He remained in that position until his death on August 14, 1897.[40]

GHOLSON, SAMUEL JAMESON—Born in Kentucky on May 19, 1808, Gholson moved to Alabama, where he obtained a law practice. He eventually settled in Aberdeen, Mississippi, where he also practiced law. Gholson quickly became very prominent prior to the Civil War, serving in the state legislature as well as two terms in the U.S. Congress and eventually as a U.S. district judge. He was also a substantial planter, owning ninety slaves in 1860 and becoming quite rich. Representing Monroe County in the secession convention, he was a firm secessionist and soon joined the Confederate war effort. He joined the Forty-Third Mississippi Infantry and was wounded at Corinth in October 1862. In May 1864 he became a brigadier general, serving mostly on cavalry duty in Mississippi under fellow convention delegate James R. Chalmers. It was in that capacity that he was wounded at the small fight at Egypt, Mississippi, losing an arm. After the war, Gholson served in the state legislature on two occasions. He died on October 16, 1883.[41]

GIBSON, ALBERT C.—Born in Mississippi around 1828, Gibson became a wealthy planter in Issaqueena County, near Skipwith's Landing. He owned a large plantation and worked eighty-seven slaves in 1860. Gibson represented Issaqueena County in the secession convention, where he voted as a straight-line secessionist. When the war began, he joined the Confederate army, serving as a lieutenant in the Issaqueena Artillery, and was captured at Fort Donelson and sent to Johnson's Island. After the war, Gibson moved across the Mississippi River to Madison Parish, Louisiana, and served in the Louisiana legislature in the 1880s. He died in 1892.[42]

GLENN, DAVID CHALMERS—Born in North Carolina around 1824, Glenn was taken to Mississippi as a teenager. He grew up in Holly Springs, studied law, and moved to Jackson. He served two terms as Mississippi's attorney general prior to the Civil War, being first elected at the young age of twenty-five. Afterward, he opened a law practice in Harrison County at Mississippi City. He represented Harrison County in the secession convention, where he played a major role and voted strictly secessionist. During the war, Glenn served in the First Mississippi Infantry and later declined a commission in the Thirty-Fourth Mississippi Infantry. He then served as a judge in A. P. Hill's corps of the Army of Northern Virginia, with the rank of colonel. After the fighting ended, Glenn returned to his law practice. He died on September 19, 1868.[43]

GWIN, WILLIAM—Born in Tennessee on February 27, 1810, Gwin later moved to Lawrence County, Mississippi, where he farmed near Boguechitto. Although of very little financial means, he was nevertheless elected to represent Lawrence County in the secession convention, where he voted completely for secession. He was too old to serve in the ranks, but lost two sons in the Confederate army. After the war, Gwin continued his farming operations. He died on January 15, 1888.[44]

HARRIS, WILEY POPE—Probably the most respected member of the convention, Harris was born in Mississippi on November 9, 1818. After studying law at the University of Virginia and in Kentucky, he became one of the foremost lawyers in the state, practicing in Jackson. Prior to the Civil War, he also served as a circuit judge, in the U.S. Congress, and as a member of the 1851 convention. Representing Hinds County in the secession convention, Harris was regarded as the elder statesman in the group and consistently voted for secession. He was one of Mississippi's delegates to the Montgomery convention, where he played a major role in drafting that constitution. He also served in the Confederate congress, being too old to serve in the ranks. After the war, Harris was involved in Reconstruction politics and formed the foremost law partnership in the state with fellow convention delegate James Z. George. He was also a member of the 1890 constitutional convention, and died on December 3, 1891.[45]

HERRING, JOHN B.—Born in Georgia on December 3, 1828, Herring later moved to Pontotoc County, Mississippi, where he farmed near Cherry Creek. He represented Pontotoc County in the secession convention and voted for all three delaying amendments, but ultimately voted for secession itself. After joining the Confederate army, he rose through the ranks of the Fifth Mississippi Infantry, ending the war as lieutenant colonel of the regiment. He was wounded in 1865. After the war, he farmed in Pontotoc County before moving to Crockett's Bluff in Arkansas County, Arkansas, where he died on August 26, 1882.[46]

HILL, ALBERT POTTS—Brother of Confederate general Daniel H. Hill, Albert P. Hill was born in South Carolina on February 15, 1819, and graduated from the University of South Carolina in 1837. He later moved to Canton in Madison County, Mississippi, where he became a lawyer, editor, and farmer, owning eighteen slaves in 1860. He had earlier served in the Mexican War. Representing Madison County in the secession convention, Hill was a firm advocate of leaving the Union. Upon entering Confederate service, he rose to captain in the Eighteenth Mississippi Infantry. He was wounded at Ball's Bluff and eventually resigned in April 1862. He was also elected colonel of a militia regiment but declined the commission. Thereafter, Hill served as a captain in Wirt Adams's cavalry regiment before becoming a colonel in the judicial branch of James Longstreet's corps of the Army of Northern Virginia. He also ran for the Confederate congress, but was not successful. After the war, Hill returned to his law practice, but died on October 15, 1868.[47]

HOLT, ALFRED C.—Born in Georgia around 1820, Holt moved to Mississippi and became a physician and planter near Woodville in Wilkinson County.

He owned six slaves in 1860. Representing Wilkinson County at the secession convention, Holt voted consistently for secession, and after war came, served as a surgeon in the Confederate army. After the war, he moved to New Orleans, where he practiced medicine. Holt died on October 12, 1881.[48]

HURST, DAVID WILEY—Born in Mississippi on July 10, 1819, Hurst became a lawyer at Liberty in Amite County before the Civil War. He also served in the Mississippi state legislature and dabbled in farming, owning nine slaves in 1860. Representing Amite County in the secession convention, Hurst voted cooperationist across the board. He immediately joined the Confederate army, however, and rose to command the Thirty-Third Mississippi Infantry as its colonel. He was wounded at Corinth in October 1862, and resigned in January 1864 to take a position as a member of the High Court of Errors and Appeals, the state's highest court. After the war, Hurst continued to serve on the high court, and as a lawyer. He died on July 10, 1882.[49]

ISOM, THOMAS DUDLEY—Born in Tennessee on September 5, 1816, Isom later moved to Oxford, Mississippi, where he practiced medicine. He was also a planter, owning twenty-nine slaves in 1860. Representing Lafayette County in the secession convention, Isom was a mild cooperationist, voting for one of the delaying amendments before voting for secession. He soon joined the army, serving as a surgeon in the Seventeenth Mississippi Infantry, but he had to resign in September 1861. After the war, Isom continued his medical practice, and was a member of the 1890 Mississippi constitutional convention. He died at Oxford on May 4, 1902.[50]

JOHNSTON, JAMES STEPTOE—A first cousin of Confederate general Joseph E. Johnston and born in Virginia on January 24, 1808, Johnston practiced law in Virginia before removing to Hinds County, Mississippi, where he continued his law practice. He served for a time as district attorney, but left his law career and became a planter in Jefferson County, near Church Hill. By 1860 Johnston owned and worked seventy-five slaves and had become very rich. Elected to represent Jefferson County in the secession convention, Johnston was a pure secessionist. Too old to fight in the war, he continued his planting activities after the conflict. He died on September 19, 1895.[51]

JOHNSTON, STEPHEN DARDEN—Born on February 6, 1812, in Georgia, Johnston later moved to DeSoto County, Mississippi, where he was a large planter, owning fifty-five slaves in 1860. Prior to the Civil War, he also became involved in politics, serving on the county board of police as well as in the state legislature. Johnston represented DeSoto County at the secession convention, where he voted for one of the delaying amendments before voting for secession itself. He was too old to join the Confederate ranks, and in fact died during the war, on August 21, 1863, apparently by falling from his horse while fleeing Federal troops.[52]

JONES, EDWARD PUGH—Born in North Carolina around 1824, Jones later removed to Sunflower County, Mississippi, near Shell Mound, and became a planter. He also served in the state legislature. Representing Sunflower County at the secession convention, Jones voted for secession. He had an active record during the war itself, serving as lieutenant colonel of the Twenty-Eighth Mississippi Cavalry. He was wounded near Franklin, Tennessee, on April 10, 1863, and became a prisoner of war. After exchange, he also served in the state legislature during the war. After the fighting ended, Jones returned to planting and became an inventor, even living in London for a time. His patents had to do with braking systems for wagons and carriages and other mechanical items. He died on April 1, 1876.[53]

KEIRN, WALTER LEAKE—Born in Mississippi on May 4, 1830, Keirn was one of the largest planters and slave owners in the secession convention. He owned 211 slaves in 1860 and was very rich. He also served as a physician in Lexington, Mississippi. Representing Holmes County in the secession convention, he voted entirely secessionist and quickly joined the Confederate army. He became lieutenant colonel of the Thirty-Eighth Mississippi Infantry and was wounded in action at Corinth. He later resigned in August 1864. After the war, Keirn returned to his planting activities, but also became involved in politics. He served in the state legislature as well as in the 1890 constitutional convention. He died on January 5, 1901.[54]

KEITH, MARSHALL M.—Born in Virginia around 1807, Keith later moved to Mississippi, where he became a physician in Decatur. He also served in the state legislature prior to the Civil War. As a delegate to the secession convention from Newton County, Keith voted the secessionist line. He was too old to join the war effort, and continued his medical practice after the war. Keith died in 1883.[55]

KENNEDY, JOHN—Born in South Carolina around 1817, Kennedy later moved to Winston County, Mississippi, operating a large plantation near

New Prospect. He owned fifty-four slaves in 1860. Representing Winston County in the secession convention, Kennedy voted consistently secessionist. He joined the Confederate army during the war, serving as a lieutenant in the Eleventh Mississippi Cavalry. He moved to Grayson County, Texas, in the 1870s, where he farmed. His date of death is unknown.[56]

KING, BENJAMIN—Born in 1822 in Mississippi, King became a lawyer in Copiah County. He also became involved in planting near Gallatin, but owned only two slaves in 1860. He represented Copiah County at the secession convention, where he voted as a strict secessionist. During the war, King became colonel of the First Mississippi Infantry State Troops. After the war, he served in the state senate, and was a candidate for governor in 1882, but Robert Lowry defeated him. He died in 1884.[57]

LAMAR, LUCIUS QUINTUS CINCINATUS—Probably the most notable of all the secession convention delegates, Lamar was a native of Georgia, born on September 17, 1825. He graduated from Emory University and joined the bar in his native state as well as engaged in planting, and he even served in the Georgia legislature. He moved to Oxford, Mississippi, in 1849, and joined the faculty of the University of Mississippi, where his father-in-law was the chancellor. He also had other interests, including planting, owning thirty-one slaves in 1860. Lamar served in the U.S. Congress, holding his seat during the chaotic secession crisis. Representing Lafayette County at the secession convention, he was the leader of the secessionists, arriving with an ordinance already written and chairing the committee of fifteen that proposed the final version. He soon joined the Confederate army, rising to the rank of colonel of the Nineteenth Mississippi Infantry. When poor health ended his active career, he became the Confederacy's minister to Russia and later a judge in A. P. Hill's corps in the Army of Northern Virginia. After the war, Lamar became a distinguished statesman, returning to his law practice and professorial duties before entering the political realm again. He was active in Mississippi's overthrow of Republican rule, served in both houses of the U.S. Congress, became Grover Cleveland's secretary of the interior, and then finished his career on the U.S. Supreme Court. He died while a member of the court on January 23, 1893.[58]

LEA, WILLIS M.—Born in North Carolina on November 5, 1802, Lea graduated from the University of North Carolina and studied medicine in Philadelphia, Pennsylvania, becoming a physician in his native state before moving to Marshall County, Mississippi. He was also a wealthy planter, owning forty-seven slaves in 1860. Representing Marshall County in the secession convention, Lea was a strong secessionist. He was too old to join the war effort, and was further disabled by a fall from his horse after the war. He died on December 8, 1879.[59]

LEWERS, THOMAS D.—Born in South Carolina in 1817, Lewers later moved to DeSoto County, Mississippi, engaging in planting around Luxahoma. He owned twenty-six slaves in 1860. Lewers represented DeSoto County in the secession convention and was an avid secessionist. During the war, he rose to the rank of lieutenant colonel in Wirt Adams's Mississippi cavalry regiment. He died on August 26, 1865.[60]

LEWIS, ALFRED E.—Born in Mississippi on January 28, 1812, Lewis soon became a prominent farmer and stock raiser around Pascagoula in Jackson County. He owned thirty-four slaves in 1860. He was also involved in local politics, serving his county as assessor, as tax collector, and eventually in the state legislature. Representing Jackson County in the secession convention, Lewis voted strictly secessionist. He was too old for the war effort, but continued his farming operations afterward. He died on December 31, 1885.[61]

MARSHALL, THOMAS ALEXANDER—Born in Kentucky on March 29, 1812, Marshall joined the bar there, but later moved to Mississippi, becoming a prominent lawyer at Vicksburg. He served in the state legislature prior to the Civil War, and likewise dabbled in planting, owning nine slaves in 1860. Representing Warren County and the large planting class along the Mississippi River in the secession convention, Marshall was a cooperationist, voting against secession. Too old to serve in the ranks, he nevertheless served in the 1865 constitutional convention, and then continued his law practice until he retired when his health broke in 1873. He died on December 21, 1893.[62]

MAYSON, JAMES HAMILTON—Born in Mississippi on June 6, 1833, Mayson graduated from the University of Mississippi in 1852 and began a successful career as a lawyer in Columbia. He grew to some wealth, owning five slaves in 1860. Representing Marion County in the secession convention, Mayson was sternly for disunion and quickly joined the Confederate army. He rose to the rank of colonel of the Seventh Mississippi Infantry before he left the army in May 1862, not being reelected to his position. After the war, Mayson continued his law career and served in the 1865 constitutional convention. He died on October 8, 1869.[63]

MCGEHEE, EDWARD F.—Brother of fellow delegate Miles H. McGehee, Edward McGehee was born in Georgia on April 6, 1816. He later moved to Mississippi and became a respected planter near Como in Panola County. He owned seventy-four slaves in 1860. Representing Panola County at the secession convention, McGehee voted for one of the delaying amendments but ultimately voted in favor of secession. He joined the Confederate ranks despite his advanced age, and became lieutenant colonel of the Twenty-Fifth Mississippi Infantry, which soon became the Second Confederate Infantry. He was wounded in the foot at Shiloh and was disabled, resigning his commission on January 1, 1863. After the war, he continued his planting endeavors. McGehee died on November 10, 1879.[64]

MCGEHEE, MILES HILL—Brother of fellow delegate Edward F. McGehee, Miles McGehee was born in Georgia on November 26, 1813. Like his brother, he moved to Mississippi and became a large planter in Bolivar County near Concordia. He was one of the largest slave owners in the convention, possessing 234 slaves in 1860. He also served in the state legislature prior to the Civil War. As a delegate to the secession convention from Bolivar County, he had defeated future Confederate general and Mississippi governor Charles Clark for the seat. McGehee did not support secession, voting for all three delaying amendments before ultimately voting for secession. Although aged in years, he nevertheless served as the quartermaster general for Mississippi's Army of 10,000 made up of militia in 1861, and also paid to outfit an entire company that would become part of the Twentieth Mississippi Infantry. He died during the war, on January 15, 1865.[65]

MILLER, ANDREW—Brother of convention delegate Hugh Reid Miller, Andrew Miller was born in South Carolina on December 6, 1801. He moved to Mississippi and began planting near Austin in Tunica County, owning twenty-six slaves in 1860. Representing Tunica County in the secession convention, Miller voted strictly secessionist, but he was far too old to join the Confederate army. He died during the war, in August 1864.[66]

MILLER, HUGH REID—Brother of fellow delegate Andrew Miller, Hugh Reid Miller was born on May 12, 1812, in South Carolina. He migrated to

Pontotoc, Mississippi, in 1835, where he became a successful lawyer and judge and also served in the state legislature. He also had some agricultural pursuits, owning ten slaves in 1860. Representing Pontotoc County in the secession convention, Miller consistently voted secessionist. He quickly joined the Confederate army, first serving as a captain in the Second Mississippi Infantry but later became colonel of the Forty-Second Mississippi Infantry. It was in that position that he was mortally wounded at Gettysburg in the railroad cut on July 1. He died several weeks later, on July 19, 1863.[67]

MYERS, PORTER JACOB—Born in 1815 in South Carolina, Myers later moved to Enon in Perry County, Mississippi. He became a small-scale farmer, owning sixteen slaves in 1860, but was prominent enough to serve in the legislature prior to the Civil War. Representing Perry County in the secession convention as a dedicated cooperationist, Myers voted for all three delaying amendments and against secession itself in the January session. He did not attend the March meeting. He was too old to serve in the war, and returned to farming after the war. He died in 1889.[68]

NEELY, OSWELL Y.—Born on October 19, 1815, in South Carolina, Neely later moved to Mississippi, where he became a prosperous planter near Scooba in Kemper County. He owned fifty-five slaves in 1860 and served in the state legislature prior to the Civil War. Representing Kemper County at the secession convention, Neely voted strictly secessionist and soon joined the Confederate army. He served in Foote's First Mississippi State Troops, a thirty-day regiment, then served in the militia again in 1864. He also sat in the Mississippi senate during the war. After the war, Neely returned to planting and died on January 30, 1872.[69]

NELSON, JAMES M.—Born in Tennessee around 1822, Nelson later moved to Pike County, Mississippi, where he served as a physician at Holmesville. He served in the state legislature prior to the Civil War, and had some agricultural pursuits, owning eight slaves in 1860. Representing Pike County at the secession convention, Nelson voted strictly secessionist and quickly joined the Confederate army, becoming a lieutenant in the Sixteenth Mississippi Infantry. He was not reelected to his position when the regiment reorganized in May 1862, so he moved to Texas and became a cavalry officer there. After the war, he returned to his medical practice. He died on August 6, 1899.[70]

ORR, JEHU AMAZIAH—Born in South Carolina on April 10, 1828, Orr moved to Mississippi with his family in 1843 but later attained an education from Princeton University, graduating in 1849. He became a prominent lawyer and planter at Houston, Mississippi, serving as district attorney and in the state legislature prior to the Civil War. He also had large agricultural pursuits, owning forty-eight slaves in 1860. Orr represented Chickasaw County in the secession convention, where he voted strictly secessionist. He represented Mississippi in the Confederate congress before becoming colonel of the Thirty-First Mississippi Infantry. He resigned that position due to sickness in March 1864 and returned to the Confederate congress. After the war, Orr returned to his law practice and served as a judge. He lived a long life, outliving all of his fellow delegates, not dying until March 9, 1921.[71]

PARKER, DANIEL H.—Born in Mississippi around 1833, Parker was a small-scale farmer around McCall's Creek in Franklin County with no slaves. He represented Franklin County in the secession convention and voted strictly cooperationist, even against secession. He soon joined the Confederate army, however, rising to the rank of captain in the Seventh Mississippi Infantry. Parker died of typhoid fever on May 12, 1862.[72]

PATTISON, ALEXANDER—Born in Tennessee on September 29, 1821, Pattison migrated to Tallahatchie County, Mississippi, where he became a large planter around Charleston. He became very well off, and owned seventy-five slaves in 1860. He represented Tallahatchie County in the secession convention and voted across the board for immediate secession. During the Civil War, Pattison served in a local state militia outfit, and returned to his agricultural pursuits after the war. He died on November 4, 1879.[73]

POWELL, ABSALOM COLUMBUS—Born in South Carolina on February 9, 1811, Powell migrated to Covington County, Mississippi, in 1835. He owned a plantation near Williamsburg, working twenty-six slaves in 1860. Representing Covington County in the secession convention, Powell voted strictly secessionist. He was too old to fight in the war, but sent a son to the army. After the war, he continued his agricultural pursuits and lived a long life, dying on April 28, 1902.[75]

POWELL, JOHN HATHORN—Born on August 30, 1800, in South Carolina, Powell moved first to Georgia and then to Jones County, Mississippi, in

1843. Prior to the Civil War, he served in a number of positions, including as postmaster, justice of the peace, and probate judge in addition to his main work as a farmer. He was not a large-scale planter, owning only three slaves in 1860. Powell represented Jones County in the secession convention and voted for two of the delaying amendments before officially agreeing to secession itself. He was too old to fight in the war, and thereafter moved to Texas. He died on September 22, 1867.[74]

RAMSEY, JAMES B.—Born in North Carolina on August 27, 1820, Ramsey moved with his family to Alabama, where he attended college at the state university in Tuscaloosa. He also went to medical school at Transylvania University, graduating in 1843. He first practiced medicine in Alabama, but eventually moved to Lauderdale County, Mississippi, where he served as a physician as well as a planter, owning thirty-three slaves in 1860. Ramsey represented Lauderdale County in the secession convention, where he supported leaving the Union despite not attending the March session. He also joined the Confederate army, serving as a surgeon in the Twelfth Mississippi Cavalry. After the war, Ramsey returned to his planting and medical practice, but later moved to Vermilion Parrish, Louisiana. He died on June 7, 1896.[76]

REYNOLDS, ARTHUR EXUM—Born on November 29, 1817, in Tennessee, Reynolds later moved to Alabama, where he studied law. He eventually moved to Tishomingo County, Mississippi. He practiced law at Jacinto and pursued other interests such as politics and planting. He served in the state senate in the 1850s and owned twenty-two slaves in 1860. Representing Tishomingo County in the secession convention, he was also one of the largest delegates, weighing well over 300 pounds. Reynolds was a firm cooperationist, voting for all three delaying amendments and against secession itself. When the majority ruled, however, he quickly joined the Confederate army, becoming colonel of the Twenty-Sixth Mississippi Infantry. He was captured at Fort Donelson and became a prisoner of war at the Old Capitol Prison in Washington, D.C. After exchange, he fought with his regiment in the Vicksburg campaign and served in the conscription bureau before being transferred to Virginia. He was wounded at Weldon Railroad near Petersburg in August 1864. He recovered, but not in time to rejoin the war. After the war, Reynolds returned to his law profession and eventually became a judge. He was elected to the U.S. Congress during Reconstruction but was not seated. He died on April 18, 1881.[77]

ROBERTS, TYRA JOHN—Born on October 15, 1806, in South Carolina, Roberts later moved to Greene County, Mississippi, and operated a farm near Vernal. He owned twenty-nine slaves in 1860. Prior to the Civil War, he was also a member of the state legislature. Representing Greene County at the secession convention, Roberts was a strong secessionist, although he missed the March session. He was too old to fight in the war, but operated a ferry on the Chickasawhay River during the conflict. After the war, he continued his agricultural pursuits. Roberts died on May 8, 1887.[78]

ROGERS, FRANCIS MARION—Born about 1821 in Georgia, Rogers later moved to Aberdeen, Mississippi, where he practiced law and served as a judge. He had other interests as well, such as politics and planting, owning sixty-five slaves in 1860. He ran for governor of Mississippi in 1853 but was defeated by John J. McRae. Rogers represented Monroe County at the secession convention, voting strictly secessionist. He quickly joined the Confederate army, becoming a captain in the Fourteenth Mississippi Infantry. He was killed in action on February 15, 1862, at Fort Donelson.[79]

SANDERS, ELIJAH H.—Born in Kentucky about 1813, Sanders later moved to Attala County, Mississippi. There, he became involved in many pursuits, including serving as sheriff, planting with thirty-six slaves in 1860, and serving in the state legislature. He became very wealthy and prominent, and represented Attala County in the secession convention, voting for all the delaying amendments and against secession itself. He was too old to join the war effort, and returned to his agricultural pursuits after the war. He died in 1886.[80]

SEMMES, FRANCIS C.—Born in Georgia about 1823, Semmes came to Mississippi in 1845, settling in Lauderdale County near Meridian. He operated a farm and represented Lauderdale County in the secession convention, where he voted strictly for secession. Too old to fight in the war, Semmes was nevertheless a conscript and served in the quartermaster department at Meridian. He also served in the state legislature during the war. After the war, Semmes returned to his farming efforts, but died in November 1867.[81]

SMART, WILLIAM B.—Born in South Carolina on April 27, 1812, Smart later moved to Hinds County, Mississippi, operating a plantation near Terry. He became wealthy, owning fifty-six slaves in 1860. He represented Hinds County in the secession convention, voting for secession continuously. Too old to fight in the ranks, Smart died on July 2, 1865.[84]

STEPHENS, MARQUIS DE LAFAYETTE—Born in Tennessee on November 9, 1829, Stephens studied medicine at the University of Louisville. He moved to Mississippi and practiced medicine in Calhoun County at Sarepta. He owned one slave in 1860. Stephens represented Calhoun County in the secession convention and voted for all three delaying amendments before finally voting for secession. He soon joined the Confederate army, first serving as a lieutenant in the Seventeenth Mississippi Infantry and then rising to the colonelcy of the Thirty-First Mississippi Infantry, often commanding the brigade to which he was attached. He was wounded in the thigh at Franklin, Tennessee, in November 1864, ending his career. After the war, Stephens became a merchant and also served in both houses of the state legislature. He died on April 15, 1911.[82]

SUMNER, WILLIAM A.—Born in South Carolina in 1828, Sumner later moved to Calhoun County, Mississippi, where he became involved in several areas of work. He listed his occupation as "varied," which included serving as circuit clerk in Pittsboro. He also owned three slaves in 1860. Sumner represented Calhoun County in the secession convention, where he voted for all three delaying amendments but for secession. He joined the Confederate army, serving as a captain in the Fourth Mississippi Infantry until wounded at Fort Donelson in February 1862. He resigned his commission in April of that year and returned home. After the war, Sumner practiced law and moved to Arkansas. He died on September 3, 1901.[83]

TAYLOR, CALEB W.—Born in Kentucky on October 6, 1811, Taylor moved to Morton, Mississippi, in 1850 by way of Alabama. He became a small-scale planter, owning only nine slaves in 1860. He represented Scott County in the secession convention, voting consistently for secession. Taylor was too old to serve in the ranks, but outfitted a company that became a part of the Twentieth Mississippi Infantry. After the war, he continued his farming pursuits. Taylor died on January 12, 1890.[85]

TERRAL, SAMUEL HEIDELBERG—Born in Mississippi on February 4, 1835, Terral attended the University of Mississippi and became a lawyer in Quitman, eventually serving as district attorney. He owned only two slaves in 1860. Terral represented Clarke County in the secession convention and voted across the board for secession. He quickly entered the Confederate army, rising to the rank of lieutenant colonel of the Thirty-Seventh Mississippi Infantry. After the war, he returned to his law practice and served as a circuit court judge as well as in the legislature. Terral died on March 20, 1903.[86]

THOMPSON, WADDY—Born in South Carolina on January 15, 1808, Thompson later moved to Flower's Place in Smith County, Mississippi, where he became involved in a number of pursuits. He listed his occupation as "Physician and Mechanic and Planter." He owned only nine slaves in 1860. Thompson represented Smith County in the secession convention and voted strictly secessionist. Too old to fight in the war, he continued his agricultural pursuits after the war, but died in 1866.[87]

THORNTON, JOHN JONES—Born in Virginia on May 10, 1826, Thornton later moved to Rankin County, Mississippi. He served as a physician, alderman, and militia officer at Brandon prior to the Civil War. He also had five slaves in 1860. Representing Rankin County at the secession convention, Thornton was an avid cooperationist, voting for all three delaying amendments and then against the ordinance of secession itself. He was the only member who flatly refused to sign the document, purposefully being absent from the convention that day. Yet he was one of the first men to join the new Confederate ranks, becoming colonel of the Sixth Mississippi Infantry. He was wounded in the thigh at Shiloh in April 1862, which ended his active career, although later in the war he was involved with the state troops. After the war, Thornton was a druggist. He died on September 12, 1886.[88]

TISON, WILLIAM HENRY HAYWOOD—Born in Alabama on November 6, 1822, Tison later moved to Itawamba County, Mississippi. He was involved in a number of pursuits, including farming, owning eleven slaves in 1860. He was also a saddler, printer, editor, U.S. marshal, and member of the state legislature prior to the Civil War. Representing Itawamba County in the secession convention, Tison voted for two of the delaying amendments before agreeing to secession. He quickly joined the Confederate ranks, first serving as a captain in the Nineteenth Mississippi Infantry and then as colonel of the Thirty-Second Mississippi Infantry. He was wounded at Resaca, Atlanta, and Franklin, all in 1864. After the war, Tison continued farming and was a storekeeper. He returned to the state legislature, eventually serving as Speaker of the house. A man with whom he had had previous fights murdered him on December 4, 1882.[89]

VAUGHAN, HENRY—Born in South Carolina on March 31, 1800, Vaughan later moved to Yazoo County, Mississippi, owning a large amount of land around Benton. The oldest member of the convention, he was also the largest slave owner, with 293 slaves in 1860. Representing Yazoo County at the secession convention, Vaughan voted straight-line secessionist. He was far too old to fight in the war and continued his planting affairs after the conflict ended. He died on December 13, 1870.[90]

WALTER, HARVEY W.—Born in Ohio on May 21, 1819, Walter came to Mississippi by way of Michigan in the late 1830s. He first taught school while reading law and joined the bar in 1840, practicing at Holly Springs. He also had some agricultural interests, owning eight slaves in 1860. Walter was also interested in politics, running unsuccessfully against John J. Pettus for governor in 1859. Representing Marshall County in the secession convention, he voted for secession the entire time and soon joined the Confederate army, even at the expense of not attending the March session. Walter served as a lieutenant in the Ninth Mississippi Infantry before becoming a member of Braxton Bragg's staff, ultimately serving as judge advocate. After the war, Walter returned to his law practice. He died on September 19, 1879, while ministering to yellow fever patients.[91]

WELSH, ISRAEL—Born in Alabama in 1822, Welsh eventually moved to Noxubee County, Mississippi, where he practiced law in Macon. He was also a planter, owning fifty-four slaves in 1860. Politics also interested him, and he served in the state legislature prior to the Civil War. Representing Noxubee County in the secession convention, Welsh voted strictly secessionist, and even missed the March session because he had joined the army. He first served as a private in the Eleventh Mississippi Infantry, but left the army after winning a seat in the Confederate congress. After the war, he continued his law career. He died on May 18, 1869.[92]

WILKINSON, GEORGE B.—Born on July 9, 1819, in Virginia, Wilkinson attended the University of Virginia as well as William and Mary. He joined the Virginia bar and practiced law in Petersburg before moving to Yazoo City, Mississippi, where he continued his law career. He also served as a judge and owned nine slaves in 1860. Representing Yazoo County at the secession convention, Wilkinson was an avid secessionist and soon joined the Confederate army. He first served as a lieutenant in the Eighteenth Mississippi Infantry, but resigned due to dysentery. Later in the war he was a judge in John C. Pemberton's army with the rank of colonel, but had to leave that position because of another bout with dysentery. After the war, Wilkinson returned to his law practice. He died on August 4, 1870.[93]

WINCHESTER, JOSIAH—Born in Massachusetts on May 22, 1814, Winchester moved to Natchez, Mississippi, where he became a lawyer and planter. He owned fifteen slaves in 1860. Representing heavily cooperationist Adams County in the secession convention, Winchester voted across the board cooperationist. He was too old to serve in the Confederate ranks, but returned to his law practice after the war, serving also as a judge. He died on September 30, 1887.[94]

WITTY, WILLIAM H.—Born in North Carolina on May 1, 1829, Witty later moved to Lodi in Choctaw County, Mississippi. He was a small farmer, owning but five slaves in 1860. Representing Choctaw County in the secession convention, Witty voted strongly secessionist and soon joined the Confederate army. He served as a captain in the Thirtieth Mississippi Infantry, being wounded in the heel at Stones River in December 1862. After recovery, he was captured at Lookout Mountain in November 1863 and was confined as a prisoner of war at Johnson's Island. After the war, Witty became a merchant and banker. He died on March 31, 1885.[95]

WOOD, JOHN W.—Born around 1821 in Virginia, Wood later moved to Kosciusko, Mississippi, where he practiced law. An avid cooperationist, he was elected to represent Attala County at the secession convention. He attended only three days and did not vote on any of the secession issues. He did attend the March session, however. He was one of two delegates who did not sign the ordinance of secession, later claiming he would not have signed even had he been in attendance. Wood did not serve in the Confederate army, and in fact moved to Union-occupied Memphis, Tennessee. After the war, he practiced law there. He died in August 1878.[96]

WOODS, THOMAS H.—The youngest member of the secession convention, Woods was born in Arkansas on March 17, 1836. He obtained an education in Massachusetts and began practicing law in DeKalb, Mississippi, in 1859. Just starting his professional life, he owned no slaves. Woods represented Kemper County in the secession convention, voting strictly secessionist. He joined the Confederate army, serving as a captain in the Thirteenth Mississippi Infantry. He was wounded at Fredericksburg in May 1863. After the war, Woods moved to Meridian and had a distinguished career as a lawyer, district attorney, state legislator, and member of the state supreme court. He died on August 10, 1910.[97]

WRIGHT, DANIEL BOONE—Born in Tennessee on February 17, 1812, Wright was educated at Cumberland University. Joining the bar in 1840, he practiced law at Salem in Tippah County, Mississippi. He was a planter as well, owning thirty-six slaves in 1860. Wright also became involved in politics, serving two terms in the U.S. Congress in the 1850s. He declined renomination and returned to his law practice. He also fought in the Seminole wars. Representing Tippah County in the secession convention, Wright was very much a secessionist. He joined the Confederate army shortly thereafter, becoming lieutenant colonel of the Thirty-Fourth Mississippi Infantry. He was wounded in the arm at Perryville in October 1862 and taken prisoner, spending time at Camp Chase in Ohio. He returned to the war after exchange and, because of his wounds, served as a judge in Nathan Bedford Forrest's cavalry with the rank of colonel. After the war, Wright returned to his law and agricultural pursuits. He died on December 27, 1887.[98]

YERGER, JACOB SHALL—Born in Pennsylvania on January 11, 1810, Yerger moved as a child to Tennessee. He later joined the Tennessee bar and practiced law in Nashville, but moved to Vicksburg, Mississippi, in 1837. He later moved to Greenville, and served in the state legislature and as a circuit judge. Representing Washington County in the secession convention, Yerger was an avid cooperationist, voting against secession. He was too old to serve in the Confederate ranks, but sent four sons to the war effort, one of whom was killed. After the war, Yerger served as president of the 1865 constitutional convention. He died on July 14, 1867.[99]

YOUNG, THOMAS P.—Born in Kentucky around 1810, Young later moved to Tishomingo County, Mississippi, operating a plantation near Corinth. He owned thirty-seven slaves in 1860. Representing Tishomingo County in the secession convention, Young voted the cooperationist line, even against secession. He soon joined the Confederate army, however, serving as the commissary officer in the Second Mississippi Infantry, with the rank of captain. After the war, Young was a bookkeeper and later moved to Grand Junction, Tennessee, where he operated a hotel. He apparently died prior to 1900.[100]

APPENDIX 2.
ELECTION RESULTS FOR CONVENTION DELEGATES, DECEMBER 20, 1860

ADAMS COUNTY[1]
*Josiah Winchester—532
*Alexander K. Farrar—530
Edward M. Blackburn—162
George W. Marshall—69

AMITE COUNTY
*David W. Hurst—382
E. M. Davis—268

ATTALA COUNTY
*Elijah H. Sanders—651
*John W. Wood—649
E. M. Wells—616
Josiah A. P. Campbell—614

BOLIVAR COUNTY
*Miles H. McGehee—202
Charles Clark—179

CALHOUN COUNTY
*Marcus D. L. Stephens—518
*William A. Sumner—506
H. L. Duncan—412
William H. Lykes—406

CARROLL COUNTY
*William Booth—830

*James Z. George—826
Jerry Robinson—59
E. R. McLean—28
J. D. McLemore—6
Scattering—1

CHICKASAW COUNTY
*Jehu A. Orr—761
*Cyrus B. Baldwin—746

CHOCTAW COUNTY
*William F. Brantley—941
*William H. Witty—934
*James H. Edwards—934
R. C. Love—591
A. G. Young—585
M. C. Sharkey—579

CLAIBORNE COUNTY
*Henry T. Ellett—322
Thomas B. Magruder—143
Richard T. Archer—23

CLARKE COUNTY
*Samuel H. Terral—546
W. B. Dozier—107
A. Carr—6
A. Brown—1

COAHOMA COUNTY
*James L. Alcorn—172
Saul N. Delaney—62

COPIAH COUNTY
*Benjamin King—799
*Philip S. Catching—798
A. P. Barry—201
Scattering—85

COVINGTON COUNTY
*Absalom C. Powell—226
G. H. Robertson—93

DESOTO COUNTY
*Stephen D. Johnston—841
*Thomas D. Lewers—825
*James R. Chalmers—817
Burford—174
Harris—140

FRANKLIN COUNTY
*Daniel H. Parker—263
William Cassidy—235

GREENE COUNTY
*Tyra J. Roberts—67

HANCOCK COUNTY
*John B. Deason—147
Green J. Wooten—83

HARRISON COUNTY
*David C. Glenn—314
L. L. Davis—1

HINDS COUNTY
*Wiley P. Harris—1,000
*Warren P. Anderson—939

*William B. Smart—916
Fulton Anderson—716
William Yerger—670
A. R. Johnston—660

HOLMES COUNTY
*James M. Dyer—768
*Walter L. Keirn—629
John J. Hooker—300
David Mitchell—2
A. M. West—2
Thomas Baines—1
Lem Doty—1
J. C. Bates—1
J. W. Wade—1
Cap Oltenbury—1

ISSAQUEENA COUNTY
*Albert C. Gibson—73
F. W. Moore—71

ITAWAMBA COUNTY
*Malachai Cummings—1,241
*Arthur B. Bullard—1,181
*Russell O. Beene—1,180
*William H. H. Tison—894
George Stovall—660

JACKSON COUNTY
*Alfred E. Lewis—194

JASPER COUNTY
*Oliver C. Dease—378
M. A. King—315
J. H. Gray—257

JEFFERSON COUNTY
*James S. Johnston—282
C. B. New—119

JONES COUNTY
*John H. Powell—166
J. M. Baylis—89

KEMPER COUNTY
*Thomas H. Woods—531
*Oswell Y. Neely—502
[A. M.] Chamberlain—76
McRae—37
R. J. Love—37
R. J. Edwards—32

LAFAYETTE COUNTY
*Thomas D. Isom—834
*Lucius Q. C. Lamar—815
Doury Robertson—161
J. S. Buford—148

LAUDERDALE COUNTY
*Francis C. Semmes—611
*James B. Ramsey—597
D. P. King—341
C. E. Rushing—255

LAWRENCE COUNTY
*William Gwin—318
Fleet T. Cooper—264

LEAKE COUNTY—No returns found
*Wallace B. Colbert

LOWNDES COUNTY
*George R. Clayton—819
*William S. Barry—811
E. B. Gaston—135
M. M. Rowen—135
Scattering—4

MADISON COUNTY
*Albert P. Hill—580
C. C. Shackelford—343

MARION COUNTY
*Hamilton Mayson—90
William Barnes Sr.—4
Lemuel Lewis—4

MARSHALL COUNTY
*Alexander M. Clayton—1,109
*Samuel Benton—1,102
*Jeremiah W. Clapp—1,097
*Harvey W. Walter—1,097
*Willis M. Lea—1,028
John W. C. Watson—1,016
John H. Record—870
Robert M. Brown—867
Arch M. Lyles—855
William Wooten—846

MONROE COUNTY
*Francis M. Rogers—893
*Samuel J. Gholson—892
Benjamin H. Shepphard—472
William H. Vasser—471

NESHOBA COUNTY
*David M. Backstrom—601
Ira N. Nash—58

NEWTON COUNTY
*Marshall M. Keith—394
O. G. Flint—144

NOXUBEE COUNTY
*Israel Welsh—383
J. J. Shelton—4
W. B. Wilborn—2

H. W. Foote—1
G. W. Edwards—1

OKTIBBEHA COUNTY
*Thomas C. Bookter—410

PANOLA COUNTY
*Edward F. McGehee—730
*John B. Fizer—722
J. M. Wallace—9
W. S. Randolph—5
John R. Dickins—2
J. C. Brahan—1
J. McGehee—1
J. J. Meek—1
F. Moore—1

PERRY COUNTY
*Porter J. Myers—71
P. McSlanulrs—66
William Jenkins—22

PIKE COUNTY
*James M. Nelson—326
William F. Quin—197

PONTOTOC COUNTY
*John B. Herring—1,280
*Robert W. Flournoy—1,230
*Hugh R. Miller—1,107
*Charles D. Fontaine—1,094
C. G. Ragan—44
W. E. Hunter—42
J. W. Bramblette—40
J. Linney—38
S. H. Taylor—1
A. Thomason—1
Jesse Westmorland—1

RANKIN COUNTY
*John J. Thornton—578
*William Denson—573
W. B. Shelby—458
J. M. Jayne—457

SCOTT COUNTY
*Caleb W. Taylor—305
E. R. Buckner—7
M. H. Lack—7
M. B. Kirkland—6
F. A. Flannaghan—3
James C. Harper—2
John Matthews Sr.—2

SIMPSON COUNTY
*William J. Douglas—270
John L. McLaurin—42
D. A. McLaurin—5

SMITH COUNTY
*Waddy Thompson—339
J. H. Wood—157

SUNFLOWER COUNTY
*Edward P. Jones—117
B. G. Humphreys—43

TALLAHATCHIE COUNTY
*Alexander Pattison—171
J. C. Stark—11

TIPPAH COUNTY
*James S. Davis—1,305
*Daniel B. Wright—1,296
*Joel H. Berry—1,290
*Orlando Davis—1,288
T. J. Murry—262
S. S. Wells—200

Irby—183
W. J. Riddle—183
W. E. Tomlinson—63
Scattering—26

TISHOMINGO COUNTY
*Arthur E. Reynolds—1,925
*John A. Blair—1,921
*Wright W. Bonds—1,916
*Thomas P. Young—1,913
B. D. Hodges—729
A. B. Dilworth—727
William M. Inge—708
L. B. Gaston—699

TUNICA COUNTY
*Andrew Miller—Number of
votes not reported

WARREN COUNTY
*Thomas A. Marshall—736
*Walker Brooke—721
W. H. McCardle—174
W. H. Johnson—151

WASHINGTON COUNTY
*Jacob S. Yerger—129
W. L. Nugent—122

WAYNE COUNTY
*William J. Eckford—121
George S. Gaines—78

WILKINSON COUNTY
*Alfred C. Holt—334
Jones S. Hamilton—306

WINSTON COUNTY—No returns
found
*William S. Bolling
*John Kennedy

YALOBUSHA COUNTY—No re-
turns found
*Francis M. Aldridge
*William R. Barksdale

YAZOO COUNTY
*George B. Wilkinson—660
*Henry Vaughan Sr.—651
C. F. Hamer—383
Frederick Smith—375

* Elected as delegate

APPENDIX 3.
MISSISSIPPI ORDINANCE OF SECESSION

AN ORDINANCE—To dissolve the Union between the State of Mississippi, and other States united with her, under the compact entitled "The Constitution of the United States of America."

The People of Mississippi, in Convention assembled, do ordain and declare, and it is hereby ordained and declared as follows, to-wit:

SECTION 1st. That all the laws and ordinances by which the said State of Mississippi became a member of the Federal Union of the United States of America, be and the same are, hereby repealed, and that all obligations on the part of said State, or the people thereof, to observe the same, be withdrawn; and that the said State doth hereby resume all the rights, functions and powers which by any of said laws or ordinances were conveyed to the government of the said United States, and is absolved from all the obligations, restraints and duties incurred to the said Federal Union, and shall from henceforth be a free, sovereign and independent State.

SEC. 2d. That so much of the first section of the seventh article of the Constitution of this State as requires members of the Legislature, and all officers, legislative and judicial, to take an oath to support the Constitution of the United States, be and the same is hereby abrogated and annulled.

SEC. 3d. That all rights acquired and vested under the Constitution of the United States, or under any act of Congress, passed in pursuance thereof, or under any law of this State, and not incompatible with this Ordinance, shall remain in force and have the same effect as if this Ordinance had not been passed.

SEC. 4th. That the people of the State of Mississippi hereby consent to form a Federal Union with such of the States as have seceded, or may secede from the Union of the United States of America, upon the basis of the present Constitution of the said United States, except such parts thereof as embrace other portions of such seceding States.

Thus ordained and declared in Convention the 9th day of January, in the Year of Our Lord One Thousand Eight Hundred and Sixty-one.

F. A. Pope,
SECRETARY
William S. Barry,
PRESIDENT

APPENDIX 4.
DECLARATION OF CAUSES

A DECLARATION

Of the immediate causes which induce and justify the secession of the State of Mississippi from the Federal Union.

In the momentous step which our State has taken of dissolving its connection with the government of which we so long formed a part, it is but just that we should declare the prominent reasons which have induced our course.

Our position is thoroughly identified with the institution of slavery—the greatest material interest of the world. Its labor supplies the product which constitutes by far the largest and most important portions of the commerce of the earth. These products are peculiar to the climate verging on the tropical regions, and by an imperious law of nature, none but the black race can bear exposure to the tropical sun. These products have become necessities of the world, and a blow at slavery, is a blow at commerce and civilization. That blow has long been aimed at the institution, and was at the point of reaching its consummation. There was no choice left us but submission to the mandates of abolition, or a dissolution of the Union, whose principles had been subverted to work out our ruin.

That we do not overstate the dangers to our institution, a reference to a few facts will sufficiently prove.

The hostility to this institution commenced before the adoption of the Constitution, and was manifested in the well-known Ordinance of 1787, in regard to the North-western territory.

The feeling increased, until, in 1819–1820, it deprived the South of more than half the vast territory acquired from France.

The same hostility dismembered Texas, and seized upon all the territory acquired from Mexico.

It has grown until it denies the right of property in slaves, and refuses protection to that right on the high seas, in the territories, and wherever the government of the United States had jurisdiction.

It refuses the admission of new slave States into the Union, and seeks to extinguish it by confining it within its present limits, denying the power of expansion.

It tramples the original equality of the South under foot.

It has nullified the Fugitive Slave Law in almost every free State in the Union, and has utterly broken the compact which our fathers pledged their faith to maintain.

It advocates negro equality, socially and politically, and promotes insurrection and incendiarism in our midst.

It has enlisted the press, its pulpit and its schools against us, until the whole popular mind of the North is excited and inflamed with prejudice.

It has made combinations and formed associations to carry out its schemes of emancipation in the States and wherever else slavery exists.

It seeks not to elevate or to support the slave, but to destroy his present condition without providing a better.

It has invaded a State, and invested with the honors of martyrdom, the wretch whose purpose was to apply flames to our dwellings, and the weapons of destruction to our lives.

It has broken every compact into which it has entered for our security.

It has given indubitable evidence of its design to ruin our agriculture, to prostrate our industrial pursuits, and to destroy our social system.

It knows no relenting or hesitation in its purposes; it stops in its march of aggression, and leaves us no room to hope for cessation or for pause.

It has recently obtained control of the Government, by the prosecution of its unhallowed schemes, and destroyed the last expectation of living together in friendship and brotherhood.

Utter subjugation awaits us in the Union, if we should consent longer to remain in it. It is not a matter of choice, but of necessity. We must either submit to degradation, and to the loss or property worth four billions of money, or we must secede from the Union framed by our fathers, to secure this as well as every other species of property. For far less cause than this, our fathers separated from the Crown of England.

Our decision is made. We follow their footsteps. We embrace the alternative of separation; and for the reasons here stated, we resolve to maintain our rights with the full consciousness of the justice of our course, and the undoubting belief of our ability to maintain it.

NOTES

PREFACE

1. "The Pro-Slavery Rebellion," March 30, 1861, Secession Subject File, Mississippi Department of Archives and History (hereafter cited as MDAH). The account can also be found in Albert D. Richardson, *The Secret Service, the Field, the Dungeon, and the Escape* (Hartford, Conn.: American Publishing, 1865), 84.

2. William W. Freehling, *The Road to Disunion: Secessionists at Bay, 1776–1854* (New York: Oxford University Press, 1990); William W. Freehling, *The Road to Disunion: Secessionists Triumphant, 1854–1861* (New York: Oxford University Press, 2007); David M. Potter, *The Impending Crisis: 1848–1861* (New York: Harper, 1976); Christopher J. Olsen, *Political Culture and Secession in Mississippi: Masculinity, Honor, and the Antiparty Tradition, 1830–1860* (New York: Oxford University Press, 2000), 5; Percy L. Rainwater, *Mississippi: Storm Center of Secession* (Baton Rouge: Louisiana State University Press, 1938), 203, 219, 222; Percy L. Rainwater, "An Analysis of the Secession Controversy in Mississippi, 1854–61," *Mississippi Valley Historical Review* 24, no. 1 (June 1937): 35–42.

3. Ralph A. Wooster, *The Secession Conventions of the South* (Princeton, N.J.: Princeton University Press, 1962); Ralph A. Wooster, "The Membership of the Mississippi Secession Convention of 1861," *Journal of Mississippi History* 16, no. 4 (October 1954): 242–257.

4. William L. Barney, *The Road to Secession: A New Perspective on the Old South* (New York: Praeger, 1972); William L. Barney, *The Secessionist Impulse: Alabama and Mississippi in 1860* (Princeton, N.J.: Princeton University Press, 1974), 38, 43, 77, 88, 189, 226–230, 296.

5. Olsen, *Political Culture and Secession in Mississippi*, 5–6, 9, 103, 169, 191, 195.

6. Luther Wesley Barnhardt, "The Secession Conventions of the Cotton South" (M.A. thesis, University of Wisconsin, 1922); John K. Bettersworth, *Confederate Mississippi: The People and Policies of a Cotton State in Wartime* (Baton Rouge: Louisiana State University Press, 1943); Bradley G. Bond, *Political Culture in the Nineteenth-Century South: Mississippi, 1830–1900* (Baton Rouge: Louisiana State University Press, 1995).

7. Barney, *Secessionist Impulse*, 296.

8. Barney, *Secessionist Impulse*, 189.

9. Bettersworth, *Confederate Mississippi*, 10–13, 19–21; Timothy B. Smith, *Mississippi in the Civil War: The Home Front* (Jackson: University Press of Mississippi, 2010), 5, 25–26.

10. Mrs. J. E. Brown, "The Secession of Mississippi," *Confederate Veteran* 39, no. 2 (February 1937): 92–94; Benjamin J. Hillman, *Virginia's Decision: The Story of the Secession Convention of 1861* (Richmond: Virginia Civil War Commission, 1964); William W.

Freehling and Craig M. Simpson, eds., *Secession Debated: Georgia's Showdown in 1860* (New York: Oxford University Press, 1992); William W. Freehling and Craig M. Simpson, eds., *Showdown in Virginia: The 1861 Convention and the Fate of the Union* (Charlottesville: University of Virginia Press, 2010); Kemp P. Battle, *The Secession Convention of 1861* (Raleigh: North Carolina Society, Daughters of the Revolutions, 1916); Wayne F. Bowers, "The First Secession Convention: A Study of the Sovereign Convention in South Carolina" (M.A. thesis, University of North Carolina at Chapel Hill, 1971); Michael P. Johnson, *Toward a Patriarchal Republic: The Secession of Georgia* (Baton Rouge: Louisiana State University Press, 1977); Carrie Helen Bently, "The Secession Convention of Virginia, 1861" (M.A. thesis, University of Texas at Austin, 1932); Clarence Phillips Denman, *The Secession Movement in Alabama* (Montgomery: Alabama State Department of Archives and History, 1933).

11. J. L. Power, "Proceedings and Debates of the Mississippi State Convention of 1861," J. F. H. Claiborne Papers, University of North Carolina (hereafter cited as UNC), 54–55; "The Debates of the Mississippi Convention," *Vicksburg Weekly Whig*, April 3, 1861.

12. Dunbar Rowland, *Courts, Judges, and Lawyers of Mississippi, 1798–1935* (Jackson, Miss.: Harderman Brothers, 1935), 318.

13. Thomas H. Woods, "A Sketch of the Mississippi Secession Convention of 1861,—Its Membership and Work," in *Publications of the Mississippi Historical Society*, ed. Franklin L. Riley (Oxford: Mississippi Historical Society, 1902), 6:103.

PROLOGUE

1. For Pettus, see Robert W. Dubay, *John Jones Pettus, Mississippi Fire-eater: His Life and Times, 1813–1867* (Jackson: University Press of Mississippi, 1975).

2. Dunbar Rowland, *Mississippi; Comprising Sketches of Counties, Towns, Events, Institutions and Persons, Arranged in Cyclopedic Form*, 3 vols. (Atlanta: Southern Historical Printing Association, 1907), 1:841–843; 1860 Mississippi Population Census; 1860 Mississippi Slave Schedules; "Alphabetical List of Members of the Mississippi State Convention," Box 8, Secession Convention Folder, Power Family Papers, MDAH; *Memorials of the Life and Character of Wiley P. Harris of Mississippi* (Jackson, Miss.: Clarion Printing Establishment, 1892), 5, 22, 26.

3. Rowland, *Mississippi*, 1:214–215; 1860 Mississippi Population Census; 1860 Mississippi Slave Schedules; "Alphabetical List of Members of the Mississippi State Convention"; Bruce S. Allardice, *Confederate Colonels: A Biographical Register* (Columbia: University of Missouri Press, 2008), 54–55.

4. Rowland, *Mississippi*, 2:22–35; Allardice, *Confederate Colonels*, 230; 1860 Mississippi Population Census; 1860 Mississippi Slave Schedules; "Alphabetical List of Members of the Mississippi State Convention"; James B. Murphy, *L. Q. C. Lamar: Pragmatic Patriot* (Baton Rouge: Louisiana State University Press, 1973); "Lucius Quintus Cincinnatus Lamar," in *Biographical Directory of the United States Congress, 1774–2005* (Washington, D.C.: Government Printing Office, 2005), 1410.

5. J. F. H. Claiborne, "The Secession Convention," n.d., J. F. H. Claiborne Papers, UNC, 2; "Col. D. C. Glenn, of Harrison," *Oxford Intelligencer*, January 16, 1861; Allardice, *Confederate*

Colonels, 165; 1860 Mississippi Population Census; 1860 Mississippi Slave Schedules; "Alphabetical List of Members of the Mississippi State Convention."

6. Ezra J. Warner, *Generals in Gray: Lives of the Confederate Commanders* (Baton Rouge: Louisiana State University Press, 1959), 103–104; 1860 Mississippi Population Census; 1860 Mississippi Slave Schedules; "Alphabetical List of Members of the Mississippi State Convention"; Olsen, *Political Culture and Secession in Mississippi*, 173.

7. "Henry Thomas Ellett," in *Biographical Directory of the United States Congress*, 1011; 1860 Mississippi Population Census; 1860 Mississippi Slave Schedules; "Alphabetical List of Members of the Mississippi State Convention"; Robert Lowry and William H. McCardle, *A History of Mississippi, From the Discovery of the Great River by Hernando DeSoto, Including the Earliest Settlement Made by the French, Under Iberville, to the Death of Jefferson Davis* (Jackson, Miss.: R. H. Henry, 1891), 477; *In Memory of Henry Thomas Ellett* (Memphis, Tenn.: Memphis Bar, 1888), 50, 61.

8. Timothy B. Smith, *James Z. George: Mississippi's Great Commoner* (Jackson: University Press of Mississippi, 2012); 1860 Mississippi Population Census; 1860 Mississippi Slave Schedules; "Alphabetical List of Members of the Mississippi State Convention"; "James Zachariah George," in *Biographical Directory of the United States Congress*, 1111.

9. Rowland, *Mississippi*, 1:62–64; Lillian A. Pereyra, *James Lusk Alcorn: Persistent Whig* (Baton Rouge: Louisiana State University Press, 1966); 1860 Mississippi Population Census; 1860 Mississippi Slave Schedules; "Alphabetical List of Members of the Mississippi State Convention."

10. Rowland, *Mississippi*, 1:308; 1860 Mississippi Population Census; 1860 Mississippi Slave Schedules; "Alphabetical List of Members of the Mississippi State Convention"; "Walker Brooke," in *Biographical Directory of the United States Congress*, 713; Woods, "Sketch of the Mississippi Secession Convention," 95.

11. Rowland, *Mississippi*, 2:1021–1022; 1860 Mississippi Population Census; 1860 Mississippi Slave Schedules; "Alphabetical List of Members of the Mississippi State Convention."

12. Allardice, *Confederate Colonels*, 372; 1860 Mississippi Population Census; 1860 Mississippi Slave Schedules; "Alphabetical List of Members of the Mississippi State Convention."

13. John W. Wood, *Union and Secession in Mississippi* (Memphis, Tenn.: Saunders, Parrish, and Whitmore, Printers, 1863); 1860 Mississippi Population Census; 1860 Mississippi Slave Schedules; "Alphabetical List of Members of the Mississippi State Convention."

CHAPTER 1.

1. *Journal of the House of Representatives of the State of Mississippi: Called Session* (Jackson, Miss.: E. Barksdale, State Printer, 1860), 3; *Journal of the Senate of the State of Mississippi: Called Session* (Jackson, Miss.: E. Barksdale, State Printer, 1860), 3; "Secession in Lafayette County," Wynn-Dockery Scrapbook, MDAH.

2. William W. Freehling, *Prelude to Civil War: The Nullification Controversy in South Carolina, 1816–1836* (New York: Oxford University Press, 1965).

3. Dubay, *John Jones Pettus*, 67; *Vicksburg Daily Whig*, December 14, 1860.

4. Donald R. Hickey, *The War of 1812: A Forgotten Conflict* (Urbana: University of Illinois Press, 1989), 255–280; *Condensed Proceedings of the Southern Convention Held at Nashville, Tennessee, June, 1850* (Jackson, Miss.: Fall and Marshall, Printers, 1850); "Delegates to the Convention of Southern States," *Jackson Mississippian*, February 10, 1860; "Letter from Hon. W. P. Harris," *Jackson Mississippian*, November 28, 1860.

5. Olsen, *Political Culture and Secession in Mississippi*, 187; Barney, *Secessionist Impulse*, 190.

6. *Journal of the Senate of the State of Mississippi*, 7; Barney, *Secessionist Impulse*, 190.

7. Rainwater, *Mississippi*, 198–200.

8. "Letter from Hon. W. P. Harris," *Jackson Mississippian*, November 28, 1860; Untitled, undated clipping in Folder 73, Clippings of Slavery and Secession, J. F. H. Claiborne Papers, UNC; *Jackson Mississippian*, November 28, 1860; "Meeting in Madison County," *Jackson Mississippian*, November 28, 1860; "Meeting in DeSoto," *Jackson Weekly Mississippian*, December 12, 1860; Thomas W. Caskey, *Caskey's Book: Lectures on Great Subjects, Selected from the Numerous Efforts of that Powerful Orator and Noble Veteran of the Cross, Thomas W. Caskey* (St. Louis: John Burns, 1884), 19–20.

9. "Secession in Lafayette County"; Untitled, undated clipping in Folder 73, Clippings of Slavery and Secession, J. F. H. Claiborne Papers, UNC; *Jackson Mississippian*, November 28, 1860; "Proceedings of a Meeting of the Citizens of Lowndes County, Mississippi, Held at Columbus, on Monday, November 19, 1860," *Jackson Mississippian*, November 28, 1860.

10. Edward Mayes, *Lucius Q. C. Lamar: His Life, Times, and Speeches, 1825–1893* (Nashville, Tenn.: Publishing House of the Methodist Episcopal Church South, 1896), 86–87; Reuben Davis, *Recollections of Mississippi and Mississippians* (Boston: Houghton, Mifflin, 1890), 391.

11. *Journal of the House of Representatives of the State of Mississippi: Called Session*, 3–6; *Journal of the Senate of the State of Mississippi*, 3–4.

12. *Journal of the House of Representatives of the State of Mississippi: Called Session*, 7–14; *Journal of the Senate of the State of Mississippi*, 5–12.

13. *Journal of the Senate of the State of Mississippi*, 5–6; "Mississippi Legislature," *Vicksburg Daily Whig*, November 27, 1860.

14. *Journal of the Senate of the State of Mississippi*, 5–7.

15. *Journal of the Senate of the State of Mississippi*, 6–9.

16. *Journal of the Senate of the State of Mississippi*, 11.

17. *Journal of the Senate of the State of Mississippi*, 11–12; "The Proposed Stay Law," *Jackson Mississippian*, December 5, 1860.

18. "The Legislature," *Jackson Weekly Mississippian*, December 5, 1860; *Journal of the Senate of the State of Mississippi*, 13–34; *Journal of the House of Representatives of the State of Mississippi: Called Session*, 15–43; "The Convention Bill," *Vicksburg Daily Whig*, November 29, 1860.

19. *Journal of the House of Representatives of the State of Mississippi: Called Session*, 16, 21, 23–24; *Journal of the Senate of the State of Mississippi*, 13, 16, 18–20; "Passage of the Convention Bill," *Jackson Mississippian*, December 5, 1860; "The Legislature," *Jackson Mississippian*, December 5, 1860; "Mississippi Legislature," *Vicksburg Daily Whig*, November 27, 1860.

20. *Journal of the House of Representatives of the State of Mississippi: Called Session*, 23–24; *Journal of the Senate of the State of Mississippi*, 18–20; "The Convention Bill," *Vicksburg Daily Whig*, November 29, 1860; "The Legislature," *Vicksburg Daily Whig*, November 29, 1860; "The Convention Bill," undated clipping in Folder 73, Clippings of Slavery and Secession, J. F. H. Claiborne Papers, UNC.

21. "Speech of Hon. L. Q. C. Lamar," *Jackson Mississippian*, December 5, 1860; Mayes, *Lucius Q. C. Lamar*, 87–88; "Correspondence," *Jackson Mississippian*, December 5, 1860; *Journal of the House of Representatives of the State of Mississippi: Called Session*, 18, 21–22, 30; Olsen, *Political Culture and Secession in Mississippi*, 188; Barney, *Secessionist Impulse*, 199, 232–233.

22. "Speech of Hon. L. Q. C. Lamar," *Jackson Mississippian*, December 5, 1860; "Correspondence," *Jackson Mississippian*, December 5, 1860; "Letter from Hon. W. P. Harris," *Jackson Mississippian*, November 28, 1860.

23. "Correspondence," *Jackson Mississippian*, December 5, 1860; *Journal of the House of Representatives of the State of Mississippi: Called Session*, 18, 21–22, 30; "The Convention Bill," *Vicksburg Daily Whig*, November 29, 1860; "Hon. J. L. Alcorn," *Jackson Weekly Mississippian*, January 2, 1861; Olsen, *Political Culture and Secession in Mississippi*, 188; Barney, *Secessionist Impulse*, 199, 232–233.

24. *Journal of the House of Representatives of the State of Mississippi: Called Session*, 17, 27, 31, 34–35; *Journal of the Senate of the State of Mississippi*, 14, 21–24.

25. "County Convention at Raymond on Saturday the 8th of December," *Jackson Weekly Mississippian*, December 5, 1860; "The Secession Spirit in Lafayette," *Oxford Intelligencer*, December 19, 1860; "The Meeting To-night," *Jackson Weekly Mississippian*, December 5, 1860; "Secession Wasn't Unanimous," *Madison County Journal*, November 12, 1998, copy in Secession Subject File, MDAH; "Meeting of Citizens of Jackson," *Jackson Weekly Mississippian*, December 12, 1860; Election Returns, 1817–2007, Secretary of State Records, RG 28, Vol. 34, Box 2445, MDAH (hereafter cited as Election Returns, 1817–2007); *Vicksburg Daily Whig*, December 11, 1860; "Warren County," *Oxford Intelligencer*, December 19, 1860; "Southern Rights Ticket," *Jackson Mississippian*, December 11, 1860; "The Union Ticket," *Jackson Mississippian*, December 11, 1860. See the December 15, 1860, *Vicksburg Whig* for other convention results.

26. "Co-operation Meeting in Madison," *Vicksburg Daily Whig*, December 14, 1860; *Vicksburg Daily Whig*, December 15, 1860; Barney, *Secessionist Impulse*, 246, 259.

27. "County Convention," *Vicksburg Daily Whig*, November 30, 1860; "For the State Convention," *Vicksburg Daily Whig*, December 14, 1860; "The Meeting of Thursday," *Vicksburg Whig*, December 1, 1860; "The Convention," *Vicksburg Daily Whig*, December 1, 1860; "County Convention," *Vicksburg Daily Whig*, December 8, 1860; "Speaking at Apollo Hall," *Vicksburg Whig*, December 11, 1860; "County Convention," *Vicksburg Daily Whig*, December 11, 1860; "Public Speaking," *Vicksburg Whig*, December 14, 1860; "Meeting of the Citizens of North Warren," *Vicksburg Whig*, December 14, 1860; "Our Ticket," *Vicksburg Daily Whig*, December 11, 1860.

28. "Is It There You Are?" *Vicksburg Whig*, December 14, 1860; "For the Convention," *Vicksburg Daily Whig*, December 11, 1860; "Hon. Thos. A. Marshall and Walker Brooke,"

Vicksburg Daily Whig, December 14, 1860; Olsen, *Political Culture and Secession in Mississippi*, 191.

29. "Mississippi State Convention," *Natchez Weekly Courier*, January 9, 1861; "Marshall County," *Oxford Intelligencer*, December 19, 1860; "County Convention at Raymond on Saturday the 8th of December," *Jackson Weekly Mississippian*, December 5, 1860; "The Meeting To-night," *Jackson Weekly Mississippian*, December 5, 1860; "Meeting of Citizens of Jackson," *Jackson Weekly Mississippian*, December 12, 1860; "Copiah County," *Oxford Intelligencer*, December 19, 1860; Election Returns, 1817–2007; "Yalobusha County," *Vicksburg Whig*, December 14, 1860. See the December 15, 1860, *Vicksburg Whig* for other convention results.

30. "Mississippi State Convention," *Natchez Weekly Courier*, January 9, 1861; Olsen, *Political Culture and Secession in Mississippi*, 193; Barney, *Secessionist Impulse*, 266; Rainwater, *Mississippi*, 179.

31. "Election in Panola County," *Weekly Panola Star*, December 27, 1860; "Delegates Elected to the Convention," *Vicksburg Weekly Whig*, January 9, 1861; "Members Elected to the Convention," *Jackson Weekly Mississippian*, January 2, 1861; Election Returns, 1817–2007.

32. Mayes, *Lucius Q. C. Lamar*, 89; "Important," *Oxford Intelligencer*, December 19, 1860; "Delegates Elected to the Convention," *Vicksburg Weekly Whig*, January 9, 1861; "Members Elected to the Convention," *Jackson Weekly Mississippian*, January 2, 1861; Election Returns, 1817–2007; "The Election," *Oxford Intelligencer*, December 26, 1860; Untitled, undated clipping in Folder 73, Clippings of Slavery and Secession, J. F. H. Claiborne Papers, UNC.

33. Rowland, *Courts, Judges, and Lawyers of Mississippi*, 322; "Public Speaking," *Jackson Mississippian*, December 11, 1860.

34. Rowland, *Courts, Judges, and Lawyers of Mississippi*, 322–323; Barney, *Secessionist Impulse*, 196–197.

35. Rowland, *Courts, Judges, and Lawyers of Mississippi*, 323–324.

36. John H. Aughey, *The Iron Furnace: Or, Slavery and Secession* (Philadelphia: William S. and Alfred Martien, 1863), 20–32; Election Returns, 1817–2007. The same accounts by Aughey appear in John H. Aughey, *Tupelo* (Lincoln: State Journal Company, Printers, 1888).

37. Aughey, *Iron Furnace*, 50; Election Returns, 1817–2007; Wood, *Union and Secession in Mississippi*, 20.

38. Election Returns, 1817–2007; "Jefferson County—The Fayette Times Says," *Vicksburg Daily Whig*, December 27, 1860; "Glorious Result in Rankin," *Vicksburg Daily Whig*, December 25, 1860; R. F. Crenshaw to Ella Austin, December 13, 1860, R. F. Crenshaw Letter, Small Manuscripts, University of Mississippi (hereafter cited as UM).

39. Benjamin G. Humphreys, "The Autobiography of Benjamin Grubb Humphreys August 26, 1808–December 20, 1882," ed. Percy L. Rainwater, *Mississippi Valley Historical Review* 21, no. 2 (September 1934): 243; Olsen, *Political Culture and Secession in Mississippi*, 192–193; Barney, *Secessionist Impulse*, 203, 208–218, 223; "Beware of Split Tickets," *Jackson Mississippian*, December 11, 1860.

40. "Patriotic Move," *Oxford Intelligencer*, January 19, 1860.

41. "Are You Ready?" *Vicksburg Daily Whig*, December 19, 1860; Barney, *Secessionist Impulse*, 268.

42. Election Returns, 1817–2007.

43. Election Returns, 1817–2007.

44. "Thanksgiving Day," *Mississippi Free Trader*, December 24, 1860; "Proclamation," *Vicksburg Daily Whig*, December 27, 1860; Percy L. Rainwater, ed., "Notes and Documents: The Civil War Letters of Cordelia Scales," *Journal of Mississippi History* 1, no. 1 (July 1939): 171, 173, 180–181; see also the Cordelia Lewis Scales Letters, MDAH; *Vicksburg Daily Whig*, November 28, 1860; *Vicksburg Daily Whig*, December 25, 1860; "The Mississippi Commissioners," *Vicksburg Daily Whig*, December 14, 1860; *Vicksburg Daily Whig*, December 28, 1860; "Appointment of Commissioners," *Oxford Intelligencer*, December 19, 1860.

CHAPTER 2

1. Woods, "Sketch of the Mississippi Secession Convention," 94–95.

2. Rowland, *Courts, Judges, and Lawyers of Mississippi*, 329; Claiborne, "Secession Convention," 5; J. L. Power, *Proceedings of the Mississippi State Convention, Held January 7th to 26th, A.D. 1861. Including the Ordinances, as Finally Adopted, Important Speeches, and a List of Members, Showing the Postoffice, Profession, Nativity, Politics, Age, Religious Preference, and Social Relations of Each* (Jackson: Power and Cadwallader, Book and Job Printers, 1861), 87; J. L. Power, "Mississippi Secession Convention," *Southern Home Journal* 3, no. 3 (April 1899): 141.

3. "The Personnel of the Mississippi State Convention," *Vicksburg Weekly Whig*, April 3, 1861; Wooster, *Secession Conventions of the South*, 26–48; Wooster, "Membership of the Mississippi Secession Convention," 242–257; "Alphabetical List of Members of the Mississippi State Convention." See also the wealth of information provided in the 1860 census population schedules and the biographical roster included as an appendix to this book. Wooster has analyzed the membership, and while my numbers fall basically in the same pattern, there are discrepancies here and there. This is attributable to the wider range of sources I have used, particularly those examined to develop the biographies found in the appendix to this book. Apparently Wooster only examined the Power document and census records, while I have investigated their lives in detailed family, county, political, and cemetery records. One example is the age of the members, which differs in some areas from Wooster. I have examined cemetery gravestones, family histories, and county will records. Sometimes the Power document's age does not agree with the census ages given, and at times neither of those agrees with headstones or death records.

4. Woods, "Sketch of the Mississippi Secession Convention," 94; "Alphabetical List of Members of the Mississippi State Convention."

5. "Alphabetical List of Members of the Mississippi State Convention."

6. "Alphabetical List of Members of the Mississippi State Convention."

7. Woods, "Sketch of the Mississippi Secession Convention," 94–95.

8. "Alphabetical List of Members of the Mississippi State Convention"; Woods, "Sketch of the Mississippi Secession Convention," 95.

9. "Delegates to the Convention of Southern States"; "Alphabetical List of Members of the Mississippi State Convention." See the biographical appendix for more detail on the preconvention political occupations of the members.

10. See the *Congressional Biographical Directory* for official biographies of these federal officials.

11. Woods, "Sketch of the Mississippi Secession Convention," 94–95; "Alphabetical List of Members of the Mississippi State Convention." See the biographical appendix for educational aspects.

12. "Alphabetical List of Members of the Mississippi State Convention"; Olsen, *Political Culture and Secession in Mississippi*, 173. See the biographical appendix for these aspects.

13. See the various 1860 Mississippi slave schedules for this information.

14. Rowland, *Courts, Judges, and Lawyers of Mississippi*, 296–297; Wooster, *Secession Conventions of the South*, 34. Further information gleaned from the 1860 slave schedules.

15. Information gleaned from 1860 population schedules.

16. "The River Counties for Co-operation," *Vicksburg Daily Whig*, December 15, 1860; *Vicksburg Whig*, January 23, 1861; "Members Elected to the Convention," *Jackson Weekly Mississippian*, January 2, 1861; Rainwater, *Mississippi*, 177, 196; "Glorious Result in Rankin," *Vicksburg Daily Whig*, December 25, 1860; *Vicksburg Daily Whig*, December 25, 1860; Barney, *Secessionist Impulse*, 263.

17. "South-East Mississippi," undated clipping in Folder 73, Clippings of Slavery and Secession, J. F. H. Claiborne Papers, UNC; "South-East Mississippi," *Jackson Mississippian*, December 11, 1860; "North Mississippi," *Jackson Mississippian*, December 11, 1860; "Panola County," *Jackson Mississippian*, December 11, 1860.

18. "Alphabetical List of Members of the Mississippi State Convention"; Wooster, *Secession Conventions of the South*, 30.

19. "Alphabetical List of Members of the Mississippi State Convention."

20. Wooster, *Secession Conventions of the South*, 35.

21. Richey Henderson, *Pontotoc County Men of Note* (Pontotoc, Miss.: Pontotoc Progress Print, 1940), 67–68; Charles D. Fontaine Subject File, MDAH; 1860 Mississippi Population Census; 1860 Mississippi Slave Schedules; "Alphabetical List of Members of the Mississippi State Convention"; Lowry and McCardle, *History of Mississippi*, 561; Olsen, *Political Culture and Secession in Mississippi*, 149–167.

22. William Henry Perrin, *Southwest Louisiana, Biographical and Historical* (New Orleans: Gulf Publishing, 1891), 301; 1860 Mississippi Population Census; 1860 Mississippi Slave Schedules; "Alphabetical List of Members of the Mississippi State Convention"; "James B. Ramsey," Ken Dupuy Files, Vermilion Parish, La.; Gary Theall, *History of Vermilion Parish*, 2 vols. (Abbeville, La.: Vermilion Historical Society, 2003), 2:456.

23. Desoto County Genealogical Society, *Desoto County Mississippi: History and Families* (Humbolt: Rose Publishing, 1999), 129; 1860 Mississippi Population Census; 1860 Mississippi Slave Schedules; "Alphabetical List of Members of the Mississippi State Convention."

24. Power, "Mississippi Secession Convention," 136; H. S. Fulkerson, *A Civilian's Recollections of the War Between the States*, ed. Percy L. Rainwater (Baton Rouge, La.: Otto Claitor, 1939), 10; Woods, "Sketch of the Mississippi Secession Convention," 94–95.

25. Dubay, *John Jones Pettus*; Delbert Hosemann, *Mississippi's Official and Statistical Register, 2008–2012* (Jackson, Miss.: Secretary of State, 2009), 74–75.

26. Rowland, *Mississippi*, 1:843, 861–862.

27. *Journal of the House of Representatives of the State of Mississippi: Called Session, January 1861* (Jackson, Miss.: E. Barksdale, 1861).

28. *Journal of the House of Representatives of the State of Mississippi, Called Session,* 3–4; *Journal of the Senate of the State of Mississippi,* 3–4.

29. See the *Biographical Directory of the United States Congress* for information on these men.

30. Election Returns, 1817–2007; "The National Crisis," *New York Times,* January 9, 1861; Power, "Mississippi Secession Convention," 139–140; Barney, *Secessionist Impulse,* 204.

31. Election Returns, 1817–2007; James Z. George to wife, January 6, 1856, James Z. George Papers, MDAH; Allardice, *Confederate Colonels,* 210.

32. B. L. C. Wailes Diary, Duke University (hereafter cited as DU); Untitled, undated clipping in Folder 73, Clippings of Slavery and Secession, J. F. H. Claiborne Papers, UNC.

33. Election Returns, 1817–2007; Rainwater, *Mississippi,* 177.

34. "Mississippi State Convention," *Natchez Weekly Courier,* January 9, 1861; "The Convention Election," *Vicksburg Daily Whig,* December 25, 1860; "The Election," *Vicksburg Daily Whig,* December 21, 1860; "The Convention Election," *Vicksburg Daily Whig,* December 27, 1860; "Delegates Elected to the Convention," *Vicksburg Daily Whig,* December 28, 1860; "The Election," *Vicksburg Evening Citizen,* December 21, 1860; "Members Elected to the Convention," *Jackson Weekly Mississippian,* January 2, 1861; *Vicksburg Whig,* January 23, 1861; "Cooperation Unconstitutional," *Vicksburg Evening Citizen,* December 21, 1860.

35. "Cooperation Unconstitutional," *Vicksburg Evening Citizen,* December 21, 1860; "The Convention Election," *Vicksburg Daily Whig,* December 25, 1860; "The Convention Election," *Vicksburg Daily Whig,* December 27, 1860; "Delegates Elected to the Convention," *Vicksburg Daily Whig,* December 28, 1860; "Delegates Elected to the Convention," *Vicksburg Weekly Whig,* January 9, 1861.

36. "Members Elected to the Convention," *Jackson Weekly Mississippian,* January 2, 1861; "States Rights Meeting in Natchez," *Jackson Weekly Mississippian,* January 9, 1861.

37. "Election of Delegates to the State Convention," *Jackson Weekly Mississippian,* January 2, 1861.

38. "States Rights Meeting in Natchez," *Jackson Weekly Mississippian,* January 9, 1861; *Vicksburg Weekly Whig,* January 9, 1861; Barney, *Secessionist Impulse,* 265.

39. R. F. Crenshaw to Ella Austin, December 13, 1860, R. F. Crenshaw Letter, Small Manuscripts, UM; "Pro-Slavery Rebellion."

40. Murphy, *L. Q. C. Lamar*; Smith, *James Z. George*; Pereyra, *James Lusk Alcorn.*

CHAPTER 3

1. Richardson, *Secret Service,* 79; James Z. George to Bettie, January 19, 1855; January 1, 10, and February 1, 1856; and January 2, 1858, James Z. George Papers, MDAH.

2. Rowland, *Mississippi,* 1:950.

3. Rowland, *Mississippi,* 1:950.

4. Rowland, *Mississippi,* 1:353–356; "Pro-Slavery Rebellion."

5. "Pro-Slavery Rebellion"; Rowland, *Mississippi*, 1:353–356.

6. Rowland, *Mississippi*, 1:353–356.

7. *Vicksburg Weekly Whig*, January 9, 1861.

8. Mayes, *Lucius Q. C. Lamar*, 89–91, 633–639; "The New Republic," *Vicksburg Daily Whig*, December 21, 1860; "Mr. Lamar's Plan of Secession," *Vicksburg Daily Whig*, December 28, 1860.

9. Mayes, *Lucius Q. C. Lamar*, 638–639.

10. Mayes, *Lucius Q. C. Lamar*, 638–639; Rowland, *Courts, Judges, and Lawyers of Mississippi*, 319; James M. McPherson, *Battle Cry of Freedom: The Civil War Era* (New York: Oxford University Press, 1988), 202–275; "Plan of a Southern Confederacy," undated clipping in Folder 73, Clippings of Slavery and Secession, J. F. H. Claiborne Papers, UNC.

11. "The Mississippi Convention," *New York Times*, January 8, 1861; "The Presidency of the Convention," *Oxford Intelligencer*, December 26, 1860; "Mississippi State Convention," *Weekly Panola Star*, January 10, 1861; "Mississippi State Convention," *Jackson Weekly Mississippian*, January 9, 1861; Rainwater, *Mississippi*, 208.

12. B. L. C. Wailes Diary, January 7, 1861, DU; "The Mississippi Convention," *New York Times*, January 9, 1861; "Mississippi State Convention," *Weekly Panola Star*, January 10, 1861; "Pro-Slavery Rebellion"; "Mississippi Convention," *Natchez Courier*, January 10, 1861; "The Convention," *Vicksburg Evening Citizen*, January 7, 1861; Power, "Mississippi Secession Convention," 199.

13. "Pro-Slavery Rebellion"; John K. Bettersworth, ed., *Mississippi in the Confederacy: As They Saw It* (Baton Rouge: Louisiana State University Press, 1961), 43–44.

14. "Pro-Slavery Rebellion."

15. "Pro-Slavery Rebellion."

16. "Pro-Slavery Rebellion."

17. Wood, *Union and Secession in Mississippi*, 20–21; *Journal of the State Convention and Ordinances and Resolutions Adopted in January, 1861, With an Appendix* (Jackson, Miss.: E. Barksdale, 1861), 3.

18. Power, "Proceedings and Debates of the Mississippi State Convention," 7; Wood, *Union and Secession in Mississippi*, 21; *Journal of the State Convention and Ordinances and Resolutions Adopted in January, 1861*, 3.

19. *Journal of the State Convention and Ordinances and Resolutions Adopted in January, 1861*, 3; "Mississippi Convention," undated clipping in Folder 73, Clippings of Slavery and Secession, J. F. H. Claiborne Papers, UNC.

20. Claiborne, "Secession Convention," 1; "Mississippi State Convention," *Jackson Weekly Mississippian*, January 9, 1861; *Journal of the State Convention and Ordinances and Resolutions Adopted in January, 1861*, 3–5.

21. *Journal of the State Convention and Ordinances and Resolutions Adopted in January, 1861*, 5–6.

22. J. L. Power, *An Account of the Siege of Vicksburg: From the Personal Diary of Col. John Logan Power and His News Report of the Mississippi Secession Convention of January 7, 1861* (Jackson, Miss.: John L. Power, 1959), A1; *Journal of the State Convention and Ordinances and Resolutions Adopted in January, 1861*, 6–7.

23. "Mississippi State Convention," *Jackson Weekly Mississippian*, January 9, 1861; *Journal of the State Convention and Ordinances and Resolutions Adopted in January, 1861*, 7; "The Mississippi Convention," *New York Times*, January 8, 1861; "Mississippi State Convention," *Weekly Panola Star*, January 10, 1861.

24. *Journal of the State Convention and Ordinances and Resolutions Adopted in January, 1861*, 3, 5; Woods, "Sketch of the Mississippi Secession Convention," 93; Rainwater, *Mississippi*, 208; Claiborne, "Secession Convention."

25. *Journal of the State Convention and Ordinances and Resolutions Adopted in January, 1861*, 7–9; *Vicksburg Weekly Whig*, January 9, 1861; "State Convention," *Vicksburg Evening Citizen*, January 7, 1861; Hugh R. Miller to George, January 14, 1861, Miller Family Papers, MDAH; Power, "Proceedings and Debates of the Mississippi State Convention," 2; Woods, "Sketch of the Mississippi Secession Convention," 97; Claiborne, "Secession Convention"; "Alphabetical List of Members of the Mississippi State Convention"; "Pro-Slavery Rebellion."

26. *Journal of the State Convention and Ordinances and Resolutions Adopted in January, 1861*, 9–10.

27. Power, "Mississippi Secession Convention," 200; *Journal of the State Convention and Ordinances and Resolutions Adopted in January, 1861*, 9; "Mississippi State Convention," *Jackson Weekly Mississippian*, January 9, 1861.

28. "Mississippi State Convention," *Jackson Weekly Mississippian*, January 9, 1861; "Mississippi Convention," *Natchez Courier*, January 10, 1861.

29. Fulkerson, *Civilian's Recollections*, 7.

30. Fulkerson, *Civilian's Recollections*, 7–9; Woods, "Sketch of the Mississippi Secession Convention," 93.

31. B. L. C. Wailes Diary, January 8, 1861, DU; "Mississippi State Convention," *Weekly Panola Star*, January 10, 1861; "The National Crisis," *New York Times*, January 9, 1861; *War of the Rebellion: A Compilation of the Official Records of the Union and Confederate Armies*, 128 vols. (Washington, D.C.: Government Printing Office, 1880–1891), Series 1, Vol. 52, Part 2:3 (hereafter cited as *OR*, with series, volume, part [where applicable], and page numbers); Bettersworth, *Confederate Mississippi*, 7; *Journal of the State Convention and Ordinances and Resolutions Adopted in January, 1861*, 10.

32. Power, "Proceedings and Debates of the Mississippi State Convention," 3–4; *Journal of the State Convention and Ordinances and Resolutions Adopted in January, 1861*, 10–11.

33. *Journal of the State Convention and Ordinances and Resolutions Adopted in January, 1861*, 12. There is some disagreement in the sources concerning when Barry announced the committee of fifteen. The official journal says January 8, but the *Jackson Weekly Mississippian* reports it on the first day, January 7. See "Mississippi State Convention," *Jackson Weekly Mississippian*, January 9, 1861; and "By Telegraph," undated clipping in Folder 73, Clippings of Slavery and Secession, J. F. H. Claiborne Papers, UNC.

34. Claiborne, "Secession Convention," 2; *Journal of the State Convention and Ordinances and Resolutions Adopted in January, 1861*, 11; David C. Glenn, "Memoranda," n.d., J. F. C. Claiborne Papers, UNC, 1; Rainwater, *Mississippi*, 208.

35. Power, "Proceedings and Debates of the Mississippi State Convention," 3; *Journal of the State Convention and Ordinances and Resolutions Adopted in January, 1861*, 10–11.

36. Claiborne, "Secession Convention," 3; "The Mississippi Convention," *New York Times,* January 9, 1861; Power, "Proceedings and Debates of the Mississippi State Convention," 3; "Second Day," *Jackson Weekly Mississippian,* January 16, 1861; *Journal of the State Convention and Ordinances and Resolutions Adopted in January, 1861,* 10–11.

37. Power, "Proceedings and Debates of the Mississippi State Convention," 3; *Journal of the State Convention and Ordinances and Resolutions Adopted in January, 1861,* 12.

38. Power, "Proceedings and Debates of the Mississippi State Convention," 4; "Second Day," *Jackson Weekly Mississippian,* January 16, 1861; Wood, *Union and Secession in Mississippi,* 23–25.

39. "Second Day," *Jackson Weekly Mississippian,* January 16, 1861; Wood, *Union and Secession in Mississippi,* 23–25; Power, "Proceedings and Debates of the Mississippi State Convention," 4.

40. "The Mississippi Convention," *New York Times,* January 9, 1861; "Second Day," *Jackson Weekly Mississippian,* January 16, 1861; Wood, *Union and Secession in Mississippi,* 23–25.

41. "Second Day," *Jackson Weekly Mississippian,* January 16, 1861; Wood, *Union and Secession in Mississippi,* 23–25.

42. Glenn, "Memoranda," 1; Wood, *Union and Secession in Mississippi,* 23.

CHAPTER 4

1. Mayes, *Lucius Q. C. Lamar,* 89. For a full biography of Lamar, see Murphy, *L. Q. C. Lamar.*

2. Election Returns, 1817–2007; Glenn, "Memoranda."

3. "The Mississippi Convention," *New York Times,* January 9, 1861; Power, *Proceedings of the Mississippi State Convention,* 8–9; "Second Day," *Jackson Weekly Mississippian,* January 16, 1861. Power records the announcement of the committee at the end of the day on January 7.

4. "Third Day," *Oxford Intelligencer,* January 23, 1861; Mayes, *Lucius Q. C. Lamar,* 637–638; Power, *Proceedings of the Mississippi State Convention,* 8–9.

5. Power, *Proceedings of the Mississippi State Convention,* 8–9.

6. B. L. C. Wailes Diary, January 9, 1861, DU; "Third Day," *Oxford Intelligencer,* January 23, 1861; Glenn, "Memoranda"; *Journal of the State Convention and Ordinances and Resolutions Adopted in January, 1861,* 13; Rainwater, *Mississippi,* 209; Power, *Proceedings of the Mississippi State Convention,* 8; Power, "Proceedings and Debates of the Mississippi State Convention," 5; Claiborne, "Secession Convention," 4.

7. "Third Day," *Oxford Intelligencer,* January 23, 1861; "Third Day," *Jackson Weekly Mississippian,* January 16, 1861; "Third Day," *Vicksburg Whig,* January 16, 1861; Power, "Proceedings and Debates of the Mississippi State Convention," 5.

8. *OR,* 4, 1:42–43; *Journal of the State Convention and Ordinances and Resolutions Adopted in January, 1861,* 119–120.

9. "Third Day," *Jackson Weekly Mississippian,* January 16, 1861.

10. Power, "Proceedings and Debates of the Mississippi State Convention," 6; "Third Day," *Jackson Weekly Mississippian,* January 16, 1861; Rainwater, *Mississippi,* 209.

11. "Third Day," *Jackson Weekly Mississippian*, January 16, 1861.

12. "Third Day," *Oxford Intelligencer*, January 23, 1861; "Third Day," *Jackson Weekly Mississippian*, January 16, 1861.

13. "Third Day," *Oxford Intelligencer*, January 23, 1861; Wood, *Union and Secession in Mississippi*, 26; Power, *Proceedings of the Mississippi State Convention*, 9; Rainwater, *Mississippi*, 209; Woods, "Sketch of the Mississippi Secession Convention," 98.

14. Woods, "Sketch of the Mississippi Secession Convention," 98; Wood, *Union and Secession in Mississippi*, 26, 30–31.

15. Wood, *Union and Secession in Mississippi*, 26–30.

16. Wood, *Union and Secession in Mississippi*, 26–30.

17. Wood, *Union and Secession in Mississippi*, 26–30.

18. "Third Day," *Oxford Intelligencer*, January 23, 1861; Woods, "Sketch of the Mississippi Secession Convention," 95; Hugh R. Miller to George, January 14, 1861, Miller Family Papers, MDAH; Fulkerson, *Civilian's Recollections*, 7–9; Claiborne, "Secession Convention."

19. *Journal of the State Convention and Ordinances and Resolutions Adopted in January, 1861*, 11; Woods, "Sketch of the Mississippi Secession Convention," 95; Hugh R. Miller to George, January 14, 1861, Miller Family Papers, MDAH; Fulkerson, *Civilian's Recollections*, 7–9; Claiborne, "Secession Convention."

20. *Journal of the State Convention and Ordinances and Resolutions Adopted in January, 1861*, 14.

21. Power, *Proceedings of the Mississippi State Convention*, 9–11.

22. Woods, "Sketch of the Mississippi Secession Convention," 99; Power, "Proceedings and Debates of the Mississippi State Convention," 7; *Journal of the State Convention and Ordinances and Resolutions Adopted in January, 1861*, 14.

23. *Journal of the State Convention and Ordinances and Resolutions Adopted in January, 1861*, 15.

24. *Journal of the State Convention and Ordinances and Resolutions Adopted in January, 1861*, 14–15. Alcorn lost Brooke and Marshall of Warren, Blair of Tishomingo, and Flournoy of Pontotoc, but he picked up Beene and Tison of Itawamba, Denson of Hinds, Dyer of Holmes, Johnston of DeSoto, McGehee of Panola, and Powell of Jones.

25. *Journal of the State Convention and Ordinances and Resolutions Adopted in January, 1861*, 15–16; Claiborne, "Secession Convention," 8.

26. Fulkerson, *Civilian's Recollections*, 7.

27. *Journal of the State Convention and Ordinances and Resolutions Adopted in January, 1861*, 15–16; Woods, "Sketch of the Mississippi Secession Convention," 100. Brooke lost Dyer of Holmes, Johnston of DeSoto, and McGehee of Panola, but gained Barksdale and Aldridge of Yalobusha, Blair of Tishomingo, Brooke and Marshall of Warren, Isom of Lafayette, and Flournoy of Pontotoc.

28. *Journal of the State Convention and Ordinances and Resolutions Adopted in January, 1861*, 16; "Third Day," *Jackson Weekly Mississippian*, January 16, 1861; Power, "Mississippi Secession Convention," 202; Claiborne, "Secession Convention," 4.

29. "Current Comment in Mississippi," *New Orleans Times Picayune*, February 3, 1895; *OR*, 4, 1:76; *Journal of the State Convention and Ordinances and Resolutions Adopted in January, 1861*, 96.

30. Power, "Mississippi Secession Convention," 201; James L. Alcorn to wife, January 15, 1861, J. L. Alcorn Papers, UNC; *Journal of the State Convention and Ordinances and Resolutions Adopted in January, 1861,* 96; Power, *Account of the Siege of Vicksburg,* A3.

31. "Prayer for the New-born Republic," January 9, 1861, Whitfield Harrington Papers, MDAH; Woods, "Sketch of the Mississippi Secession Convention," 95–97; Mayes, *Lucius Q. C. Lamar,* 92; "Third Day," *Oxford Intelligencer,* January 23, 1861; *OR,* 4, 1:76–77.

32. Power, "Proceedings and Debates of the Mississippi State Convention," 7; "Third Day," *Jackson Weekly Mississippian,* January 16, 1861; Fulkerson, *Civilian's Recollections,* 7–9.

33. Fulkerson, *Civilian's Recollections,* 7; Power, "Mississippi Secession Convention," 201; "Third Day," *Jackson Weekly Mississippian,* January 16, 1861; Power, *Proceedings of the Mississippi State Convention,* 68.

34. *Journal of the State Convention and Ordinances and Resolutions Adopted in January, 1861,* 16; Mayes, *Lucius Q. C. Lamar,* 91–92; Bettersworth, *Mississippi in the Confederacy,* 31; *OR,* 4, 1:77; "The Disunion Movement," *New York Times,* January 10, 1861. The members voting for Brooke's amendments but not for secession were Herring, Stephens, Sumner, McGehee of Bolivar, Powell, Denson, Beene, Tison, Alcorn, Brooke, Flournoy, Barksdale, Aldridge, and Isom. The two who voted against secession and against Alcorn's amendment were Marshall and Blair.

35. "Prayer for the New-born Republic"; Woods, "Sketch of the Mississippi Secession Convention," 95; Mayes, *Lucius Q. C. Lamar,* 92; "Third Day," *Jackson Weekly Mississippian,* January 16, 1861; *OR,* 4, 1:76–77.

36. "Third Day," *Oxford Intelligencer,* January 23, 1861; "Third Day," *Jackson Weekly Mississippian,* January 16, 1861.

37. "Current Comment in Mississippi," *New Orleans Times Picayune,* February 3, 1895; "Third Day," *Jackson Weekly Mississippian,* January 16, 1861; *Journal of the State Convention and Ordinances and Resolutions Adopted in January, 1861,* 16; Mayes, *Lucius Q. C. Lamar,* 91–92; Bettersworth, *Mississippi in the Confederacy,* 31; "The Disunion Movement," January 10, 1861, *New York Times;* Power, *Account of the Siege of Vicksburg,* A4-A5. John L. Power years later described it as a white star. See Power, "Mississippi Secession Convention," 202.

38. Wood, *Union and Secession in Mississippi,* 31; "By Telegraph," undated clipping in Folder 73, Clippings of Slavery and Secession, J. F. H. Claiborne Papers, UNC; "Third Day," *Jackson Weekly Mississippian,* January 16, 1861; Mayes, *Lucius Q. C. Lamar,* 91–92; Bettersworth, *Mississippi in the Confederacy,* 31; Power, "Mississippi Secession Convention," 202; "Third Day," *Oxford Intelligencer,* January 23, 1861; "The Disunion Movement," January 10, 1861, *New York Times.*

39. "Current Comment in Mississippi," *New Orleans Times Picayune,* February 3, 1895; Power, *Account of the Siege of Vicksburg,* A5; "The Bonnie Blue Flag," *New Orleans Times Picayune,* February 4, 1895; Power, "Mississippi Secession Convention," 203. Power later put the song in type.

40. "Third Day," *Natchez Courier,* January 15, 1861; "Hon. J. A. Blair, of Tishomingo," *Natchez Courier,* January 10, 1861; *Natchez Courier,* January 22, 1861; *Vicksburg Whig,* January 16, 1861; "Mississippi Is Out!," *Oxford Intelligencer,* January 9, 1861; "Mississippi and Alabama Out of the Union," *Weekly Panola Star,* January 10, 1861; Davis, *Recollections*

of Mississippi and Mississippians, 401–402; James Fontaine Maury Diary, January 9, 1861, UNC; "Circular of Bishop Green of Mississippi," *Vicksburg Evening Citizen*, January 17, 1861; Barney, *Secessionist Impulse*, 312.

41. Fulkerson, *Civilian's Recollections*, 7–9; Rainwater, *Mississippi*, 211, 216.

42. *OR*, 4, 1:76; *Journal of the State Convention and Ordinances and Resolutions Adopted in January, 1861*, 14–16.

43. Statistics gleaned from 1860 census population and slave schedules.

44. "Alphabetical List of Members of the Mississippi State Convention."

45. *Journal of the State Convention and Ordinances and Resolutions Adopted in January, 1861*, 17.

46. Fulkerson, *Civilian's Recollections*, 7–9; Rainwater, *Mississippi*, 211, 216; "Third Day," *Oxford Intelligencer*, January 23, 1861; Barney, *Secessionist Impulse*, 245; *OR*, 4, 1:77.

CHAPTER 5

1. B. L. C. Wailes Diary, January 10, 1861, DU; Olsen, *Political Culture and Secession in Mississippi*, 15.

2. Thomas B. Webber Diary, January 9, 1861, DU.

3. Richardson, *Secret Service*, 80; James L. Alcorn to wife, January 15, 1861, J. L. Alcorn Papers, UNC; Charles D. Fontaine to Sally Ann, January 13 and 20, 1861, Fontaine Family Papers, MDAH; Hugh R. Miller to George, January 14, 1861, Miller Family Papers, MDAH.

4. *OR*, 1, 52, 2:4; *Congressional Globe*, 36th Congress, 2nd Session, 345, 352; Davis, *Recollections of Mississippi and Mississippians*, 401.

5. Power, *Proceedings of the Mississippi State Convention*, 16; *Journal of the State Convention and Ordinances and Resolutions Adopted in January, 1861*, 17.

6. Power, *Proceedings of the Mississippi State Convention*, 16; *Journal of the State Convention and Ordinances and Resolutions Adopted in January, 1861*, 17.

7. Power, *Proceedings of the Mississippi State Convention*, 16; *Journal of the State Convention and Ordinances and Resolutions Adopted in January, 1861*, 17.

8. Power, *Proceedings of the Mississippi State Convention*, 16; *Journal of the State Convention and Ordinances and Resolutions Adopted in January, 1861*, 17.

9. Power, *Proceedings of the Mississippi State Convention*, 16; *Journal of the State Convention and Ordinances and Resolutions Adopted in January, 1861*, 17, 237–239.

10. Glenn, "Memoranda," 1; Power, *Proceedings of the Mississippi State Convention*, 16; *Journal of the State Convention and Ordinances and Resolutions Adopted in January, 1861*, 17.

11. *Journal of the State Convention and Ordinances and Resolutions Adopted in January, 1861*, 17.

12. "Fourth Day," *Jackson Weekly Mississippian*, January 16, 1861; *Journal of the State Convention and Ordinances and Resolutions Adopted in January, 1861*, 17–18; Power, *Proceedings of the Mississippi State Convention*, 16–17; Power, "Proceedings and Debates of the Mississippi State Convention," 8–9.

13. "Fourth Day," *Jackson Weekly Mississippian*, January 16, 1861; *Journal of the State Convention and Ordinances and Resolutions Adopted in January, 1861*, 17–18; Power,

Proceedings of the Mississippi State Convention, 16–17; Power, "Proceedings and Debates of the Mississippi State Convention," 9.

14. B. L. C. Wailes Diary, January 11–12, 1861, DU; "Fourth Day," *Jackson Weekly Mississippian*, January 16, 1861; *Journal of the State Convention and Ordinances and Resolutions Adopted in January, 1861*, 18.

15. Power, "Proceedings and Debates of the Mississippi State Convention," 9; "Fourth Day," *Jackson Weekly Mississippian*, January 16, 1861.

16. *Journal of the State Convention and Ordinances and Resolutions Adopted in January, 1861*, 18–19; Power, *Proceedings of the Mississippi State Convention*, 17.

17. "Fourth Day," *Jackson Weekly Mississippian*, January 16, 1861; Power, "Proceedings and Debates of the Mississippi State Convention," 10; *Journal of the State Convention and Ordinances and Resolutions Adopted in January, 1861*, 19; Power, *Proceedings of the Mississippi State Convention*, 18.

18. Hugh R. Miller to George, January 14, 1861, Miller Family Papers, MDAH; *Journal of the State Convention and Ordinances and Resolutions Adopted in January, 1861*, 19; Power, *Proceedings of the Mississippi State Convention*, 18.

19. "Fifth Day," *Jackson Weekly Mississippian*, January 16, 1861; *Journal of the State Convention and Ordinances and Resolutions Adopted in January, 1861*, 19–20.

20. Power, "Proceedings and Debates of the Mississippi State Convention," 12–13; *Journal of the State Convention and Ordinances and Resolutions Adopted in January, 1861*, 19–20.

21. Power, *Proceedings of the Mississippi State Convention*, 18; *Journal of the State Convention and Ordinances and Resolutions Adopted in January, 1861*, 20; "Fifth Day," *Jackson Weekly Mississippian*, January 16, 1861.

22. "Fifth Day," *Jackson Weekly Mississippian*, January 16, 1861; Power, *Proceedings of the Mississippi State Convention*, 18; Power, "Proceedings and Debates of the Mississippi State Convention," 10–11; *Journal of the State Convention and Ordinances and Resolutions Adopted in January, 1861*, 20.

23. Power, *Proceedings of the Mississippi State Convention*, 18; "Fifth Day," *Jackson Weekly Mississippian*, January 16, 1861.

24. "Fifth Day," *Jackson Weekly Mississippian*, January 16, 1861; Power, *Proceedings of the Mississippi State Convention*, 82–83; Power, "Proceedings and Debates of the Mississippi State Convention," 11.

25. *Journal of the State Convention and Ordinances and Resolutions Adopted in January, 1861*, 19–20; Power, *Proceedings of the Mississippi State Convention*, 18, 69; James L. Alcorn to wife, January 15, 1861, J. L. Alcorn Papers, UNC. Barry also appointed a "temporary Executive Committee" of Alcorn, Alexander Clayton, Harris, Francis M. Rogers of Monroe County, and Alfred C. Holt of Wilkinson.

26. "Fifth Day," *Jackson Weekly Mississippian*, January 16, 1861; *Journal of the State Convention and Ordinances and Resolutions Adopted in January, 1861*, 20; Power, *Proceedings of the Mississippi State Convention*, 18–19, 69–70.

27. Power, "Proceedings and Debates of the Mississippi State Convention," 13; *Journal of the State Convention and Ordinances and Resolutions Adopted in January, 1861*, 21; Barney, *Secessionist Impulse*, 307.

28. *Journal of the State Convention and Ordinances and Resolutions Adopted in January, 1861*, 21; "Fifth Day," *Jackson Weekly Mississippian*, January 16, 1861; Charles B. Dew, *Apostles of Disunion: Southern Secession Commissioners and the Causes of the Civil War* (Charlottesville: University Press of Virginia, 2001), 45; James Fontaine Maury Diary, January 11, 1861, UNC. For Burt's full address, see Power, "Proceedings and Debates of the Mississippi State Convention," 14; *OR*, 4, 1:77.

29. *Journal of the State Convention and Ordinances and Resolutions Adopted in January, 1861*, 21; "Sixth Day," *Jackson Weekly Mississippian*, January 16, 1861; "Seventh Day," *Jackson Weekly Mississippian*, January 16, 1861.

30. Power, "Proceedings and Debates of the Mississippi State Convention," 14; "Fifth Day," *Jackson Weekly Mississippian*, January 16, 1861; *Journal of the State Convention and Ordinances and Resolutions Adopted in January, 1861*, 21–22; "Sixth Day," *Jackson Weekly Mississippian*, January 16, 1861.

31. "Sixth Day," *Jackson Weekly Mississippian*, January 16, 1861; *Mississippi Free Trader*, January 22, 1861; *Journal of the State Convention and Ordinances and Resolutions Adopted in January, 1861*, 22; "Seventh Day," *Jackson Weekly Mississippian*, January 16, 1861.

32. *Journal of the State Convention and Ordinances and Resolutions Adopted in January, 1861*, 22; "Sixth Day," *Jackson Weekly Mississippian*, January 16, 1861.

33. *Journal of the State Convention and Ordinances and Resolutions Adopted in January, 1861*, 23; Power, "Proceedings and Debates of the Mississippi State Convention," 15; "Sixth Day," *Jackson Weekly Mississippian*, January 16, 1861; *Mississippi Free Trader*, January 22, 1861.

34. Power, "Proceedings and Debates of the Mississippi State Convention," 15; Power, *Proceedings of the Mississippi State Convention*, 20; "Sixth Day," *Jackson Weekly Mississippian*, January 16, 1861.

35. *Journal of the State Convention and Ordinances and Resolutions Adopted in January, 1861*, 22; "Sixth Day," *Jackson Weekly Mississippian*, January 16, 1861.

36. *Journal of the State Convention and Ordinances and Resolutions Adopted in January, 1861*, 22–23; "Sixth Day," *Jackson Weekly Mississippian*, January 16, 1861.

37. "Sixth Day," *Jackson Weekly Mississippian*, January 16, 1861; Richard Beeman, *Plain, Honest Men: The Making of the American Constitution* (New York: Random House, 2009), 99–100, 108–109, 117, 124, 140, 158, 160, 171, 277.

38. Power, "Proceedings and Debates of the Mississippi State Convention," 16–17; "Sixth Day," *Jackson Weekly Mississippian*, January 16, 1861.

39. "Sixth Day," *Jackson Weekly Mississippian*, January 16, 1861.

40. Power, "Proceedings and Debates of the Mississippi State Convention," 4; William R. Barksdale to Ferrell, January 18, 1861, William R. Barksdale Letters, MDAH.

CHAPTER 6

1. B. L. C. Wailes Diary, January 14, 1861, DU; James Fontaine Maury Diary, January 14, 1861, UNC; Power, *Proceedings of the Mississippi State Convention*; 21; "The Convention," *Vicksburg Evening Citizen*, January 14, 1861; "Seventh Day," *Jackson Weekly Mississippian*, January 16, 1861.

2. For overviews of these periods, see Gordon S. Wood, *Empire of Liberty: A History of the Early Republic, 1789–1815* (New York: Oxford University Press, 2009); and Daniel Walker Howe, *What Hath God Wrought: The Transformation of America, 1815–1848* (New York: Oxford University Press, 2007).

3. "Political," *Vicksburg Evening Citizen*, March 30, 1861.

4. McPherson, *Battle Cry of Freedom*, 689–692.

5. "Seventh Day," *Jackson Weekly Mississippian*, January 16, 1861; Power, *Proceedings of the Mississippi State Convention*, 21; Power, "Proceedings and Debates of the Mississippi State Convention," 16; *Journal of the State Convention and Ordinances and Resolutions Adopted in January, 1861*, 20–25, 138–139; "Mississippi Convention," *Vicksburg Whig*, January 23, 1861.

6. "Seventh Day," *Jackson Weekly Mississippian*, January 16, 1861; *Journal of the State Convention and Ordinances and Resolutions Adopted in January, 1861*, 146–147; Power, *Proceedings of the Mississippi State Convention*, 70–72; Power, "Proceedings and Debates of the Mississippi State Convention," 16–17.

7. "Military Board," *Vicksburg Whig*, January 23, 1861; "Military," *Natchez Courier*, January 22, 1861; "Military Board," undated clipping in Folder 73, Clippings of Slavery and Secession, J. F. H. Claiborne Papers, UNC; *Journal of the State Convention and Ordinances and Resolutions Adopted in January, 1861*, 225.

8. "Mississippi Convention," *Vicksburg Whig*, January 23, 1861; *Journal of the State Convention and Ordinances and Resolutions Adopted in January, 1861*, 22–23, 25–26; "Seventh Day," *Jackson Weekly Mississippian*, January 16, 1861.

9. Power, "Proceedings and Debates of the Mississippi State Convention," 17–18.

10. Power, "Proceedings and Debates of the Mississippi State Convention," 18–19; "Mississippi Convention," *Vicksburg Whig*, January 23, 1861; *Journal of the State Convention and Ordinances and Resolutions Adopted in January, 1861*, 22–23, 25–26; "Seventh Day," *Jackson Weekly Mississippian*, January 16, 1861.

11. Rainwater, *Mississippi*, 191; Hugh R. Miller to George, January 14, 1861, Miller Family Papers, MDAH; Charles D. Fontaine to John, January 21, 1861, Fontaine Family Papers, MDAH; James L. Alcorn to wife, January 15, 1861, J. L. Alcorn Papers, UNC; Woods, "Sketch of the Mississippi Secession Convention," 93, 100.

12. "Guns for the State," *Vicksburg Whig*, January 23, 1861; "Military Movements in Lowndes County," *Vicksburg Whig*, January 23, 1861; "Quitman Artillery," *Vicksburg Whig*, January 23, 1861; "The Downing Rifles," *Vicksburg Whig*, January 23, 1861; "Military Spirit," *Vicksburg Evening Citizen*, January 14, 1861; W. Ivie Westbrook to John J. Pettus, January 14, 1861, Mississippi Governor, John J. Pettus, Correspondence and Papers, 1859–1863, Series 757, MDAH; Absalom F. Dantzler to wife, January 20, 1861, Absalom F. Dantzler Papers, DU; W. H. McClanahan to Joseph D. Stapp, January 14, 1861, Joseph D. Stapp Papers, DU.

13. *Vicksburg Evening Citizen*, January 14, 1861; "From the Seat of War," *Vicksburg Evening Citizen*, January 14, 1861; Charles D. Fontaine to Sally Ann, January 12, 1861, Fontaine Family Papers, MDAH; Michael B. Ballard, *Vicksburg: The Campaign That Opened the Mississippi River* (Chapel Hill: University of North Carolina Press, 2004), 9; B. L. C. Wailes Diary, January 19, 1861, DU.

14. "Seventh Day," *Jackson Weekly Mississippian*, January 16, 1861; *Journal of the State Convention and Ordinances and Resolutions Adopted in January, 1861*, 26; Power, *Proceedings of the Mississippi State Convention*, 21; "Mississippi Convention," *Vicksburg Whig*, January 23, 1861; Power, "Proceedings and Debates of the Mississippi State Convention," 19.

15. B. L. C. Wailes Diary, January 14–17, 1861, DU; James Fontaine Maury Diary, January 15–19, 1861, UNC; *Laws of the State of Mississippi Passed at a Called Session of the Mississippi Legislature Held in the City of Jackson, January, 1861, Constitution Revised* (Jackson, Miss.: E. Barksdale, 1861); *Journal of the House of Representatives of the State of Mississippi: Called Session, January 1861*, 3; Absalom F. Dantzler to wife, January 20, 1861, Absalom F. Dantzler Papers, DU; "The Legislature," *Mississippi Free Trader*, January 22, 1861; "The Convention," *Vicksburg Evening Citizen*, January 14, 1861; "Damage to the Southern Road," *Vicksburg Evening Citizen*, January 17, 1861; "Let the Convention Be Moved to Vicksburg," *Vicksburg Evening Citizen*, January 15, 1861; "The Legislature," *Vicksburg Whig*, January 23, 1861; William R. Barksdale to Ferrell, January 18, 1861, William R. Barksdale Letters, MDAH.

16. "The Legislature," *Mississippi Free Trader*, January 22, 1861; "The Convention," *Vicksburg Evening Citizen*, January 14, 1861; "Damage to the Southern Road," *Vicksburg Evening Citizen*, January 17, 1861; "Let the Convention Be Moved to Vicksburg," *Vicksburg Evening Citizen*, January 15, 1861; "The Legislature," *Vicksburg Whig*, January 23, 1861; William R. Barksdale to Ferrell, January 18, 1861, William R. Barksdale Letters, MDAH.

17. "News of the Morning," *Natchez Courier*, January 26, 1861; Absalom F. Dantzler to wife, January 17 and 20, 1861, Absalom F. Dantzler Papers, DU.

18. Absalom F. Dantzler to wife, January 17 and 20, 1861, Absalom F. Dantzler Papers, DU; "Military," *Natchez Courier*, January 22, 1861.

19. *Journal of the State Convention and Ordinances and Resolutions Adopted in January, 1861*, 27; Power, *Proceedings of the Mississippi State Convention*, 94–95, 111; Glenn, "Memoranda," 1; Power, "Proceedings and Debates of the Mississippi State Convention," 20–21.

20. Glenn, "Memoranda," 1–2; *Journal of the State Convention and Ordinances and Resolutions Adopted in January, 1861*, 27; Power, *Proceedings of the Mississippi State Convention*, 94–95, 111.

21. *Journal of the State Convention and Ordinances and Resolutions Adopted in January, 1861*, 27; Power, *Proceedings of the Mississippi State Convention*, 94–95, 111.

22. Power, "Proceedings and Debates of the Mississippi State Convention," 21; "Affairs in Mississippi," *Mississippi Free Trader*, January 28, 1861; *Journal of the State Convention and Ordinances and Resolutions Adopted in January, 1861*, 20, 22, 27–28.

23. Claiborne, "Secession Convention," 4; Woods, "Sketch of the Mississippi Secession Convention," 100; *Journal of the State Convention and Ordinances and Resolutions Adopted in January, 1861*, 120–122; Rainwater, *Mississippi*, 211–212; Power, *Proceedings of the Mississippi State Convention*, 23; "Signing the Ordinance," *Vicksburg Whig*, January 23, 1861; *Journal of the State Convention and Ordinances and Resolutions Adopted in January, 1861*, 36; "Mississippi Convention," *Vicksburg Whig*, January 23, 1861; "Affairs in Mississippi," *Mississippi Free Trader*, January 28, 1861; *Mississippi Free Trader*, January 22, 1861.

24. Woods, "Sketch of the Mississippi Secession Convention," 100; *Journal of the State Convention and Ordinances and Resolutions Adopted in January, 1861*, 120–122; Power, "Mississippi Secession Convention," 206; Rainwater, *Mississippi*, 211–212; Power, *Proceedings of the Mississippi State Convention*, 23; "Signing the Ordinance," *Vicksburg Whig*, January 23, 1861; *Journal of the State Convention and Ordinances and Resolutions Adopted in January, 1861*, 36; "Mississippi Convention," *Vicksburg Whig*, January 23, 1861; "Affairs in Mississippi," *Mississippi Free Trader*, January 28, 1861; *Mississippi Free Trader*, January 22, 1861; "Mississippi Ordinance of Secession Signed," *Memphis Daily Appeal*, January 22, 1861.

25. "Mississippi Convention," *Vicksburg Whig*, January 23, 1861; *OR*, 4, 1:42–43; *Journal of the State Convention and Ordinances and Resolutions Adopted in January, 1861*, 28–29, 31–32. See the Ordinance of Secession Subject File, MDAH, for a facsimile of the signed ordinance.

26. William M. Brooks to John J. Pettus, January 11, 1861, and John C. McGehee to John J. Pettus, January 21, 1861, both in Mississippi Governor, John J. Pettus, Correspondence and Papers, 1859–1863, Series 757, MDAH; *Journal of the State Convention and Ordinances and Resolutions Adopted in January, 1861*, 28–29; Charles D. Fontaine to Sally Ann, January 12, 1861, Fontaine Family Papers, MDAH; Power, "Proceedings and Debates of the Mississippi State Convention," 21.

27. "Affairs in Mississippi," *Mississippi Free Trader*, January 28, 1861.

CHAPTER 7

1. B. L. C. Wailes Diary, January 16, 1861, DU.

2. B. L. C. Wailes Diary, January 25, 1861, DU; "The State Convention," *Natchez Daily Courier*, January 22, 1861; Power, *Proceedings of the Mississippi State Convention*, 23–24, 74–77; *Journal of the State Convention and Ordinances and Resolutions Adopted in January, 1861*, 29–31; "Mississippi Convention," *Vicksburg Whig*, January 23, 1861.

3. "The State Convention," *Natchez Daily Courier*, January 22, 1861; Power, *Proceedings of the Mississippi State Convention*, 23–24, 74–77; *Journal of the State Convention and Ordinances and Resolutions Adopted in January, 1861*, 29–31; Power, "Proceedings and Debates of the Mississippi State Convention," 22–23.

4. Power, "Proceedings and Debates of the Mississippi State Convention," 23; Glenn, "Memoranda," 4; Power, *Proceedings of the Mississippi State Convention*, 23–24; *Journal of the State Convention and Ordinances and Resolutions Adopted in January, 1861*, 29–31.

5. Glenn, "Memoranda," 4; Claiborne, "Secession Convention," 8–9; Power, "Proceedings and Debates of the Mississippi State Convention," 23–24; Power, *Proceedings of the Mississippi State Convention*, 23–24, 79–81, 95–98; *Journal of the State Convention and Ordinances and Resolutions Adopted in January, 1861*, 29–31.

6. Power, *Proceedings of the Mississippi State Convention*, 23–24, 79–81, 95–100; *Journal of the State Convention and Ordinances and Resolutions Adopted in January, 1861*, 29–31; "The State Convention," *Natchez Daily Courier*, January 22, 1861; Power, "Proceedings and Debates of the Mississippi State Convention," 25.

7. Power, *Proceedings of the Mississippi State Convention*, 23–24, 79–81, 95–100; *Journal of the State Convention and Ordinances and Resolutions Adopted in January, 1861*, 29–31;

"The State Convention," *Natchez Daily Courier*, January 22, 1861; Power, "Proceedings and Debates of the Mississippi State Convention," 25.

8. "Mississippi Convention," *Vicksburg Whig*, January 23, 1861; *Journal of the State Convention and Ordinances and Resolutions Adopted in January, 1861*, 32.

9. "Mississippi Convention," *Vicksburg Whig*, January 23, 1861; *Journal of the State Convention and Ordinances and Resolutions Adopted in January, 1861*, 32–35.

10. William R. Barksdale to Ferrell, January 18, 1861, William R. Barksdale Letters, MDAH; "Mississippi Convention," *Vicksburg Whig*, January 23, 1861; Power, "Proceedings and Debates of the Mississippi State Convention," 23, 29–30; Power, *Proceedings of the Mississippi State Convention*, 25, 104–110.

11. "Mississippi Convention," *Vicksburg Whig*, January 23, 1861; Power, *Proceedings of the Mississippi State Convention*, 25, 104–110; Power, "Proceedings and Debates of the Mississippi State Convention," 23.

12. Power, *Proceedings of the Mississippi State Convention*, 25, 104–110; "Mississippi Convention," *Vicksburg Whig*, January 23, 1861.

13. "Mississippi Convention," *Vicksburg Whig*, January 23, 1861; Power, "Proceedings and Debates of the Mississippi State Convention," 30.

14. Power, "Proceedings and Debates of the Mississippi State Convention," 31; *Journal of the State Convention and Ordinances and Resolutions Adopted in January, 1861*, 33.

15. Glenn, "Memoranda," 1–2; "Mississippi Convention," *Vicksburg Whig*, January 23, 1861; Power, *Proceedings of the Mississippi State Convention*, 25.

16. Glenn, "Memoranda," 1–2; "Mississippi Convention," *Vicksburg Whig*, January 23, 1861; Power, *Proceedings of the Mississippi State Convention*, 25; Power, "Proceedings and Debates of the Mississippi State Convention," 28, 32.

17. Power, *Proceedings of the Mississippi State Convention*, 26; "Mississippi Convention," *Vicksburg Whig*, January 23, 1861; Power, "Proceedings and Debates of the Mississippi State Convention," 33; *Journal of the State Convention and Ordinances and Resolutions Adopted in January, 1861*, 35–36.

18. Power, *Proceedings of the Mississippi State Convention*, 26, 78–79, 93; "Mississippi Convention," *Vicksburg Whig*, January 23, 1861; *Journal of the State Convention and Ordinances and Resolutions Adopted in January, 1861*, 35–36; Power, "Proceedings and Debates of the Mississippi State Convention," 33.

19. *Journal of the State Convention and Ordinances and Resolutions Adopted in January, 1861*, 35–36; "Mississippi Convention," *Vicksburg Whig*, January 23, 1861.

20. "Mississippi Convention," *Vicksburg Whig*, January 23, 1861; *Journal of the State Convention and Ordinances and Resolutions Adopted in January, 1861*, 36–37; Power, *Proceedings of the Mississippi State Convention*, 27.

21. "Mississippi Convention," *Vicksburg Whig*, January 23, 1861; Power, *Proceedings of the Mississippi State Convention*, 72–74.

22. Power, "Proceedings and Debates of the Mississippi State Convention," 34; Power, *Proceedings of the Mississippi State Convention*, 73; "Mississippi Convention," *Vicksburg Whig*, January 23, 1861.

23. "Mississippi Convention," *Vicksburg Whig*, January 23, 1861; Power, *Proceedings of the Mississippi State Convention*, 28; Power, "Proceedings and Debates of the Mississippi State Convention," 36.

24. Power, *Proceedings of the Mississippi State Convention*, 28; *Journal of the State Convention and Ordinances and Resolutions Adopted in January, 1861*, 38.

25. *Journal of the State Convention and Ordinances and Resolutions Adopted in January, 1861*, 37–40; "Mississippi Convention," *Vicksburg Whig*, January 23, 1861; Power, *Proceedings of the Mississippi State Convention*, 29; Power, "Proceedings and Debates of the Mississippi State Convention," 36.

26. Charles D. Fontaine to Sally Ann, January 13, 1861, and Charles D. Fontaine to John, January 21, 1861, both in Fontaine Family Papers, MDAH; Power, *Proceedings of the Mississippi State Convention*, 110.

27. "Mississippi Convention," *Vicksburg Whig*, January 23, 1861; "The Legislature," *Vicksburg Whig*, January 23, 1861; Power, "Proceedings and Debates of the Mississippi State Convention," 33.

28. "The Unfavorable Weather," *Natchez Courier*, January 26, 1861; *Natchez Courier*, January 22, 1861.

CHAPTER 8

1. B. L. C. Wailes Diary, January 21–23, 1861, DU; James Fontaine Maury Diary, January 21–26, 1861, UNC; *Congressional Globe*, 36th Congress, 2nd Session, 345, 487; Lynda Lasswell Crist, ed., *The Papers of Jefferson Davis*, 12 vols. (Baton Rouge: Louisiana State University Press, 1971-), 7:15; Charles D. Fontaine to John, January 21, 1861, Fontaine Family Papers, MDAH; *Journal of the State Convention and Ordinances and Resolutions Adopted in January, 1861*, 135; "The State Convention," *Natchez Daily Courier*, January 22, 1861; Absalom F. Dantzler to wife, January 20, 1861, Absalom F. Dantzler Papers, DU; Power, *Proceedings of the Mississippi State Convention*, 30.

2. "Seventh Day," *Jackson Weekly Mississippian*, January 16, 1861.

3. *Natchez Courier*, January 22, 1861; Power, "Mississippi Secession Convention," 138; Power, *Proceedings of the Mississippi State Convention*, 30; Power, "Proceedings and Debates of the Mississippi State Convention," 36; *Journal of the State Convention and Ordinances and Resolutions Adopted in January, 1861*, 40–42.

4. Power, "Proceedings and Debates of the Mississippi State Convention," 37; *Journal of the State Convention and Ordinances and Resolutions Adopted in January, 1861*, 41; Power, *Proceedings of the Mississippi State Convention*, 77–79, 92.

5. *Journal of the State Convention and Ordinances and Resolutions Adopted in January, 1861*, 42; William R. Barksdale to Ferrell, January 18, 1861, William R. Barksdale Letters, MDAH.

6. Glenn, "Memoranda," 4; Power, *Proceedings of the Mississippi State Convention*, 30; *Journal of the State Convention and Ordinances and Resolutions Adopted in January, 1861*, 42.

7. Power, *Proceedings of the Mississippi State Convention*, 30; *Journal of the State Convention and Ordinances and Resolutions Adopted in January, 1861*, 42–43.

8. "Mississippi Convention," *Vicksburg Whig*, January 30, 1861; *Journal of the State Convention and Ordinances and Resolutions Adopted in January, 1861*, 43–46.

9. "Mississippi Convention," *Vicksburg Whig*, January 30, 1861.

10. *Journal of the State Convention and Ordinances and Resolutions Adopted in January, 1861*, 43–46; "Mississippi Convention," *Vicksburg Whig*, January 30, 1861.

11. Power, *Proceedings of the Mississippi State Convention*, 30; "Correspondence of the Whig," *Vicksburg Whig*, January 30, 1861.

12. Power, *Proceedings of the Mississippi State Convention*, 30; Power, "Proceedings and Debates of the Mississippi State Convention," 39; *Journal of the State Convention and Ordinances and Resolutions Adopted in January, 1861*, 46–50; "Mississippi Convention," *Vicksburg Whig*, January 30, 1861.

13. Power, "Proceedings and Debates of the Mississippi State Convention," 39; Power, *Proceedings of the Mississippi State Convention*, 30, 111; *Journal of the State Convention and Ordinances and Resolutions Adopted in January, 1861*, 46–50.

14. Glenn, "Memoranda," 1–3; "Mississippi Convention," *Vicksburg Whig*, January 30, 1861; Power, "Proceedings and Debates of the Mississippi State Convention," 40; Power, *Proceedings of the Mississippi State Convention*, 30, 101–103, 111; *Journal of the State Convention and Ordinances and Resolutions Adopted in January, 1861*, 46–50.

15. "Mississippi Convention," *Vicksburg Whig*, January 30, 1861; Power, *Proceedings of the Mississippi State Convention*, 30, 101–103, 111; *Journal of the State Convention and Ordinances and Resolutions Adopted in January, 1861*, 46–50; Glenn, "Memoranda," 1–3.

16. *Journal of the State Convention and Ordinances and Resolutions Adopted in January, 1861*, 132–134.

17. *Journal of the State Convention and Ordinances and Resolutions Adopted in January, 1861*, 50–51; "Mississippi Convention," *Vicksburg Whig*, January 30, 1861; Power, "Proceedings and Debates of the Mississippi State Convention," 42.

18. James L. Alcorn to wife, January 15, 1861, J. L. Alcorn Papers, UNC; "Mississippi Convention," *Vicksburg Whig*, January 30, 1861; *Journal of the State Convention and Ordinances and Resolutions Adopted in January, 1861*, 51, Nota Bena; *Vicksburg Whig*, January 30, 1861; Power, *Proceedings of the Mississippi State Convention*, 106–107.

19. James L. Alcorn to wife, January 15, 1861, J. L. Alcorn Papers, UNC; "Mississippi Convention," *Vicksburg Whig*, January 30, 1861; *Journal of the State Convention and Ordinances and Resolutions Adopted in January, 1861*, 51, Nota Bena; *Vicksburg Whig*, January 30, 1861; Power, *Proceedings of the Mississippi State Convention*, 106–107.

20. *Journal of the State Convention and Ordinances and Resolutions Adopted in January, 1861*, 51–53; William R. Barksdale to Ferrell, January 18, 1861, William R. Barksdale Letters, MDAH.

21. Power, *Proceedings of the Mississippi State Convention*, 32; "Mississippi Convention," *Vicksburg Whig*, January 30, 1861; James L. Alcorn to wife, January 15, 1861, J. L. Alcorn Papers, UNC; *Journal of the State Convention and Ordinances and Resolutions Adopted in January, 1861*, Nota Bena.

22. Power, *Proceedings of the Mississippi State Convention*, 31–32; *Journal of the State Convention and Ordinances and Resolutions Adopted in January, 1861*, 53–57; Woods, "Sketch of the Mississippi Secession Convention," 101.

23. "Mississippi Convention," *Vicksburg Whig,* January 30, 1861; *Journal of the State Convention and Ordinances and Resolutions Adopted in January, 1861,* 57–58; Power, *Proceedings of the Mississippi State Convention,* 32; "Mississippi Convention," *Washington, D.C., National Republican,* January 26, 1861.

24. *Vicksburg Whig,* January 30, 1861.

25. "Correspondence of the Whig," *Vicksburg Whig,* January 30, 1861; "Mississippi Convention," *Vicksburg Whig,* January 30, 1861; *Journal of the State Convention and Ordinances and Resolutions Adopted in January, 1861,* 59, 122–126.

26. "Correspondence of the Whig," *Vicksburg Whig,* January 30, 1861; "Mississippi Convention," *Vicksburg Whig,* January 30, 1861; *Journal of the State Convention and Ordinances and Resolutions Adopted in January, 1861,* 59, 122–126.

27. "The Military Bill and Our Army Officers," *Vicksburg Whig,* January 30, 1861; Power, "Proceedings and Debates of the Mississippi State Convention," 44; "Jeff Davis' Aspiration," *Vicksburg Daily Whig,* December 15, 1860; Power, *Proceedings of the Mississippi State Convention,* 32; "Mississippi Convention," *Vicksburg Whig,* January 30, 1861; *Journal of the State Convention and Ordinances and Resolutions Adopted in January, 1861,* 59–63.

28. "The Military Bill and Our Army Officers," *Vicksburg Whig,* January 30, 1861; "Mississippi Convention," *Washington, D.C., National Republican,* January 26, 1861.

29. *Vicksburg Whig,* January 30, 1861; *Natchez Courier,* January 9, 1861; "Hill City Cadets," *Vicksburg Whig,* January 30, 1861; *Vicksburg Evening Citizen,* January 15, 1861; "The New Orleans Delta of Saturday," *Vicksburg Whig,* January 30, 1861; "From Pensacola," *Vicksburg Whig,* January 30, 1861; "Mississippi Students Leaving a Tennessee College," *Vicksburg Whig,* January 30, 1861.

CHAPTER 9

1. B. L. C. Wailes Diary, January 24–25, 1861, DU; "Pro-Slavery Rebellion."

2. *Journal of the State Convention and Ordinances and Resolutions Adopted in January, 1861,* 63; "Mississippi State Convention," *Natchez Courier,* January 29, 1861.

3. Power, *Proceedings of the Mississippi State Convention,* 33; *Journal of the State Convention and Ordinances and Resolutions Adopted in January, 1861,* 63–64; "Mississippi Convention," *Vicksburg Whig,* January 30, 1861.

4. "Mississippi Convention," *Vicksburg Whig,* January 30, 1861; *Journal of the State Convention and Ordinances and Resolutions Adopted in January, 1861,* 64–66; Power, "Proceedings and Debates of the Mississippi State Convention," 45–46; Power, *Proceedings of the Mississippi State Convention,* 33–34, 86–89.

5. Power, "Proceedings and Debates of the Mississippi State Convention," 47; Power, *Proceedings of the Mississippi State Convention,* 35–36, 90–92; "Mississippi Convention," *Vicksburg Whig,* January 30, 1861; *Journal of the State Convention and Ordinances and Resolutions Adopted in January, 1861,* 66–67.

6. Glenn, "Memoranda," 4; Power, *Proceedings of the Mississippi State Convention,* 88–90.

7. "Mississippi Convention," *Vicksburg Whig,* January 30, 1861; Power, "Proceedings and Debates of the Mississippi State Convention," 48.

8. B. L. C. Wailes Diary, January 25, 1861, DU; "Mississippi Convention," *Vicksburg Whig*, January 30, 1861; Power, "Proceedings and Debates of the Mississippi State Convention," 48; *Journal of the State Convention and Ordinances and Resolutions Adopted in January, 1861*, 67–69; Power, *Proceedings of the Mississippi State Convention*, 36.

9. "Mississippi Convention," *Vicksburg Whig*, January 30, 1861; *Journal of the State Convention and Ordinances and Resolutions Adopted in January, 1861*, 69–73; Power, *Proceedings of the Mississippi State Convention*, 85–86, 92; Power, "Proceedings and Debates of the Mississippi State Convention," 49.

10. *Journal of the State Convention and Ordinances and Resolutions Adopted in January, 1861*, 73; Power, *Proceedings of the Mississippi State Convention*, 37.

11. "Reconstruction," *Vicksburg Whig*, January 30, 1861; *Journal of the State Convention and Ordinances and Resolutions Adopted in January, 1861*, 73–77; "Mississippi Convention," *Vicksburg Whig*, January 30, 1861; Power, *Proceedings of the Mississippi State Convention*, 37–38; "Military," *Natchez Courier*, January 22, 1861; Power, "Proceedings and Debates of the Mississippi State Convention," 52.

12. B. L. C. Wailes Diary, January 25–26, 1861, DU; James Fontaine Maury Diary, January 24–26, 1861, UNC; *Journal of the State Convention and Ordinances and Resolutions Adopted in January, 1861*, 73.

13. B. L. C. Wailes Diary, January 26, 1861, DU; James Fontaine Maury Diary, January 25–26, 1861, UNC; "Mississippi Convention," *Vicksburg Whig*, January 30, 1861; *Journal of the State Convention and Ordinances and Resolutions Adopted in January, 1861*, 77; "Mississippi Convention—Last Day," *Natchez Courier*, January 31, 1861.

14. *Journal of the State Convention and Ordinances and Resolutions Adopted in January, 1861*, 77, 144.

15. "Mississippi Convention," *Vicksburg Whig*, January 30, 1861; *Journal of the State Convention and Ordinances and Resolutions Adopted in January, 1861*, 77–78, 84–85; Power, *Proceedings of the Mississippi State Convention*, 41–42; Power, "Proceedings and Debates of the Mississippi State Convention," 54.

16. Glenn, "Memoranda," 3; "Adjournment of the Convention," *Vicksburg Whig*, January 30, 1861; Power, *Proceedings of the Mississippi State Convention*, 39; *Journal of the State Convention and Ordinances and Resolutions Adopted in January, 1861*, 79–80, 143; "Mississippi Convention," *Vicksburg Whig*, January 30, 1861; Power, "Proceedings and Debates of the Mississippi State Convention," 53.

17. Power, *Proceedings of the Mississippi State Convention*, 40; *Journal of the State Convention and Ordinances and Resolutions Adopted in January, 1861*, 80, 134.

18. "Mississippi Convention," *Vicksburg Whig*, January 30, 1861; *Journal of the State Convention and Ordinances and Resolutions Adopted in January, 1861*, 81–83, 126–132, 136–142; Power, *Proceedings of the Mississippi State Convention*, 40.

19. "The Cabinet," *Vicksburg Whig*, January 30, 1861; Power, *Proceedings of the Mississippi State Convention*, 40–44; *Journal of the State Convention and Ordinances and Resolutions Adopted in January, 1861*, 82–84, 88, 135–136, 145.

20. Power, *Proceedings of the Mississippi State Convention*, 40; Bettersworth, *Confederate Mississippi*, 10; *Journal of the State Convention and Ordinances and Resolutions Adopted*

in January, 1861, 82–83, 86–88; Power, "Proceedings and Debates of the Mississippi State Convention," 55.

21. Power, *Proceedings of the Mississippi State Convention,* 44; Woods, "Sketch of the Mississippi Secession Convention," 93; *Journal of the State Convention and Ordinances and Resolutions Adopted in January, 1861,* 90.

22. "The Mississippi Convention," *Oxford Intelligencer,* January 30, 1861; Power, *Proceedings of the Mississippi State Convention,* 40.

23. "Pro-Slavery Rebellion"; *OR,* 4, 1:76.

24. Fulkerson, *Civilian's Recollections,* 7.

25. Power, "Proceedings and Debates of the Mississippi State Convention," 27.

CHAPTER 10

1. James R. Chalmers to John J. Pettus, March 2, 1861; J. B. Fizer to John J. Pettus, March 11, 1861; and O. C. Dease to John J. Pettus, March 12, 1861, all in Mississippi Governor, John J. Pettus, Correspondence and Papers, 1859–1863, Series 757, MDAH; "Public Meeting," *Paulding Eastern Clarion,* March 29, 1861.

2. Charles D. Fontaine to John J. Pettus, February 23, 1861; Hugh R. Miller to John J. Pettus, March 8, 1861; and John J. Pettus to William S. Barry, March 25, 1861, all in Mississippi Governor, John J. Pettus, Correspondence and Papers, 1859–1863, Series 757, MDAH.

3. Alex W. Randall to John J. Pettus, January 21, 1861; "Joint Resolutions of the General Assembly of the State of Ohio," January 12, 1861; "Joint Resolutions on the State of the Union," February 2, 1861; Oliver P. Morton to John J. Pettus, unreadable date; and Unknown to John J. Pettus, February 2, 1861, all in Mississippi Governor, John J. Pettus, Correspondence and Papers, 1859–1863, Series 757, MDAH.

4. *Journal of the State Convention and Ordinances and Resolutions Adopted in January, 1861,* 150, 165, 202; Barney, *Secessionist Impulse,* 204. See also Dew, *Apostles of Disunion.*

5. William R. Smith, *The History and Debates of the Convention of the People of Alabama Begun and Held in the City of Montgomery, on the Seventh Day of January, 1861: In Which is Preserved the Speeches of the Secret Sessions and Many Valuable State Papers* (Atlanta: Wood, Hanleiter, Rice, 1861), 130; *Journal of the State Convention and Ordinances and Resolutions Adopted in January, 1861,* 164, 175–176, 199, 208; Power, "Mississippi Secession Convention," 139–140; *Journal of the Proceedings of the Convention of the People of Florida Begun and Held at the Capitol in the City of Tallassee on Thursday January 3, A.D. 1861* (Tallahassee: Office of the Floridian and Journal, 1861); *Journal of the Secession Convention of Texas 1861* (Austin, Tex.: Austin Printing, 1912).

6. *Journal of the State Convention and Ordinances and Resolutions Adopted in January, 1861,* 149, 184, 189, 191, 194, 208; "The Mississippi Commission to Arkansas," undated clipping in Folder 73, Clippings of Slavery and Secession, J. F. H. Claiborne Papers, UNC.

7. Rowland, *Courts, Judges, and Lawyers of Mississippi,* 95; *Journal of the State Convention and Ordinances and Resolutions Adopted in January, 1861,* 27, 180, 196; J. Thomas Scharf, *History of Delaware: 1609–1888,* 2 vols. (Philadelphia: L. J. Richards, 1888), 1:331.

8. *Journal of the State Convention and Ordinances and Resolutions Adopted in January, 1861,* 149–220; Dew, *Apostles of Disunion,* 80; Barney, *Secessionist Impulse,* 204.

9. *Journal of the State Convention and Ordinances and Resolutions Adopted in January, 1861*, 150, 171–172, 177, 187, 203, 220; Barney, *Secessionist Impulse*, 234.

10. "Honorable Wm. Barksdale," *Mississippi Democrat*, April 6, 1861; February 12, 1861, entry, Minutes of the Military Board, January 29, 1861–November 23, 1861, RG 9, Series 394, Box 416, MDAH; *Orders of the Military Board of the State of Mississippi* (Jackson: Mississippi Book and Job Printing Office, 1861), 3–10; Dunbar Rowland and H. Grady Howell Jr., *Military History of Mississippi: 1803–1898, Including a Listing of All Known Mississippi Confederate Military Units* (Madison, Miss.: Chickasaw Bayou Press, 2003), 37; *Journal of the State Convention and Ordinances and Resolutions Adopted in March, 1861, With an Appendix* (Jackson, Miss.: E. Barksdale, 1861), 85, 87, 94–95; *Journal of the House of Representatives of the State of Mississippi: At a Called Session Thereof, Held in the City of Jackson, July and August, 1861* (Jackson, Miss.: E. Barksdale, 1861), 9.

11. "Editorial Correspondence," *Vicksburg Weekly Whig*, April 3, 1861; Rowland, *Mississippi*, 1:146–147; Davis, *Recollections of Mississippi and Mississippians*, 405–407. For more on the lesser-known members, see the various biographies in Bruce S. Allardice, *More Generals in Gray* (Baton Rouge: Louisiana State University Press, 1995).

12. *Journal of the Congress of the Confederate States of America, 1861–1865*, 7 vols. (Washington, D.C.: Government Printing Office, 1904–5), 1:15; William C. Davis, *"A Government of Their Own": The Making of the Confederacy* (New York: Free Press, 1994), 46.

13. *Journal of the Congress of the Confederate States of America, 1861–1865*, 1:11; Davis, *"Government of Their Own,"* 73–74, 438–439; "Autobiography of J. A. P. Campbell," March 2, 1914, J. A. P. Campbell Papers, UNC. Campbell made no mention of his absence from this first session in his autobiography.

14. Power, *Proceedings of the Mississippi State Convention*, 105; Davis, *"Government of Their Own,"* 60, 85–86, 91, 102, 241.

15. Davis, *"Government of Their Own,"* 18, 26.

16. For Davis, see William C. Davis, *Jefferson Davis: The Man and His Hour, a Biography* (New York: Harper Collins, 1991).

17. *Journal of the State Convention and Ordinances and Resolutions Adopted in January, 1861*, 74–75.

18. McPherson, *Battle Cry of Freedom*, 202–275; Davis, *"Government of Their Own,"* 17.

19. Davis, *"Government of Their Own,"* 61, 63–64, 82–84.

20. *Journal of the Congress of the Confederate States of America, 1861–1865*, 1:22; Davis, *"Government of Their Own,"* 83–89.

21. Davis, *"Government of Their Own,"* 69, 101, 117–118.

22. *Journal of the Congress of the Confederate States of America, 1861–1865*, 1:31; Davis, *"Government of Their Own,"* 69, 101, 117–118.

23. J. T. Harrison to wife, February 17, 1861, J. T. Harrison Papers, UNC; *Journal of the Congress of the Confederate States of America, 1861–1865*, 1:40, 63.

24. William S. Barry to John J. Pettus, February 12 and March 6, 1861, Mississippi Governor, John J. Pettus, Correspondence and Papers, 1859–1863, Series 757, MDAH.

25. J. T. Harrison to wife, February 17, 1861, J. T. Harrison Papers, UNC; *OR*, 4, 1:81; Davis, *"Government of Their Own,"* 181; "Mississippi—Seceded January 9, 1861," *Confederate*

Veteran 35, no. 2 (February 1927): 73; *Journal of the Congress of the Confederate States of America, 1861–1865*, 1:40, 44, 85.

26. J. T. Harrison to wife, February 17, 1861, J. T. Harrison Papers, UNC.

27. *Journal of the Congress of the Confederate States of America, 1861–1865*, 1:78, 91, 98, 121–122, 125, 132.

28. Davis, *"Government of Their Own,"* 124, 225–229, 257, 260.

29. Davis, *"Government of Their Own,"* 224–225, 256–257.

30. William S. Barry to John J. Pettus, March 6 and 11, 1861, Mississippi Governor, John J. Pettus, Correspondence and Papers, 1859–1863, Series 757, MDAH.

31. Rowland, *Courts, Judges, and Lawyers of Mississippi*, 325.

CHAPTER 11

1. William S. Barry to John J. Pettus, March 11, 1861, Mississippi Governor, John J. Pettus, Correspondence and Papers, 1859–1863, Series 757, MDAH.

2. "A Call for Troops," *Weekly Panola Star*, March 28, 1861; "Editorial Correspondence," *Vicksburg Weekly Whig*, April 3, 1861; *Journal of the State Convention and Ordinances and Resolutions Adopted in March, 1861*, 26, 37; Woods, "Sketch of the Mississippi Secession Convention," 102; Power, "Proceedings and Debates of the Mississippi State Convention," 48; Rowland and Howell, *Military History of Mississippi*, 52, 196–197.

3. *Journal of the State Convention and Ordinances and Resolutions Adopted in March, 1861*, 25–26, 45.

4. "Pro-Slavery Rebellion"; *Journal of the State Convention and Ordinances and Resolutions Adopted in March, 1861*, 3. See the various editions of the *Oxford Intelligencer*, March 27 and April 3, 1861; *Vicksburg Evening Citizen*, March 30, 1861; *Weekly Panola Star*, March 28, 1861; and *Vicksburg Weekly Whig*, March 27, 1861, for examples of newspaper coverage.

5. "Mississippi State Convention," *Vicksburg Weekly Whig*, March 27, 1861; Glenn, "Memoranda," 3; *Journal of the State Convention and Ordinances and Resolutions Adopted in March, 1861*, 3–4, 24.

6. "Editorial Correspondence," *Vicksburg Weekly Whig*, April 3, 1861; *Journal of the State Convention and Ordinances and Resolutions Adopted in March, 1861*, 4–20.

7. Glenn, "Memoranda," 3; Rowland, *Courts, Judges, and Lawyers of Mississippi*, 325.

8. "Editorial Correspondence," *Vicksburg Weekly Whig*, April 3, 1861; *Journal of the State Convention and Ordinances and Resolutions Adopted in March, 1861*, 21; Glenn, "Memoranda," 3.

9. Power, "Proceedings and Debates of the Mississippi State Convention," 43; "Mississippi State Convention," *Vicksburg Weekly Whig*, March 27, 1861; *Journal of the State Convention and Ordinances and Resolutions Adopted in March, 1861*, 21; "Editorial Correspondence," *Vicksburg Weekly Whig*, April 3, 1861; Glenn, "Memoranda," 3.

10. Glenn, "Memoranda," 3; "Mississippi State Convention," *Vicksburg Weekly Whig*, March 27, 1861; Bettersworth, *Confederate Mississippi*, 20; *Journal of the State Convention*

and Ordinances and Resolutions Adopted in March, 1861, 21–22; Power, "Proceedings and Debates of the Mississippi State Convention," 18.

11. Davis, *"Government of Their Own,"* 295; *Journal of the State Convention and Ordinances and Resolutions Adopted in March, 1861,* 22; "Mississippi State Convention," *Vicksburg Weekly Whig,* March 27, 1861.

12. *Journal of the State Convention and Ordinances and Resolutions Adopted in March, 1861,* 22.

13. *Journal of the State Convention and Ordinances and Resolutions Adopted in March, 1861,* 22; "Editorial Correspondence," *Vicksburg Weekly Whig,* April 3, 1861.

14. "Editorial Correspondence," *Vicksburg Weekly Whig,* April 3, 1861; *Journal of the State Convention and Ordinances and Resolutions Adopted in March, 1861,* 22–23.

15. Glenn, "Memoranda," 3; *Journal of the State Convention and Ordinances and Resolutions Adopted in March, 1861,* 23–24; "Editorial Correspondence," *Vicksburg Weekly Whig,* April 3, 1861.

16. "Editorial Correspondence," *Vicksburg Weekly Whig,* April 3, 1861; Glenn, "Memoranda," 3.

17. Glenn, "Memoranda," 3; "Editorial Correspondence," *Vicksburg Weekly Whig,* April 3, 1861; *Journal of the State Convention and Ordinances and Resolutions Adopted in March, 1861,* 24.

18. Wood, *Union and Secession in Mississippi,* 37; *Journal of the State Convention and Ordinances and Resolutions Adopted in March, 1861,* 24.

19. *Journal of the State Convention and Ordinances and Resolutions Adopted in March, 1861,* 24–25, 46; Wood, *Union and Secession in Mississippi,* 37.

20. B. L. C. Wailes Diary, March 27, 1861, DU; James Fontaine Maury Diary, March 27, 1861, UNC; Glenn, "Memoranda," 4; *Journal of the State Convention and Ordinances and Resolutions Adopted in March, 1861,* 26–27.

21. B. L. C. Wailes Diary, March 28, 1861, DU; *Journal of the State Convention and Ordinances and Resolutions Adopted in March, 1861,* 28–31.

22. Wood, *Union and Secession in Mississippi,* 38; *Journal of the State Convention and Ordinances and Resolutions Adopted in March, 1861,* 28–29.

23. *Journal of the State Convention and Ordinances and Resolutions Adopted in March, 1861,* 29–31.

24. *Journal of the State Convention and Ordinances and Resolutions Adopted in March, 1861,* 30; Power, "Proceedings and Debates of the Mississippi State Convention," 18.

25. Glenn, "Memoranda," 3; Power, "Proceedings and Debates of the Mississippi State Convention," 30.

26. Power, "Proceedings and Debates of the Mississippi State Convention," 19; "Pro-Slavery Rebellion." The reporter misnamed D. B. Wright as "D. B. Moore of Tippah," but cross-referencing the speech with other sources definitively makes Wright his subject.

27. Power, "Proceedings and Debates of the Mississippi State Convention," 18, 30–33, 43; Glenn, "Memoranda," 3.

28. B. L. C. Wailes Diary, March 29, 1861, DU; James Fontaine Maury Diary, March 29, 1861, UNC; "The State Convention," *Vicksburg Weekly Whig,* April 3, 1861; *Journal of the State Convention and Ordinances and Resolutions Adopted in March, 1861,* 31–32.

29. Power, "Proceedings and Debates of the Mississippi State Convention," 44–46; *Journal of the State Convention and Ordinances and Resolutions Adopted in March, 1861,* 33, 36.

30. "The State Convention," *Vicksburg Weekly Whig,* April 3, 1861; *Journal of the State Convention and Ordinances and Resolutions Adopted in March, 1861,* 33–35; Power, "Proceedings and Debates of the Mississippi State Convention," 45.

31. Glenn, "Memoranda," 3; *Journal of the State Convention and Ordinances and Resolutions Adopted in March, 1861,* 35–37; OR, 4, 1:210; "The State Convention," *Vicksburg Weekly Whig,* April 3, 1861; Power, "Proceedings and Debates of the Mississippi State Convention," 46–47.

32. *Journal of the State Convention and Ordinances and Resolutions Adopted in March, 1861,* 36; Glenn, "Memoranda," 3; Power, "Proceedings and Debates of the Mississippi State Convention," 47.

33. B. L. C. Wailes Diary, March 30, 1861, DU; "The State Convention," *Vicksburg Weekly Whig,* April 3, 1861; *Journal of the State Convention and Ordinances and Resolutions Adopted in March, 1861,* 37–39, 40, 45–46; "Correspondence of the Whig," *Vicksburg Weekly Whig,* April 3, 1861.

34. Power, "Proceedings and Debates of the Mississippi State Convention," 50; "Correspondence of the Whig," *Vicksburg Weekly Whig,* April 3, 1861; *Journal of the State Convention and Ordinances and Resolutions Adopted in March, 1861,* 25, 40–47; Glenn, "Memoranda," 4.

35. "Correspondence of the Whig," *Vicksburg Weekly Whig,* April 3, 1861; Power, "Proceedings and Debates of the Mississippi State Convention," 53.

36. "Adjournment of the State Convention," *Vicksburg Weekly Whig,* April 3, 1861; *Journal of the State Convention and Ordinances and Resolutions Adopted in March, 1861,* 46, 48.

CHAPTER 12

1. J. T. Harrison to wife, February 17, 1861, J. T. Harrison Papers, UNC; Power, "Proceedings and Debates of the Mississippi State Convention," 18, 30, 44.

2. "Affairs in Mississippi," *Mississippi Free Trader,* January 28, 1861.

3. Woods, "Sketch of the Mississippi Secession Convention," 102.

4. David S. Heidler and Jeanne T. Heidler, eds., *Encyclopedia of the American Civil War: A Political, Social, and Military History,* 5 vols. (Santa Barbara, Calif.: ABC-CLIO, 2000), 1:486–487; McPherson, *Battle Cry of Freedom,* 430–431, 611–612.

5. Bell Irvin Wiley, *The Life of Johnny Reb: The Common Soldier of the Confederacy* (Indianapolis: Bobbs-Merrill, 1943), 331; Wood, *Union and Secession in Mississippi,* 55–56; McPherson, *Battle Cry of Freedom,* 430–431, 611–612; "Correspondence of the Whig," *Vicksburg Weekly Whig,* April 3, 1861; Rowland, *Courts, Judges, and Lawyers of Mississippi,* 328.

6. See the biographical appendix for statistics.

7. Rowland, *Mississippi,* 2:1021–1022.

8. Rowland, *Mississippi*, 1:215–216. See Kenneth W. Noe, *Reluctant Rebels: The Confederates Who Joined the Army after 1861* (Chapel Hill: University of North Carolina Press, 2010), for an examination of the differences between those who joined in 1861 and 1862.

9. Power, "Proceedings and Debates of the Mississippi State Convention," 48. See the various delegates' Compiled Service Records for war service.

10. Smith, *James Z. George*, 44–84. See the biographical appendix for information on military and political service.

11. Estate of Warren P. Anderson, Deceased, Case #1823, Chancery Court Files, Hinds County Courthouse, Second Judicial District, Raymond; "Warren P. Anderson," *Jackson Weekly Mississippian*, September 25, 1861.

12. Timothy B. Smith, "Secession at Shiloh: Mississippi's Convention Delegates and Their State's Defense," *Hallowed Ground* (Spring 2012): 16–22. See the Compiled Service Records for the individual details surrounding each delegate.

13. *Prentiss County, Mississippi: History and Families* (Paducah, Miss.: Turner Publishing, 2002), 101. See the Compiled Service Records for the individual details surrounding each delegate.

14. Desoto County Genealogical Society, *Desoto County Mississippi*, 129. See the Compiled Service Records for the individual details surrounding each delegate.

15. Andrew Miller headstone, Pontotoc City Cemetery, Pontotoc, Miss.; Warner, *Generals in Gray*, 26–27. See the Compiled Service Records for the individual details surrounding each delegate.

16. James Edmonds Saunders, *Early Settlers of Alabama* (New Orleans: L. Graham and Son, 1899), 451; *OR*, 1, 49, 1:210. See the Compiled Service Records for the individual details surrounding each delegate.

17. *OR*, 1, 49, 1:210; Smith, *James Z. George*, 84. See the Compiled Service Records for the individual details surrounding each delegate.

18. See the Compiled Service Records for the individual details surrounding each delegate.

19. Rowland, *Courts, Judges, and Lawyers of Mississippi*, 296–297. See the real estate and personal wealth statistics from the 1860 and 1870 census returns for each delegate.

20. "Debates of the Mississippi Convention," *Vicksburg Weekly Whig*, April 3, 1861; Power, *Account of the Siege of Vicksburg*, A5; J. T. Harrison to wife, February 17, 1861, J. T. Harrison Papers, UNC; Power, *Proceedings of the Mississippi State Convention*, 111; Jennie Newsom Hoffman, "A History of Winston County" (n.p.: WPA, 1938), 83, 159; William T. Lewis, *The Centennial History of Winston County, Mississippi* (Pasadena, Tex.: Globe, 1972), 107–109; James Alex Baggett, *The Scalawags: Southern Dissenters in the Civil War and Reconstruction* (Baton Rouge: Louisiana State University Press, 2003), 48.

21. *OR*, 1, 24, 2:530–531; "One Warren Countian Voted for Secession, One Voted Against," *Vicksburg Daily Post*, April 30, 2000, copy in Secession Subject File, MDAH.

22. Fulkerson, *Civilian's Recollections*, 9; Rowland, *Mississippi*, 2:415.

23. *OR*, 4, 1:77; Olsen, *Political Culture and Secession in Mississippi*, 15.

24. *Journal of the State Convention and Ordinances and Resolutions Adopted in January, 1861*, 16, 28.

25. For more on states' rights, see Frank L. Owsley, *States Rights in the Confederacy* (Chicago: University of Chicago Press, 1925).

26. Smith, *Mississippi in the Civil War*, 33, 43.

27. *OR*, 4, 1:115–116; Bettersworth, *Confederate Mississippi*, 60–75, 89.

28. *OR*, 4, 1:77.

29. Woods, "Sketch of the Mississippi Secession Convention," 102. For the Lost Cause, see Gaines M. Foster, *Ghosts of the Confederacy: Defeat, the Lost Cause, and the Emergence of the New South* (New York: Oxford University Press, 1987).

30. Rowland, *Courts, Judges, and Lawyers of Mississippi*, 318–319, 324–325.

31. Rowland, *Courts, Judges, and Lawyers of Mississippi*, 326–327.

32. Rowland, *Courts, Judges, and Lawyers of Mississippi*, 326–327.

33. "Mississippi's Secession Ordinance," *New York Times*, January 29, 1899.

34. "Prized Civil War Booty Discovered at Department of Archives," *Jackson Clarion Ledger*, February 1, 1981, copy in Ordinance of Secession Subject File, MDAH; "Old Confederate Document Found in Lombard Library," n.d., Ordinance of Secession Subject File, MDAH.

EPILOGUE

1. Power, *Proceedings of the Mississippi State Convention*, 80.

2. Rowland, *Courts, Judges, and Lawyers of Mississippi*, 327; Smith, *James Z. George*, 83.

3. *Report of the Joint Select Committee To Inquire into the Conditions of Affairs in the Late Insurrectionary States* (Washington, D.C.: Government Printing Office, 1872), 74–75, 601; Baggett, *Scalawags*, 48; M. G. Abney, "Reconstruction in Pontotoc County," in *Publications of the Mississippi Historical Society* (Oxford: Mississippi Historical Society, 1910), 11:234; Power, "Mississippi Secession Convention," 200; James Z. George to L. Q. C. Lamar, May 3, 1874, L. Q. C. Lamar and Edward Mayes Papers, MDAH; *Congressional Record*, vol. 12, Part 1: 161–167 (hereafter cited as *CR*, with volume, part, and page numbers); *CR*, 13, 4:3463; *CR*, 16, 1:624, 684; *CR*, 26, 3:2935; *CR*, 15, 3:2376; *CR*, 13, 4:3462.

4. Willie D. Halsell, "James R. Chalmers and 'Mohoneism' in Mississippi," *Journal of Southern History* 10, no. 1 (February 1944): 37–58; Bradley G. Bond, "Edward C. Walthall and the 1880 Senatorial Nomination: Politics of Balance in the Redeemer Era," *Journal of Mississippi History* 50 (February 1988): 1–20; Willie D. Halsell, "Democratic Dissensions in Mississippi, 1878–1882," *Journal of Mississippi History* 2 (July 1940): 123–135; Willie D. Halsell, "The Bourbon Period in Mississippi Politics, 1875–1890," *Journal of Southern History* 11, no. 4 (November 1945): 519–537.

5. Rowland, *Mississippi*, 1:910–911; "Henry Thomas Ellett," 1011; Smith, *James Z. George*, 89, 117–121; http://house.louisiana.gov/H_PDFdocs/HouseMembers1808_2012.pdf; William S. Speer, *Sketches of Prominent Tennesseans, Containing Biographies and Records of Many of the Families Who Have Attained Prominence in Tennessee* (Nashville, Tenn.: Albert B. Tavel, 1888), 40–41; *Commissioners of Patents' Journal*, No. 2348, July 4 and September 15, 1876, 2172; Henderson, *Pontotoc County Men of Note*, 67–68; Charles D. Fontaine Subject File, MDAH.

6. Smith, *James Z. George*; Murphy, *L. Q. C. Lamar*; Pereyra, *James Lusk Alcorn*; Warner, *Generals in Gray*, 46; *Journal of the Proceedings of the Constitutional Convention of the State of Mississippi, Begun at the City of Jackson on August 12, 1890, and Concluded November 1, 1890* (Jackson, Miss.: E. L. Martin, 1890), 5–7.

7. Rowland, *Mississippi*, 1:214–215, 308; Rowland, *Mississippi*, 2:1021–1022; Allardice, *Confederate Colonels*, 165, 373; Israel Welsh Subject File, MDAH; *A History of Rankin County Mississippi* (Brandon, Miss.: Rankin County Historical Society, 1984), 1:42; Warner, *Generals in Gray*, 32–33; William F. Brantley Subject File, MDAH; *In Memory of Henry Thomas Ellett*, 9, 89.

8. Woods, "Sketch of the Mississippi Secession Convention," 104.

9. "Mississippi's Secession Ordinance," *New York Times*, January 29, 1899.

10. Rowland, *Courts, Judges, and Lawyers of Mississippi*, 318–319, 324–325.

APPENDIX 1.

1. Rowland, *Mississippi*, 1:62–64; Pereyra, *James Lusk Alcorn*; 1860 Mississippi Population Census; 1860 Mississippi Slave Schedules; "Alphabetical List of Members of the Mississippi State Convention." For more on Alcorn, see the James L. Alcorn and Family Papers, MDAH, and the J. L. Alcorn Papers, UNC.

2. Lowry and McCardle, *History of Mississippi*, 611; 1860 Mississippi Population Census; 1860 Mississippi Slave Schedules; "Alphabetical List of Members of the Mississippi State Convention." For more on Aldridge, see the Francis Marion Aldridge Papers, MDAH.

3. Estate of Warren P. Anderson, Deceased, Case #1823, Chancery Court Files, Hinds County Courthouse, Second Judicial District, Raymond; "Warren P. Anderson," September 25, 1861, *Jackson Weekly Mississippian*; 1860 Mississippi Population Census; 1860 Mississippi Slave Schedules; "Alphabetical List of Members of the Mississippi State Convention"; Lowry and McCardle, *History of Mississippi*, 489–490.

4. David M. Backstrom headstone, Backstrom Cemetery, Neshoba County, Mississippi; 1860 Mississippi Population Census; 1860 Mississippi Slave Schedules; "Alphabetical List of Members of the Mississippi State Convention"; Theresa T. Rideout, ed., *Our Links to the Past: Cemetery Records of Neshoba County, MS* (Philadelphia, Miss.: Neshoba County Library, 1998), iv, 10.

5. Cyrus B. Baldwin Obituary, *Staunton Spectator*, March 19, 1867; Cyrus B. Baldwin Compiled Service Record, National Archives and Records Administration (hereafter cited as NARA); 1860 Mississippi Population Census; 1860 Mississippi Slave Schedules; "Alphabetical List of Members of the Mississippi State Convention"; Cyrus B. Baldwin headstone, Soul Chapel Cemetery, Chickasaw County, Miss.

6. Rowland, *Mississippi*, 1:214; 1860 Mississippi Population Census; 1860 Mississippi Slave Schedules; "Alphabetical List of Members of the Mississippi State Convention." For more on Barksdale, see the William R. Barksdale Papers, MDAH.

7. Rowland, *Mississippi*, 1:214–215; 1860 Mississippi Population Census; 1860 Mississippi Slave Schedules; "Alphabetical List of Members of the Mississippi State Convention";

Allardice, *Confederate Colonels*, 54–55; *OR*, 1, 49, 1:210. For a Barry letter, see William T. S. Barry Letter, UM.

8. Lowry and McCardle, *History of Mississippi*, 495, 561; 1860 Mississippi Population Census; 1860 Mississippi Slave Schedules; "Alphabetical List of Members of the Mississippi State Convention."

9. Warner, *Generals in Gray*, 26–27; 1860 Mississippi Population Census; 1860 Mississippi Slave Schedules; "Alphabetical List of Members of the Mississippi State Convention."

10. Rowland, *Mississippi*, 3:85–86; Joel H. Berry headstone, Baldwin Masonic Cemetery, Baldwin, Miss.; 1860 Mississippi Population Census; 1860 Mississippi Slave Schedules; "Alphabetical List of Members of the Mississippi State Convention"; William Cathcart, *The Baptist Encyclopedia: A Dictionary of the Doctrines, Ordinances, Usages, Confessions of Faith, Sufferings, Labors, and Successes, and of the General History of the Baptist Denomination in All Lands. With Numerous Biographical Sketches of Distinguished American and Foreign Baptists, and a Supplement* (Philadelphia: Lewis H. Everts, 1881), 97.

11. Rowland, *Mississippi*, 3:114–116; 1860 Mississippi Population Census; 1860 Mississippi Slave Schedules; "Alphabetical List of Members of the Mississippi State Convention"; John A. Blair headstone, Glenwood Cemetery, Tupelo, Miss.

12. Hoffman, "History of Winston County," 83, 159; 1860 Mississippi Population Census; 1860 Mississippi Slave Schedules; "Alphabetical List of Members of the Mississippi State Convention."

13. *Prentiss County, Mississippi*, 101; 1860 Mississippi Population Census; 1860 Mississippi Slave Schedules; "Alphabetical List of Members of the Mississippi State Convention"; Lowry and McCardle, *History of Mississippi*, 588.

14. Rowland and Howell, *Military History of Mississippi*, 555; 1860 Mississippi Population Census; 1860 Mississippi Slave Schedules; "Alphabetical List of Members of the Mississippi State Convention"; 1870 Tunica County Mississippi Census.

15. *Carroll County, Mississippi: History and Families* (Humboldt, Tenn.: Rose Publishing, 2001), 66; 1860 Mississippi Population Census; 1860 Mississippi Slave Schedules; "Alphabetical List of Members of the Mississippi State Convention."

16. Warner, *Generals in Gray*, 32–33; 1860 Mississippi Population Census; 1860 Mississippi Slave Schedules; "Alphabetical List of Members of the Mississippi State Convention"; William F. Brantley Subject File, MDAH.

17. Rowland, *Mississippi*, 1:308; 1860 Mississippi Population Census; 1860 Mississippi Slave Schedules; "Alphabetical List of Members of the Mississippi State Convention"; "Walker Brooke," 713.

18. 1860 Mississippi Population Census; 1860 Mississippi Slave Schedules; "Alphabetical List of Members of the Mississippi State Convention"; *Journal of the Congress of the Confederate States of America, 1861–1865*, 2:64, 75; Chancery Court to C. H. Whitfield, April 24, 1873, Packet No. 337, Chancery Court Archives, Itawamba County Courthouse.

19. Lowry and McCardle, *History of Mississippi*, 470, 573; 1860 Mississippi Population Census; 1860 Mississippi Slave Schedules; "Alphabetical List of Members of the Mississippi State Convention"; Philip S. Catching headstone, Catchings Cemetery, Copiah County, Miss.; *OR*, 4, 1:565.

20. Warner, *Generals in Gray*, 46; 1860 Mississippi Population Census; 1860 Mississippi Slave Schedules; "Alphabetical List of Members of the Mississippi State Convention"; Lowry and McCardle, *History of Mississippi*, 466, 448. For more on Chalmers, see James R. Chalmers Letter, Louisiana State University (hereafter cited as LSU).

21. 1860 Mississippi Population Census; 1860 Mississippi Slave Schedules; "Alphabetical List of Members of the Mississippi State Convention"; Speer, *Sketches of Prominent Tennesseans*, 40–41; Jeremiah W. Clapp Obituary, *Memphis Commercial Appeal*, September 8, 1898; Jeremiah W. Clapp headstone, Elmwood Cemetery, Memphis, Tenn. For more on Clapp, see the J. W. Clapp Collection, UM.

22. Rowland, *Mississippi*, 1:453–454; 1860 Mississippi Population Census; 1860 Mississippi Slave Schedules; "Alphabetical List of Members of the Mississippi State Convention"; John N. Waddel, *Memorials of Academic Life: Being An Historical Sketch of the Waddel Family, Identified Through Three Generations With the History of the Higher Education in the South and Southwest* (Richmond, Va.: Presbyterian Committee of Publication, 1891), 289. See also the A. M. Clayton Letter, UM.

23. Rowland, *Mississippi*, 1:454; 1860 Mississippi Population Census; 1860 Mississippi Slave Schedules; "Alphabetical List of Members of the Mississippi State Convention"; Gideon Dowse Harris, *Harris Geneology* (Columbus, Miss.: Keith Printing, 1914), 90.

24. Allardice, *Confederate Colonels*, 105; 1860 Mississippi Population Census; 1860 Mississippi Slave Schedules; "Alphabetical List of Members of the Mississippi State Convention."

25. *Biographical and Historical Memoirs of Mississippi, Embracing and Authentic and Comprehensive Account of the Chief Events in the History of the State, and a Record of the Lives of Many of the Most Worthy and Illustrious Families and Individuals*, 2 vols. (Chicago: Goodspeed Publishing, 1891), 1:607–608; 1860 Mississippi Population Census; 1860 Mississippi Slave Schedules; "Alphabetical List of Members of the Mississippi State Convention"; "The Family of B. Y. Cummings," *Northeast Mississippi Historical & Genealogical Society Quarterly* 19, no. 1 (September 1998): 21.

26. Rowland, *Mississippi*, 3:206–207; 1860 Mississippi Population Census; 1860 Mississippi Slave Schedules; "Alphabetical List of Members of the Mississippi State Convention"; Orlando Davis Subject File, MDAH; Orlando Davis headstone, Hillcrest Cemetery, Holly Springs, Miss.

27. James S. Davis Obituary, *Nashville Christian Advocate*, January 17, 1880; 1860 Mississippi Population Census; 1860 Mississippi Slave Schedules; "Alphabetical List of Members of the Mississippi State Convention."

28. Lowry and McCardle, *History of Mississippi*, 502, 548, 569, 577; 1860 Mississippi Population Census; 1860 Mississippi Slave Schedules; "Alphabetical List of Members of the Mississippi State Convention."

29. Allardice, *Confederate Colonels*, 124; Lowry and McCardle, *History of Mississippi*, 523; 1860 Mississippi Population Census; 1860 Mississippi Slave Schedules; "Alphabetical List of Members of the Mississippi State Convention"; Rowland and Howell, *Military History of Mississippi*, 29.

30. *History of Rankin County Mississippi*, 1:42; 1860 Mississippi Population Census; 1860 Mississippi Slave Schedules; "Alphabetical List of Members of the Mississippi State Convention"; William Denson headstone, Pisgah Cemetery, Rankin County, Miss.

31. Rowland and Howell, *Military History of Mississippi*, 73; 1860 Mississippi Population Census; 1860 Mississippi Slave Schedules; "Alphabetical List of Members of the Mississippi State Convention."

32. Lowry and McCardle, *History of Mississippi*, 493; 1860 Mississippi Population Census; 1860 Mississippi Slave Schedules; "Alphabetical List of Members of the Mississippi State Convention"; James M. Dyer headstone, Oddfellows Cemetery, Lexington, Miss.

33. Rowland and Howell, *Military History of Mississippi*, 66; John C. Rietti, *Military Annals of Mississippi: Military Organizations Which Entered the Service of the Confederate States of America from the State of Mississippi* (N.p.: n.p., 1895), 167; 1860 Mississippi Population Census; 1860 Mississippi Slave Schedules; "Alphabetical List of Members of the Mississippi State Convention"; William J. Eckford Compiled Service Record, NARA.

34. Lowry and McCardle, *History of Mississippi*, 457; 1860 Mississippi Population Census; 1860 Mississippi Slave Schedules; "Alphabetical List of Members of the Mississippi State Convention"; James H. Edwards headstone, Bethlehem Cemetery, Ackerman, Miss.

35. "Henry Thomas Ellett," 1011; 1860 Mississippi Population Census; 1860 Mississippi Slave Schedules; "Alphabetical List of Members of the Mississippi State Convention"; Lowry and McCardle, *History of Mississippi*, 477. For more on Ellett, see the Ellett-Jefferies Family Papers, MDAH.

36. Alexander K. Farrar headstone, King Cemetery, Adams County, Miss.; 1860 Mississippi Population Census; 1860 Mississippi Slave Schedules; "Alphabetical List of Members of the Mississippi State Convention"; Winthrop D. Jordan, *Tumult and Silence at Second Creek: An Inquiry into a Civil War Slave Conspiracy*, rev. ed. (Baton Rouge: Louisiana State University Press, 1996), 258, 323. For more on Farrar, see the Alexander K. Farrar Papers, LSU.

37. John B. Fizer headstone, Long Cemetery, Robertson County, Tenn.; 1870 Robertson County, Tennessee Census; 1860 Mississippi Population Census; 1860 Mississippi Slave Schedules; "Alphabetical List of Members of the Mississippi State Convention."

38. *Report of the Joint Select Committee To Inquire into the Conditions of Affairs in the Late Insurrectionary States*, 74–75, 601; 1860 Mississippi Population Census; 1860 Mississippi Slave Schedules; "Alphabetical List of Members of the Mississippi State Convention"; Baggett, *Scalawags*, 48; Abney, "Reconstruction in Pontotoc County," 234.

39. Henderson, *Pontotoc County Men of Note*, 67–68; Charles D. Fontaine Subject File, MDAH; 1860 Mississippi Population Census; 1860 Mississippi Slave Schedules; "Alphabetical List of Members of the Mississippi State Convention"; Lowry and McCardle, *History of Mississippi*, 561; Charles D. Fontaine headstone, Pontotoc City Cemetery, Pontotoc, Miss. For more on Fontaine, see the Fontaine Family Papers, MDAH.

40. Smith, *James Z. George*; 1860 Mississippi Population Census; 1860 Mississippi Slave Schedules; "Alphabetical List of Members of the Mississippi State Convention", "James Zachariah George," 1111.

41. Warner, *Generals in Gray*, 103–104; 1860 Mississippi Population Census; 1860 Mississippi Slave Schedules; "Alphabetical List of Members of the Mississippi State Convention." See also the Samuel J. Gholson Letter, USM.

42. Albert C. Gibson Compiled Service Record, NARA; http://house.louisiana.gov/H_PDFdocs/HouseMembers1808_2012.pdf; Albert C. Gibson Probate File 405, Madison Parrish Courthouse; 1860 Mississippi Population Census; 1860 Mississippi Slave Schedules; "Alphabetical List of Members of the Mississippi State Convention."

43. Allardice, *Confederate Colonels*, 165; 1860 Mississippi Population Census; 1860 Mississippi Slave Schedules; "Alphabetical List of Members of the Mississippi State Convention." For more on Glenn, see the David Chalmers and Archibald Glenn Papers, MDAH.

44. William Gwin headstone, Gwin Family Cemetery, Bouge Chitto, Miss.; 1860 Mississippi Population Census; 1860 Mississippi Slave Schedules; "Alphabetical List of Members of the Mississippi State Convention."

45. Rowland, *Mississippi*, 1:841–843; 1860 Mississippi Population Census; 1860 Mississippi Slave Schedules; "Alphabetical List of Members of the Mississippi State Convention."

46. Rowland and Howell, *Military History of Mississippi*, 164; Lowry and McCardle, *History of Mississippi*, 561; 1860 Mississippi Population Census; 1860 Mississippi Slave Schedules; "Alphabetical List of Members of the Mississippi State Convention"; John B. Herring headstone, Crokett's Bluff Cemetery, Arkansas County, Ark.

47. Allardice, *Confederate Colonels*, 195; 1860 Mississippi Population Census; 1860 Mississippi Slave Schedules; "Alphabetical List of Members of the Mississippi State Convention."

48. Alfred C. Holt Obituary, *Woodville Republican*, October 15, 1881; 1860 Mississippi Population Census; 1860 Mississippi Slave Schedules; "Alphabetical List of Members of the Mississippi State Convention"; James G. Hollandsworth, *Portrait of a Scientific Racist: Alfred Holt Stone of Mississippi* (Baton Rouge: Louisiana State University Press, 2008), 33–34.

49. Rowland, *Mississippi*, 1:910–911; 1860 Mississippi Population Census; 1860 Mississippi Slave Schedules; "Alphabetical List of Members of the Mississippi State Convention"; Allardice, *Confederate Colonels*, 208; Lowry and McCardle, *History of Mississippi*, 635.

50. Skipworth Historical and Genealogical Society, *History of Lafayette County, MS* (Dallas: Curtis Media Corporation, 1986), 387; 1860 Mississippi Population Census; 1860 Mississippi Slave Schedules; "Alphabetical List of Members of the Mississippi State Convention"; Julia Kendel, "Reconstruction in Lafayette County," in *Publications of the Mississippi Historical Society* (Oxford: Mississippi Historical Society, 1913), 13:231–232.

51. *Biographical and Historical Memoirs of Mississippi*, 1:1044–1046; 1860 Mississippi Population Census; 1860 Mississippi Slave Schedules; "Alphabetical List of Members of the Mississippi State Convention"; James S. Johnston headstone, Christ Episcopal Church Cemetery, Jefferson County, Miss.

52. Desoto County Genealogical Society, *Desoto County Mississippi*, 129; 1860 Mississippi Population Census; 1860 Mississippi Slave Schedules; "Alphabetical List of Members of the Mississippi State Convention."

53. Lowry and McCardle, *History of Mississippi*, 580; Rowland and Howell, *Military History of Mississippi*, 444; 1860 Mississippi Population Census; 1860 Mississippi Slave Schedules; "Alphabetical List of Members of the Mississippi State Convention"; Edward P. Jones headstone, Canton Cemetery, Canton, Miss.; *Commissioners of Patents' Journal*, No. 2348, July 4 and September 15, 1876, 2172.

54. "An Account of Manuscripts, Papers, and Documents in Private Hands," in Riley, *Publications of the Mississippi Historical Society*, 5:245; 1860 Mississippi Population Census; 1860 Mississippi Slave Schedules; "Alphabetical List of Members of the Mississippi State Convention"; "Deaths and Obituaries," *Journal of the American Medical Association* 36, no. 3 (January 19, 1901): 199; Walter L. Keirn headstone, Oddfellows Cemetery, Lexington, Miss.

55. A. J. Brown, *History of Newton County from 1834 to 1894* (Jackson, Miss.: Clarion Ledger, 1894), 325; 1860 Mississippi Population Census; 1860 Mississippi Slave Schedules; "Alphabetical List of Members of the Mississippi State Convention."

56. Rowland and Howell, *Military History of Mississippi*, 809; 1860 Mississippi Population Census; 1860 Mississippi Slave Schedules; "Alphabetical List of Members of the Mississippi State Convention"; Grayson County, Texas, 1880 Census.

57. "Account of Manuscripts, Papers, and Documents in Private Hands," 5:245; 1860 Mississippi Population Census; 1860 Mississippi Slave Schedules; "Alphabetical List of Members of the Mississippi State Convention."

58. Rowland, *Mississippi*, 2:22–35; Allardice, *Confederate Colonels*, 230; 1860 Mississippi Population Census; 1860 Mississippi Slave Schedules; "Alphabetical List of Members of the Mississippi State Convention"; Murphy, *L. Q. C. Lamar*; "Lucius Quintus Cincinnatus Lamar," 1410. For more on Lamar, see the L. Q. C. Lamar and Edward Mayes Papers, MDAH; and the L. Q. C. Lamar Papers, UNC. See also the L. Q. C. Lamar Letter, UM.

59. Lea Family Papers, UNC; *Biographical and Historical Memoirs of Mississippi*, 2:264; 1860 Mississippi Population Census; 1860 Mississippi Slave Schedules; "Alphabetical List of Members of the Mississippi State Convention"; Joan E. Cashin, *A Family Venture: Men and Women on the Southern Frontier* (New York: Oxford University Press, 1991), 134; Willis M. Lea headstone, Hillcrest Cemetery, Holly Springs, Miss.

60. Rowland and Howell, *Military History of Mississippi*, 384; 1860 Mississippi Population Census; 1860 Mississippi Slave Schedules; "Alphabetical List of Members of the Mississippi State Convention"; Thomas D. Lewers headstone, Fredonia Cemetery, Panola County, Miss.

61. Cyril Edward Cain, *Four Centuries on the Pascagoula: History and Genealogy of the Pascagoula River Country*, 2 vols. (State College, Miss.: n.p., 1953), 1:164; Cain, *Four Centuries on the Pascagoula*, 2:5, 136, 213–214; 1860 Mississippi Population Census; 1860 Mississippi Slave Schedules; "Alphabetical List of Members of the Mississippi State Convention."

62. *Biographical and Historical Memoirs of Mississippi*, 2:400; 1860 Mississippi Population Census; 1860 Mississippi Slave Schedules; "Alphabetical List of Members of the Mississippi State Convention"; Frank E. Everett Jr., *Vicksburg Lawyers Prior to the Civil War* (N.p.: n.p., n.d.), 62–65.

63. Allardice, *Confederate Colonels*, 230; 1860 Mississippi Population Census; 1860 Mississippi Slave Schedules; "Alphabetical List of Members of the Mississippi State Convention."

64. Rowland and Howell, *Military History of Mississippi*, 263; 1860 Mississippi Population Census; 1860 Mississippi Slave Schedules; "Alphabetical List of Members of the Mississippi State Convention"; Saunders, *Early Settlers of Alabama*, 451.

65. Rowland and Howell, *Military History of Mississippi*, 368, 628; Wirt A. Williams, ed., *History of Bolivar County, Mississippi* (Jackson, Miss.: Herderman Brothers, 1948), 145–146, 472–473; 1860 Mississippi Population Census; 1860 Mississippi Slave Schedules; "Alphabetical List of Members of the Mississippi State Convention"; Saunders, *Early Settlers of Alabama*, 451.

66. Andrew Miller headstone, Pontotoc City Cemetery, Pontotoc, Miss.; 1860 Mississippi Population Census; 1860 Mississippi Slave Schedules; "Alphabetical List of Members of the Mississippi State Convention."

67. Allardice, *Confederate Colonels*, 274; 1860 Mississippi Population Census; 1860 Mississippi Slave Schedules; "Alphabetical List of Members of the Mississippi State Convention." For more on Miller, see the Hugh Reid and Susan Walton Miller Family Papers, MDAH; and the Miller Family Papers, UM.

68. Robert J. McSwain Jr., *Descendants of Early Settlers of Perry County, Mississippi* (Carrollton, Miss.: Pioneer Publishing, 2006), 145; 1860 Mississippi Population Census; 1860 Mississippi Slave Schedules; "Alphabetical List of Members of the Mississippi State Convention"; Lowry and McCardle, *History of Mississippi*, 556.

69. Rowland and Howell, *Military History of Mississippi*, 545; Oswell Y. Neely headstone, Old Scooba Cemetery, Kemper County, Miss.; 1860 Mississippi Population Census; 1860 Mississippi Slave Schedules; "Alphabetical List of Members of the Mississippi State Convention"; Lowry and McCardle, *History of Mississippi*, 510.

70. Rowland and Howell, *Military History of Mississippi*, 74; Lowry and McCardle, *History of Mississippi*, 442, 559; 1860 Mississippi Population Census; 1860 Mississippi Slave Schedules; "Alphabetical List of Members of the Mississippi State Convention"; James M. Nelson Obituary, *Magnolia Gazette*, August 9, 1899.

71. Allardice, *Confederate Colonels*, 295; 1860 Mississippi Population Census; 1860 Mississippi Slave Schedules; "Alphabetical List of Members of the Mississippi State Convention." For more on Orr, including an autobiography, see the J. A. Orr Papers, MDAH.

72. Rowland and Howell, *Military History of Mississippi*, 181; 1860 Mississippi Population Census; 1860 Mississippi Slave Schedules; "Alphabetical List of Members of the Mississippi State Convention"; Daniel H. Parker Compiled Service Record, NARA.

73. Alexander Pattison headstone, Old Masonic Cemetery, Charleston, Miss.; 1860 Mississippi Population Census; 1860 Mississippi Slave Schedules; "Alphabetical List of Members of the Mississippi State Convention"; Confederate Grave Registrations, MDAH.

74. *Echoes From Our Past: History-Military-Churches-Families*, 2 vols. (Jones County, Miss.: Jones County Genealogical and Historical Organization, 2006), 1:505; 1860 Mississippi Population Census; 1860 Mississippi Slave Schedules; "Alphabetical List of Members of the Mississippi State Convention"; John H. Powell headstone, Balch Cemetery, Johnson County, Tex.

75. *Biographical and Historical Memoirs of Mississippi*, 2:605; 1860 Mississippi Population Census; 1860 Mississippi Slave Schedules; "Alphabetical List of Members of the Mississippi State Convention"; June Ellis email to author, December 8, 2010.

76. Perrin, *Southwest Louisiana*, 301; 1860 Mississippi Population Census; 1860 Mississippi Slave Schedules; "Alphabetical List of Members of the Mississippi State Convention"; Ken Dupuy telephone conversation with author, 2010; Theall, *History of Vermilion Parish*, 2:456.

77. Allardice, *Confederate Colonels*, 320; 1860 Mississippi Population Census; 1860 Mississippi Slave Schedules; "Alphabetical List of Members of the Mississippi State Convention"; Allardice, *More Generals in Gray*, 196–197.

78. Lowry and McCardle, *History of Mississippi*, 479; 1860 Mississippi Population Census; 1860 Mississippi Slave Schedules; "Alphabetical List of Members of the Mississippi State Convention"; T. J. Roberts headstone, Old Rosemary Cemetery, Greene County, Miss.

79. "Account of Manuscripts, Papers, and Documents in Private Hands," 5:256; 1860 Mississippi Population Census; 1860 Mississippi Slave Schedules; "Alphabetical List of Members of the Mississippi State Convention."

80. Lowry and McCardle, *History of Mississippi*, 444; 1860 Mississippi Population Census; 1860 Mississippi Slave Schedules; "Alphabetical List of Members of the Mississippi State Convention"; Jim H. Wallace, *A History of Kosciusko and Attala County* (n.p.: L. L. Henderson, 1967), 3–5.

81. *Biographical and Historical Memoirs of Mississippi*, 2:736–737; 1860 Mississippi Population Census; 1860 Mississippi Slave Schedules; "Alphabetical List of Members of the Mississippi State Convention"; Lowry and McCardle, *History of Mississippi*, 518.

82. Allardice, *Confederate Colonels*, 356; 1860 Mississippi Population Census; 1860 Mississippi Slave Schedules; "Alphabetical List of Members of the Mississippi State Convention." See also the M. D. L. Stephens Manuscript, UM.

83. Rowland and Howell, *Military History of Mississippi*, 544; 1860 Mississippi Population Census; 1860 Mississippi Slave Schedules; "Alphabetical List of Members of the Mississippi State Convention"; William A. Sumner headstone, Hanegan Robinson Cemetery, Hempstead County, Ark.; 1870 Hempstead County, Arkansas Census.

84. William B. Smart headstone, Dabney Family Cemetery, Raymond, Miss.; 1860 Mississippi Population Census; 1860 Mississippi Slave Schedules; "Alphabetical List of Members of the Mississippi State Convention."

85. *Biographical and Historical Memoirs of Mississippi*, 2:878; Eugene Richard Brown, "A History of Scott Co. Mississippi" (M.A. thesis, Mississippi College, 1967), 15–17; 1860 Mississippi Population Census; 1860 Mississippi Slave Schedules; "Alphabetical List of Members of the Mississippi State Convention"; Caleb W. Taylor headstone, Morton City Cemetery, Morton, Miss.

86. *Biographical and Historical Memoirs of Mississippi*, 2:887–889; 1860 Mississippi Population Census; 1860 Mississippi Slave Schedules; "Alphabetical List of Members of the Mississippi State Convention"; Samuel H. Terral headstone, Quitman Cemetery, Quitman, Miss. For eulogies of Terral upon his death, see the Samuel H. Terral Papers, MDAH. For his time at Ole Miss and in the war, see the Samuel Terral Letters, UM.

87. William Harold Graham email to author, November 13, 2010; 1860 Mississippi Population Census; 1860 Mississippi Slave Schedules; "Alphabetical List of Members of the Mississippi State Convention."

88. Allardice, *Confederate Colonels*, 372; 1860 Mississippi Population Census; 1860 Mississippi Slave Schedules; "Alphabetical List of Members of the Mississippi State Convention." For more on Thornton, see the John J. Thornton Scrapbooks, MDAH.

89. Allardice, *Confederate Colonels*, 373; 1860 Mississippi Population Census; 1860 Mississippi Slave Schedules; "Alphabetical List of Members of the Mississippi State Convention."

90. Henry Vaughan headstone, Medley Cemetery, Yazoo County, Miss.; 1860 Mississippi Population Census; 1860 Mississippi Slave Schedules; "Alphabetical List of Members of the Mississippi State Convention."

91. Rowland, *Mississippi*, 2:894–895; 1860 Mississippi Population Census; 1860 Mississippi Slave Schedules; "Alphabetical List of Members of the Mississippi State Convention"; James Daniel Lynch, *The Bench and Bar of Mississippi* (New York: E. J. Hale and Son, 1881), 487–492. See also the H. W. Walter Collection, UM.

92. Israel Welsh Subject File, MDAH; 1860 Mississippi Population Census; 1860 Mississippi Slave Schedules; "Alphabetical List of Members of the Mississippi State Convention."

93. Allardice, *Confederate Colonels*, 396; 1860 Mississippi Population Census; 1860 Mississippi Slave Schedules; "Alphabetical List of Members of the Mississippi State Convention."

94. Matilda Gresham, *Life of Walter Quintin Grisham, 1832–1895*, 2 vols. (Chicago: Rand McNally, 1919), 1:251; 1860 Mississippi Population Census; 1860 Mississippi Slave Schedules; "Alphabetical List of Members of the Mississippi State Convention"; Josiah Winchester headstone, Natchez City Cemetery, Natchez, Miss. For more on Winchester, see the Winchester Family Papers, University of Texas.

95. Rowland and Howell, *Military History of Mississippi*, 668; Confederate Grave Registrations, MDAH; 1860 Mississippi Population Census; 1860 Mississippi Slave Schedules; "Alphabetical List of Members of the Mississippi State Convention"; *History of Montgomery County, Miss.* (Dallas: Curtis Media, 1993), 66; William H. Witty headstone, Oakwood Cemetery, Winona, Miss.

96. Wood, *Union and Secession in Mississippi*; 1860 Mississippi Population Census; 1860 Mississippi Slave Schedules; "Alphabetical List of Members of the Mississippi State Convention"; John W. Wood Obituary, *Memphis Appeal*, August 14 and 18, 1878.

97. Rowland, *Mississippi*, 2:990; Rowland, *Courts, Judges, and Lawyers*, 119–121; 1860 Mississippi Population Census; 1860 Mississippi Slave Schedules; "Alphabetical List of Members of the Mississippi State Convention"; Thomas H. Woods headstone, Rose Hill Cemetery, Meridian, Miss.

98. "Daniel Boone Wright," in *Biographical Directory of the United States Congress*, 2202; 1860 Mississippi Population Census; 1860 Mississippi Slave Schedules; "Alphabetical List of Members of the Mississippi State Convention"; Allardice, *Confederate Colonels*, 408–409.

99. Rowland, *Mississippi*, 2:1021–1022; 1860 Mississippi Population Census; 1860 Mississippi Slave Schedules; "Alphabetical List of Members of the Mississippi State Convention."

100. Rowland and Howell, *Military History of Mississippi*, 40; 1860 Mississippi Population Census; 1860 Mississippi Slave Schedules; "Alphabetical List of Members of the Mississippi State Convention"; 1870 Alcorn County, Mississippi Census; 1880 Hardeman County, Tennessee Census.

APPENDIX 2.

1. Candidates and number of votes gleaned from Election Returns, 1817–2007. Returns for Leake, Winston, and Yalobusha counties were not found. Some returns only listed one candidate and the number of votes received, indicating there was no contested election. One county, Tunica, only reported the winner with no vote total. Several of the handwritten documents were extremely difficult to read, but every effort has been made to cross-reference the names with 1860 census records. In doing so, several discrepancies regarding name spelling were found. In a few instances, the writing was so illegible that no similarity could be found in the census records. On those rare occasions, the names are spelled as best deciphered.

BIBLIOGRAPHY

MANUSCRIPTS

Duke University
   Absalom F. Dantzler Papers
   Joseph D. Stapp Papers
   B. L. C. Wailes Diary
   Thomas B. Webber Diary

Hinds County Courthouse, Second Judicial District, Chancery Court Files
   Estate of Warren P. Anderson, Deceased, Case #1823

Itawamba County Courthouse, Chancery Court Files
   Packet No. 337

Louisiana State University
   James R. Chalmers Letter
   Alexander K. Farrar Papers

Madison Parrish, Louisiana, Courthouse
   Albert C. Gibson Probate File 405

Mississippi Department of Archives and History
   James L. Alcorn and Family Papers
   Francis Marion Aldridge Papers
   William R. Barksdale Letters
   David Chalmers and Archibald Glenn Papers
   Confederate Grave Registrations
   Ellett-Jefferies Family Papers
   Fontaine Family Papers
   James Z. George Papers
   Whitfield Harrington Papers
   L. Q. C. Lamar and Edward Mayes Papers
   Miller Family Papers

Minutes of the Military Board, January 29, 1861–November 23, 1861, RG 9, Series 394,
    Box 416
Mississippi Governor, John J. Pettus, Correspondence and Papers, 1859–1863, Series 757
J. A. Orr Papers
Power Family Papers
Cordelia Lewis Scales Letters
Secretary of State Records
    Election Returns, 1817–2007
Subject Files
    William F. Brantley
    Orlando Davis
    Charles D. Fontaine
    Ordinance of Secession
    Secession
    Secession Jumbo
    Israel Welsh
Samuel H. Terral Papers
John J. Thornton Scrapbooks
Wynn-Dockery Scrapbook

National Archives and Records Administration
    1860 Mississippi Population Census
    1860 Mississippi Slave Schedules
    Compiled Service Records
        Cyrus B. Baldwin
        William J. Eckford
        Albert C. Gibson
        Daniel H. Parker

University of Mississippi
    Miller Family Papers
    Small Manuscripts
        William T. S. Barry Letter
        J. W. Clapp Collection
        A. M. Clayton Letter
        R. F. Crenshaw Letter
        L. Q. C. Lamar Letters
        Ordinance of Secession
            Facsimile of Ordinance of Secession
            Published announcement of Secession by Power & Cadwallader, Jackson, Miss.
        M. D. L. Stephens Manuscript
        H. W. Walter Collection
    Samuel Terral Letters

University of North Carolina
  J. L. Alcorn Papers
  J. A. P. Campbell Papers
  J. F. H. Claiborne Papers
    Clippings of Slavery and Secession
    Manuscripts on Secession
    J. F. H. Claiborne, "The Secession Convention"
    J. L. Power, "Proceedings and Debates of the Mississippi State Convention of 1861:
  First Session"
    J. L. Power, "Proceedings and Debates of the Mississippi State Convention of 1861:
  Second Session"
      David C. Glenn, "Memoranda"
  J. T. Harrison Papers
  L. Q. C. Lamar Papers
  Lea Family Papers
  James Fontaine Maury Papers

University of Southern Mississippi
  Samuel J. Gholson Letter

University of Texas
  Winchester Family Papers

NEWSPAPERS

Charleston Mercury
Fayette Times
Jackson Clarion Ledger
Jackson Mississippian
Jackson Weekly Mississippian
Madison County Journal
Magnolia Gazette
Memphis Appeal
Memphis Commercial Appeal
Memphis Daily Appeal
Mississippi Democrat
Mississippi Free Trader
Nashville Christian Advocate
Natchez Courier
Natchez Weekly Courier
New Orleans Times Picayune
New York Times
Oxford Intelligencer

Paulding Eastern Clarion
Staunton Spectator
Vicksburg Daily Post
Vicksburg Daily Whig
Vicksburg Evening Citizen
Vicksburg Weekly Whig
Washington, D.C., National Republican
Weekly Panola Star
Woodville Republican

PUBLISHED PRIMARY SOURCES

Aughey, John H. *The Iron Furnace: Or, Slavery and Secession*. Philadelphia: William S. and Alfred Martien, 1863.

———. *Tupelo*. Lincoln, Miss.: State Journal, Printers, 1888.

Bettersworth, John K., ed. *Mississippi in the Confederacy: As They Saw It*. Baton Rouge: Louisiana State University Press, 1961.

Caskey, Thomas W. *Caskey's Book: Lectures on Great Subjects, Selected from the Numerous Efforts of that Powerful orator and Noble Veteran of the Cross, Thomas W. Caskey*. St. Louis: John Burns, 1884.

Commissioners of Patents' Journal, No. 2348, July 4 and September 15, 1876.

Condensed Proceedings of the Southern Convention Held at Nashville, Tennessee, June, 1850. Jackson, Miss.: Fall and Marshall, Printers, 1850.

Congressional Globe.

Congressional Record.

Crist, Lynda Lasswell, et al., eds. *The Papers of Jefferson Davis*, 12 vols. Baton Rouge: Louisiana State University Press, 1971–.

Davis, Reuben. *Recollections of Mississippi and Mississippians*. Boston: Houghton, Mifflin, 1890.

"Deaths and Obituaries." *Journal of the American Medical Association* 36, no. 3 (January 19, 1901): 198–199.

Fulkerson, H. S. *A Civilian's Recollections of the War Between the States*. Ed. Percy L. Rainwater. Baton Rouge, La.: Otto Claitor, 1939

Hooker, Charles E. *Confederate Military History: Mississippi*. Atlanta: Confederate Publishing, 1899.

Humphreys, Benjamin G. "The Autobiography of Benjamin Grubb Humphreys August 26, 1808–December 20, 1882." Ed. Percy L. Rainwater. *Mississippi Valley Historical Review* 21, no. 2 (September 1934): 231–255.

In Memory of Henry Thomas Ellett. Memphis, Tenn.: Memphis Bar, 1888.

Journal of the Congress of the Confederate States of America, 1861–1865. 7 vols. Washington, D.C.: Government Printing Office, 1904–1905.

Journal of the House of Representatives of the State of Mississippi: At a Called Session Thereof, Held in the City of Jackson, July and August, 1861. Jackson, Miss.: E. Barksdale, 1861.

Journal of the House of Representatives of the State of Mississippi: Called Session. Jackson, Miss.: E. Barksdale, State Printer, 1860.

Journal of the House of Representatives of the State of Mississippi: Called Session, January 1861. Jackson, Miss.: E. Barksdale, 1861.

Journal of the Proceedings of the Constitutional Convention of the State of Mississippi, Begun at the City of Jackson on August 12, 1890, and Concluded November 1, 1890. Jackson, Miss.: E. L. Martin, 1890.

Journal of the Proceedings of the Convention of the People of Florida Begun and Held at the Capitol in the City of Tallassee on Thursday January 3, A.D. 1861. Tallahassee: Office of the Floridian and Journal, 1861.

Journal of the Secession Convention of Texas 1861. Austin, Tex.: Austin Printing, 1912.

Journal of the Senate of the State of Mississippi: Called Session. Jackson, Miss.: E. Barksdale, State Printer, 1860.

Journal of the State Convention and Ordinances and Resolutions Adopted in January, 1861, With an Appendix. Jackson, Miss.: E. Barksdale, 1861.

Journal of the State Convention and Ordinances and Resolutions Adopted in March, 1861, With an Appendix. Jackson, Miss.: E. Barksdale, 1861.

LaBree, Benjamin. *The Confederate Soldier in the Civil War.* Louisville, Ky.: Prentice Press, 1897.

Laws of the State of Mississippi Passed at a Called Session of the Mississippi Legislature Held in the City of Jackson, January, 1861, Constitution Revised. Jackson, Miss.: E. Barksdale, 1861.

Mayes, Edward. *Lucius Q. C. Lamar: His Life, Times, and Speeches, 1825–1893.* Nashville, Tenn.: Publishing House of the Methodist Episcopal Church South, 1896.

Memorial Addresses on the Life and Character of James Z. George (Late a Senator from Mississippi) Delivered in the Senate and House of Representatives. Washington, D.C.: Government Printing Office, 1898.

Memorials of the Life and Character of Wiley P. Harris of Mississippi. Jackson, Miss.: Clarion Printing Establishment, 1892.

Orders of the Military Board of the State of Mississippi. Jackson, Miss.: Mississippi Book and Job Printing Office, 1861.

Power, J. L. *An Account of the Siege of Vicksburg: From the Personal Diary of Col. John Logan Power and His News Report of the Mississippi Secession Convention of January 7, 1861.* Jackson, Miss.: John L. Power, 1959.

———. "Mississippi Secession Convention." *Southern Home Journal* 3, no. 3 (April 1899): 135–143.

———. "Mississippi Secession Convention." *Southern Home Journal* 3, no. 4 (May 1899): 199–207.

———. *Proceedings of the Mississippi State Convention, Held January 7th to 26th, A.D. 1861. Including the Ordinances, as Finally Adopted, Important Speeches, and a List of Members, Showing the Postoffice, Profession, Nativity, Politics, Age, Religious Preference, and Social Relations of Each.* Jackson, Miss.: Power and Cadwallader, Book and Job Printers, 1861.

Report of the Joint Select Committee To Inquire into the Conditions of Affairs in the Late Insurrectionary States. Washington, D.C.: Government Printing Office, 1872.

Richardson, Albert D. *The Secret Service, the Field, the Dungeon, and the Escape.* Hartford, Conn.: American Publishing, 1865.

Rietti, John C. *Military Annals of Mississippi: Military Organizations Which Entered the Service of the Confederate States of America from the State of Mississippi.* N.p.: n.p., 1895.

Rowland, Dunbar. *Courts, Judges, and Lawyers of Mississippi, 1798–1935.* Jackson, Miss.: Harderman Brothers, 1935.

Smith, William R. *The History and Debates of the Convention of the People of Alabama Begun and Held in the City of Montgomery, on the Seventh Day of January, 1861: In Which is Preserved the Speeches of the Secret Sessions and Many Valuable State Papers.* Atlanta: Wood, Hanleiter, Rice, 1861.

War of the Rebellion: A Compilation of the Official Records of the Union and Confederate Armies. 128 vols. Washington, D.C.: Government Printing Office, 1880–1891.

Wood, John W. *Union and Secession in Mississippi.* Memphis, Tenn.: Saunders, Parrish, and Whitmore, Printers, 1863.

Woods, Thomas H. "A Sketch of the Mississippi Secession Convention of 1861,—Its Membership and Work." In *Publications of the Mississippi Historical Society,* ed. Franklin L. Riley, 6:91–104. Oxford: Mississippi Historical Society, 1902.

SECONDARY SOURCES

Abney, M. G. "Reconstruction in Pontotoc County." In *Publications of the Mississippi Historical Society.* Oxford: Mississippi Historical Society, 1910.

"An Account of Manuscripts, Papers, and Documents in Private Hands." In *Publications of the Mississippi Historical Society,* ed. Franklin L. Riley. Oxford: Mississippi Historical Society, 1902.

Allardice, Bruce S. *Confederate Colonels: A Biographical Register.* Columbia: University of Missouri Press, 2008.

———. *More Generals in Gray.* Baton Rouge: Louisiana State University Press, 1995.

Baggett, James Alex. *The Scalawags: Southern Dissenters in the Civil War and Reconstruction.* Baton Rouge: Louisiana State University Press, 2003.

Ballard, Michael B. *Vicksburg: The Campaign That Opened the Mississippi River.* Chapel Hill: University of North Carolina Press, 2004.

Barney, William L. *The Road to Secession: A New Perspective on the Old South.* New York: Praeger, 1972.

———. *The Secessionist Impulse: Alabama and Mississippi in 1860.* Princeton, N.J.: Princeton University Press, 1974.

Barnhardt, Luther Wesley. "The Secession Conventions of the Cotton South." M.A. thesis, University of Wisconsin, 1922.

Battle, Kemp P. *The Secession Convention of 1861.* Raleigh: North Carolina Society, Daughters of the Revolutions, 1916.

Beeman, Richard. *Plain, Honest Men: The Making of the American Constitution.* New York: Random House, 2009.

Bently, Carrie Helen. "The Secession Convention of Virginia, 1861." M.A. thesis, University of Texas at Austin, 1932.

Bettersworth, John K. *Confederate Mississippi: The People and Policies of a Cotton State in Wartime.* Baton Rouge: Louisiana State University Press, 1943.

Biographical and Historical Memoirs of Mississippi, Embracing and Authentic and Comprehensive Account of the Chief Events in the History of the State, and a Record of the Lives of Many of the Most Worthy and Illustrious Families and Individuals. 2 vols. Chicago: Goodspeed Publishing, 1891.

Biographical Directory of the United States Congress, 1774–2005. Washington, D.C.: Government Printing Office, 2005.

Bond, Bradley G. "Edward C. Walthall and the 1880 Senatorial Nomination: Politics of Balance in the Redeemer Era." *Journal of Mississippi History* 50 (February 1988): 1–20.

———. *Political Culture in the Nineteenth-Century South: Mississippi, 1830–1900.* Baton Rouge: Louisiana State University Press, 1995.

Bowers, Wayne F. "The First Secession Convention: A Study of the Sovereign Convention in South Carolina." M.A. thesis, University of North Carolina at Chapel Hill, 1971.

Brown, A. J. *History of Newton County from 1834 to 1894.* Jackson, Miss.: Clarion Ledger, 1894.

Brown, Eugene Richard. "A History of Scott Co. Mississippi." M.A. thesis, Mississippi College, 1967.

Brown, Mrs. J. E. "The Secession of Mississippi." *Confederate Veteran* 39, no. 2 (February 1937): 92–94.

Cain, Cyril Edward. *Four Centuries on the Pascagoula: History and Genealogy of the Pascagoula River Country.* 2 vols. State College, Miss.: n.p., 1953.

Carroll County, Mississippi: History and Families. Humboldt, Tenn.: Rose Publishing, 2001.

Cashin, Joan E. *A Family Venture: Men and Women on the Southern Frontier.* New York: Oxford University Press, 1991.

Cathcart, William. *The Baptist Encyclopedia: A Dictionary of the Doctrines, Ordinances, Usages, Confessions of Faith, Sufferings, Labors, and Successes, and of the General History of the Baptist Denomination in All Lands. With Numerous Biographical Sketches of Distinguished American and Foreign Baptists, and a Supplement.* Philadelphia: Lewis H. Everts, 1881.

Davis, William C. *"A Government of Their Own": The Making of the Confederacy.* New York: Free Press, 1994.

———. *Jefferson Davis: The Man and His Hour, a Biography.* New York: Harper Collins, 1991.

Denman, Clarence Phillips. *The Secession Movement in Alabama.* Montgomery: Alabama State Department of Archives and History, 1933.

Desoto County Genealogical Society. *Desoto County Mississippi: History and Families.* Humbolt, Miss.: Rose Publishing, 1999.

Dew, Charles B. *Apostles of Disunion: Southern Secession Commissioners and the Causes of the Civil War.* Charlottesville: University Press of Virginia, 2001.

Dubay, Robert W. *John Jones Pettus, Mississippi Fire-eater: His Life and Times, 1813–1867.* Jackson: University Press of Mississippi, 1975.

Echoes From Our Past: History-Military-Churches-Families. 2 vols. Jones County, Miss.: Jones County Genealogical and Historical Organization, 2006.

Everett, Frank E., Jr., *Vicksburg Lawyers Prior to the Civil War*. N.p.: n.p., n.d.

"The Family of B. Y. Cummings." *Northeast Mississippi Historical & Genealogical Society Quarterly* 19, no. 1 (September 1998): 21–22.

Foster, Gaines M. *Ghosts of the Confederacy: Defeat, the Lost Cause, and the Emergence of the New South*. New York: Oxford University Press, 1987.

Freehling, William W. *Prelude to Civil War: The Nullification Controversy in South Carolina, 1816–1836*. New York: Oxford University Press, 1965.

———. *The Road to Disunion: Secessionists at Bay, 1776–1854*. New York: Oxford University Press, 1990.

———. *The Road to Disunion: Secessionists Triumphant, 1854–1861*. New York: Oxford University Press, 2007.

Freehling, William W., and Craig M. Simpson, eds. *Secession Debated: Georgia's Showdown in 1860*. New York: Oxford University Press, 1992.

———. *Showdown in Virginia: The 1861 Convention and the Fate of the Union*. Charlottesville: University of Virginia Press, 2010.

Gresham, Matilda. *Life of Walter Quintin Grisham, 1832–1895*. 2 vols. Chicago: Rand McNally, 1919.

Halsell, Willie D. "The Bourbon Period in Mississippi Politics, 1875–1890." *Journal of Southern History* 11, no. 4 (November 1945): 519–537.

———. "Democratic Dissensions in Mississippi, 1878–1882." *Journal of Mississippi History* 2 (July 1940): 123–135.

———. "James R. Chalmers and 'Mohoneism' in Mississippi." *Journal of Southern History* 10, no. 1 (February 1944): 37–58.

Harris, Gideon Dowse. *Harris Geneology*. Columbus, Miss.: Keith Printing, 1914.

Heidler, David S., and Jeanne T. Heidler, eds. *Encyclopedia of the American Civil War: A Political, Social, and Military History*. 5 vols. Santa Barbara, Calif.: ABC-CLIO, 2000.

Henderson, Richey. *Pontotoc County Men of Note*. Pontotoc, Miss.: Pontotoc Progress Print, 1940.

Hickey, Donald R. *The War of 1812: A Forgotten Conflict*. Urbana: University of Illinois Press, 1989.

Hillman, Benjamin J. *Virginia's Decision: The Story of the Secession Convention of 1861*. Richmond: Virginia Civil War Commission, 1964.

History of Montgomery County, Miss. Dallas: Curtis Media, 1993.

A History of Rankin County Mississippi. Vol. 1. Brandon, Miss.: Rankin County Historical Society, 1984.

Hoffman, Jennie Newsom. "A History of Winston County." N.p.: WPA, 1938.

Hollandsworth, James G. *Portrait of a Scientific Racist: Alfred Holt Stone of Mississippi*. Baton Rouge: Louisiana State University Press, 2008.

Hosemann, Delbert. *Mississippi's Official and Statistical Register, 2008–2012*. Jackson, Miss.: Secretary of State, 2009.

Howe, Daniel Walker. *What Hath God Wrought: The Transformation of America, 1815–1848*. New York: Oxford University Press, 2007.

Johnson, Michael P. *Toward a Patriarchal Republic: The Secession of Georgia.* Baton Rouge: Louisiana State University Press, 1977.

Jordan, Winthrop D. *Tumult and Silence at Second Creek: An Inquiry Into a Civil War Slave Conspiracy.* Rev. ed. Baton Rouge: Louisiana State University Press, 1996.

Kendel, Julia. "Reconstruction in Lafayette County." In *Publications of the Mississippi Historical Society.* Oxford: Mississippi Historical Society, 1913.

Lewis, William T. *The Centennial History of Winston County, Mississippi.* Pasadena, Tex.: Globe Publishers, 1972.

Lowry, Robert, and William H. McCardle. *A History of Mississippi, From the Discovery of the Great River by Hernando DeSoto, Including the Earliest Settlement Made by the French, Under Iberville, to the Death of Jefferson Davis.* Jackson, Miss.: R. H. Henry, 1891.

Lynch, James Daniel. *The Bench and Bar of Mississippi.* New York: E. J. Hale and Son, 1881.

McPherson, James M. *Battle Cry of Freedom: The Civil War Era.* New York: Oxford University Press, 1988.

McSwain, Robert J., Jr., *Descendants of Early Settlers of Perry County, Mississippi.* Carrollton, Miss.: Pioneer Publishing Company, 2006.

"Mississippi——Seceded January 9, 1861." *Confederate Veteran* 35, no. 2 (February 1927): 73.

Murphy, James B. *L. Q. C. Lamar: Pragmatic Patriot.* Baton Rouge: Louisiana State University Press, 1973.

Noe, Kenneth W. *Reluctant Rebels: The Confederates Who Joined the Army after 1861.* Chapel Hill: University of North Carolina Press, 2010.

Olsen, Christopher J. *Political Culture and Secession in Mississippi: Masculinity, Honor, and the Antiparty Tradition, 1830–1860.* New York: Oxford University Press, 2000.

Owsley, Frank L. *States Rights in the Confederacy.* Chicago: University of Chicago Press, 1925.

Pereyra, Lillian A. *James Lusk Alcorn: Persistent Whig.* Baton Rouge: Louisiana State University Press, 1966.

Perrin, William Henry. *Southwest Louisiana, Biographical and Historical.* New Orleans: Gulf Publishing, 1891.

Potter, David M. *The Impending Crisis: 1848–1861.* New York: Harper, 1976.

Prentiss County, Mississippi: History and Families. Paducah, Ky.: Turner Publishing, 2002.

Rainwater, Percy L. "An Analysis of the Secession Controversy in Mississippi, 1854–61." *Mississippi Valley Historical Review* 24, no. 1 (June 1937): 35–42.

———. *Mississippi: Storm Center of Secession.* Baton Rouge: Louisiana State University Press, 1938.

———, ed. "Notes and Documents: The Civil War Letters of Cordelia Scales." *Journal of Mississippi History* 1, no. 1 (July 1939): 169–181.

Rideout, Theresa T. ed. *Our Links to the Past: Cemetery Records of Neshoba County, MS.* Philadelphia, Miss.: Neshoba County Library, 1998.

Rowland, Dunbar. *Mississippi; Comprising Sketches of Counties, Towns, Events, Institutions and Persons, Arranged in Cyclopedic Form.* 3 vols. Atlanta: Southern Historical Printing Association, 1907.

Rowland, Dunbar, and H. Grady Howell Jr. *Military History of Mississippi: 1803–1898, Including a Listing of All Known Mississippi Confederate Military Units.* Madison, Miss.: Chickasaw Bayou Press, 2003.

Saunders, James Edmonds. *Early Settlers of Alabama.* New Orleans: L. Graham and Son, 1899.

Scharf, J. Thomas. *History of Delaware: 1609–1888.* 2 vols. Philadelphia: L. J. Richards, 1888.

Skipworth Historical and Genological Society. *History of Lafayette County, Miss.* Dallas: Curtis Media, 1986.

Smith, Timothy B. *James Z. George: Mississippi's Great Commoner.* Jackson: University Press of Mississippi, 2012.

———. *Mississippi in the Civil War: The Home Front.* Jackson: University Press of Mississippi, 2010.

———. "Secession at Shiloh: Mississippi's Convention Delegates and Their State's Defense." *Hallowed Ground* (Spring 2012): 16–22.

Speer, William S. *Sketches of Prominent Tennesseans, Containing Biographies and Records of Many of the Families Who Have Attained Prominence in Tennessee.* Nashville, Tenn.: Albert B. Tavel, 1888.

Theall, Gary. *History of Vermilion Parish.* 2 vols. Abbeville, La.: Vermilion Historical Society, 2003.

Waddel, John N. *Memorials of Academic Life: Being An Historical Sketch of the Waddel Family, Identified Through Three Generations With the History of the Higher Education in the South and Southwest.* Richmond, Va.: Presbyterian Committee of Publication, 1891.

Wallace, Jim H. *A History of Kosciusko and Attala County.* N.p.: L. L. Henderson, 1967.

Warner, Ezra J. *Generals in Gray: Lives of the Confederate Commanders.* Baton Rouge: Louisiana State University Press, 1959.

Wiley, Bell Irvin. *The Life of Johnny Reb: The Common Soldier of the Confederacy.* Indianapolis: Bobbs-Merrill, 1943.

Williams, Wirt A., ed. *History of Bolivar County, Mississippi.* Jackson, Miss.: Herderman Brothers, 1948.

Wood, Gordon S. *Empire of Liberty: A History of the Early Republic, 1789–1815.* New York: Oxford University Press, 2009.

Wooster, Ralph A. "The Membership of the Mississippi Secession Convention of 1861." *Journal of Mississippi History* 16, no. 4 (October 1954): 242–257.

———. *The Secession Conventions of the South.* Princeton, N.J.: Princeton University Press, 1962.

PERSONAL COMMUNICATION

Ken Dupuy, telephone conversation with author, 2010.

June Ellis, email to author, December 8, 2010.

William Harold Graham, email to author, November 13, 2010.

INDEX

Printed in the United States
By Bookmasters